IN THE SHADOW
OF THE POORHOUSE

IN THE SHADOW OF THE POORHOUSE

A Social History
of Welfare in America

MICHAEL B. KATZ

BasicBooks
A Division of HarperCollinsPublishers

Library of Congress Cataloging-in-Publication Data

Katz, Michael B.
  In the shadow of the poorhouse.

  Includes index.
  1. Public welfare—United States—History. 2. Social
service—United States—History. 3. United States—
Social policy. I. Title.
HV91.K349 1986   362.5'8'0973   85–73875
ISBN 0–465–03225–7 (cloth)
ISBN 0–465–03226–5 (paper)

© 1986 BasicBooks, A Division of HarperCollins Publishers
Designed by Vincent Torre
Printed in the United States of America
91 RRD 9 8 7 6 5

CONTENTS

PART III

FROM THE WAR ON POVERTY TO
THE WAR ON WELFARE

ACKNOWLEDGMENTS

This book started several years ago with research made possible by a grant from the Center for Studies of Metropolitan Problems of the National Institute of Mental Health (Grant No. RO1MH3250). It was written primarily in two places: first, at Clioquossia in Oquossoc, Maine. I remain, as always, appreciative of my family, friends, and neighbors there for their tolerance, support, and willingness to divert me when I need it. The other location was the Shelby Cullom Davis Center at Princeton University, where I was privileged to spend the academic year 1984–85. I am grateful to the center's director, Lawrence Stone, for inviting me and providing an intellectually stimulating environment. The University of Pennsylvania granted me a study leave, which made it possible for me to remain for a full year at the center.

In November 1984, Theda Skocpol invited me to a conference on the development of America's welfare state at the University of Chicago, which had a major influence on the way I thought about this book. Subsequent conversations with her and her associate, Ann Shola Orloff, have been exceptionally helpful. Their forthcoming work will lift American discussion of the welfare state to a new level. Daniel Rodgers read a large portion of the manuscript at a time when I desperately needed feedback; Viviana Zelizer read a draft of the whole book and helped me think about its revision. I also have been informed and stimulated by conversations with many colleagues, among whom Michael Frisch, David Garland, Gary Gerstle, and Christophe Sachsse deserve special mention.

This book began as a coauthored volume with Susan Davis and Mark Stern. The exigencies of academic schedules made continued collaboration impossible, but their contributions to the research and formulation of ideas have been essential. Steven Fraser of Basic Books has been an acute, creative, and tough editor, as well as an amazingly fast reader. This book is much better for his efforts. The flaws that remain after all this help are purely my responsibility.

Edda Katz and Sarah Katz offered their customary support, patience, and encouragement. I am particularly grateful for the good humor with which they bore my absence at the Davis Center.

INTRODUCTION

Nobody likes welfare. Conservatives worry that it erodes the work ethic, retards productivity, and rewards the lazy. Liberals view the American welfare system as incomplete, inadequate, and punitive. Poor people, who rely on it, find it degrading, demoralizing, and mean. None of these complaints are new; they echo nearly two centuries of criticism. In truth, American welfare hardly qualifies as a system. Diffused through every layer of government; partly public, partly private, partly mixed; incomplete and still not universal; defeating its own objectives, American welfare practice is incoherent and irrational. Still, this crazy system resists fundamental change. What is the source of its resilience? How are we to understand the persistence of a welfare system so thoroughly disliked and so often and authoritatively criticized? The answer rests in its past. American welfare practice has been constructed in layers deposited during the last two centuries. Despite accretions and extensions, it has served a consistent and useful set of purposes; its strength derives from its symbiosis with American social structure and political economy. This book sketches its social history.

Four major structural features mark American welfare practice. First is the division between public assistance and social insurance. Public assistance is means-tested relief. It is what we usually think of as welfare. Its major contemporary examples are Aid to Families with Dependent Children (AFDC) and General Assistance. Social insurance is not means tested. It is an entitlement for everyone eligible by virtue of fixed, objective criteria, such as age, disability, or unemployment, and its benefits cross class lines. The great current example, of course, is social security. The division between social insurance and public assistance has bifurcated social welfare along class lines. With a strong, articulate middle-class constituency, social insurance, especially social security, carries no stigma, and its expanded benefits have reduced drastically the amount of poverty among the elderly. Public assistance, which has become synonymous with welfare, is, of course, restricted to the very poor. Its recipients carry the historic stigma of the unworthy poor, and, as a consequence, they are treated meanly. Their

4 Purposes shaping Amer. Welfare System

benefits, which do not lift them out of poverty, remain far below those paid by social security.[1]

(2) Local variation is American welfare's second feature. In colonial times, relief was a local responsibility, administered within a town, county, or parish. In the nineteenth century, state governments tried to make practice more uniform within their jurisdictions, but, even then, a dazzling variety of local, as well as state, differences remained, and the assumption of new responsibilities by the federal government during the New Deal did not wipe out local variation. States remained responsible for setting benefit levels, even when they received federal funds, and the disparity in welfare benefits between states continues today. Another way to put the persistence of local variation is this: welfare practice has always been mediated by the complex structure of American federalism. As a consequence, the formulation of coherent national welfare policy remains extraordinarily difficult, and the amount and kind of assistance offered poor people varies by where they live.[2]

(3) Third, governments accomplish many public purposes through private agents. Boundaries between public and private always have been protean in America. The definition of public as applied to social policy and institutions has never been fixed and unambiguous. In the colonial period, towns often contracted for the care of the poor with individuals. In the nineteenth century, they subsidized schools, hospitals, reformatories, orphanages, and other institutions. Within the last twenty years, governments increasingly have delivered social services by purchasing them from private agencies. Welfare practice, in short, is part of what Alan Wolfe terms the "franchise state." Not all franchise holders act in the best interests of their clients, as Medicare and Medicaid frauds make clear. In fact, franchising encourages the confusion of service with profit making and removes important public tasks—and a lot of money—from public oversight and scrutiny (as the recent defense contracting scandals reveal vividly). At the same time, the scramble for public dollars pushes private agencies away from challenging, innovative activities and toward conservative, routine programs tailored to government specifications.[3]

(4) Fourth, the American welfare state is incomplete, which is why I call it the semiwelfare state. America remains the only advanced Western democracy without national health insurance or family allowances. Welfare coverage is neither universal nor comprehensive. Social welfare expenses consume a much smaller share of the Gross National Product than in other wealthy nations, and ideological resistance to social welfare remains far more virulent.

Despite—and in some cases because of—its limits, social welfare practice has served important purposes throughout American history. The first three— relief of misery, preservation of social order and discipline, and regulation of the labor market—seem universal in Western societies. The fourth, political

Introduction

mobilization, is more distinctively American. The humanitarian goals of welfare have always been obvious, although those who consider them exclusive or paramount miss other important roles. Time and again, welfare has been extended or redesigned to promote social order by appeasing protest or disciplining the poor. The escalation of benefits after the great urban riots in the 1960s is one particularly vivid recent example. Another is the attempt in the late forties and fifties to reduce out-of-wedlock births among black women by tightening the "suitable home" provisions of Aid to Dependent Children (ADC). Welfare has also been deployed to regulate labor markets by manipulating work incentives. In practice, this has meant goading working-class men and women to labor hard for low wages by frightening them with the prospect of a subhuman and stigmatized descent into the ranks of paupers.

For a long time, welfare's political role reflected the structure of American urban politics. With public authority weak and limited, the local ward leaders who ran city governments retained political power by returning services for votes. Outdoor relief—grocery orders, fuel, or small amounts of cash—helped cement the allegiance of the poor; lucrative contracts to supply poorhouses, fees for local doctors hired to treat their inmates, and the circulation of enough cash to sustain grocers and tavernkeepers won the loyalty of small businessmen and professionals. Since the New Deal, the federal government has used the distribution of welfare benefits, especially to urban minorities and the rural poor, to build political support. Conversely, also for nearly two centuries, critics, casting themselves as reformers, have mobilized different sources of political support by attacking welfare. (Ronald Reagan is only one in a line of politicians whose antiwelfare rhetoric has helped carry them into office.)[4]

Although these four purposes have always shaped American welfare practice, their relative prominence has varied with economic conditions, political climate, and social structure. Even more, they have always been inconsistent with each other, and the unresolved tensions between them have undercut virtually all attempts to formulate coherent welfare policy. In the nineteenth century, for instance, reformers who wanted to reduce taxes and discipline the poor by ending outdoor relief clashed with local manufacturers who wanted to keep their labor force from migrating in slack seasons, merchants who profited from poor relief, and politicians with a constituency in poor neighborhoods. Within poorhouses, decent care for the poor conflicted with the objective of deterring the poor from asking for relief and making them willing to work hard for low wages. Indeed, of all their contradictions, the most glaring and debilitating has been the incompatibility of policies that simultaneously preach compassion and stress deterrence. It should be no surprise that deterrence usually has won.

Other themes run through the history of welfare. One is the stigma attached to extreme poverty in America. In the land of opportunity, poverty has seemed not only a misfortune but a moral failure. Another is the meaning of welfare reform: with few exceptions, its operating definition has been a reduction in benefits. Most often, the target has been the so-called ablebodied poor, whom welfare reformers for the last two centuries have tried to purge from the rolls of relief. Their relative failure only underscores the futility—and ideological baggage—of the persistent attempt to draw a sharp line between the very poor and everybody else.

Relief or welfare policy has never been inevitable. Always, policies and practices have emerged from a choice among alternative possibilities. Early in the nineteenth century, relief policy deliberately stressed poorhouses, even though they turned out to be more expensive and administratively cumbersome than outdoor relief. Later in the century, reformers moved children out of poorhouses and away from their parents because they wanted to break up poor families. Just as easily, they could have built decent family quarters in poorhouses or, most cheaply of all, supported families with outdoor relief. In the Great Depression, President Franklin D. Roosevelt, despite pleas from key members of his administration and social workers, among others, took the government out of the business of relief, in which it had been engaged for about two years, and left hundreds of thousands of people hungry and desperate. The selection of welfare policy, as these examples show, has reflected social values and the purposes welfare was to serve. However, whatever these official goals, poor people have managed, at least partly, to subvert them and to turn institutions and practices to their own purposes. Indeed, the resilience of the poor, their capacity to survive and resist, is the only major note of cheer in the depressing past that characterizes American welfare.

This book sets welfare in the context of American social history and outlines its story. It is, in part, a tale of transformation, of how social policy responded to the great shifts in America's social and economic structure from the nascent capitalism of the late eighteenth and early nineteenth centuries, through the nation's industrialization and the great era of corporate capital in the early twentieth century, to the current period of deindustrialization and the emergence of a service economy. Part I is called "The Poorhouse Era" because, although more people received help outside than inside institutions, poorhouses symbolized the spirit and intent of welfare practice. At first, they were, indeed, welfare's cutting edge as reformers responded to new forms of dependence and heightened problems of social discipline and labor force control during the early spread of capitalist social and economic relations. Chapter 1 shows why poorhouses became the preferred response to extreme poverty and why they failed to meet their goals. Chapter 2 highlights the resilience of *outdoor relief*, noninstitutional public assistance, despite reformers' hostility, and describes how and why it survived the late nineteenth-century war against it. Chapter 3 focuses on the voluntary

Introduction

sector: antebellum private philanthropy and a post–Civil War theory, *scientific charity*, deployed amid the tensions of Gilded Age America to justify newly hardened policies toward the poor. Chapter 4 returns to poorhouses and shows how their transformation fostered the development of large orphanages, huge custodial mental hospitals, flophouses, and public old-age homes.

Part II covers the great era of corporate capital from roughly the 1890s through the 1930s, when replacements for the failed earlier nineteenth-century policies, especially poorhouses and scientific charity, became urgent and the impotence of state and local governments before the great problems of dependence became unmistakable. Its focus is the creation of what I have called the semiwelfare state, whose structure was completed by the New Deal. It deals with the special problem of children and, then, the implications for welfare of attempts to reorganize cities, labor markets, and the nature of government. Chapter 5 situates the great reform movement of the late nineteenth century, *child-saving*, in its social context and reveals how the resolution of debates about the appropriateness of institutions for children, the role of government in their lives, and the preservation of families resulted in new social policies toward children, including the intrusion of state authority into family relations. Chapter 6 traces the interconnections between early twentieth-century municipal reform and the development of both urban welfare systems and professional urban experts: reformers, social workers, and public welfare officials. Chapter 7 shows how attempts to reorganize labor markets in the same period fueled the development of welfare capitalism and early forms of social insurance. Chapter 8 locates the emergence of the semiwelfare state in the New Deal's reorganization of the national government and its relations to its citizens.

In both parts I and II chapters for the most part are thematic rather than chronological. It seemed to me more useful and interesting to explicate great themes in welfare's history than to scatter them throughout a strictly narrative account. (The result is some overlap, which is inescapable, but I hope not too intrusive.) Part III traces the relation of social welfare to some of the great themes of post–World War II experience: the civil rights movement, the urban crisis, deindustrialization, and the emergence of a new structure of poverty. My main concern in the last two chapters is to offer an interpretation of the war on poverty, the expansion of social welfare, and what I call the current war on welfare and to show how they flow from and reflect the larger history of welfare in America. The last chapter ends with my speculations about the future of welfare and the components of more adequate social policies.[5]

If readers take only two major ideas from this book, I would like them to be these: first, American public welfare has a very old history. Public funds have always relieved more people than private ones. Voluntarism never was and never will be an adequate answer to the problem of dependence. By contrast, despite all its flaws, government has been, and can be again, a great source of social progress in America. Second, welfare policy results from choices among alternative possibilities. We have the resources, competence, and ideas to transform social welfare in America. The real question is how much we care. If we fail to eliminate poverty, hunger, malnutrition, and bad housing, we will have made our answer clear.

PART I

THE
POORHOUSE
ERA

1 The Origins and Failure

of the Poorhouse

Throughout the century before the New Deal, the poorhouse dominated the structure of welfare—or, as it was called then, relief. Although despised, dreaded, and often attacked, the poorhouse endured as the central arch of public welfare policy. Even in the twentieth century it did not disappear. Instead, through a gradual transformation it slid into a new identity: the public old-age home. Its history shows clearly how decent and compassionate care of the poor has always remained subordinate to both low taxes and the other great purposes that have guided relief. American welfare has remained within the shadow of the poorhouse. Poorhouses, which shut the old and sick away from their friends and relatives, were supposed to deter the working class from asking for poor relief. They were, in fact, the ultimate defense against the erosion of the work ethic in early industrial America. Miserable, poorly managed, underfunded institutions, trapped by their own contradictions, poorhouses failed to meet any of the goals so confidently predicted by their sponsors.[1]

In both England and America, local communities helped destitute people in their homes—a form of assistance known as outdoor relief—long before the first almshouse had been built. Even more, despite a century of sustained attack, outdoor relief refused to disappear. Indeed, throughout the nineteenth century, many more people—in most places three, four, or more times as many—received public outdoor relief in any year as were admitted to poorhouses. Still, the number of people affected offers only one measure with which to judge whether a practice is fundamental. Another is its role in policy, and in both Britain and

America the poorhouse was the cutting edge of poor relief policy in the late eighteenth and early nineteenth centuries, advocated by Utilitarians in England and forward-looking architects of state policy in America.

Poverty

Myths of abundance in early American history notwithstanding, poverty was a serious and growing problem. Indeed, no clear line separated ordinary working people from those in need of help, because periodic destitution was one structural result of the great social and economic transformations in American life. The reasons for this prevalence of poverty vary, although most of them may be traced in one way or another to the organization of work.

Increasingly, throughout the early nineteenth century, most people worked for someone else during their entire adult lives. "Nothing more clearly distinguishes the years in which the factory system was built from the modern age, inured to its ranks of wage and salary earners," writes Daniel Rodgers, "than that the simple fact of employment should have deeply disturbed so many Americans." This spread of wage labor can be traced in various ways: through an analysis of the proportion of workers simply called "laborers" on the New York City assessment rolls between 1750 and 1850 (the proportion rose from 6 percent to 27 percent); through manuscript censuses and city directories (which show the numerical domination of most trades by wage laborers at a ratio of ten or eleven employees for each proprietor by at least the middle of the century); or by the spread of trade unions, labor newspapers, and working-class militancy as early as the 1830s. (In Philadelphia, the General Trades Union, a loose organization of unskilled and skilled workers, staged successful collective actions in the 1830s until they were decimated by the severe depression of 1837.)[2]

The uneven character of economic development complicates attempts to generalize about the relations between the history of work and poverty. Throughout the first half of the nineteenth century, handcrafts coexisted with manufactured goods; goods were produced in homes as well as in factories. Some large workplaces were collections of hand workers; in some the work was subdivided into its component parts; a few introduced steam-driven machinery. Even within the same trades, widely different work settings and manufacturing processes coexisted. Nonetheless, everywhere, a reorganization of economic life eroded the position of independent journeymen artisans. For whatever their work setting, almost all of them became wage laborers, employees rather than independent craftsmen owning their raw materials and tools and selling their products directly. As wage workers, they lost the flexibility that had marked artisan manufacture. Most also lost their skill monopoly as the logic of production subdivided work into smaller components that required less skill and less time to learn.[3]

As young men entered trades with increased ease, apprenticeships shortened or disappeared, and a glutted labor market led to lower wages. In fact, to keep their wages as low as possible, employers often fired apprentices as soon as their term expired so that they could avoid paying them adult journeyman wages.[4] Two factors intensified the problems of apprentices and adult artisans thrown out of work. One was the absence of any cushion against unemployment. Very few workers could save enough to tide them over a prolonged period of unemployment, and, without aid from their families, their alternatives were to seek relief or to travel in search of work. Here the ecology of home and workplace— the second factor—came into play. Until very late in the nineteenth century, most working people had to live within walking distance of their jobs. Few could afford the early forms of public transportation such as the horse-drawn street railways introduced in many cities in the 1860s. Because most workplaces were relatively small, most workers found only a limited number of jobs within walking distance of their homes, and, as a consequence, losing a job often meant traveling to find new work. This is one reason historians have found extraordinary population mobility everywhere in nineteenth century America. (Recent studies rarely have discovered more than a third of households remaining in the same town or city for at least a decade around the middle of the nineteenth century.) People on the road looking for work usually had almost no money. Often hungry and desperate, they sometimes sought relief in poorhouses or from public officials. In this way, transiency helped swell the roles of public relief.[5]

Sometimes, mechanization also drove people to relief. Consider the example of threshing machines in New York, where in 1853 an observer wrote:

> It is not very long since all the grain raised in this State was threshed out with flails. It requires no intellect whatever to perform this labor; any one, not a perfect idiot, can stand and pound upon the floor of a barn. This employment was usually relied on by laborers for their winter's employment. Now there is scarcely a farmer to be found who threshes with a flail. Threshing machines are everywhere used, and have completely cut off this source of winter employment.

The replacement of hand threshing by machines underlines the existence of rural, as well as urban, poverty. Nearly every county, rural or urban, had its poorhouse. One source of rural poverty was the mechanization of agriculture, which reflected the increased influence of market forces during the first half of the nineteenth century. In the Genesee Valley, observes Hannon, after 1925, commercial wheat production "was accompanied by rapid population growth, increased average farm size, a decline in self-sufficient household production, a shortening of the average tenant contract to one year, a decline in the tenancy rate, and increased use of seasonal labor." In 1857, the editor of a local newspaper explained that "after employment for a few weeks or months," farm laborers "were left to beg, steal, or go the poorhouse. . . . This has been the situation of farm laborers in western New York for the past ten or twenty years." As the manufacture of domestic goods—clothes, small home furnishings, and so on— began to move out of homes and into shops and factories, farm women lost an important source of supplementary income. In fact, Hannon found the decline of home manufacture, far more than either industrialization or urbanization, associated with rising rates of pauperism in antebellum New York. Another source of rural poverty was the pressure of population on land, especially in long-settled areas of the East where the productivity of land had declined and farmers had run out of land to subdivide for their children. Rural poverty arose, too, from periodic crop failures caused by bad weather or insects, as in the Kansas "Grasshopper Scourge" (1874–75) that left many families destitute, or the droughts and crop failures in the same state between 1885 and 1895.[6]

Everywhere, the seasonality of work menaced working-class security, and poorhouse populations swelled during winter months. Much unskilled labor took place outdoors: unloading ships, digging canals, building railways. In cold climates where lakes and canals froze, all this employment ended in the winter. So did most construction work, another major source of employment.[7]

For most people work remained unsteady as well as seasonal. Because the availability of work varied with demand, few manufacturers employed a consistent number of workers throughout the year, and very few people found steady work. As much as low wages, this irregular employment—in the urban South as well as in the North—often dropped families into poverty. The great periodic depressions had the same effect. During each depression, thousands of workers, their jobs lost, were left without resources, dependent on relatives, friends, or charity. At times, even the well-to-do were plunged into poverty, and many workers fled cities. Others stayed and suffered. During one depression in antebellum Philadelphia, laborers worked for fifty cents a day; the wages of handloom weavers were slashed; the demand for domestic servants and seamstresses declined; and everywhere, disease, hunger, and destitution stalked the streets.[8]

The availability of work for every ablebodied person who really wants a job is one of the enduring myths of American history. In fact, work was no more universally available in the early and mid-nineteenth century than it is today, as unskilled and semiskilled workers overstocked urban labor markets. In 1822, Josiah Quincy, addressing the Grand Jury of Suffolk County, Massachusetts, pointed to the 700 men "for whom work cannot be obtained" on the books of Boston's Employment Society. "These men long for work; they anxiously beg for it; yet it is not to be found." In 1828, Matthew Carey, attacking the proposed abolition of outdoor relief in Philadelphia, observed:

> Many citizens entertain an idea that in the present state of society in this city, every person able and willing to work may procure employment; that all those who are thus employed, may earn a decent and comfortable support; and that if not the whole, at least the chief part of the distresses of the poor, arises from idleness, dissipation, and worthlessness.

Nothing could be further from the truth, wrote Carey. Even in the "most prosperous times," he pointed out, "some trades and occupations" always were "depressed," and a "deficiency of employment" consumed the modest savings of the most "frugal and industrious."[9]

Carey highlighted another great source of poverty: the low wages paid women. Some philanthropic societies had attempted to help women—especially widows—by starting workshops where they could earn money sewing. Other women earned a little money sewing for individual masters. Carey showed that even the philanthropists did not pay women enough to survive. Even so, work was so scarce that every time contracts for making clothes for soldiers were announced, "the applications" were "too numerous to be supplied." Women in the urban South faced similar problems, as the editor of the Richmond *Daily Dispatch* pointed out in 1857. Women compelled "to make their living by their industry," he observed, were paid far less than men: fifty or sixty cents a day was considered enough to make a woman "entirely independent," and some with children to support, were "actually making up shirts and drawers for 6¼ cents each."[10]

Carey also traced the relation among the wretched wages paid male workers, their working conditions, and the growth of poverty. Thousands of laborers, he pointed out, "travel hundreds of miles in quest of employment on canals" at less than a dollar a day, paying "a dollar and a half or two dollars per week for their board, leaving families behind, depending on them for support." Often, they worked "in marshy grounds, where they" breathed "pestiferous miasmata" that destroyed "their health, often irrecoverably." They returned "to their poor families, broken hearted, and with ruined constitutions, with a sorry pittance, most laboriously earned" and took to their beds "sick and unable to work." Still, their places filled quickly with other men desperate for any work. Hundreds were "most laboriously employed on turnpikes, working from morning till night, at from half a dollar to three quarters per day, exposed to the broiling sun in summer, and all the inclemency of our severe winters." Always there was "a redundance of wood pilers in our cities, whose wages are so low, that their utmost efforts do not enable them to earn more than from thirty-five to fifty cents per day." Even the "painful situation of a watchman" was an "object of desire." There never was "a want of scavengers"; nor was there any work "whatever, how disagreeable, or loathsome, or dangerous, or deleterious soever it may be, or however reduced the wages," that did not "find some persons willing to follow it, rather than beg or steal."[11]

Usually low to begin with, wages frequently were reduced. For instance, in one Philadelphia cotton mill, handloom weavers making cotton ticking earned one dollar per cut in 1820, seventy cents in 1833, and sixty cents in 1840. When wages were reduced, Walter Channing pointed out in 1843, the effect was not only to lessen "the amount paid to each" but also to discharge "from regular employment a certain number of operatives." The net effect left large numbers of people suddenly "without the means of subsistence for themselves, and for their families. These last, after no very long time, must become dependent on foreign aid for support. They are made paupers."[12]

With figures from the Board of Canal Comissioners, Carey calculated an annual income for a laborer consisting of 10 months' work at $12 per month, 2 months' work at $5 per month, and a wife's annual income of $13. The total, which implied the availability of work throughout the year, was $143. As he stressed, this total income did not allow *"for one day's want of employment of the husband, or one day's sickness of him or his wife!"* Against the income he set a modest budget, 50 cents a week for rent, a total of $65.20 for food, $24 for clothes for the couple and $16 for their two children. With fuel and a few other expenses this bare bones budget totaled $145.74, more than they could expect to earn. Without "allowance of one day or one dollar for sickness, or want of employment," both of which were common, with no provision for unemployment, Carey's hypothetical family still could not quite match income and expenses. Their plight would have been worse, Carey pointed out, had he increased the number of their children, which would not have been unreasonable. The same results, he said, would emerge from calculating the income and expenses of the laborers on the railroad. Nor was the plight of weavers any better.[13]

Carey was right to stress the role of sickness, because illness was a major cause of destitution. A great many almshouse inmates were sick, and in histories of families on relief, illness almost always stands out as a major theme. The reasons are not hard to find. Work was dangerous and unhealthy; diets were inadequate; sanitary conditions in cities were dreadful; medical care was poor. When men took sick and died, they usually left no life insurance and few assets, and their widows had almost no way short of prostitution to support their families. Some widows with young children combined help from family, friends, and charity with sweated work sewing or washing. But when they took sick—and

8

not surprisingly they often did—they had no alternatives to private charity, relief, or the poorhouse. Families often survived by putting all possible members to work. Even young children were expected to help by taking care of their younger brothers and sisters, collecting bits of fuel from the streets, wharves, and woods, or by begging. Those families in which at least one person remained well enough to work survived best.[14]

Landlords and grocers often helped by giving credit that enabled poor people to weather periods of unemployment or sickness. (Indeed, the role of credit as a form of relief never has received the attention it deserves from students of poverty.) Yet, often no one could earn any money. Fathers were dead or sick; mothers were consumed with the care of very young children or ill; children were too young to work, sick themselves, or had left home. To be sure, kin were expected to help each other, and charity workers almost always tried to find relatives who could assist a family before they gave it very much relief. But most poor families only had very poor relatives with no surplus to share. In other cases, kin lived too far away from each other to be of any help.[15]

Problems intensified in old age. Men did not retire. They worked until they were fired or could continue no longer. Women, who usually outlived their husbands, inherited almost nothing. A few men had small life insurance policies, and a fortunate minority of working-class people had bought and paid for a home. Otherwise, elderly people usually lived with their children. With no savings, no pension, no social security, or if they lacked children willing or able to care for them, old people often found themselves completely destitute.[16]

Immigration also intensified the problem of poverty. Between 1820 and 1860 more than five million immigrants entered the United States. Although it seems unlikely that foreign countries, as protesters claimed at the time, were dumping their paupers on American shores, the massive antebellum immigration—especially because of the Irish famine in the 1840s and early 1850s—did exacerbate the problem of poverty and poor relief. Many immigrants had used up all their money simply to get to America; some arrived sick from the trip; others could not find work; many, contemporaries said, "had been accustomed to receiving relief in their old homes, and so were not abashed to ask for it when they came to the New World." And, of course, immigrants helped overstock the labor market for unskilled work. (However, it is crucial to remember that without massive immigration America would have lacked an adequate labor *dependence* supply to build its infrastructure of canals, railroads, and turnpikes. American *on immigrants* homes would have lacked domestic servants, and American factories would have *as laborers* lacked enough hands.)[17]

Even this cursory overview shows why poverty was a major problem in early and mid-nineteenth century America. The great transformation of social and economic structure disrupted social relations and created a class of highly mobile wage laborers subject to irregular, seasonal, dangerous, unhealthy, often badly paid work. Even in the urban South, "the incidence of poverty increased throughout the antebellum period." Public policy made no provision for the periodic unemployment endemic to the emerging system, no provision for the women left widows, or for the elderly without families. Those in need of relief were young men thrown out of apprenticeships or looking for work, unemployed household heads with families, widows without working children, and those sick and elderly people without kin who could care for them. Crises were woven into the very fabric of working-class experience, and periods of dependence were normal. They were integral to the structure of social and economic life. With luck, some people pulled themselves out. They got well or found work. Others were not so fortunate. Working-class experience was a continuum; no clear line separated the respectable poor from paupers. This is why all attempts to divide the poor into classes and all policies based on those divisions ultimately failed. In no instance was the failure more spectacular than in the history of the poorhouse.[18]

Poorhouses and Other Social Institutions

Poorhouses were one among a set of social institutions invented or redesigned early in the nineteenth century, all of which embodied similar assumptions and strategies. Together, they were a collective response to the great transformation of social experience that both frightened and exhilarated women and men confronted with the task of raising families, earning a living, and shaping public life at a time when old expectations crumbled, past practice offered few reliable guides, and the future remained unpredictable, even, to a very real extent, unimaginable.

Few formal, specialized institutions existed in colonial America. Criminals, for instance, were not punished by long jail sentences. Rather, they were held in jail only until trial; if found guilty, they were punished by fines, whipping, or execution. The mentally ill were cared for by their families or dumped in the few large almshouses built in the eighteenth century. The poor were cared for largely through some form of outdoor relief or auctioned off to local farmers. Poor strangers were told to leave town. Children of the poor learned to read in a variety of ways: at home, in small dame schools, or in town schools that they attended irregularly.

The Origins and Failure of the Poorhouse

By 1850, all of this had changed. Specialized institutions had been founded to care for the mentally ill, to rehabilitate juvenile delinquents, to educate the blind, deaf, and dumb, and to eradicate ignorance. New penitentiaries had been built on novel principles, and even almshouses became instruments of social policy.[19]

The new institutions all rested on optimistic assumptions about the possibilities of reform, rehabilitation, and education. Their sponsors believed that institutions could improve society through their impact on individual personalities. Because of their environmental sources, crime, pauperism, ignorance, and mental illness—which observers at the time usually confounded as different manifestations of an underlying and pathological condition of dependence—could be eradicated. Even intemperance could be treated in institutions because it originated in causes extrinsic to individual character, most often a faulty family life in childhood and an absence of religious and secular education. Institutions would seal off individuals from the corrupting, tempting, and distracting influences of the world long enough for a kind but firm regimen to transform their behavior and reorder their personalities. Even poorhouses shared in this rehabilitative vision; they would suppress intemperance, the primary cause of pauperism, and inculcate the habit of steady work.

The institutional explosion burst forth from both voluntary and state sponsorship; dotted the landscape with both residential asylums and nonresidential schools; and eventually encompassed almost everyone. (Many institutions were founded by philanthropists or voluntary groups and then taken over by the state; in some cases, philanthropists gave money to states to start new institutions; states, on the other hand, often gave money to voluntary associations to perform public functions, for instance, to run the educational system for New York City. This all points not only to the intermingling of voluntary and state activity but also to the very different, protean definition of *public* in early American history.) Early nineteenth century institutional development was defined by the creation of formal organizations to build or reform the character of distinct categories of clients: the mentally ill, criminals, juvenile delinquents, paupers, and children. This use of secular institutions as deliberate agencies of social policy, their specialization, and their emphasis on the formation or reformation of character represented a new and momentous development in modern history.[20]

What accounts for this institutional explosion? How are we to interpret the sudden emergence of the institutional state in early nineteenth century America? Answers are both general and specific. Each institution responded to a specific set of concerns. However, all of them confronted problems inherent in the great transformation of social experience that accompanied the emergence of capitalism in America.

The new institutions were heavy artillery in an assault on popular culture

11

that accompanied the diffusion of wage labor as the template for human relations. Consider two great issues: the problem of time and work discipline and the question of universal standards. Wage labor breaks the noneconomic ties between employers and employees. It frees workers by setting them adrift. An exchange of labor for money, nothing more, governs their relation to their employers. Wages depend on the price of finished products, local labor markets, and the demand for goods. Within wage labor, time is essential. Except for piece work, time is the unit through which labor is measured and paid. Wasted time costs employers extra money, raises the cost of finished goods, and lowers their competitive position in the market. For these reasons, it is imperative that workers labor steadily and efficiently.

All this may seem commonplace. But remember that wage work was novel in the early nineteenth century and that, even more than wages, time and work discipline were at the heart of conflicts between masters and workers. Flexible work schedules had defined the artisan life. In weaving, to take one example, each month masters gave out material to be woven. During the month weavers could organize their work as they wished, and many worked hardest at the end of the month when their work was due. Cordwainers traditionally took "blue Monday," a holiday that extended the weekend but interfered with masters' increasing demands for reliable, steady output; cabinetmakers, too, largely set their own work schedules.[21]

The transformation of casual, episodic, and flexible work patterns into steady, punctual, and predictable labor underlay many of the key struggles surrounding the creation of a working class in both England and North America, and through their emphasis on time and work discipline all of the new social institutions took a leading role in these conflicts.[22] As an example, consider public schools. In their early reports, even public school boards in small towns and villages discussed no question as often as punctual and regular attendance. Sometimes they even advocated locking the school door at the start of the day, turning away latecomers who had trudged miles through the snow. Within every other institution, order, predictability, and work also were central. Penitentiaries stressed a rigid, mechanical, "machine-like" schedule. Reform schools, "large congregate institutions with workshop routines," had unbending programs. The "orderly, predictable, and regular" routine in early mental hospitals was itself part of the therapy. And the work ethic—as will become clear—is what poorhouses were all about.[23]

An emphasis on universal standards also joined the culture of wage labor to the emergence of social institutions. Reformers assaulted the personalistic, ascriptive basis of much public life and advocated its replacement with universal standards that stressed achievement. Merit, or worthiness, should be defined by productive capacity, the ability to do a job better than someone else, or by meeting a bureaucratic standard, such as passing an examination. Above all, rewards should be earned, not distributed on the basis of kinship, friendship, patronage, or some other particularistic relation. Everywhere, reformers wanted to classify: to divide children into grades with clear criteria for promotion; to sort the poor into moral categories; to classify the insane; to grade prisoners and delinquents and demarcate clear standards for passage from one category to another. Rewards should be distributed by clear criteria applied without favor to everyone who fell into one of the narrow and proliferating categories through which nineteenth century policy entrepreneurs viewed their world. All of this reflected what Christopher Lasch has called the emergence of a "single standard of honor." The corollary, as Harry Braverman pointed out, was disposing of the rest as cheaply and conveniently as possible through the creation of institutions that cleared the marketplace of all but the economically active and productive.[24]

Despite their key role in a general cultural offensive, each new social institution had goals of its own. Each responded to a social problem exacerbated or redefined by the great social and economic transformation of the age. In the case of poorhouses, the problem was the forces that made poverty a major problem in late eighteenth and early nineteenth century America and the dramatic increase in the number of poor people asking for relief.

Pauperism and Relief Before the Poorhouse

Throughout the colonial period and the early nineteenth century, poor relief policy in England profoundly influenced American practice. On both sides of the Atlantic, rising expenses for relief and anxieties about both labor supplies and social order stimulated searching reexaminations of poor laws. Reformers predicted that the replacement of outdoor relief with poorhouses would curb the demand for relief, check the threatened demoralization of the poor, avoid interference with labor supplies, and inculcate a work ethic. However, reformers never managed to eliminate outdoor relief completely, and their great innovation—poorhouses—proved an abject failure.

Early American poor relief, it is important to stress, drew heavily on English precedents. In fact, four principles inherited from England underlay the local practice. First, poor relief was a public responsibility, usually assigned to officials called overseers of the poor. Second, it was profoundly local. Each parish in England organized its own system of relief and retained responsibility for its

influenced by English 4 principles

13

own people, even when they had temporarily moved away. This made the question of legal residence, or settlement, the most contentious practical problem in aid to the poor. Kin responsibility, the third principle, denied public aid to individuals with parents, grandparents, adult children, or grandchildren who could take them into their homes. Finally, concerns about children and about work were combined in legislation that authorized overseers to apprentice the children of paupers to farmers and artisans who agreed to train and care for them in their homes.[25]

At first, the colonies more or less copied the major features of English legislation. In fact, Rhode Island merely stated that the basis of its poor law would be 43 Elizabeth (the basis of the Elizabethan poor law). In America, as in England, poor relief was a local (at first township, later usually county) responsibility assigned to overseers of the poor. (In the South, until after the Revolution, the parish remained the unit for relief, which was administered by the Anglican clergy.) Relief policy, also as in England, authorized overseers only to aid those poor with a settlement and to bind out children of paupers as apprentices.[26]

Poorhouses were only one of the four methods of poor relief practiced in most states. As late as 1851, in a report to the Rhode Island legislature, Thomas Hazard found all four within that small state.

> 1st. By venduing [auctioning or selling] them to the lowest bidder. 2nd. By contracting for their maintenance, with an individual, or individuals, through the agency of a committee or otherwise. 3d. By placing all the poor in one Asylum, owned by the town. 4th. By placing all such in an asylum as are bereft of home and friends, and administering out-door relief to such as have.

Although detailed practices varied greatly, the mixture of auction, contract, outdoor relief, and poorhouses, described by Thomas Hazard in Rhode Island in 1851, existed in most colonies a century earlier, although auctioning was less common in the South. It was mainly larger towns and cities that had built poorhouses (Boston, 1664; Salem, 1719; Portsmouth, New Hampshire, 1716; Newport, Rhode Island, 1723; Philadelphia, 1732; New York City, 1736; Charlestown, 1736; Providence, 1753; Baltimore, 1773). Smaller towns and villages usually followed the other practices.[27] The worst of these practices—and all other writers on poor relief seem to agree—was the first. "When stripped of all disguises, selling the poor to the lowest bidder is simply offering a reward for the most cruel and avaricious man that can be found to abuse them." The poor were auctioned most often in country towns, because it was a cheap way to care for them and because there were too few poor to make an almshouse practical.[28]

In time, most places chose poorhouses. However, despite their alleged economy—one of their principal selling points—in Britain and America it invariably cost more to keep paupers in almshouses than to support them in their homes. As with criminals or the mentally ill today, institutions have been an expensive response to a social problem. Given their cost and the availability of cheaper alternatives, the reasons state and local governments clung so long to poorhouses as the cornerstone of public relief are not transparent.[29]

Of course, not every town or county chose among alternatives in quite the same way. Everywhere, practices differed within the same state: towns and counties spent different amounts to help the destitute, varied the balance between indoor and outdoor relief, and ran their poorhouses differently. Despite variations, the contours of poor relief paralleled each other in critical ways from Maine to North Carolina, from Rhode Island, New York, and Pennsylvania to Kansas, Indiana, and Michigan. Poor relief history, therefore, exemplifies one of the great themes of American social experience: the continuities in institutional patterns across a sprawling, decentralized, and diverse nation. Looked at this way, the issue is not diversity. Rather, it is this: all over the country those nineteenth century Americans who controlled social policy made similar choices about poor relief. We should try to understand why.[30]

By the end of the eighteenth century, the two general patterns of relief were the township system of New England and the county system of Pennsylvania. The latter, which made the county rather than the town responsible for the poor, eliminated many settlement disputes, which had arisen between towns within the same county. In fact, Pennsylvania's poor laws became the most influential in the new nation because they were copied in the Northwest Territories and, subsequently, in the states created out of them. The Pennsylvania legislation was enabling, not mandatory. Counties asked for and were granted permission to build poorhouses. Except for New York, which passed a mandatory law, this was the pattern in most of the country. Nonetheless, even without coercion, the poorhouse became a familiar institution during the first decades of the nineteenth century. By the Civil War poorhouses had spread from cities and the more densely populated seaboard to rural towns and counties throughout most of the settled regions of the country, North and South. In the South, rural counties often abandoned their poorhouses in the first decades of the nineteenth century. With most of the dependent members of the population the responsibility of the slaveholders who owned them, official relief rates in the South remained, of course, much lower than in the North.[31]

When state reports in Massachusetts, New York, Pennsylvania, and New Hampshire in the 1820s all advocated almshouses as the major public policy for poor relief, they drew not only on English theory and practice, about which they were very well informed, but on American experience with almshouses in the preceding two decades. So uniformly positive were the towns with almshouses, that officials everywhere felt confident about recommending a shift away from existing, noninstitutional relief. The American pattern that emerged did not simply imitate English practice. The English attempted to ban all outdoor relief to ablebodied paupers. In America, only Delaware seriously tried to prohibit outdoor relief for any group. Moreover, not only did America lack a national system, but practices within states remained varied and permissive, and, as a consequence, arrangements differed among towns and counties within the same states.[32]

What, exactly, did poorhouse advocates hope to accomplish and why did poor law reform appear so urgent? First, in the early decades of the nineteenth century, state and local officials everywhere claimed pauperism was rising at an alarming rate. In 1821, a Massachusetts Committee, chaired by Josiah Quincy (hereafter Quincy Report), reported that "the increase of the pauper burden [in Massachusetts] has exceeded, in a given number of years, the proportion of the increase of the pauper burden of Great Britain." About 6 years later the secretary of New Hampshire wrote of the "rapid increase in the number of paupers supported by the public, and in the expense of supporting them."[33]

Relief roles grew most in cities. Yates, secretary of state of New York, pointed to the "dense population" of New York City "and of the large villages and towns, which, from their convenient situation for navigation and commerce, allure to their haunts and recesses, the idle and dissolute of every description." In the same year, the mayor of Schenectady pointed out "that cities are the great resorts for the straggling and vagrant poor, who although having no permanent settlement amongst us, still at times call loudly for relief and assistance." Unlike some social fears, the increase in the number and expense of paupers was tangible. In contrast to moral decay, lax family discipline, a decline in civility, or, even, to some extent the safety of the streets, it was not nebulous or largely a product of perception. Rather, it was concrete, measurable, translated into tax dollars. Because poor rates (taxes for poor relief) often were billed separately from other taxes, taxpayers immediately felt every increase in municipal expenses.[34]

As they reluctantly paid the mounting poor rates, early nineteenth century taxpayers tried to account for the increase in pauperism, and they developed a clear explanation. They placed some of the blame on the growth of cities and immigration. Even more, they stressed the role of intemperance. But the real villains were existing public poor relief practice and the indiscriminate generosity of private charity. In Massachusetts, the Quincy Report (1821) concluded, "That of all the causes of pauperism, intemperance, in the use of spiritous liquors, is the most powerful and universal." Three years later the articulate overseer of the poor in Albany claimed, "that if any measure could be devised, to diminish the use of spiritous liquors, the condition of the poor would at once be improved; for it is doubtless the principal cause of the suffering of a large proportion of the poor." European countries, many observers believed, increased America's problem by dumping their paupers on its shore. In 1850, for instance, the mayor of Bangor, Maine, argued that only the federal government could prevent European countries from assessing "a tax upon the property of this country sufficient for the maintenance of all the paupers on the face of the earth." In 1827, the Philadelphia Board of Guardians of the Poor wrote, "One of the greatest burthens that falls upon this corporation, is the maintenance of the host of worthless foreigners, disgorged upon our shores," and in the 1850s, to take a final example, a well-informed observer noted that one cause "for the increase of pauperism amongst us . . . is the increase of our foreign population."[35]

Despite immigration, the growth of cities, and drink, to many observers the great source of pauperism lay within poor relief practice itself. For private charity and outdoor relief encouraged idleness by undermining the relation between work and survival. To nineteenth century observers, the poor laws interfered with the supply of energy available for productive labor by draining the working class of its incentive. Paupers were living proof that a modestly comfortable life could be had without hard labor. Their dissipation was a cancer demoralizing the poor and eroding the independence of the working class.

Overseers of the poor in Beverly, Massachusetts, claimed that poor relief encouraged "idleness" and "improvidence." "The idle will beg in preference to working; relief is extended to them without suitable discrimination. They are not left to feel the just consequences of their idleness." Meanwhile, the "industrious poor" were "discouraged by observing that bounty bestowed upon the idle, which they can only obtain by the sweat of their brow." Massachusetts's climate made saving for winter necessary. If the poor spent all their money in the summer, in winter they would "be in want. This improvidence may be and often is encouraged by the facility with which relief is obtained." The Yates Report in New York put forth as "propositions very generally admitted" that "our poor laws are manifestly defective in principle, and mischievous in practice, and that under the imposing and charitable aspect of affording relief exclusively to the poor and infirm, they frequently invite the ablebodied vagrant to partake of the same bounty." Poor relief practices operated "as so many invitations to become beggars."[36]

Indiscriminate charity and outdoor relief eroded more than the will to work. They also destroyed character. When the poor started to think of relief "as a right," they began to count on it "as an income." All "stimulus to industry and economy" was "annihilated, or weakened" while "temptations to extravagance and dissipation . . . increased." As a consequence, "The just pride of

reason for growth of the poor

17

independence, so honorable to a man, in every condition" was "corrupted by the certainty of public provision."[37]

Even more, Charles Burroughs warned, the generous public aid that had begun to teach the poor that relief was a right promoted militancy and eroded the deference that should govern class relations. "The poor tax," he asserted, made relief impersonal. It was paid "without any comparative rememberance of the poor." At the same time, as poor people began to claim relief "as an obligation" owed to their "wretched condition," they became "jealous about the proper administration of the poor laws, and the encroachments [on their] . . . prerogatives." They started to "utter the language of discontent, complaint, and even vengeance." The indifference of the taxpayers and the militance of the poor widened "the breach between [them] . . . and the affluent. . . . The poor look to the rich, as hard hearted oppressors . . . and the rich look to the poor, as so many poachers in their domains."[38]

None of the critics of poor relief, it must be stressed, proposed to eliminate poverty. To most people of the time, the idea would have been preposterous. Even in America, the vast majority would have to scrabble hard for a living. Nor was the issue redistributing wealth; rather, it was this: how to keep the genuinely needy from starving without breeding a class of paupers who chose to live off public and private bounty rather than to work. These were the goals most commentators felt current poor relief practice defeated.

As the Quincy Report made clear, policy assumed the existence of two classes of paupers.

> 1. The impotent poor; in which denomination are included all, who are wholly incapable of work, through old age, infancy, sickness or corporeal debility. 2. The able poor; in which denomination are included all, who are capable of work, of some nature, or other; but differing in the degree of their capacity, and in the kind of work, of which they are capable.

No one should hesitate to help the first class of poor. Christian charity and ordinary human compassion made their care a clear duty, although it was not so clear where and by whom they should be aided. The real issue concerned the ablebodied poor. According to the Quincy Report, all the "evils" attributable to the current system of poor relief could be traced to the same root: "the difficulty of discriminating between the able poor and the impotent poor and of apportioning the degree of public provision to the degree of actual impotency." The able poor, so it was assumed, should fend for themselves. Indeed, it is only a slight exaggeration to say that the core of most welfare reform in America since the early nineteenth century has been a war on the ablebodied poor: an attempt to define, locate, and purge them from the roles of relief.[39]

18

The Origins and Failure of the Poorhouse

Perhaps the difficulty of drawing the line between the ablebodied and impotent poor led Yates, in New York, to use a different definition: the distinction between the permanent poor, "or those who are regularly supported, during the whole year, at the public expense," and the occasional or "temporary poor . . . who receive occasional relief, during a part of the year chiefly in the autumn or winter." However the poor were divided, the problem that eluded all commentators was finding a satisfactory way to limit relief to a portion of those who asked for help. As the seemingly straightforward behavioral categories proposed by Quincy and Yates proved difficult to put into practice, observers turned increasingly toward moral distinctions. Charles Burroughs pointed the way to the newer distinction in 1834 when he attempted to distinguish poverty from pauperism. Poverty was an "unavoidable evil, to which many are brought from necessity, and in the wise and gracious Providence of God." Poverty resulted not from "our faults" but from "our misfortunes," and the poor should "claim our tenderest commiseration, our most liberal relief." But pauperism was a different story. "Pauperism is the consequence of wilful error, of shameful indolence, of vicious habits. It is a misery of human creation, the pernicious work of man, the lamentable consequence of bad principles and morals." Relief to the poor was charity; relief to paupers increased "the evil in a tenfold degree." (Later in the century, Burroughs's moral categories were formalized into the distinction between the "worthy" and "unworthy" poor.)[40]

In the South, explanations of poverty among whites sometimes blurred the familiar distinction between worthy and unworthy poor. For distinctions of race ultimately proved more important than those of class. Whatever else it accomplished, poor relief was supposed to shore up white supremacy by assuring even needy whites a standard of living and work superior to blacks. "The *leitmotif* of the Southern public relief system," writes Bellows, "was to give definition to the role of the white laborer in the urban economy. Even in indigency and unemployment, a distinction had to exist between the white hireling and the black slave if the grand illusion of white supremacy was not to be eroded at its base." As a consequence, white Southerners often transmuted the distinction between worthy and unworthy poor into a division between neighbors and strangers. "Fear of strangers, vagrants and vagabonds better describes the antipathy aimed at some indigents of the city, rather than horror at their personal conduct."[41]

Critics also attacked two other major features of poor relief: the practice of auctioning off the poor and settlement laws. The case against auctions had two sides. One was its brutality. In New York, the Yates Report concluded, "The poor, when farmed out, or sold, are frequently treated with barbarity and neglect by their keepers," and "in more than one instance" the "cruelty and torture" inflicted by keepers had killed the paupers with whose care they were charged. Even more graphically, Abijah Hammond, in an address to the agricultural society of Westchester County in October, 1820, thundered:

> Most of the poor are *sold*, as the term is, that is, *bid off*, to those who agree to support them on the lowest terms, to purchasers nearly as poor as themselves, who treat them in many instances more like brutes than like human beings; and who, instead of applying the amount received from the poor-master, for the comfort of the pauper, spend it to support their own families, or, which is too often the case, in purchasing ardent spirits; under the maddening influence of which, they treat these wretched pensioners, and not unfrequently their own wives and children, with violence and outrage.[42]

infers abuse

Nonetheless—and this was the other criticism—the poor sometimes turned the system of auction or sale to their own advantage. Families sometimes put in the low bid for their own relatives because they were willing or able to care for them with very little extra money. When this happened, public funds subsidized a modestly comfortable life for dependent people with their kin. To poor law critics, these subsidies were an outrageous abuse of the taxpayers. The supervisor of Hunter, New York, wrote:

> Every pauper has more or less relations in the town, who seem to feel that it is a fine thing to get some money from the town, and yet keep the poor themselves. They dread the idea of their being sent to a house of industry, because they lose the money they draw from the town. Hence they raise a clamor against such a project, and enlist with them all the connexions of the pauper, his neighbors, etc. and the plan is defeated.[43]

Here is a hint that the attempt to replace older methods of relief with poorhouses met popular resistance in America as well as in Britain, where local opposition, especially in northern England, frequently was fierce. Although American historians have not studied this topic, there is no reason to believe that American working people understood the meaning of reformed poor laws less well than their British counterparts. Poorhouses, they heard, were designed to enforce discipline and help regulate labor markets and wages. Their advocates wanted to remove people too poor, sick, or old to care for themselves from their friends and families and put them into a harsh, degrading institution. In these circumstances, resistance became neither venal nor unreasonable. Poor people found allies in their resistance to poorhouses among the professionals and merchants who profited from their business and among the justices of the peace and overseers of the poor who earned at least some of their living from the unreformed system. As the Yates Report pointed out:

The Origins and Failure of the Poorhouse

The interests of the physician and the shopkeeper or merchant, in those towns in which the alms-house might not be located, would perhaps be affected by the proposed system [of county almshouses], and some hostilities might arise from that source. . . . in some towns the local feelings and interests of justices, overseers and constables may also be arrayed in some degree against this plan; nor is it the least item in the objections that will probably be made, that the paupers themselves and their connexions, and those who derive a profit from supporting the paupers, or expect to derive it, will also indulge in feelings hostile to the system.[44]

Except for the South, settlement remained the other great problem with the poor laws. Towns often spent more money ridding themselves of paupers than they would have spent supporting them. Aside from the trouble and expense of endless litigation, the system often was cruel, for old and sick paupers frequently were shipped from town to town, even in the middle of winter. The Yates Report estimated that one-ninth of all the taxes raised for poor relief were spent "in the payment of fees of justices, overseers, lawyers and constables" who decided and administered settlement questions. Part of the problem lay in the laws themselves, which were "so technical, numerous, and complicated, if not obscure, that even eminent counsel" often could not "determine questions arising" from them. What then could be expected from the decisions of local officials "unlearned in our laws"? The Albany overseer of the poor explained that the local constable charged with sending the poor on their way had to advance his own money to support and transport them. Often, he was not reimbursed for several months, sometimes not for a year, and, even then, his accounts were often examined in "a most rigid and . . . unjustifiable" way. For this reason, the constable tried to "rid himself of [paupers] at the least possible expense," and, as a result, the individual pauper was "bandied about from constable to constable, not unfrequently from one extremity of the state to another, generally in feeble health, and during the inclemency of the winter season."[45]
-   Although unsatisfactory for everyone, the mix of outdoor relief, the auction of paupers, and their transport from town to town was especially harsh on children. According to the Yates Report, "The education and morals of the children of paupers, (except in alms houses) are almost wholly neglected. They grow up in filth, idleness, ignorance and disease, and many become early candidates for the prison or the grave. The evidence on this head is too voluminous even for reference." Although many adult poor had passed beyond redemption, their children were quite another matter. By failing to intervene between parents and their children, reformers argued, the state had abandoned—temporarily, as it turned out—the opportunity to break the mechanism through which pauperism and its allies, crime and ignorance, perpetuated each other. This inability to break the cycle of pauperism added urgency to appeals for reform.[46]

21

The Case for the Poorhouse

Both the Quincy and Yates reports rejected the views of those English political economists who advocated the total abolition of all poor relief. They found such a draconian solution offensive and contrary to American sentiment. Rather, they recommended replacing most forms of outdoor relief, the auction, and the contract system with a network of almshouses (or poorhouses). Within the almshouses, work—especially farm labor—would be mandatory for all inmates neither too sick nor too feeble, and both idleness and alcohol would be prohibited. Ablebodied men would be pruned rigorously from the relief roles; begging would be barred and punished; children would be schooled; and settlement laws would be greatly simplified.[47]

Especially in England, the replacement of outdoor relief with poorhouses has echoed through time as a cruel solution to the problem of pauperism. And so it was. But in America, the goals of poorhouse sponsors were not entirely repressive. For they reflected an attempt to mitigate the harshness of contemporary poor relief practice by ending the auctioning of the poor to the lowest bidder and stopping the shunting of the poor from town to town regardless of their health or the weather. To their sponsors, poorhouses appeared an ideal way to accomplish a broad array of economic, disciplinary, rehabilitative, and humanitarian objectives.

Poorhouses had very clear goals: they were supposed to check the expense of pauperism through cheaper care and by deterring people from applying for relief. According to the Quincy Report, all the towns that had already built a poorhouse "without exception claimed a reduction in their expenses." In New York, the Yates Report estimated the annual cost of a pauper in an almshouse at twenty to thirty-five dollars and on outdoor relief not less than thirty-three to sixty-five dollars; if the pauper was old or sick, outdoor relief would cost at least eighty or one hundred dollars each year. County poorhouses, it was also argued, would spread the financial burden of relief more evenly among rural and urban areas, in contrast to the current system under which urban areas often paid three times as much as rural ones. Another projected benefit of a county poorhouse system was its contribution to the reduction of settlement problems. "The expenses of removals from extreme parts, and the consequent grievous litigation, as well as the payment of the innumerable host of officers, would be avoided."[48]

As for cutting the cost of poor relief through deterrence, consider the experience of New Bedford, Massachusetts, with its poorhouse. Since its construction the town had "experienced a diminution of that class of vagrants who have for years annoyed us." Before the poorhouse, the town's poor had been helped with outdoor relief, and very often people applied "for assistance for supporting their aged and infirm relations." With the opening of the poorhouse, "their applications" had "almost entirely ceased." Once people knew "that every Pauper must be removed to the Poor House, many causes combined to prevent their application for assistance." Franklin, New York, expected that a poorhouse would "in a great measure, deter many persons from applying for relief, except in cases of absolute necessity." "The prohibition against alcohol and mandatory work," predicted Charles Burroughs, "will deter many intemperate wretches, and lazy vagrants from seeking admission to these walls" and act "as a stimulant on their industry and moral feelings."[49]

Poorhouses were expected to do more than cut the expense of poor relief and deter potential paupers from asking for help. In the North—but much less so in the South—they also were supposed to transform the behavior and character of their inmates. Every town, an official from Pepperell, Massachusetts, pointed out, harbored "a class of people naturally disposed to be lazy and indolent." When boarded with private families, they indulged their habits, caring only for "what is sufficient to nourish the body," passing "their time in sloth and inactivity." But put "these characters" in a poorhouse, and "you find they are uneasy and discontented. A degree of pride begins to operate in their bosom; this proves an incentive to exertion; they quit their station and shift for themselves." Under the influence of a poorhouse superintendent who made them work and watched their behavior, paupers would "possibly in time become renovated." At the same time, poorhouses would strike a blow at intemperance, the great immediate cause of pauperism, first by prohibiting alcohol, second by deterrence. For magistrates should be given authority "to send any person, on view, found intoxicated, or in the habit of intoxication, for a certain period, to labor in a house of industry."[50]

Almshouses, their advocates predicted confidently, also would improve the lives of pauper children. Pauper children outside of almshouses, observed the Yates Report, were "not only brought up in ignorance and idleness"; their "health" was "precarious," and, often, they died "prematurely." Just the reverse happened in almshouses. Children's "health and morals" were "alike improved and secured," and they received "an education to fit them for future usefulness." For all these reasons, to its sponsors the poorhouse seemed a just, humane alternative to the practice of boarding out the poor. As one official from a New York town claimed, "The *infirm* could be more readily healed—the *idiot* more humanely provided for—the *lunatic* more securely kept, and the *youth* better prepared for society."[51]

Poorhouse advocates believed they had good grounds for optimism. Although poorhouses were novel, enough of them existed to compile a swelling body of evidence about their virtues. The verdict appeared unanimous. Every town or city that had established a poorhouse before the early 1820s reported a reduction in the cost of poor relief and an improved moral climate. Yates's survey of pauperism throughout the country concluded, "where the poor-house system has prevailed for the greatest length of time, and to the greatest extent, the ratio of pauperism, and of the amount of expense is less than it is in any other state in which that system has been more recently or partially introduced." This is why Pennsylvania, Delaware, Rhode Island, and Virginia had the lowest ratios of paupers in the country. At a local level, to take only one example, the supervisor of Brookhaven, New York, estimated that the establishment of a poorhouse in 1817 had reduced expenses for pauperism by one-third.[52]

Poorhouse advocates even exuded optimism about paupers' ability to produce their own food and do other useful work. Salem, Massachusetts, for instance, appears to have been especially successful at employing its poorhouse inmates. The town had opened a new almshouse in 1816. In the next year, about 18 acres of land were broken up and planted, producing 4,391 pounds of pork (of which 2,000 pounds were sold for $280), 1,000 bushels of turnips, and 2,700 bushels of potatoes. Besides farming, inmates worked at "spinning, weaving, coopering, the manufacture of small articles of cabinet furniture, making the wood work of all the tools used on the farm, corn brooms, etc. etc." All the shoes worn by the inmates had been made in the almshouse as had most of the clothes. Picking oakum, probably the major employment of paupers in most almshouses, was "restricted to those who are confined to their rooms by age and infirmity, or are otherwise incapable of hard labor." Even New York City reported a large and varied product from its almshouse inmates, and as late as 1843, Walter Channing could write glowingly about the industry in Boston's Almshouse.[53]

The optimism of early almshouse sponsors and administrators contradicts most reports made only a few years later. Clearly, in their early years, it was at least plausible to think of almshouses positively, as humane, reformatory institutions, reducing expenditures for poor relief and checking the growth of a demoralized pauper class. But it is difficult to believe that even in these early years the picture was quite as cheery as poor law reformers would have had their contemporaries believe. For one example, recall the hints of opposition, the local resistance to poorhouses. From the start, poorhouses were not popular institutions. Nor were they supposed to be. Here is the heart of the issue. Irreconcilable contradictions had been stamped into the foundations of almshouses. The almshouse was to be at once a refuge for the helpless and a deterrent to the ablebodied; it was supposed to care for the poor humanely and to discourage them from applying for relief. In the end, one of these poles would have to prevail. The almshouse was to be both a voluntary institution, entered with no more coercion than the threat of starvation, and, in some cases, a penal institution for vagrants and beggars. Asserting that poverty was not a crime, almshouse sponsors protested against the inhumanity of existing poor relief practices such as auctioning the poor or shunting them around from town to town. At the same time, their own comments confounded crime and poverty. Not least, they expected institutions designed to house only the most helpless and infirm paupers to be hives of industry and productivity. If the almshouses worked, the aged and infirm would be held hostage to the war on ablebodied paupers. In essence, social policy advocated shutting up the old and sick away from their friends and relatives to deter the working class from seeking poor relief. In this way, fear of the poorhouse became the key to sustaining the work ethic in nineteenth century America.

The Failure of the Poorhouse

By the 1850s, almost every major institution founded in the early nineteenth century had lost its original promise. For a short time it had appeared that most of them would work in the way their promoters had predicted. Early mental hospitals reported astonishing rates of cure; reform schools allegedly transformed young delinquents; and poorhouses purportedly slowed the growth of pauperism and sheltered the helpless. But within several years this early optimism faded. Mental hospitals did not cure; prisons and reform schools did not rehabilitate; public schools did not educate very well; and poorhouses did not check the growth of outdoor relief or promote industry and temperance. A preoccupation with order, routine, and cost replaced the founders' concern with the transformation of character and social reform. Everywhere, reform gave way to custody as the basis of institutional life.[54]

Poorhouses had degenerated especially badly. A select committee of the New York State Senate visited the state's poorhouses in 1856 and issued a scathing indictment. "The poor houses throughout the State," wrote the committee, "may be generally described as badly constructed, ill-arranged, ill-warmed, and ill-ventilated. The rooms are crowded with inmates; and the air, particularly in the sleeping apartments, is very noxious, and to casual visitors, almost insufferable." Sometimes forty-five inmates slept in one dormitory "with low ceilings, and sleeping boxes arranged in three tiers one above another." Within poorhouses good health was an "impossibility." Almost none of them had adequate hospital

[handwritten margin notes: "physical plant inadequate" and "unhealthy"]

25

facilities, and the sick were "even worse cared for than the healthy." Medical attendance was "inadequate" and physicians "poorly paid." Sometimes inmates died with no medical attention at all. One county poorhouse that averaged 137 inmates reported 36 deaths in the previous year, "yet none of them from epidemic or contagious disease," a death rate that indicated "most inexcusable negligence." With almost no classification of their inmates, men and women mingled freely during the day and, even, at night. As a result, many of the births in poorhouses were "the offspring of illicit connections." Petty graft exacerbated the problem of poorhouse administration. In two counties the contractor who supplied the poorhouse was "allowed to profit by all the labor which he could extort from the paupers." In both these cases, the contractor was also one of the superintendents of the poor and in one case, even, the superintendent of the poorhouse himself. In 1857, in Charleston, South Carolina, shocked commissioners of the poor reported:

> The Yard was uncleansed—the surface drains filled with offensive matter—the Privies in a most filthy state—the floors most unwashed, many of the windows obscured by apparently many months accumulation of dust and cobwebs—nearly all the beds and bedding in a disgustingly neglected state, and in some localities, swarming with vermin.[55]

Managerial problems in poor relief began with the office of overseer of the poor. So unpopular was the job that it sometimes took fines to force men to serve. In Philadelphia, for example, until the late 1820s men usually did not serve as Guardians of the Poor for more than a year. Only when paid, full-time officials assumed more of the day-to-day burden of handling applications for relief and investigating the merit of individual cases, did guardians begin to accept longer terms. Philadelphia's guardians disliked most dealing with the outdoor poor. However, some of them managed to win a potentially lucrative place among the managers of the almshouse, who often sold the institution supplies.[56]

Indeed, because superintendents or overseers of the poor often used their offices as sources of graft, petty corruption infected the administration of poor relief. In New York State, said one experienced observer, one of the superintendents of the poor usually was a "country merchant" and two were farmers. They divided the "purchasing of supplies" among themselves. The merchant sold the poorhouse its meat and other articles from his own store at the "highest retail prices," charging even "for the very wrapper and twine" used to package the goods. He had little incentive to "restrain waste and extravagance" because the more he sold, the larger his profits. Farmers also had their own intricate fiddles that brought them a "nice profit." The whole process of supplying poorhouses, in fact, was "reduced to a regular system in most counties in the State."

The Origins and Failure of the Poorhouse

Petty corruption proved hard to eradicate. Almost forty years later in the 1890s, Amos Warner included in his complaints about poor relief administration "dishonest or wasteful mismanagement of funds."[57]

Warner also pointed to the limited ability of most poorhouse keepers and described how job pressures drove even well-meaning men to brutality. With "dreary work, small pay, and practically no general recognition" for their services, whatever their quality, "a sensitive, high-minded, ambitious man" was not likely to accept the job, and, "almost of necessity," the typical keeper was "a tolerably stolid, unsympathetic person, and one who had not been very successful in other lines." Unfortunately, the job usually exceeded his abilities. He was sent "a miscellaneous assortment of the diseased, defective, and incapable" and told to care for them without "the proper facilities." Although the county "cut his appropriations to the lowest possible point," he did not complain for fear of losing his job. Most of the inmates, moreover, were "bad-tempered, unreasonable, and inveterately querulous. They would complain no matter what might be done for them." In these circumstances, he gradually came to feel that "it does not matter what is done for them—that anything is good enough for them." The result was brutality. "He becomes brutal unconsciously, and almost in self-defense. After a few years he does, without question, things that would have seemed absolutely awful to him when he first entered his duties."[58]

Managerial inferiority

In North Carolina, even in the early twentieth century, it was not "unusual to find a superintendent" who belonged "to a class only slightly superior to most of his inmates." Rarely could he be compared with "the other officials of the county." He was "not the type of man who could be elected register of deeds or clerk of the court." His wife, of course, usually belonged "to the same class as he." In 1922, a survey of poorhouse superintendents in eighty counties found that seventy-four had less than a high school education. "The only superintendent who had any college training" had been "removed because he did not belong to the same political faction as the county commissioners." Many superintendents were "practically illiterate," and a few could not read and write. Most—sixty-nine of eighty—had been farmers, and thirty had been tenant farmers. The eleven nonfarmers "came from various occupations—merchant, salesman, carpenter, mason, jailer, policeman, 'moonshiner.' "[59]

Like other new service professions that developed during the nineteenth century, poorhouse administration had to forge an occupational identity. The first school systems, penitentiaries, reform schools, mental hospitals, and poorhouses could not draw on a pool of trained administrators or a body of technical and managerial knowledge. In each case, however, as officials created a new role and accumulated practical experience, they developed their own organizations, journals, and training procedures. As a result, by the early twentieth century, each new service activity had generated a new profession: school superintendent, penologist, psychiatrist, social worker, public welfare official. Each of these professions originated in practice, that is, from the attempt to build and run novel institutions.[60]

In New York State, the Annual Convention of the County Superintendents of the Poor, which met first in 1870, was a loosely knit organization that held annual conventions, published its proceedings, and sometimes lobbied the state legislature. Over the years, its proceedings show the gradual development of an occupational identity, fostered, especially late in the century, by attacks on county poorhouses and attempts to remove the insane to state institutions. A few superintendents, who held their jobs for many years (such as the one from Rochester), obviously were well read in contemporary literature about pauperism and poor relief, and they tried to run their own institutions professionally and to stimulate their colleagues throughout the state to higher standards. Indeed, by 1913 the County Convention felt sufficiently professional to change its name to the New York Association of Public Welfare Officials.

Nonetheless, probably no more than a few poorhouses were very well administered. Small county poorhouses had few staff besides the keeper or superintendent and his wife. Cities such as Philadelphia or New York developed elaborate hierarchies for administering their large poorhouses, but these, too, were understaffed. Medical care, always insufficient, sometimes was left to local doctors for whom the poorhouse offered a lucrative and steady source of income—and a source of contention among local physicians who sometimes underbid one another for the contract. Occasionally, as in Philadelphia, medical students provided much of the medical care. Professional nurses were almost nonexistent, and most of the nursing was done by other inmates.[61]

Inmates, in fact, did a great deal of the routine work around poorhouses. They not only nursed other inmates and gardened but also often cooked, cleaned, sewed, and did other small jobs. Inmates virtually ran the larger poorhouses, as in Philadelphia, where they greatly outnumbered the paid staff. With inmates serving as attendants, officials had little control over life on the wards, and large poorhouses turned into rowdy, noisy places in which discipline was almost impossible. According to Clement, in Philadelphia some of the inmates formed their own organizations; others fought with each other; and the city's ethnic tensions erupted into conflicts within the almshouse. Other inmates peddled small goods—"pins, needles, thread, and other small personal articles"—to one another while the "gatekeepers peddled drugs, fruits, and candy." (Inmates were supposed to turn all their money over to the agent who admitted them; so the medium of exchange remains unclear.) Even liquor was easily available. Doctors failed to hide the keys to the liquor cabinet; the inmates stole liquor from the managers' private stock; employees smuggled in liquor which they sold; and doctors prescribed a great deal of liquor as medicine. In 1825–26, for example,

28

they authorized the purchase of 1,624 gallons for the hospital, or an average of one-half gallon for every person admitted during the year. This easy availability of liquor, of course, defeated attempts to curb the intemperance thought to be the major immediate cause of pauperism.[62]

The ease with which inmates could enter or leave almshouses made discipline problems worse. Despite a rule that required inmates to work off the cost of their care, in Philadelphia inmates left the almshouse easily: they went to an official who checked their records and, usually, finding nothing amiss, handed them their clothes and allowed them to leave. (Inside the almshouse all the inmates had to wear the same uniform.) Warner complained of the "laxness" of admission and discharge policies. Because everyone was "entitled to be saved from starvation and death and exposure," anyone could enter an almshouse. But the almshouse, after all, was not a penal institution and it "was in the interest of no one to have persons there who" could "support themselves outside." This meant that inmates virtually could discharge themselves at will; "the door swings . . . outward or inward with the greatest ease." As a result, the almshouse became a temporary refuge for the degenerate poor, "a winter resort for tramps . . . a place where the drunkard and the prostitute" recuperated "between debauches." The open-door policy, as characteristic of Charleston as of Philadelphia, had spawned a class of almshouse recidivists. Citing a study in Hartford, Warner reported the case of one woman who "came and went thirteen times in twenty-two and one-half months."[63]

A failure to classify inmates underlay the administrative problems of poorhouses. Critics throughout the century complained that many poorhouses did not separate paupers by age, condition, sex, and color; allowed the worthy poor to mingle with the degraded; and failed to send the insane or other handicapped inmates to special institutions. In 1855, a New York critic complained that the "poor of all classes and colors, all ages and habits, partake of a common fare, a common table, and a common dormitory." Respectable widows who found themselves in poorhouses as a result of financial "misfortunes" had to sit at the same table as "a negro wench . . . and a filthy prostitute." Nearly forty years later, Warner charged, "Probably a majority of the grave evils which could be charged at the present time to the American almshouse have their origin in a lack of proper classification," by which he meant both the reluctance to remove some categories of people—children and the insane particularly—to special institutions as well as the failure to sort out the inmates who remained. He recommended classification by color, "separation of the sexes," "isolation of defectives," "special provision for the sick," and "classification by age . . . and . . . character." Classification remained a defect in poorhouses well into the twentieth century. Writing in the mid-1920s, Harry C. Evans claimed, "The poor-farm is our human dumping ground into which go our derelicts of every

29

description. Living in this mass of insanity and depravity, this prison place for criminals and the insane, are several thousand children and respectable old folk, whose only offense is that they are poor."[64]

One other problem made classification impossible and prevented the poorhouse from reaching any of its goals other than deterrence. That, of course, was the cheapness that governed poor relief, what Warner called the "culpable stinginess . . . of the appropriating power, resulting in inadequate or unhealthful food, lack of proper building, heating apparatus, clothing and so forth." Everywhere, the real concern of public officials was to keep poor relief as inexpensive as possible. In the end, all the various goals of poor law reform throughout the century could be sacrificed, as long as taxes for poor relief went down.[65]

Within poorhouses, the insane suffered especially badly. Often treated abusively, the insane poor were "confined" to "cells and sheds," that were "wretched abodes, often wholly unprovided with bedding." For the most part, male attendants looked after female inmates; sometimes they whipped inmates; in other cases they chained them in their "loathsome cells." "In some poor houses, the committee found lunatics, both male and female, in cells, in a state of nudity. The cells were intolerably offensive, littered with the long accumulated filth of the occupants, and with straw reduced to chaff by long use as bedding, portions of which, mingled with the filth, adhered to the persons of the inmates and formed the only covering they had." Children, however, worried the New York Senate committee most. Outside of New York City and Kings County (Brooklyn), at least thirteen hundred children lived in the state's poorhouses, "enough, in these nurseries, if not properly cared for, to fill some day all the houses of refuge and prisons of the State."[66]

Nor did most poorhouse superintendents manage to find useful work for their inmates. In fact, "idleness" remained "a great evil," most notable during the winter "when the houses are crowded, where there is little out door work to be done, and when the inmates are in the most vigorous state to do full work." In most poorhouses, the best source of work, farming or gardening, was "unavailable in the winter, just at the time when a rigid work-test is most essential." Work remained a problem that plagued poorhouse administrators throughout the century. Writing in 1894, Amos Warner pointed out how much more it usually cost to "set the inmates of an almshouse to work than their work is worth." They could be supported "more cheaply in idleness," he said. Finding work for women inmates, however, was easier. There were "relatively so few" of them that they usually could be put to work usefully "taking care of the house and in doing the laundry-work and sewing."[67]

In the Philadelphia almshouse, managers repeatedly tried to organize profitable factories run by inmates. They never succeeded. Only a minority of inmates were healthy enough or strong enough to work; often goods were produced

30

more cheaply outside the almshouse; and inmates had few skills. Nonetheless, managers clung to the importance of work for its moral as well as its economic returns. In the 1820s, they sold the poorhouse horses and instead constructed tread wheels with which to punish inmates. When there were too few men and women who needed punishment because they were lazy or had venereal disease, the managers used mentally ill inmates to work the tread wheels. Despite their inefficiency and a committee's recommendation to replace them with steam-driven machinery, most officials wanted to keep the tread wheels to deter the poor from seeking public relief.[68]

Disturbed by the idleness of most poorhouse inmates, the New York Commissioners of Public Charities observed "that pauper labor still remains very far behind what it should be in productiveness." Even discounting the sick and old, inmates did not earn a third of the cost of their support. Given this situation, the commissioners urged sentencing the ablebodied and others convicted of minor offenses to special workhouses for as long as possible (at least 3 months), where they would be made to "labor systematically" and be taught a trade. In Kansas, the discipline on poor farms was penal. A visitor found inmates forbidden to speak to each other, "except concerning their work," and if they "became unruly, a jail room was used. . . . They were also sometimes deprived of their meals as a punishment." These examples show how social policy confounded crime and poverty. Extreme poverty among ablebodied men itself was a crime that justified their detention; criminals differed so little from ablebodied paupers that they could be sentenced to the same institution. Work was important, first, because wherever possible paupers should earn their support. Second, it could help make paupers independent by teaching them a trade. But most of all, it deterred shirkers from applying for public relief.[69]

In his letters on pauperism, "Franklin," a well-informed New York newspaper correspondent, unintentionally highlighted the ambiguities in the stress on work within poorhouses. Whether work returned a profit ultimately was irrelevant; any work was better than none because its greatest value was deterring others from seeking public relief. Everywhere, noted Franklin, paupers earned only a tiny amount. The average for New York State was $3.15 per year; in Boston, it was $4.73; in Philadelphia, $4.71; in Essex County, Massachusetts, $4.53. Only Providence, Rhode Island, where paupers annually averaged $16.37, stood out as an exception. Not only did paupers in Providence earn more, but the city supported more paupers who, for one reason or another, were incapable of working. The Providence Poorhouse rigidly enforced "the rule . . . that every one able to work must work." If no profitable work was available, "they set them at something which is not profitable, at all events they must be kept employed." During his last visit, Franklin had seen "a party of men carrying wood from one corner of the yard to another and piling it there; when it was all removed it was brought back again and piled in the old place." This sort of practice rid "Providence of all lazy drones, such as infest our poor houses to a great degree." "Franklin" had begun his argument by stressing the need to increase the profitability of pauper labor, but he slipped without transition into the virtues of labor, any hard labor, for its own sake. In the end, it was deterrence, not profitability, that mattered.[70]

Satisfactory work arrangements rarely existed. Work's deterrent, educational, and moneymaking purposes contradicted each other, and the large share of old, sick, and disabled inmates left only a minority able to labor. The most successful work was farming, and poorhouses often were built in the country with farms attached to them. Indeed, in many states they were called poor-farms rather than poorhouses. In some instances, superintendents who were both good managers and good farmers ran productive farms that grew a large share of the inmates' food. Even in Philadelphia, the farm attached to the poorhouse was relatively successful. However, in many instances, farms, like manufacturing operations, were failures. In 1872, for example, Dr. C. T. Murphey, criticized the failure of the farms attached to North Carolina's poorhouses. "If it be possible to contemplate any one feature more than another of the faulty management of our houses," he wrote, "it is the neglect and want of proper cultivation of vegetable gardens." At least half of the inmates' food could be grown on one well-cultivated acre, but the year's crops were "barely sufficient" for "the overseer and his family, and apples and fruit during their season (so abundant in North Carolina)" were "regarded as a great luxury by the inmate poor, and . . . seldom found among them either as a relish or food." Poorhouse farms often failed because in the summer when they needed ablebodied labor, healthy younger men left to work elsewhere. Indeed, poorhouses remained most crowded in the winter when they could offer their inmates little outdoor work. This is why even most country poorhouses failed to employ their inmates usefully.[71]

Poorhouses not only failed to find work for their inmates; they did not even manage to reduce the expense of poor relief. Despite the confident predictions of their founders in the 1820s, it proved more expensive to support someone in a poorhouse than on outdoor relief. The New York Senate Committee pointed out that "half the sum requisite" to support a person in a poorhouse "would often save them from destitution, and enable them to work in their households and their vicinity, sufficiently to earn the remainder of their support during the inclement season when indigence suffers the most." Dirty, dangerous, brutal, demoralizing, and expensive, poorhouses had become "unsuitable refuges for the virtuous poor, and mainly places of confinement for the degraded." Poor inmates received worse treatment than criminals, worse even than animals. "Common domestic animals are usually more humanely provided for than the paupers in some of these institutions; where the misfortune of poverty is visited with greater deprivations of comfortable food, lodging, clothing, and warmth and ventilation than constitute the usual penalty of crime."[72]

The New York Senate Committee did not evaluate how well poorhouses played their other role. For they had been founded not only to care for the indigent and helpless but to deter the poor from asking for relief. No one was supposed to want to go to a poorhouse. By their very existence, poorhouses were supposed to spur the working class to independence. Most commentators implied that poorhouses succeeded as deterrents, but the actual situation was more complex. In the 1850s, one poor relief critic argued that poorhouses had made the poor "less independent than they had been twenty years" earlier. In the 1830s, he said, "there was a strong repugnance on the part of the poor to go to the County house, or to accept public relief in any form," and they would suffer an "astonishing" amount "rather than become a public charge." Equally "astonishing" was "the extent to which they carried the science of frugality." Now, the poor had become "more wasteful," with "less sense of shame in living on the public." Public policy bore much of the blame for this demoralization of the poor, for it was common to hear the inmates in county poorhouses "discussing the merits of Poor Houses in different parts of the State, just as fashionable travelers discuss the merits of the Ocean House at Newport, or the United States at Saratoga." Paupers had begun to think of "County Houses as places of rest and repose, intended to shield them from effort and labor" and could see no reason not to "avail themselves of their comforts without scruple, as often and as long as it suits their convenience."[73]

One lesson observers learned was the incompatibility of deterrence and compassion: the spread of fear and the kindly treatment of decent poverty could not coexist. One or the other always prevailed. This was the reason poorhouse critics increasingly argued for the separation of the ablebodied into special workhouses. By dividing the inmates into the ablebodied and deserving two separate policies could exist: one harsh, punitive, and centered on work, the other more compassionate and generous. However, very few places managed to create both a workhouse and an almshouse, and, in any event, in practice, the division of individual cases rarely was as easy as commentators implied. Some people were helpless because they were sick, insane, or old. But for others, the line was not nearly so clear. Maintaining two institutions, moreover, would have strained the administrative capacity and financial resources of towns and counties already reluctant to provide more than the most minimal support, even for the impotent poor. Even more, occasional bursts of sentiment aside, poorhouses were not supposed to do more than keep old and helpless inmates from starvation. They existed to deter the impotent as well as the ablebodied poor from seeking their shelter. Whether some poorhouses chose compassion over deterrence in the mid-nineteenth century and so encouraged homeless men to seek them out is not the main point. Most poorhouses offered few comforts or attractions. By the close of the century, at the latest, dread of the poorhouse was virtually universal. In the end, deterrence won.

By ignoring the contradiction in poorhouse goals, the New York Senate Committee could retain some optimism, a faith that honest, capable management could turn poorhouses around. But poorhouse managers needed support, and the committee, worried about public neglect, complained that citizens generally showed "little interest in the condition even of those" poorhouses "in their immediate neighborhood." Even people who took a "great interest in human suffering" never visited poorhouses and were "entirely uninformed" of the horrors that lurked in a "county house almost at their own doors." A correspondent to the Savannah *Republican* made a similar criticism of public involvement with poorhouses in the urban South. In the last analysis, the New York Senate Committee concluded, this "apparent indifference on the part of the citizens" accounted for the "miserable state to which these houses have fallen." Twelve years later, in 1869, the newly appointed Commissioners of Public Charity reviewed the state's poorhouses and found them in much the same condition as had the earlier Senate committee. Quoting at length from the committee's report, the commissioners observed, "the condition of things twelve years ago corresponds with our representations today." They pointed out that the Senate committee had criticized the "little interest taken by citizens in the counties in the condition of the poorhouses" and attributed much of their miserable state to "this apparent indifference." Though the committee had made "a strong and urgent appeal to the benevolent to look into the condition of the poor," there had been "little, if any, response."[74]

The commissioners' complaints about public indifference reflected a growing fear that the well-to-do had abandoned their public responsibilities. Not only the corruption of politics but the decay of public institutions and the emergence of a militant, undeferential working class, so it was argued, resulted from the withdrawal of educated, well-off citizens from an active role in local government, the oversight of public institutions, and their former close and personal contact with the poor. The commissioners hammered at public indifference by pointing out that paying taxes did "not include the whole sphere of duty of the citizen to the community of which he is a member. He should take part at least in a general oversight of its municipal management, and constitute himself a moral policeman in home affairs."[75]

The reassertion of the citizen as "moral policeman"—a major theme of late nineteenth-century history, reflected in scientific charity, the temperance movement, and the wars against sexuality—helped shape the history of poorhouses. "Moved by considerations of a purely benevolent character," reported the commissioners in 1872, "some public spirited citizens of Westchester county, acting under the suggestions of Miss Louisa L. Schuyler, have taken initiatory steps looking toward a local supervision of its poor house, by the organization of a local visiting committee." The criticism of indifference had worked; the women of Westchester County became the nucleus of a new organization, the New York State Charities' Aid Association, a coalition of county associations of well-to-do citizens, mainly women, whose members attempted to stimulate improvements in local poorhouses through systematic visiting. As might be expected, poorhouse keepers did not always welcome their new observers. In fact, the Westchester visitors at first were denied entrance to the poorhouse. Using its influence, however, the association turned to the state legislature and, within a year, had sponsored a bill granting them access to poorhouses. Their success revealed the power and influence of their members, the close, complex relations between the state and voluntarism, and the indistinct boundaries between public and private that have always been a feature of American life.[76]

The watchfulness of the State Charities' Aid Association failed to transform poorhouses into decent, compassionate refuges for the destitute. Not only in New York but throughout the country, trapped by their contradictory purposes, undercut by poor management and inadequate funds, poorhouses never could find useful work for their inmates or offer the old, sick, and helpless, not to mention the ablebodied unemployed, much more than a roof and escape from death by starvation. Nor did they reduce pauperism or cut the cost of poor relief. In fact, despite the diffusion of poorhouses, the volume of outdoor relief continued to grow.

2   Outdoor Relief

Recurrent attacks on outdoor relief throughout American history have repeated the same stale myths: most of those on relief do not need help; what they do need is an incentive to work; those truly in need of assistance can be helped best by private charity. None of these familiar points have ever been valid, and their repetition in the face of massive contradictory evidence shows that relief, or welfare, rarely has had humane, effective alleviation of suffering as its primary goal. Anxieties about social order and discipline, worries about labor supply, resentment of taxes, and political ambition all have fueled relief policy. In fact, political ambition has driven the supporters of relief as well as its critics, for American urban politics has always been about the "distribution of goods and services." Ward politicians used outdoor relief to cement loyalty. Local manufacturers depended on it to sustain their workforce during slack seasons. Local merchants profited from contracts to supply poorhouses, from grocery orders given to the poor, and from cash spent on drink. Physicians earned money by caring for paupers at public expense. Thus, when reformers attempted to abolish outdoor relief, they bumped up against a complex network linking the poor, some local businessmen and professionals, and ward politicians in an exchange of welfare, cash, and votes. Late nineteenth century attempts to abolish outdoor relief—both those which succeeded and those which failed—thereby highlighted relief's mixed public/private economy and its key role in the politics of American cities.[1]

TABLE 2.1

Costs of Outdoor Relief and Poorhouses: New York State, 1840–90

Year	Outdoor Relief (No.)	Poorhouses (No.)	Outdoor Relief ($)	Poorhouses ($)
1840	11,937	14,315	120,159	269,103
1850	63,764	37,203	314,517	492,100
1860	174,403	39,563	524,943	351,820
1870	105,843	64,070	976,560	1,731,677
1880	70,667	89,909	749,267	1,712,581
1890	47,399	60,172	737,671	3,175,775

NOTE: Outdoor relief = numbers recorded as received "temporary relief." Poorhouse = number received in poorhouses during the year, number born in poorhouses during year, and number present in poorhouses on December 1.
SOURCE: Annual reports of the New York secretary of state on expenses of pauperism.

The Resilience of Outdoor Relief

Despite the predictions of their sponsors, poorhouses did not end public outdoor relief. With a few exceptions, most towns, cities, and counties helped more people outside of poorhouses than within them. Nonetheless, hostility to outdoor relief, which remained strong, escalated in the 1870s into a fierce attack. Some cities abolished public outdoor relief; others reduced the amount they gave. In the end, it proved easier to eliminate or reduce relief than to remove the reasons that made people ask for help, and by the early twentieth century most authorities reluctantly had admitted that outdoor relief played an indispensable role in the alleviation of human misery.

The persistence of outdoor relief could be illustrated with statistics from almost any state, even North Carolina, South Carolina, and Georgia. However, the statistics from New York, which are particularly complete from an early date (1839), were reported in reasonably consistent categories throughout the nineteenth century. (The figures do not show what form outdoor relief took. In some places, small amounts of cash were given; in others, relief was in kind, mainly food; nearly everywhere it included fuel during the winter; a number of cities also established souphouses in the first half of the nineteenth century.) Table 2.1 illustrates the numbers of people in New York who received outdoor relief and the number in poorhouses at decade intervals between 1840 and 1890 and the amounts spent for each type of relief within the state.[2] The table reveals that tens of thousands of people received outdoor relief throughout the century and highlights the enormous growth in their number during the 1840s, the decade of the great Irish famine immigration. Earlier in the century, the number receiving outdoor relief and the number helped in poorhouses were rather close, but they began to grow apart during the 1840s. By 1850, almost twice as many people received outdoor relief as were assisted in almshouses; by 1860, that ratio had more than doubled. Nonetheless, only in 1860 did towns and counties spend more on outdoor relief than on almshouses. The reason is that almshouse care, as the table shows, was much more expensive. By 1870, a decline had started in the number receiving outdoor relief, but the expense of both indoor and outdoor relief had mushroomed. Within the decade, the cost of outdoor relief had nearly doubled to $1 million, and the cost of almshouses had risen almost six times to nearly $2 million. (Figures during the height of the depression that began in 1873 would show a rise in the numbers, too, as would figures during most depressions.)

The figures for 1880 register the effect of the attack on relief that began in the 1870s. Outdoor relief had dropped; the almshouse population had increased; and the cost of relief, especially indoor relief, had gone down. By 1890, fewer people in New York received outdoor relief than in 1850 and fewer than in 1860 were in almshouses, whose costs had skyrocketed once again. (The declining numbers in almshouses should not be read as a drop in the problem of dependence. Many who had previously been inmates had been transferred to other institutions and others were driven out, as chapter 4 will show.) In a speech to the county superintendents of the poor, one leading poor law reformer pointed out that in 1870, when the population of New York State was less than 4.5 million, outdoor relief cost over $900 thousand; in 1896, with the population of the state about 7 million, the cost had dropped to about $843 thousand. The largest reduction had been in cities, not in the countryside. Indeed, country districts paid six times as much in outdoor relief as cities. The reason lay in the movement against outdoor relief sponsored by wealthy professionals in cities across the state.[3]

Despite the overall pattern, within New York State individual counties differed in the balance they struck between indoor and outdoor relief. Table 2.2 compares Erie County (mainly Buffalo), which remained relatively generous with relief; Kings County, (primarily Brooklyn), which was the first major city to abolish outdoor relief; and rural Oswego County. The number of people aided in Erie County remained relatively stable between 1850 and 1890 as did the number in Oswego after 1860. (Of course, the proportion helped went down because population increased.) However, in Kings County the number given both indoor and outdoor relief jumped enormously between 1850 and 1860 and in the next decade, too. A massive cutback in relief within Kings County followed. In 1880 and 1890, no one received public outdoor relief there, and the number in the poorhouse remained relatively steady. To take

TABLE 2.2
Relief Practices in Three New York Counties,
1850–90

Year County	Temporary Relief (No.)	Poorhouses (No.)
1850		
Erie	8,084	1,373
Kings	7,336	2,669
Oswego	292	265
1860		
Erie	6,238	1,444
Kings	19,261	6,291
Oswego	2,839	237
1870		
Erie	7,870	1,369
Kings	38,170	11,688
Oswego	2,643	244
1880		
Erie	4,828	2,123
Kings	0	7,028
Oswego	1,950	228
1890		
Erie	6,360	2,279
Kings	0	11,164
Oswego	2,235	385

SOURCE: Annual reports of the New York secretary of state on expenses of pauperism.

another example, relief practice varied widely in Indiana. In one county, 1 of every 13 people received public relief. In an adjoining and similar county, the proportion was 1 in 208. "Great differences in the proportionate amount of relief given," said Ernest Bicknell, secretary of the Indiana State Board of Charities, were "to be found, not only between adjoining counties and between counties which, though not contiguous, are similar in almost every respect, but also between adjoining townships in most of the counties."[4]

In Philadelphia in 1877, 8,147 people received outdoor relief and 2,387 were in the poorhouse. As late as 1917, 36,901 people received outdoor relief in Pennsylvania in a year when the state spent more than $4 million on its poorhouses. Clearly, outdoor relief persisted despite the hostility it generated and the partial success of attacks. Although year-by-year figures would show some correlation between the numbers on outdoor relief and economic conditions, fluctuations in the relief rolls resulted as much from policy as from the business cycle. Public outdoor relief did not decline in the late nineteenth century because of prosperity. In fact, until 1893, even recessions failed to stimulate spending. Outdoor relief decreased because of a national campaign launched against it.[5]

Attacks on Outdoor Relief

Public officials and would-be reformers periodically had attacked outdoor relief since the late eighteenth century. In Philadelphia, the first controversy took place in 1769, only to be repeated in 1774 and 1793, when the major form of outdoor relief ("outpensions") was abolished. In 1828, legislation eliminated outdoor relief in the city. (It was resumed when municipal finances improved and social conditions grew worse, in the 1840s.) In New York, reformers also—though less successfully—attacked outdoor relief in the 1820s.[6]

Arguments against outdoor relief remained depressingly similar throughout the century, as opponents trumpeted the same fears and predictions of catastrophe over and over again. Here is one by George Arnold, minister-at-large to the poor in New York City. Arnold figured out that the average amount of outdoor relief given each outdoor pauper was sixty-five cents, a "paultry pittance," which in most cases could have been "saved out of needless expenditures." For this tiny amount,

> more than twenty thousand persons were degraded to the condition of public paupers, deprived of their feelings of honourable independence and self-respect, and, together with many others who were rejected applicants for relief, were exposed to a powerful temptation to practice deception and fraud, had their fears of the consequences of idleness, improvidence, and vice, at least greatly lessened, and were many of them undoubtedly prepared to become ultimately, inmates of the alms-house or the penitentiary.

The demoralization of the poor through the erosion of independence and self-respect; the spread of idleness and the loss of the will to work; the promotion of immorality in all its ugly forms; and the increase in public costs through the growth of poorhouses and jails; these, so its opponents believed, were the consequences of outdoor relief. Other fears probably lurked a bit more below the surface. An Irish observer pointed out what many others undoubtedly thought in the 1820s, "No poor-law can be otherwise than injurious which interferes directly with the labour-market, and this of America does so even now, by giving relief in aid of wages."[7]

Outdoor Relief

One recurrent—even to this day—peculiarity about the attacks on outdoor relief is the lack of correspondence between the actual demography of relief and reformers' images. In the nineteenth century, most of the people helped with outdoor relief were widows, children, old people, or the sick. Very few had the capacity to work. Indeed, with the demography of outdoor relief as a backdrop, most arguments against it make very little sense. For instance, in New Bedford, Massachusetts, in 1853, 280 families with 1,098 persons received outdoor relief. In only 52 instances did officials label intemperance as the cause of need; for 60 families the problem was "want of employment"; 80 were sick or old; the rest were headed by women whose husbands had died, gone to sea, or left them. From 1811 to 1829 in Philadelphia, "between 86 and 91 percent of those on the outdoor relief rolls were females. Of these women, an 1814–15 census reveals that roughly two-thirds were single persons who were sick, disabled, or aged. The remaining one-third were single mothers (most of whom were widows), each of whom had two to three children to support." In Pennsylvania in 1875, of the 11,100 people who received outdoor relief, 12.5 percent were men, 40 percent women, and the rest children less than 16 years old. Of the adults, 55 percent were widowed and 35 percent single; 94 percent were reported as either abstinent or "moderate drinkers." Nearly half were illiterate and about 45 percent had been born in America. For 25 percent, destitution had been caused by "old age or permanent disability"; for nearly 49 percent the reason was "death, absence, or desertion of husband or father"; for nearly another quarter it was "temporary sickness or want of work of male heads of families and single men." Only 1 percent were "single women" and half that many were "insane persons and idiots" helped outside of institutions.[8]

Clearly, helpless widows and old people were not the major objects of the war on outdoor relief. Even the fiercest opponents of relief would have had difficulty predicting their imminent demoralization or associating their relief with interference in wages and labor supplies. Rather, the target was the minority who by some definition could be called ablebodied. Even though they were usually only a small fraction of those assisted outside poorhouses, although their numbers swelled during depressions, the presence of these potential workers on relief rolls upset many officials and reformers throughout the century. When they were unable to prune ablebodied men from outdoor relief, some cities tried to put them to work in various ways, from breaking stone and chopping wood to—in New York City—developing public works projects. Some reformers advocated the creation of Houses of Industry where the ablebodied would work during the day. Even more, opponents feared not just the people on relief but those who might be. Outdoor relief was dangerous not because of whom it helped but because of the lesson it taught by example. Its very existence was a threat to productivity, morality, and the tax rate, because the respectable working

41

class just might learn the possibility of life without labor. As with poorhouses, policy again held the sick and helpless hostage to fears about social order and the need for a dependable, industrious workforce willing to labor for low wages.[9]

Relief as a Public/Private Venture

The number of cities that abolished or reduced outdoor relief in the last two decades of the century gives one measure of the success of the campaign against it. The most thorough estimate of what cities had done was made in 1899 by Frederic Almy, secretary of the Buffalo Charity Organization Society. Almy assessed the relation between public and private relief in a two-part article in *The Charities Review*. Did the existence of municipal outdoor relief, he asked, retard private charity? Or, put another way, did the absence or abolition of public outdoor relief stimulate private philanthropy? To answer the question he gathered data from the forty cities in the United States whose populations exceeded 100,000. City statistics showed how much public relief existed, but accurate private statistics proved much more elusive. Working with local directories and informants, the best Almy felt he could accomplish was a ranking of cities into four groups, from high to low. His data show, first, how successful the opponents of outdoor relief had been. Ten of the forty largest cities no longer gave outdoor relief, and three others gave only "trifling" amounts. Truly, if the entire war had not been won, relief's opponents could claim many individual victories.[10]

The relations between public and private relief, however, were not quite as neat as Almy would have liked, though they were reasonably strong for cities that either had abolished outdoor relief or were very generous with private charity. None of the cities where private charity was "liberal" ranked high on public outdoor relief, and in eight of the nine cities that gave no public outdoor aid and for which figures could be compiled, private charity was either "considerable" or "liberal." Even though little relation between public and private assistance existed in the other cities, Almy argued that "A correspondence or balance between the amounts of public and private relief appears to be established."[11]

In fact, his figures show a wide variation in the amount of relief available in different cities across the country. The per capita amount of private relief varied from a high of thirty-four cents in Syracuse to a low of three cents in

42

Philadelphia. Per capita outdoor relief was twenty-eight cents in Buffalo, thirteen cents in Scranton, five cents in Baltimore, and no relief in Philadelphia. The case against outdoor relief was national; reformers made the same arguments everywhere. Only the results differed dramatically. What accounted for the differences in the ways cities responded? First, as Almy himself noted, "In northern cities the severe winters increase the expense of the poor, and at the same time stop the outdoor work upon which common labor is so dependent." Of the six cities that gave the most public outdoor relief, "six were not only northern . . . but also lake cities, in which the closing of navigation through the winter months throws many out of employment." Three of them also were "materially affected by the closing of the Erie Canal." All of them had "a large class with whom winter non-employment is almost the normal condition." More than the survival of the poor was at issue in the lake ports. Local manufacturers and shippers whose operations slowed in the winter often wanted to keep their workforce close by, and outdoor relief helped assure that they would have a labor force available in the spring when the lakes and canals thawed. In 1869, the director of the Chicago Relief and Aid Society stressed the civic importance of aid to unemployed workers whose "labor is needed here in the summer" but who could not "go elsewhere in the winter."[12]

Other factors probably influenced the nature and amount of relief in individual cities. One of them may have been the amount of work available for women. In Brooklyn and Philadelphia, both of which abolished relief, relatively high proportions of women worked outside their homes. In Buffalo, where relief remained generous by the standards of the time, relatively few women were employed. Wages from working wives and children may have kept families alive during the periodic unemployment experienced by most men, and local politicians may have voted to abolish outdoor relief only when they knew that families had a way to supplement their incomes. Another factor could have been the structure of elites. Controversies over outdoor relief throughout the century pitted wealthy professionals against local merchants, public officials, other professionals who served the poor, and manufacturers in need of seasonal labor. The relative size and strength of these groups probably varied with city size, which is why reformers succeeded much more often in very large cities. Of course, local political struggles also shaped the nature of relief.[13]

Almy's study had an implicit purpose. He wanted to reinforce the case against outdoor relief by showing that private charity could meet all of the needs of the poor, even in the largest cities. In the cities where outdoor relief had been abolished, many people with whom he corresponded as he prepared his study spoke "with satisfaction of the fact that in their cities there was no public outdoor aid." Indeed, no one who wrote to him favored it. The secretary of the Associated Charities of Washington, D.C., wrote, "When you consider," how

43

many of "our population . . . are poor colored people, you can easily imagine how large a public outdoor relief fund might become if we had one . . . we are very much better off without it, and when I say 'we,' I mean the poor people just as much as the taxpayers." A physician from Philadelphia wrote Almy that there was "no need whatever in this city for the restoration of municipal outdoor relief" because the "private benevolence of our citizens is sufficient to supply all needs." From Baltimore, one of the most important figures in the modern history of social work, Julia Richmond, told Almy "that the anxiety of those who fear to abolish public outdoor aid is like the dread of taking babies from overheated rooms into the fresh air."[14]

Almy's study made private charity appear more capable than it was. In fact, even in Almy's Buffalo at the time he gathered the data for his articles, private sources paid less of the cost of dependence than public ones, and, in truth, no sharp line divided the two spheres. In Buffalo, as throughout the country, relief was, as it usually has been in America, a public/private venture. Relief practices in Buffalo showed the intermingling of public and private, the local financial basis, and the contradictions—the gap between professed concern and actual contributions, the mix of innovation and resistance—that marked approaches to dependence in nineteenth century cities.

Almy's Buffalo was an important city in the history of philanthropy. It was the site of the first YMCA (1854) and the first American Charity Organization Society (1878, discussed in chapter 3). It also was the first city to appoint paid agents to place dependent children in families. Yet, despite its commitment to current trends in charity, Buffalo's leading citizens never could abolish public outdoor relief. Indeed, Buffalo gave more outdoor relief than most large cities, and its payments per capita, much to the horror of its charity reformers, remained among the most generous in the country. Only one newspaper supported outdoor relief, but its opponents never could convince enough local politicians that private sources would take care of the worthy poor. Official skepticism was justified. The Charity Organization Society complained that it was easier to identify and counsel the worthy poor than to find someone willing to give them aid and that the money raised for relief by private sources was inadequate. Indeed, Almy's Charity Organization Society had a hand-to-mouth existence, and almost always ran a deficit that once even forced it to dismiss four of its agents.[15]

Erie County's residential institutions formed a complex network with several components: two state institutions, The Thomas Asylum for Orphan and Destitute Indian Children and Buffalo State Hospital; the almshouse; dispensaries providing cheap or free medical care and twelve hospitals; four residential schools; several homes for the aged; and even more orphanages. The superintendent of the poor, two public agents, and various private agents actively attempted to

44

place dependent children in foster families. Aside from the sheer size and complexity of this list, two points about institutions and relief should be stressed. First is the mixture of public and private resources. Not only did both public and private institutions exist, but private institutions received large amounts of public funds, either directly from the state or from boards of supervisors or counties and towns who paid for the inmates they sent on a per capita basis. Orphanages flourished because children, who could no longer be placed in almshouses, had to be sent to special institutions of the same denomination as their parents. Similar mixtures appeared, too, in the budgets of the homes for the aged and hospitals.[16]

Clearly, the state, county boards of supervisors, and local governments made extensive use of private facilities. The economy of dependence was mixed. Indeed, most private institutions could not have remained in business without the fees of inmates paid by public sources. The income of institutions throughout New York State also mixed private and public funds. In 1900, these institutions and agencies received $17,312,326. Of this amount, $1,169,326 was cash on hand. Another $8,728,943 came from public sources: the state, county boards of supervisors, and towns and cities. The latter spent by far the largest share, $4,545,249. Of the remainder, definitely all but $1,604,607 (classified as from "other" sources, probably private) came from nonpublic sources such as fees, donations, legacies, interest, dividends, and benefits. Thus, roughly half of the budget used to relieve dependence directly came from private sources. However, these amounts do not include the millions of dollars spent on jails, prisons, and mental institutions, which, although inspected by other state agencies, also relieved dependence and were integral components of New York's welfare apparatus.[17]

Not only was the budget for relief a mixture of public and private. It also was intensely local, as the preceding figures show. Most of the private funds came from local sources as did more than half of the public ones. In New York State at the turn of the century at least three-quarters of the funds used for the relief of dependence came from towns and cities. If the county is included in the definition of local, the proportion rises, at a minimum, to seven-eighths. The state inspected the private institutions and agencies it funded and required annual reports. The State Charities Aid Association, a private organization, sent volunteers to investigate public institutions on a regular basis. At the same time, public officials made use of private resources to accomplish public tasks. Most notably, the city of Buffalo asked the Charity Organization Society (COS) to investigate individuals requesting outdoor relief. Until financial problems at the end of the century forced it to discontinue the practice, the COS tried to investigate all cases, whether requested or not, and it continued to examine as many as it could, even with its more limited resources. This pattern of cooperation

45

had existed since the inception of the COS, which, in its early years, had used city police officers to examine applications for relief.

The other major point about relief is the role of the Catholic community. First, Catholics gave exceptionally large amounts for relief. Indeed, many of the nonpublic institutions were affiliated with the Catholic church. It is difficult to quantify the proportion of institutional, nonpublic relief provided by Catholic facilities in Buffalo, but it is unlikely that it was less than 50 percent. Given the relative poverty of the Catholic community, these efforts made on behalf of the needy are truly impressive. Moreover, Catholics and Protestants did cooperate in a number of ways. The first hospital in the city, the highly respected Sisters of Charity, was used in its early years by both Catholics and Protestants; the COS stressed its cooperation with Catholic churches; and the city employed both a Protestant and a Catholic agent to place children in homes.

Everywhere relief had a mixed economy. In practice, throughout most of America it was a public/private venture. The precise configuration of relief arrangements varied from state to state, indeed from county to county, but almost everywhere complex funding and administrative arrangements blurred the boundary between public and private. This variation was one implicit message of Almy's study. Another was that outdoor relief remained a very live issue everywhere; otherwise he would not have taken such trouble to try to show why private charity by itself could care for the needy.

Brooklyn and the War Against Outdoor Relief

A crisis in outdoor relief brought about by a combination of economic depression and municipal corruption gave Brooklyn reformers the chance to put ideology into practice. With a bold stroke, they eliminated outdoor relief in one of America's largest cities. Although opponents of outdoor relief triumphed in New York City and Philadelphia at just about the same time, the ideological zeal of Brooklyn's reformers, their prominence, and their eagerness to publicize their achievements, gave their experiment national significance. Everywhere, reformers of similar persuasion held up the Brooklyn experience as proof that outdoor relief could be abolished with no increase in the suffering of the poor.

The reform leader, Mayor Seth Low, interpreted Brooklyn's achievements as a classic tale of disinterested reform routing the municipal corruption that fed venal politicians and starved the needy. Not surprisingly, the story is more complex. Within Kings County (which Brooklyn dominated), a complicated network of institutions specializing in the care and custody of various sorts of dependents had developed since the 1830s. At the same time, many small private and religious societies developed philanthropic institutions or took part in charitable work. Reformers called Brooklyn "the paupers' paradise."[18]

Outdoor relief had been customary in New York State for a long time. The New York Poor Laws intended it as support for old or sick people who could not be placed in a poorhouse or who should not be forced to leave their homes. But in most places, including Brooklyn, it also served to tide people over periods of unemployment, prevent starvation, speed tramps on their way, and, undoubtedly insure some votes. State law fragmented the authority to appropriate money for all Brooklyn's institutions and for temporary outdoor relief between a County Board of Supervisors and the Commissioners of Charity. The commissioners distributed relief and supervised the institutions; the county board controlled all expenditures and made recommendations to the Board of Estimate about the amount of money needed for both purposes. Thus, the commissioners planned expenses, gave out the money, hired people, and directed work, but they relied entirely (with recourse only to the state legislature) on the supervisors for approval of their spending plans and contracts as well as for cash. Ever since the 1860s, relations between the commissioners and supervisors had been antagonistic, and the war against outdoor relief was part of a decade-long struggle by the supervisors to either eliminate or control the commissioners completely.

Relief rolls grew rather slowly before the 1870s, although they did jump in periods of distress, especially during the winter of 1865 with the turmoil that followed the end of the war. After 1865, the number aided declined again until 1870, when it jumped once more, only to subside in the next few years. When the effect of the depression that started in 1873 began to register on relief rolls in 1874, the number aided grew once again and continued to climb until the abolition of relief in 1878. Nonetheless, during these years, the amount of money spent on relief did not grow as fast as the number aided, and per capita expense actually declined. Aid was almost never cash, even though one might well think otherwise from reformers' accounts. Rather, aid usually consisted of food or coal, but never both during the same week. Only family heads, usually men, could apply for relief, and each family of four could receive only one dollar's worth of food or fuel to last a week. Even with the falling price of food and fuel in the mid-seventies, this was a pitiful amount. (An unskilled laborer at this time might expect to earn at least $1.00 or $1.25 per day.) This meager aid included no "luxuries," only flour, potatoes, or rice. By the 1870s, critics attacked the inclusion of tea and sugar in the food package. At the same time, they debated whether or not to give out coal. It was cheaper than food, went further, and was easy to distribute, but people sold it for cash to buy other commodities. The average family of four probably received aid only for about 3 weeks every year, and the total number assisted included dependents as well as family heads. Also, because the number aided probably reflects disbursements rather than individuals, the true number of families assisted was much smaller than reformers implied, far less, certainly, than the one in ten that Low cited in his attempt to show the massive corruption and demoralization that had infected the process of relief.

Certainly, there was corruption in poor relief, and it was not a negligible problem. Still, it was not simply a combination of corruption with increased numbers that stimulated the attack on outdoor relief. In Brooklyn, the abolition of outdoor relief had a wider constituency than voluntarists who wanted to extend their influence or impose their ideas on public policy. Rather, in committees, public meetings, and newspapers, advocates argued for abolition largely as a tax issue. Whether it was the most realistic or effective way to end taxes, which were driven up more by debt service on municipal improvements, is not the point. The abolition of outdoor relief became a symbolic crusade against public spending and waste. Recall that even though the number on relief had been growing, the actual expense of relief had not increased very much. The increased number of poor people who received help during the depression of the 1870s received smaller amounts each year. The struggle between the commissioners and supervisors for control over the administration and finance of poor relief had started before the worst years of the decade. The high points of this conflict were the occasionally successful attempts of the supervisors to impeach, remove, and jail individual commissioners for malfeasance in office. This long-standing drive to weaken the commissioners, combined with hostility to increased taxes, formed the context for the reform campaign with its focus on outdoor relief.

In part, the struggle between the commissioners and supervisors reflected an ongoing conflict between Republicans and Democrats for control of the city. Republicans were consolidating their control over the Board of Supervisors and attacking sources of Democratic patronage whenever they could. The Republican assault on the Democratic machine included a tax revolt, which found its most convenient and corrupt-looking target in the poor establishment. Wealthy, prominent charity reformers, usually also Republicans and sometimes involved in more partisan struggles as well, joined the assault on the commissioners. The coalition included Low, who was a young, independently wealthy Republican whose grandfather had founded the Brooklyn Association for Improving the Condition of the Poor (BAICP), on whose board many of his family members had served. Another key leader was Ripley Ropes, whose brother Reuben was president of the BAICP. Ripley Ropes was first a county supervisor and later

48

county representative to the State Board of Charities. Both Low and Ropes used the political capital from the abolition of outdoor relief to build their later careers.

The Republican-reform coalition planned its campaign against the commissioners with some care. First, it managed the election of Ropes and other BAICP antipublic relief people to the Board of Supervisors. Then, it had BAICP members appointed volunteer visitors in the service of the Charities Commissioners. The Charities Commissioners had experimented unsuccessfully with hired visitors (proto-case workers) in 1871, but paying visitors had added greatly to the cost of relief and seemed to encourage the distribution of aid rather than to weed out the unworthy. The commissioners hoped that the volunteer visitors, who began work in 1874–75, would take over some of their work and reduce costs. Invested with authority by the commissioners, the visitors began to collect information about the distribution of relief and the condition of the poor. To the dismay of the commissioners, who had not realized where the visitors' sympathies lay, the visitors appeared before the supervisors in 1876 and testified that outdoor relief was superfluous, wasteful, corrupting, and, under New York law, illegal. Low and Ropes urged the supervisors to end outdoor relief and promised to use their own money to relieve anyone whose needs could not be met through private charity. The commissioners could only disagree and ask for the usual appropriation for the winter.

Commissioners and those supervisors with large working-class and poor constituencies argued against the abolition of outdoor relief and reached a compromise with the rest of the supervisors. As an experiment, outdoor relief would be phased out over a two-year period. Only coal would be distributed in 1876–77 and nothing the following year. To insure their control, the supervisors suggested that any orders and contracts for coal be cosigned by the voluntary visitors as well as by the commissioners. In this way, they hoped to strengthen their control, drive away paupers, and reeducate the worthy poor.

The commissioners were trapped because they had no legal authority to make contracts or appropriate money. Nonetheless, they resisted sharing their limited authority with the volunteer visitors. Although they had agreed to distribute only coal, the commissioners backed away from the new plan during the winter of 1876–77 because, they said, people were starving. Even the mayor suggested public works (a scheme exposed by the city's leading newspaper, the *Eagle*, as a "communistic evil"), and some of the supervisors were forced to change their position because their offices filled with poor people, who also surrounded their houses and begged them to open the warehouses where food was stored. Despite the reformers' control of the Board of Supervisors' critical Supply Committee, in mid-January the board voted an emergency appropriation for food.[19]

The commissioners' refusal to cooperate with the new plan and the supervisors' vote for emergency funds for food enraged the voluntarists, who denounced outdoor relief and its supporters in newspaper editorials and council chambers. Despite pressure from the newspapers, Ropes, other reformers, the Central Tax Payers' Association, and even Father Fransoli of the St. Vincent de Paul Society, also a critic of public outdoor relief, the pivotal supervisor refused to change his vote. Eventually, the city's storehouses opened and the commissioners distributed small amounts of flour and potatoes. The Board of Supervisors punished them by taking the extra appropriation for food out of their salaries.

When the new fiscal year began in December, 1878, the commissioners had no funds. They were unable even to buy coal for their offices. At every turn, investigations, suits, and salary cut-offs hampered their work. In their war on waste and fraud, the supervisors even cut off seventy nurses' salaries and delayed appropriations for food and medicine for people in the city's institutions. They investigated the purchase of mosquito netting for the orphan asylum and sued the commissioners for violation of the emergency spending act when they bought Thanksgiving turkeys for almshouse inmates. The most important charge of corruption was the allegation that Commissioner Demas Strong had transported almshouse inmates to the polls to vote for him in the annual election.

All through December and early January the fight between commissioners and supervisors continued. In the end, the commissioners lost. With their number reduced to two and their responsibilities restructured, the commissioners no longer were an effective force. Public outdoor relief ended, and voluntarists took over the distribution of aid. Like the commissioners they had attacked, the voluntarists used depots to distribute small amounts of food after a careful investigation of applicants. They also opened shops where poor women earned their alms by sewing on a piecework basis and wood-yards where men earned theirs chopping wood. They claimed success. The number aided, they said, dropped 50 percent when cases of fraud had been detected. No worthy and needy person, they argued, had suffered by the abolition of public outdoor relief.

But were they right? What happened to the poor who lost their relief? When Dr. Thomas Norris reported on the Brooklyn experiment to the county superintendents, he told a very different story than Low. Although private charity might meet the needs of the few who needed help in small towns, in big cities "very many more cases require help than private benevolence can reach." This, he said, had been the situation in Brooklyn during the last winter when outdoor relief was abolished.

As to the entire withdrawal of temporary assistance, the experience of last winter showed that it would have been a saving to afford some. Many families were obliged to break up, the parents or parent going to the poorhouse, and the children to the asylums for care, at the expense of the county, costing in some instances, forty dollars a month; whereas, one or two dollars' worth of food a week, during the winter, given by the public, would have sufficed to keep them together in their own little homes.

Small amt could have kept families together

Norris was right. By 1880, the number of children placed with agencies or in orphan asylums had skyrocketed. Parents coped with the abolition of outdoor relief by breaking up their families. Between 1879 and 1880, the number of children placed with the Catholic Orphan Asylum nearly doubled from 898 in 1877 to 1,683 in 1879 and 1,640 in 1880. Local magistrates cooperated with hard-pressed parents by committing their children to institutions. Angered by the way these local courts frustrated their attempt to lower the city's burden of dependency, in 1881 Brooklyn's reformers persuaded the state legislature to transfer the power of commitment from the magistrates to the commissioners.[20]

children ~ asylums doubled

There is no systematic way to find out what happened to people who had depended on relief, but the fragments of evidence that exist make the following account likely. First, some people with other sources of income had received outdoor relief as a form of political patronage. This practice stopped. Next, economic recovery opened up more jobs, which absorbed some of the unemployed. Some men who could not find work turned to petty crime; others slept in the police station; some managed to have themselves arrested as vagrants—arrests for vagrancy increased 50 percent in 1879—and spent the winter in and out of jail, where, at least, they had a bed and food; and some left Brooklyn for cities and towns with more generous policies. In time, hunger and cold caught up with many people, who turned for help to the city's hospitals. However, relatively few more went to the local poorhouse, because it already was jammed to capacity. Families turned first to familiar sources of credit: landlords, grocers, and kin. By borrowing and pawning what few valuables they had, they managed to survive a year or so. But after awhile, they exhausted all sources of income. With no money and no prospect of a job, they sent their children to agencies and asylums, with the hope of retrieving them when their fortunes improved. With their children away, women could seek jobs as live-in domestic servants, and husbands and wives could split up to look for work. Indeed, the years when public officials and charity reformers complained most about an increase in tramps coincided with the general cutback in outdoor relief throughout the country. Most tramps, in fact, were men in their twenties and thirties who had been on the road a relatively short time looking for work.[21]

Clearly, when Low reported that no one had suffered, he exaggerated. The great forces that made dependence endemic in working-class life did not disappear because wealthy Brooklyn reformers and Republicans denied they existed. Letters to newspapers, protests reported by public officials, and the

Low exaggerated many people did suffer

pressures on other institutions that helped needy people all showed that hunger, homelessness, and destitution did not evaporate when Brooklyn abolished public outdoor relief. Years later, one of the directors of the poor in Pennsylvania tried to find out what had happened when Brooklyn and other towns and cities abolished outdoor relief in the late nineteenth century. "As bearing upon the allegation that outdoor relief can be abolished without substitute and without hardship," the letters he received showed that where it had been tried, "it has been found necessary either to revert, or to shift the burden" to other "shoulders."[22]

Of what significance was the Brooklyn experiment? First, it shows the complex politics of relief, even within local governments. Although reformers knew that per capita spending for relief had gone down and that many people suffered from extreme poverty, they ignored both points in their public statements. In the end, they probably saved the city only a trivial amount of money. But they did succeed in other ways. On a personal level, Ropes and Low launched themselves on successful political careers. Even more, the reformer-Republican coalition wrested control of an important set of municipal functions from Democrats with a base in working-class constituencies. As such, the abolition of outdoor relief was part of the wider municipal reform campaign that surfaced all around the country in the same years. (Municipal reform and its relation to welfare is discussed in chapter 6.) There is no mistaking the class character of the campaign, with its wealthy patrician leadership on one side and its political machines with their working-class constituencies on the other. Nonetheless, class was not a straightforward factor in the controversies over outdoor relief. For relief had become one medium linking ward politicians, small businessmen and professionals, and the poor through the exchange of the food, cash, and votes on which each depended for survival. In the end, its role in local politics, labor markets, and economies, as much as the suffering it alleviated, secured outdoor relief its fixed, if unwelcome, place in most American communities.

The Defense of Outdoor Relief

Outdoor relief had no passionate, articulate champions, and the wealthy professionals who led the attack against it encountered little ideological opposition. Still, the most ardent critics of outdoor relief did not deal on a day-to-day basis with poor people who needed help, and most of those who did, county super-

outdoor relief –
didn't like it, but
couldn't do without
it.

intendents of the poor, found relief a much more complex issue. They understood the arguments against outdoor relief; they saw it abused all around them; but they knew they could not do without it. As they debated the role of outdoor relief with each other, the county superintendents developed a defense that was neither elegant, theoretical, nor consistent, but it was grounded in experience, and it did provide them with a rough guide to practice.

In New York, and probably elsewhere, county superintendents were caught between opposing forces. The new, aggressive charity reformers pushed them to "raise the standard of equipment and administration in public institutions" and to tighten up their relief practices. Conservative local officials, on the other side, failed to give them enough money and resisted change. Taxpayers complained about taxes for poor relief, while the poor, their friends, and local merchants protested when individual families were refused relief or when superintendents tried to introduce tougher standards. Even wealthy, well-intentioned women created problems because they championed the cause of poor families and tried to intercede on their behalf with the superintendents or local politicians.[23]

Given the conflicting forces at work on them, ambivalence colored most of the superintendents' discussions of relief. Time and again, they began their speeches or comments at conventions by trotting out all the familiar criticisms only to end up by stressing the necessity of outdoor relief. George McGonegal, superintendent of the poor in Monroe County, told his colleagues, "I believe out-door relief, as a rule, does more harm than good. Its worst feature is in its pauperizing tendencies." Still, he lamented, "it seems impossible to do away with it entirely." Lawrence Dutcher, superintendent of Poughkeepsie, agreed. "This question of outdoor relief," he told the convention, "is one having many sides. We cannot dispose of it in a sweeping way, either by denouncing it altogether or advocating its continuance without reservation, caution, or qualification. . . . I discourage those who come to me for relief as much as possible, nevertheless, I am obliged to help them." It would be wrong "to allow the worthy poor to go unrelieved," but not a dollar of public money "should be expended more than the stern realities of the case demand, and no larger [longer] than the actual pressing necessities require."[24]

Outdoor relief's great virtue was simple: it prevented starvation. "We should discourage it as much as possible," advised one superintendent, acknowledging his familiarity with contemporary ideas about poor relief, "but there are cases when it would be inhuman and wrong to deny it." Although he disapproved "of temporary relief as a general rule," observed the superintendent from Albany in 1876, "everybody" knew that "the last two winters" had "been exceptionally hard on the poor and laboring classes. They have been without employment and cannot get it. Now, what are you going to do with a man with a family of small children depending on him, with whom there is nothing in the world the matter except that he can't work." There were many unemployed men "suffering for want of bread. It would not do to let the children starve."[25]

Unlike most of the reformers, county superintendents could not ignore dependence brought on by unemployment, harsh winters, industrial accidents, and the disasters common to working-class life. The applications for relief they received registered the impact of seasonal employment, economic cycles, and personal tragedy. The superintendent of Suffolk County illustrated the problem. In the winter of 1886–87, he had aided 134 "county paupers—usually known as tramps." Many of these men had been employed during the summer in brick yards and factories where they earned $1.25 per day and paid $4.00 for board. With periodic layoffs included, "how much" was "left to keep them from actual want during the long winter ... when they" were "utterly unable to find employment." Without help, they would starve.[26]

The superintendents liked to make their point by using specific cases to illustrate the inescapable need for outdoor relief. The two most common types were the family man thrown out of work or injured and the worthy widow. One superintendent, who proclaimed his opposition to outdoor relief in the same speech, wrote about a family of seven children he had been asked to help. He had been born in the same town as the husband and knew the family and its circumstances. On a Friday night the man took sick, and on Sunday he died. "Do you mean to tell me," asked the superintendent, "I am not going to rent a room and put that woman in there, with her own children, for less than it would cost to send those children to the orphan asylum?"[27]

The superintendent's reluctance to send the widow to the poorhouse and her children to an asylum reflects two other themes in the defense of outdoor relief: the fear of pauperization and the high cost of institutional relief. Over and over again, superintendents cited cases where, they claimed, a few dollars helped a family stay out of the poorhouse, regain its independence, and avoid the demoralization fostered by institutional life. "We think it lowers a man to bring him to the poor house," reported one superintendent about opinion in his county. "It takes his manhood away from him. We prefer to urge such to find work for themselves, and give them a very little temporary aid if need be." The "question," said the next speaker, is not whether a man was "able-bodied; but when destitute, unable to get any employment, shall he be allowed to starve to death?" The issue was how best to help him. "If by giving him a small amount to bridge over the winter and towards spring you have him earning his living," outdoor relief was preferable to the demoralization threatened by sending him to "the county house."[28]

It did cost much less to support a family on outdoor relief than to send its members to institutions. One superintendent pointed out that the two large

Pro-outdoor. relief [handwritten margin note]

54

villages in his county had "a great many widows with from one to six or eight children." He found "it a great deal cheaper to grant them from one to three dollars a week . . . than to take them to the county house." The situation had been made more complex by the 1875 law ordering children out of poorhouses. Now, institutional relief meant breaking up a family by sending the parent or parents to the poorhouse and the children to orphan asylums, which were even more expensive. "The very moment the law of 1875 . . . was passed," reported Mr. Goodale from Orange County, "that very moment the supervisors of Orange county recommended out-door relief." The problem was that "the cost of maintaining the children in orphan asylums, the cost of their transportation there was so great as to lead the board of supervisors to favor the idea of out-door relief, as a family could be kept together in that way so much cheaper."[29]

In fact, with only a little outdoor relief families could stay together. "My opinion," said one superintendent, "is that there is no better way of taking care of these children than to keep them at home and provide for them there." He didn't "believe in sending them two or three hundred miles away from the parents simply because there has been a husband dead, or a mother washing next door." He recommended that every county care for its own children. "I believe it is the best plan and the cheapest too." In the 1870s this superintendent's position was more controversial than might appear from his sentimental rhetoric. By no means did most public officials and reformers concede that the children of the very poor were best left with their parents. Because they could not deny that institutions were expensive, they responded by emphasizing the long-range cost to society rather than the short-range expense to the county. Children of paupers left with their families would breed families of dependents and criminals whose cost to society in economic as well as moral terms would far outweigh the short-term expense of supporting them for a while in an orphan asylum.[30]

Even if they overcame their reservations and tried to cut off all outdoor relief, reported superintendents, they could not succeed. Community pressure would force them to back down. A coalition of the poor, their friends and relatives, and the merchants who enjoyed their business made a raucous, militant, and effective constituency for outdoor relief, sensitive to any variation in county policy or its application to individual cases. "The minute you get into a town and undertake to send away to the almshouse a widow woman with five or six children," said one superintendent, "the people up and say, 'Why you ain't going to take these people to the poor house, are you?' " "We have one difficulty to contend with in our section of the country," said another superintendent, "which . . . may be experienced by other Superintendents also—*public opinion*. The Overseers of the Poor fear to send persons to the Alms-house unless they are compelled to do so. The relatives do not like to have them taken away from home and confined in the County House." Whenever he tried to cut off outdoor

55

aid—which consisted of orders for groceries—observed the superintendent of Allegany County, he encountered "two opposing interests; the recipient of the aid, and the merchant on whom the order for supplies is drawn, in fact, the greatest obstacle is . . . the latter." The problem also was political, because overseers of the poor were elected officials. A "great deal" of outdoor relief was given, suggested one superintendent, "to accommodate merchants—men who help to elect Overseers of the Poor and perhaps superintendents. They want to be accommodated by trade and I think that in many cases there is a great deal of money thrown away in this connection."[31]

Wealthy, philanthropic women posed another obstacle to the efficient administration of relief, according to the superintendents. Often, applicants refused relief by the superintendent of the poor would take their case to women, who, out of misguided sympathy, pressured their husbands and local politicians. Tramps, said one superintendent, "know just enough to start tears of sympathy in the eyes of the ladies." Superintendent J. B. White of Onandaga complained that he had been called "hard hearted" when he refused the appeal of "Christian ladies" to aid outdoor paupers. A policy of turning away tramps, said another superintendent, would "never get a single vote from the ladies."[32]

Even when they started out to discuss outdoor relief as a question of principle, the superintendents slipped quickly into a discussion of specific problems. Unable or reluctant to erect a strong intellectual defense of outdoor relief, yet unwilling or unable to give it up, superintendents who spoke on the issue redefined it over and over again as an administrative problem. They voted down every motion that called for its abolition and devoted their attention, instead, to the real, practical questions that confronted them every day. How much and for how long should aid be given? To whom should it be given? Should it be cash or in kind? How could the amount of relief be minimized? The superintendents sought a compromise between the opponents of relief and the community forces that supported it, and they found it in a constant attempt to reassert the distinction between the worthy and unworthy poor. Only the worthy, they said, should be helped. By the exercise of adequate discrimination, the cost of relief could be minimized and the objectives of charity, justice, economy, and the promotion of independence all served. The means they advocated, aside from their own knowledge of who in the community truly deserved help, was the work test. Especially for strangers, nothing would certify worthiness as well as the willingness to break stone. At the same time, they recognized that many people turned to relief because they could not find work, and, by the 1880s, the superintendents had started to endorse employment offices and, in some cases, even public works.[33]

The secretary of the State Board of Charities, Charles Hoyt, summed up the circumstances in which outdoor relief could be given in a way that most superintendents would have endorsed.

1 In cases of sickness, or accident, when the person may not be in condition to be removed to the alms-house or hospital.
2 In cases of aged and infirm persons dependent upon relatives able and willing to nurse and care for them, but without the pecuniary ability to meet the whole expense of their support.
3 In cases of pestilence, failure of crops, producing temporary distress, or commercial revulsions throwing large numbers of persons, for the time being, out of employment.
4 In cases where the head of a family is removed by death, or prostrated by sickness, and there is good reason to believe that the family, by being thus held together, may ultimately become self-supporting.

Even with a clear typology of eligibility, "every possible safeguard" had to be thrown around the administration of outdoor relief to "check abuses." The circumstances of recipients should be "re-examined" frequently; all officials who distributed aid should be "experienced and intelligent"; as far as possible, the "work . . . should be removed from . . . party politics"; and the relief, "as far as possible," should be "temporary." Under no circumstances, should outdoor relief be used "to furnish the means of vicious indulgence or encourage improvidence and idleness."[34]

In the end, the superintendents proved more accurate than the reformers who advocated the abolition of outdoor relief. The forces that drove people to dependence—unemployment, sickness, death, crop failure—frustrated the prediction that public outdoor relief could be abolished with no increase in suffering. At the same time, in most places relief remained too closely tied to local politics, too long established as custom, too subject to popular demand for reformers ever to successfully do away with it completely. Even Frederic Almy admitted, in 1911, "After more than ten years of opposition to public outdoor relief, I find myself still yearning for it."[35]

3   The Theory and Practice

of Scientific Charity

After about 1870, leading voluntarists twisted the familiar strands of poor relief doctrine into a tough new theory, which they called *scientific charity*. In the public sector, the result of their attempt to impose it on policy was the abolition or reduction of outdoor relief across the country. In the private sector, it was the formation of charity organization societies that attempted to rationalize and systematize philanthropy. Reformers wanted to do more than cut expenses and purge the ablebodied from relief. To these familiar goals, they added a new element: a concerted drive to make relief primarily private. Alarmed by the disorder of American cities in the last third of the nineteenth century, frightened by the spectre of a militant, organized, and undeferential working class, the charity organizers responded as harshly as employers and governments confronted with similar problems. The task charity organizers set themselves was to teach the poor that they had no rights. Afraid that relief was turning into a right, the new reformers put all their energy into transforming it back into charity.

Volunteers and Poverty Before Scientific Charity

In the early decades of the nineteenth century, men and women in villages, towns, and cities across the country organized associations dedicated to the eradication of vice, crime, ignorance, and poverty. If energy and optimism had

58

been enough, a moral and social revolution would have swept across America. However, they proved no more able to relieve America's destitute than to eradicate prostitution and intemperance or to reduce crime. In time, the optimistic, evangelical Protestant thrust of early American reform retreated as voluntarism, like state activity, became more secular, bureaucratized, and professional, and charity became scientific.

Despite its commitment to innovation, scientific charity drew on the legacy of antebellum voluntarism for its method, friendly visiting; its key distinction, the difference between the worthy and unworthy poor; its enemy, outdoor relief; and its personnel, well-to-do Protestant women. Virtually everyone who has written about Jacksonian America has commented on its myriad voluntary associations. In fact, most historians concentrate on voluntarism and ignore the public's important, contentious role. Nonetheless, given its mixed public/private economy, no history of American social welfare can ignore voluntarism's successive confrontations with poverty. Indeed, Americans organized themselves for almost every purpose, and the list of their associated activities almost defies categorization.[1] Within this variety, seven strands or themes stand out in the history of the relation between voluntarism and poverty in the years between the early republic and the Gilded Age (roughly, 1800–70). They are (1) the organized response to social and economic crisis; (2) the role of evangelical Protestantism, especially before about 1840; (3) the response of the Catholic church; (4) ethnic and occupational group self-help; (5) the use of education; (6) the "moral-social control tradition" (to use Paul Boyer's apt phrase);[2] and (7) the relation between voluntarism, sisterhood, and feminism.

Whenever emergencies struck cities, leading citizens quickly organized associations designed to aid the poor. In New York, the first emergency association was the Samaritan Society, founded to cope with a relief crisis in 1805. A similar organization, the General Committee of the Benevolent Associates for the Relief of the Poor, tried to relieve the poor during the Embargo Crisis of 1807–09, and others appeared during crises in 1809, 1813, and 1817. Associations of citizens who divided themselves into ward committees usually founded these emergency relief organizations. They stressed the importance of visiting the families they helped and often tried to spread religion along with alms. They concerned themselves with the immediate problems of the poor and paid little attention to the underlying causes of destitution or the long-term needs of their clients, and when the emergency to which they had responded ended, most of them disbanded. Similar temporary relief associations sprang up in cities during every nineteenth-century crisis.[3]

Charity, of course, always was a religious duty, but the religious impulse that underlay work with the poor intensified in the wake of the Second Great Awakening. "Beginning with the late 1780's and 1790's," writes Carroll Smith

59

Rosenberg, "a wave of revivals swept across frontier America." From the frontier it spread eastward, "reshaping the religious life of entire areas of New England and New York State," converting "ministers, prominent merchants, and lawyers, college presidents, faculty and students." In the wake of the revival, church membership increased from about one person in fifteen in 1800 to one in eight by 1835. The number of adult members of Methodist churches grew from about 87,000 in 1802 to 196,000 in 1812, and 362,000 in 1836.[4]

The revivals stimulated "the organization of countless missionary societies" whose purpose was to "spread God's word to the unbelieving." Their goal was nothing less than "the conversion of the world to evangelical Protestantism and the remaking of the home society into a nation pure and Christian." Evangelicals at first sought to bring the poor spiritual, not material, relief. The theology of the Second Great Awakening "rejected rigid predestination" and argued that all men could be saved. "Christ died," ministers said, "not for the elect alone, but for all men," and they instructed "all Christians to practice universal or 'disinterested benevolence'—dedication to human improvement in imitation of divine example." Through the spread of evangelical piety, converts might "regenerate the whole of society, might indeed bring the millennium." With this impulse, evangelicals went into poor districts to distribute Bibles and, later, tracts. In 1816, the local groups that had begun to distribute Bibles in Philadelphia, Boston, and New York soon after 1800 joined together to form the American Bible Society. Within local societies, women played the key role in Bible distribution because, as a nineteenth century historian of the American Bible Society observed, "This work is peculiarly fitted to her nature and assorts most beautifully with the character given of devoted females in the time of Christ." However, because of its length and complexity, the Bible proved a difficult "instrument for the moral guidance of the masses," and, by the 1820s and 1830s, Bible societies had lost their momentum.[5]

Tract societies replaced the Bible societies. Tracts were short, cheap, and simple pamphlets that could be easily distributed and read. Started in Britain, tract societies, which, like the Bible societies, hoped to reach the poor, appeared in American cities as early as 1812. In May, 1825, representatives from local groups met to form the American Tract Society. Soon, tracts were big business. By 1846, the American Tract Society had a "new five-story, fifty-six room" headquarters in New York, where thirty printers operated seventeen of the latest printing presses and nearly one hundred other employees worked in the bindery. By 1850, the American Tract Society produced about 5 million tracts every year. Although tracts were sent in bulk shipments to "Sunday schools, poorhouses, prisons, orphanages, and immigration depots," in many cities the local tract societies visited families systematically.[6]

By visiting the poor, many of the volunteers who distributed tracts came into close contact with poverty for the first time, and each year, the Tract Society distributed more "temporal goods" and permitted its visitors to "pay rent, to bring food and clothing to the destitute, and to find jobs for the unemployed." Even though its role expanded, the Tract Society began to lose its early optimism and, after the mid-1830s, began to blame the poor themselves for their misery. By the 1840s, their sense of despair only fueled by the depression of 1837, "many businessmen and others" argued for "the urgent need for more activist and forceful programs of slum uplift and control." Indeed, the task confronting the society appeared so large that its executive committee ordered a major policy change in the 1840s when it "decided to hire salaried full-time workers to labor exclusively with the very poor and the immigrant." Twenty years earlier, the society's founders had believed that "all Christians must serve as missionaries"; by the 1840s its leading members had transmuted their commitment of time and personal contact into money. The new, salaried, male agents quickly became experts not only in religion but in "job placement, wage scales, public health, and the coordination of the city's numerous charities." As their numbers increased, the number of volunteer visitors declined. By 1870, the number of employed missionaries had risen to forty and the number of volunteers dropped to thirty-one. As the society's range of activities continued to expand, it "ceased to hope or even work for the conversion of all New Yorkers." Instead, it tried to help many of the city's poor.[7]

The Second Great Awakening had other philanthropic implications as well. In New York, city missions, the Female Missionary Society for the Poor of the City of New-York, and the Young Men's Missionary Society, all grew directly out of the revivals. Evangelical impulses also underlay the early temperance movement, attacks on prostitution, the organization of Sunday schools, and attempts to convert prisoners, orphans, and delinquents, even, indeed especially, when they were Catholic. Out of self-defense, therefore, the Catholic church began to build its own institutional network in antebellum cities.[8]

Catholics brought with them to America an approach to social reform that differed greatly from evangelical Protestantism. They "defined social reform in a very traditional and conservative manner" as "basically carrying out the corporal works of mercy" to "the poor, the hungry, and the homeless. It was a crusade of charity and not one of social change." At once less aggressive and far more reluctant to use the state, Catholic charity also was less judgmental, more ready to help, less quick to condemn. Individual efforts of Catholic clergy, like Father Varela, pastor of Transfiguration, famous for his "unselfish work with the poor and sick," reflected "the traditional approach of Catholic benevolence" as did the parish societies attached to most churches. The principal Catholic relief organization was the St. Vincent de Paul Society, first founded in France and imported to the United States in 1846. An association of laymen, the society

61

stressed visiting poor families in their homes "to minister to their physical wants as far as means will admit and to give such counsel for their spiritual good as circumstances may require and to look after male orphans when they shall have left the asylum." In contrast to the evangelical Protestants who visited poor families, the society's members "sought to alleviate the suffering of the poor rather than to prevent it."[9]

A well-grounded "fear of Protestant proselytizing" drove Catholics to create their own orphan asylums, hospitals, and homes for young women. As early as 1817, a Roman Catholic orphanage opened in New York City; Catholic sisters started the first hospital in Buffalo, New York, and directed St. Vincent's Hospital in New York, founded in 1849, as well as hospitals in other cities; in 1863, New York's Catholics built the Catholic Protectory for delinquent and neglected children to counteract the influence of the Children's Aid Society. The organization of Catholicism in America had an ethnic basis; "each immigrant group coming to the United States brought its own missionaries and its own traditions and institutions of charity." As a consequence, language differences and ethnic rivalries divided the American Catholic church. In New York, for instance, the English-speaking sisters who ran St. Vincent's "could not communicate satisfactorily with the German Catholics" who organized their own hospital, St. Francis, and, in 1850, opened their own orphan asylum, as did French Catholics in 1858. Later in the century, to take another example, the Italian Missionary Sisters of the Sacred Heart ran hospitals in New York, Chicago, and Philadelphia " designed especially for work among Italian immigrants." (Until well into the twentieth century, Catholic parochial schools were also organized according to ethnicity.) These efforts made by the Catholic church to help the sick and needy can only be described as heroic. An immigrant, working-class institution, the Catholic church lacked the resources available to the Protestant community. Even so, it built major institutions and devoted a great share of its resources to the poor. If it were possible to measure such things, I suspect a comparison would show that the Catholic church spent a greater proportion of its resources on charity than did Protestant denominations.[10]

In one sense, Catholic charity was an example of the mutual self-help practiced by virtually every immigrant group. Most of these efforts had two purposes. One was "social and fraternal"; the other to help "indigent members and recent arrivals." The first immigrant self-help society in New York City was the Scots Charitable Society (1744). Not only the destitution of many immigrants, but both public and private relief regulations that tied eligibility to length of residence, gave these societies special importance. Occupational groups—indeed, virtually every major trade—also often organized associations to help their members and their families. These occupational benevolent societies,

62

claims Mohl, created "the nucleus for nascent labor organization in New York City" and, undoubtedly, elsewhere as well.[11]

As the Catholic church understood very well, education played a strategic role in the voluntarists' campaign to reach and reform the poor. In some instances, denominational schools (often, early in the century, aided with tax money) provided the only free education available. Even more closely tied to Protestantism were the Sunday schools that erupted all over the country early in the nineteenth century. In 1825, an American Sunday School Union survey found that about one-third of the six to fifteen-year-old children in Philadelphia attended Sunday school; and an 1829 survey in New York City "showed that some 9,000 or about 41 percent, of all children aged four to fifteen were in Sunday school." (According to the same survey, only 5,700 children attended public schools.) Other cities reported similar, high enrollments.[12] Early Sunday schools were not, as Sunday schools are today, places where only religion is taught. Rather, they stressed the teaching of reading as well as scripture. They were an alternative, not a supplement, to other forms of elementary schooling, which were either unavailable to the poor or too expensive. Sunday schools emphasized moral even more than secular instruction because they felt that in the cities "traditional agencies of child nurture were failing," and none was as inadequate as the families of the poor, to whom "Sunday school spokesmen often betrayed hostility, even contempt." Therefore, according to Boyer, they deliberately and explicitly attempted to "promote deferential and disciplined patterns of behavior based on an image of society as stable, orderly, and securely hierarchical."[13]

From early in the nineteenth century, therefore, conversion remained only one goal woven through reformers' attempts to reach the poor, and in time its prominence faded as crime, poverty, vice, and ignorance seemed to threaten more imminent disaster than irreligion. Even at the height of evangelical zeal, social purposes always intertwined with religious goals as reformers began to visit the poor. In the 1840s, continued urban growth, massive Irish immigration, the increasing separation of classes within cities, a sense that crime and immorality threatened to engulf American cities, and a perception that earlier efforts to reach the poor had not worked very well all combined to fuel the creation of new voluntary associations devoted, to be sure, to the spread of Christianity but with a more secular emphasis on "urban moral and social control." Within these new organizations, paid, full-time staff replaced part-time volunteers; targeted, limited objectives contrasted with the broader spheres of action claimed by the older evangelical associations; and careful, hierarchical administrative arrangements guided day-to-day work. Urban social reform, in short, had taken the road to professionalism and bureaucracy.[14] Although associations to relieve the poor emerged in many cities during these years, the New York Association for Improving the Condition of the Poor, founded in 1843 by Robert M. Hartley, a wealthy Presbyterian merchant, was the most visible. Its early leaders, largely businessmen and professionals, included "some of the greatest bankers and merchant princes of the day." Although "deeply Protestant (especially Presbyterian), the AICP was officially nonsectarian, and few ministers were among the leaders." With an elaborate, hierarchical organization, the AICP "administrative structure" included Hartley, who was secretary and general agent, "a figurehead president and vice-president, a 100-member board of managers, district supervisors and advisory committees . . . and a cadre of paid male visitors."[15]

The AICP began its work with two convictions about urban poverty: namely, that it "was (1) a massive threat to social stability and (2) the direct consequence of individual depravity." Its goal was "to awaken the poor to the flaws of character that underlay their degradation and lead them to change their ways." Because the causes of poverty were primarily moral, the means for their eradication had to be moral as well. This is why the visitor was so central to the association's strategy.[16]

In 1843, home visiting was not an entirely new strategy. It derived from the work of a Scottish theologian, Thomas Chalmers, whose first major American disciple was the Boston Unitarian minister Joseph Tuckermann, founder of the Society for the Prevention of Pauperism, in 1835. To a limited extent, visiting had been tried in the 1830s in Philadelphia and Cincinnati, and it had been part of the American Sunday School Union's strategy as well. However, with the AICP, home visiting moved center stage where it became the "institutional mechanism for transmitting the values of the city's middle and upper strata downward into the ranks of the poor."[17]

In the late antebellum years, the AICP began to decline, and by the 1870s, Hartley had begun to complain that "the New York AICP had become simply another almsgiving body, with its larger vision of systematic visitation, detailed record keeping, and an unflagging commitment to moral uplift a thing of the past." In Baltimore, the AICP had become no more than a "paper program." One reason for its relative failure was the association's inability to overcome the rivalries among the various organizations that gave relief in the city. With relief available from many sources, it was impossible to avoid duplication and give relief and counsel on a systematic basis. Another source of decline was the AICP's personnel policy. By its dependence on a paid, male staff, the AICP denied itself access to the greatest source of energy animating antebellum philanthropy: women volunteers.[18]

Everywhere, in antebellum America women were the shock troops of charity. In most towns and cities, a Female Charitable Society or Ladies Benevolent Society, dedicated to the relief of widows and run by women, was among the

64

first associations. Women also usually ran the early orphan asylums scattered throughout the country, and when the evangelical impulse unleashed by the Second Great Awakening found an outlet in association building, women, converted in much greater numbers than men, led the way.[19]

women managed asylums

Within the new associations women, as Smith Rosenberg observes, "found ways to expand the roles traditionally allotted them."[20] As Susan Lebsock shows through a detailed and fascinating history of voluntarism in Petersburg, Virginia, "gender really mattered" in the organization of relief and reform. There, men left poor relief to the town's women until about 1850. Young, educated mothers, eager for activity, first responded to the town's social problems by organizing an orphan asylum for girls, in 1813. As an "affirmation of women's role as friend in need," the asylum gave "institutional form and public importance" to the most positive features of "women's sphere." For these "upper-middle-class women," nothing gave quite as much "focus to that special combination of sisterhood and ambition." By managing the asylum, women increased their sense of importance and competence. Although, at first, women had collected dues from the members of the asylum association, men had raised money on their behalf. However, by the 1820s, the "women took over most of the fundraising, discovering in the process their capacity to raise large sums of money." When the men who ran the town abolished outdoor relief in 1823, women church members tried to fill some of the void with increased benevolent associations, and until 1858, "voluntary, organized charity was the exclusive province of women."[21]

On the surface, it seemed as though men and women had solved the problem of how to live in the separate spheres to which reigning social ideas had relegated them. However, in the 1850s the town's men showed that they "thought they had conceded too much." One indication of male resentment was the "persistent failure" of the men who kept church records to "acknowledge women's collective contributions." Even more direct, in 1858 men reclaimed organized charity when they started their own association for poor relief, an Association for Improving the Condition of the Poor complete with paid agent, officers, and board of managers, all male. In the same year, Methodist men assumed control of the female orphan asylum that their wives had been running for a decade, and the town's women began to "participate in several new organizations," which "were run by men, with the women playing well-defined auxiliary roles." Other developments indicated that women's roles had changed, too. The question of whether women should speak in front of mixed audiences was finally settled with women the losers, and women began to be referred to as Mrs. John Smith rather than Mary Smith. Although their role in the organization and conduct of voluntary associations had increased the public autonomy of women, the male takeover of the 1850s erased "in symbol and in organizational structure, the appearance of autonomous action by women in the public sphere."[22]

By the Civil War, relations between voluntarism and poverty had been transformed. Their evangelical, feminine tone had been transmuted into a harsher, moralistic, bureaucratic, male proto-professional campaign aimed more at the behavior of the poor than at their souls. Catholics had mounted a counteroffensive against Protestant institutions that tried to convert as well as to help or reform Catholic inmates. Yet, despite the outpouring of voluntarism, poverty, crime, and immorality appeared more prevalent than ever. Nor had public efforts proved any more successful. Poorhouses were awful pits that failed to meet almost any of their objectives; outdoor relief remained pervasive and expensive; innovative social institutions such as state mental hospitals or public school systems failed to transform the character or behavior of the poor. Clearly, the situation called for new approaches. The first response was the attempt to privatize assistance through the abolition of outdoor relief, as in Brooklyn, and the introduction of charity organizations in cities around the country. Underlying both was a doctrine that welded the familiar elements of poor law reform into a hard new form called scientific charity.

Scientific Charity and the Theory of Charity Organization

The completion of the transcontinental railroad; the formation of Standard Oil; the emergence of the first important national union (the Knights of Labor); and the great railroad strike—all events that happened in 1877 and 1878—illustrate the great transformation of American social and economic life in the North and West. The strike was the most extensive and violent ever to have occurred in American history. As workers captured train yards, blocked all movement along the rails, and seized power in some towns, fear of insurrection spread among the country's manufacturing and commercial leaders. Indeed, ever since the draft riots of 1863 and the Paris Commune in 1871, fear had stalked America's business class. Although the terrible depression that began in 1873, the worst yet in American history, had exposed the fragility of American prosperity and industrial growth, neither the government nor business was able or willing to grapple with the fundamental reasons for periodic depressions or to try to alleviate the distress they caused. Unwilling to deal with the structural

66

roots of unemployment, observers invented a new and derogatory noun—
tramps—with which to dismiss its most visible casualties: the men wandering
around the country in search of work.

As a consequence, in the 1870s, social relations assumed a menacing new
form. With good reason, writers of every political persuasion began to refer
routinely to the division of American social structure into two great classes:
capital and labor. In the North, technological innovation, factory size, trusts and
monopolies, and the spatial segregation of classes within sprawling cities all
changed the way in which people lived, worked, and interacted with each other.
In the South, the end of slavery, the extension of civil and political rights to
blacks, and the spread of capitalist agriculture through the enclosure of common
lands and the consolidation of large farms, all combined to alter irrevocably the
social and economic life of the region. Within cities, not only did the number
of people asking for relief grow at an alarming rate; their insistent demands
showed that many of them had learned to regard relief as a right, not as an act
of charity. In the same years, Southern white leaders feared the stirring militance
among newly enfranchised blacks.[23]

Capital answered the threats that besieged it with harsh measures. For the
first time, the federal government sent in armed troops to end a strike. After
the strike, the government built arsenals in major cities to insure prompt defense
against urban uprisings. In the Compromise of 1877, the Republicans traded
the protection of Southern blacks for the presidency. In the North, public officials
and private reformers launched a major campaign against tramps. Cities abolished
or reduced outdoor relief, and their civic leaders advocated new measures to
reverse class estrangement, rid the streets of beggars, and eliminate the interference with the labor market created, so they thought, by indiscriminate charity.
Their instruments were charity organization societies; their theory, scientific
charity.

From its inception, contradictions plagued scientific charity. Charity organization society agents and visitors were supposed to be both investigators
and friends. They were to inspire confidence and radiate warmth as they intruded
into the most intimate details of their clients' lives. They were to be welcome
guests in the homes of people who had no choice but to receive them, if they
wanted to eat or keep warm. Even more, the concept of charity organization
was hopelessly anachronistic. It diagnosed the great social problem of its day as
the chasm that had opened between classes, which it proposed to close through
human contact. In industrializing cities full of wage workers, charity organization
proposed deference as the mode of social control long after its social base had
disappeared. Nor did its method fit its goals. Over and over again, charity organization's sponsors claimed their overriding goal was to restore the very poor
to independence. Dependence on private or public charity was their great enemy.

Yet, their very method taught dependence, because only an outward show of deference merited relief. Any display of independence they translated into ingratitude, and gratutude was everything. Clients had to show their appreciation cheerfully; they had to accept the advice so freely offered; they could not resist attempts of agents or visitors to reorder their lives. In fact, increased dependence became the price of continued support. In the end, the Charity Organization Society as much as those villains of their drama, purveyors of indiscriminate charity, taught the poor to be paupers.[24]

The major American statement of scientific charity was *Public Relief and Private Charity* by Josephine Shaw Lowell, published in 1884. The major statement of the principles and methods of charity organization was A *Handbook of Charity Organization* by the Reverend S. Humphreys Gurteen, written 2 years earlier. Despite a wide area of agreement between them—the menace of public outdoor relief, the importance of voluntarism, the necessity of charity organization—the two authors represented the poles of interest in reform. Lowell, tough, sharp, and perceptive, dedicated her adult life to social reform. Her overriding commitment to improving the condition of the poor led her through scientific charity to the left wing of respectable reform. Always precise and to the point and never sentimental, Lowell could sound mean, in fact, tougher than she was. Gurteen's rhetoric, by contrast, vacillated between a mawkish sentimentalism and a harsh, punitive tone. Never could a reader or listener forget for very long that Gurteen's overriding goal, as he was fond of saying, was "repression."[25]

Josephine Shaw Lowell (1843–1905) was the daughter of a prominent Boston family with serious social reform commitments. Her parents belonged to Theodore Parker's Unitarian Church; their friends included James Russell Lowell and Margaret Fuller; her father contributed to the Brook Farm literary journal; and the family had an articulate record as radical abolitionists. Because of her mother's illness, the family moved to Long Island in 1847 and, from there, traveled in Europe for almost 5 years. When the Civil War came, her father sponsored relief efforts for Southern blacks and helped organize the Freedmen's Bureau. Her brother, Robert Gould Shaw, led the first black regiment (which was raised in Massachusetts) and was killed in action. Not long afterward, her husband of a few months, Charles Russell Lowell (nephew of James Russell Lowell), also was killed. At the age of twenty, Josephine Shaw Lowell found herself a widow, pregnant with what would be her only daughter.

Soon after her husband's death and the birth of her daughter, Lowell started on her energetic career as a professional reformer. She worked for the Sanitary Commission and became the chief fundraiser for the National Freedmen's Relief Association. With a friend, she inspected schools for blacks in Virginia. In 1872, she helped found the New York State Charities Aid Association. In her capacity as an association visitor, she discovered the horrors of the local jail and almshouse and wrote a series of devastating reports, which she followed with a statewide study of ablebodied paupers. In recognition of her ability, in 1876, Governor Samuel Tilden appointed her to the State Board of Charities as its only woman member. On the board, she proved an indefatigable worker. Largely as a consequence of her reports and speeches, the state created a House of Refuge for Girls in 1886 and an asylum for feebleminded women in 1885. Another one of her major campaigns, which succeeded in 1886, aimed to place a matron in every police station.

After she completed a report on "waste and duplication" in New York's "privately financed relief societies," Lowell helped organize the New York Charity Organization Society (1882) and served as its "guiding spirit" for 25 years. Nonetheless, within a few years, she realized that the major cause of poverty among ablebodied people was low wages and, in 1890, left the Board of State Charities to spend more of her time on labor problems. She helped found the Consumer's League of New York, which tried to organize boycotts of employers who sweated their labor; encouraged workers to form unions; supported the Homestead Strike in 1892; and wrote a book advocating concil-iation, by which she meant binding arbitration, as the key to improving wages without strikes. She was active, too, in the municipal reform movement directed against Tammany Hall in the 1890s, organized the Women's Municipal League, campaigned for Civil Service Reform, and helped lead the opposition to the war in the Philippines.[26]

Calling charity "our science," Lowell claimed that philanthropic experience around the world had developed a body of hard, definitive principles about poverty, charity, and relief. The "task of dealing with the poor and degraded," she wrote, "has become a science, and has its well defined principles, recognized and conformed to, more or less closely, by all who really give time and thought to the subject." Scientific charity was not only a set of principles that guided action; it also was a method for gathering the data with which to further develop the laws of charity and reform. Charity organization societies, their leaders felt, should study as well as help the poor. In New York, the Charity Organization Society meticulously classified its cases and mapped their distribution by streets and even houses. When its organizing secretary, Charles Kellogg, found that the distribution of cases by type in Boston and New York was practically identical, he reported, excitedly, that "these striking coincidences . . . in cities having so many diverse conditions, and at times so far apart as to forbid the theory that the similarity is due to contemporaneous financial and industrial causes" showed definitively that there were "laws governing charity as fixed as those which underlie any other department of social or political economy, and that Organized Charity is the way, and the only way to discover and apply them."[27]

relief is not a right or entitlement

To Lowell and her contemporary charity reformers no one should look on relief as a right or entitlement. "It is not right," she said, "to tax one part of the community for the benefit of another part; it is not right to take money by law from one man and give it to another, unless for the benefit of both." Therefore, money spent on relief could only be justified by its reciprocal benefits. Nonetheless, a civilized community, she observed, had an obligation to prevent its members from dying as a result of hunger or cold. The problem, therefore, was how to alleviate destitution without the bad side effects that usually accompanied relief and charity. Any solution had to meet five criteria:

1 To provide that no one shall starve, or shall suffer for the absolute physical necessaries of life.
2 To make this provision in such a way as shall do as little moral harm as possible, both to the recipient of relief and to the community at large.
3 To use every means to render the necessity for relief of short duration.
4 To take as small a sum from the tax-paying (that is the working) part of the community as is consistent with the accomplishment of the first three objectives.
5 To convince the community that all these objects are attained, and that consequently, they need not take upon themselves the provision of the necessaries of life for those who have no direct or personal claim upon them.[28]

Although in theory outdoor relief seemed to meet these goals, real experience, she said, showed exactly the opposite. (To buttress her point she quoted at length from Malthus and the English Poor Law Commissioners of 1832.) In the United States, the great proof, she observed, was the abolition of outdoor relief in Brooklyn, which, she claimed, quoting Seth Low, had not increased the suffering of the poor. Indeed, outdoor relief, she believed, only increased the misery of the poor, and failed to meet every one of her objectives.[29]

Lowell thought of her campaign *against* outdoor relief and *for* charity organization as radical. This is the thread that connects her family's abolitionist activity, her work on charity organization, and her later support of labor. To her, almsgiving and public outdoor relief represented old, outmoded practices, while she advocated a rigorous, fresh application of the latest ideas about poverty and relief. There was, she said, a "fundamental difference in the mental attitude" of the old and the new charity. The old charity believed in doles and found it "a natural condition" that some part of the community "should not be self-supporting." Its patrons even found it "desirable that there should be 'the poor' to look after," and they accepted other people's destitution "with calmness" as "inevitable facts, and to satisfy their own feelings of pity they offer inadequate doles." The other, modern approach thought of every instance "of poverty as a wrong, an unnatural evil and one which" it "should use every effort to eradicate." Although its leaders were shocked to learn "that men should be unable

old charity vs New

70

to live by their labor," they did not hand out "doles" because they knew that they might "often retard or entirely prevent the energetic action" necessary for very poor people "to lift themselves out of their difficulties."[30]

How, then, should relief be distributed? In brief, everyone aided by the public should be sent to an institution, and outdoor relief should come only through private charity. Asylums for delinquent and feebleminded women, Lowell believed, would reduce drastically the reproduction of a degraded, pauper class. However, indoor relief should do more than prevent the reproduction of a pauper class or repel everyone not starving or "in extremity." Rather, relief should try to "insure a distinct moral and physical improvement on the part of all those . . . forced to have recourse to it." That is "discipline and education" should be "inseparably associated with any system of relief." Only in an institution could the public turn relief into a moral and educational force.[31]

With public relief restricted to institutions, only private charity should aid those who remained outside. Public outdoor relief had "none of the redeeming features of private charity, because there is nothing personal or softening in it." Charity, almsgiving, and public outdoor relief, Lowell argued, were very different activities. Charity had four distinctive characteristics: first, it had to be "voluntary." If a "benefit . . . could not be avoided," it was not charity. Second, "the person to whom we exercise charity cannot have an acknowledged personal claim upon us." When someone fulfills duties as a parent or child or master, these actions are not charity, even though they may be "kind, just, fair, and considerate." Third, charity extended beyond good intentions; it had to be "kind action—it must accomplish good to the object of it." Finally, "charity must be exercised toward a person in an inferior circumstance to those of his benefactor. We cannot be charitable to our equals—in the sense of the word with which we are dealing." Given these characteristics, all official and public relief was "put outside the pale of charity" because it was not voluntary. Equally, but less obvious, "all indiscriminate almsgiving and all systematic dole giving" were not charity because they actually harmed the people they were supposed to help by destroying their character, depressing wages, exciting false hopes, and killing the capacity for self-support. All charity, she emphasized, should "tend to raise the character and elevate the moral nature, and so improve the condition of those toward whom it is exercised." The great rule of charity was, "that the best help of all is to help people to help themselves."[32]

To Lowell, the greatest character defect was idleness, which she found in the rich as often as in the poor. Although she had no means with which to root out idleness among the rich, to those who gave charity she said the key was the application of a labor test. No ablebodied man who refused a labor test—chopping wood or breaking stone—should get a cent. The more difficult decisions concerned the families of drunks who refused to reform or men who refused the

[margin notes: According to Lowell / 4 characterists of charity / ① ② ③ ④ / Reasons public relief is not charity / ✗]

71

labor test. To aid them, she said, only would spread the impression that a man could stop working with impunity and count on charity to feed his family. Certainly, his family would suffer if it were refused charity, but, observed Lowell, it would suffer under any circumstances. (The most constructive suggestion she could offer wives of drunks was to leave their husbands and sue for support.)[33]

Despite the sharp line she drew between public relief and private charity, Lowell did not want to dissociate the two completely. They had a reciprocal relation in which each assured the other's honesty and efficiency through inspection. Private groups should inspect public institutions; public agencies should inspect those run by the private groups. As a frequent visitor to institutions, Lowell provided a one-woman example of her principles in action. As a member of the private State Charities Aid Association she inspected poorhouses and prisons, and as a member of the State Board of Charities, she helped with the oversight of the state's voluntary agencies. Indeed, no one person better illustrated the blurred boundaries between public and private in nineteenth century America.[34]

Tough-minded and unsentimental, Lowell spent relatively little time outlining specific administrative procedures and organizational details. Nonetheless, she did stress the importance of charity organization. However carefully an individual, or even single association, tried to distribute its charity, she observed, in modern cities it was impossible to know each applicant or to ferret out imposters who went from charity to charity collecting help. The only answer was organization.[35]

Lowell concentrated on the theoretical basis for charity organization and specified few practical details about its application. However, anyone wanting to start a charity organization society could find concrete advice in S. Humphreys Gurteen's *Handbook of Charity Organization*, a disjointed and repetitive collection of Gurteen's speeches and pamphlets together with practical suggestions, sample forms, by-laws, constitution, and bibliography. Stephen Humphreys Gurteen, born in England, was the son of an Anglican clergyman, who died when he was very young. He was educated partly in Paris and then at Cambridge University. For a while he worked in a settlement with Edward Denison in London's East End, and, afterward, for the Charity Organization Society in London, which had been founded in 1869. In the 1870s, he migrated to America to begin a career as a "man of letters" around New York University, but he soon exchanged the literary life for a career in law and became a student in Judge Amasa Parker's law office in Albany. However, when he learned that law practice would require him to renounce his allegiance to the queen, he decided to change professions and went to Hobart College, where he taught classics. At Hobart, his interests shifted to religion, and, soon, he took orders and went to Buffalo as assistant to the pastor of St. Paul's Church.

72

The Theory and Practice of Scientific Charity

After the depression of 1873, Gurteen preached a series of sermons titled "phases of charity," which led to the reestablishment of St. Paul's Guild, a defunct organization whose purpose was to give alms and advice. In 1877, with the guild as a base and his London experience as a guide, Gurteen persuaded businessmen in Buffalo to start a Charity Organization Society, the first in America. As the idea of charity organization spread throughout the country, Gurteen helped other cities (including Toledo to which he moved as rector of Trinity Church) reorganize their philanthropy. However, the climate in Toledo damaged his health and he migrated to Davenport, Iowa, as assistant to Bishop Perry in Griswold College. There, he resumed his old interest in literature and wrote books on Arthurian romances until his death in 1898.[36]

Gurteen decided to publish a handbook on charity organization to answer the deluge of questions from all over the country. Because none of the society's administrative details and operating procedures had ever been published in one place, a handbook, he felt, "seemed to meet a real want of the present day."[37] The surge of interest in charity organization reflected an international preoccupation with pauperism; "scarcely any one of the great problems affecting the public good" had taken "as strong a hold upon the national mind of Europe, or indeed upon the minds of the more intelligent portion of our own people, as the question of the prevention of the pauperization of the poor." By themselves, churches and voluntary associations had proved inadequate to stem the flood of pauperism, and municipal systems everywhere worked badly.[38]

The problem had two roots. One was ecological: the separation of classes within cities. "There is," he claimed, "a terrible chasm already existing between the rich and the poor; a chasm which is becoming wider and wider as the years roll by, and for the existence of which the well-to-do of the country are chiefly responsible." A trip through any very poor city district would show "large families huddled together in tenements and shanties which barely afford protection from wind and storm; dwellings where the laws of health are defied, where the most ordinary sanitary arrangements are unknown, and where 'boards of health' fail to penetrate. . . . beds innocent of clothing; human forms, even those of children, shivering in rags; hunger written upon care-worn faces; and despair everywhere triumphant." Within these homes lurked "an immorality as deep as" their "poverty," a "moral atmosphere as pestilential as the physical." This is the disease the well-to-do had allowed to infect American cities.[39]

Charity—both private and public—was the other root of pauperism. Official charity's "mechanical movement" left the "heart untouched" and fostered "habits of dependence, destroying manliness and self-respect," making "pauperism a permanent institution, a positive profession." At the same time, the mass of "organized societies and noble-hearted individuals" each worked independently of the others and created a staggering, uncoordinated array of societies, homes,

73

schools, and associations that only encouraged fraud and dependence.[40]

If unchecked, pauperism would continue to grow into a monster, ensnaring more and more of the honest poor in its tentacles, until it became society's master and destroyed the very foundations of civilized life. Indiscriminate charity, he wrote, "unmans" the individual, "by destroying all self respect and independence and ambition." It "encourages idleness and unthriftiness and improvidence." As for the home, it "disintegrates the family and loosens the bonds of relationship, so that the duties of parents to children, and children to parents are held in light esteem . . . it weakens the responsibilities of more distant kinship" so that well-to-do people were only too ready to "throw the burden of the support of indigent relations on State, city or private charity." The poor knew little of the "home-idea" and "few memories of home, follow the children of the poor into afterlife." In sum, "we are allowing the most hallowing of all social influences to rot."[41]

Although his wallow in the muck of domestic sentimentality allowed Gurteen to turn up images calculated to revolt and frighten his listeners, he went on to argue that the worst consequence of all was the effect of indiscriminate charity and pauperism on society. For "the treatment of pauperism" was "a matter that" bore "directly upon our own homes, and our own safety in life and property." Gurteen began his attempt to frighten well-to-do Buffalo Episcopalians with an analogy between Frankenstein and poor relief. He wrote how in the "romance of Frankenstein" a young German student created a grotesque "monster of huge proportions" that, given life, craved for "human *sympathy*; he learns, he becomes conscious of his own *deformity*, and unable to escape the burden of such a life, wreaks a series of acts of terrible revenge" on his maker. Within this tale, says Gurteen, lurked a "momentous *moral* truth," exemplified by the fall of Rome. Rome had "created the monster 'pauperism' " through its indiscriminate policies of relief, which became the "fatal factor" in its collapse. Now, Americans had taken the same road. Gurteen used two examples. One was the draft riots in New York City in 1863, which shook the city "to its very center." He, himself, had watched the "revolting spectacle of 5,000 women and children sweeping down the leading avenue of the city in the darkness of night, the lurid flames of a hundred torches disclosing a scene of wild license scarcely surpassed by any single incident of the French revolution." The other example was the riots, by which he means the events around the strike, in the summer of 1877, " 'that yawning chasm of Communism opened at our feet.' " Whatever "may have contributed to the cause of the riots," argued Gurteen, "whatever differences may have characterized the actors in one or other of" them, the "*root* of the trouble lay in" the current "system of leaving pauperism to take care of itself; of widening instead of narrowing the chasm between the rich and the poor."[42]

The Theory and Practice of Scientific Charity

The answer, he said, was the plan of charity organization pioneered in London. Charity organization meant "the intelligent co-operation of all classes in the community, independently of creed or nationality, and the co-operation of all charitable institutions in the city with one another, and with the distributors of official relief." The first object of charity organization, he stressed, using one of his favorite images, was "the repressing of pauperism." Other goals—"improving the condition of the honest poor"; promoting "provident schemes to aid the struggling poor to be self-supporting"; and "the reform of social abuses"— though important, ranked lower.[43]

Charity organization societies repressed pauperism by organizing their work around five cardinal principles.

1   There must be no exclusion of any person or body of persons on account of religious creed, politics or nationality.
2   There must be no attempt at proselytism on the part of the Agents or others employed by the Organization.
3   There must be no interference with any existing benevolent societies; each society must retain its autonomy intact; its rules, funds, modes of operation and everything which gives it individuality.
4   There must be no relief given by the Organization itself, except in very urgent cases.
5   There must be no sentiment in the matter. It must be treated as a business scheme, if success is to attend its operations.[44]

The repression of pauperism, these principles underscored, took precedence over the saving of souls. If pauperism were to be routed, churches and voluntary associations would have to submerge their rivalries for the common good and create one umbrella organization to coordinate all charitable activity within the city. Proselytizing would only flame religious rivalries and arouse resentment among the poor. Charity organization societies were to be the first great secular organizations of urban philanthropy.

The ideal charity organization society would coordinate, investigate, and counsel. It would not give material relief. Gurteen's blueprint called for each city to create a central council of leading business and professional men— ideally, without clergy—to administer the affairs of the society and to appoint a central agent or organizing secretary to oversee the work in the city as a whole. Most actual operations would be decentralized into a series of districts. To stay clear of municipal politics and corruption—a subject very much on the minds of charity reformers—district boundaries should not be coterminous with wards. In Buffalo, Gurteen said, "We avoided the *ward* divisions, considering that they were the very worst that could be adopted, from their political bearings."[45]

A paid agent would run the operation in each district. All cooperating churches and associations were supposed to send relief applicants to the appro-

Principles of charity organization Societies.

priate district office, where the agent, after a visit to their homes and a thorough investigation, would report back to a district committee, which would decide whether the applicant deserved help and the form help should take. If the committee recommended material relief, it was supposed to send the applicant to the appropriate church or charity. In no case was the agent to give applicants anything other than temporary help to tide them over until the committee met. The committee and agent also would appoint a friendly visitor, a volunteer, whose role was to work with the family. The central office was to supplement the work of the districts by bringing agents together for conferences, sponsoring citywide innovations, investigating social conditions, maintaining a central registry of relief open to all agencies in the city, and developing a labor register that would help the unemployed find work.[46]

"The visitation of the poor at their homes," Gurteen stressed, was "an essential feature of the plan." The "chief need to the poor to-day," he asserted, was "not almsgiving, but the *moral support of true friendship*—the possession of a real friend, whose education, experience, and influence, whose general knowledge of life, or special knowledge of domestic economy are placed at the service of those who have neither the intelligence, the tact nor the opportunity to extract the maximum of good from their slender resources." Visitors were not to mix relief with advice; they were not to sully their relation with either alms or religion. They were to make friends with their families and help them along the road to independence. Still, a thread of coercion wove its way through the relation between visitor and family, because visitors were supposed to make sure that families followed the good advice they were offered; that they used relief wisely; that their morality remained beyond question; and that they obeyed all laws, especially those that required their children to attend school or to refrain from work. If the dwelling or neighborhood were "not respectable," the visitor should tell the family to move. If the family did not realize that work was a duty and seemed "perfectly content" with its poor relief, the visitor had an "imperative duty" to "point out, in a firm but loving spirit, the degrading tendency of a life of dependence and the real dignity of honest work." If the family was entitled to relief, the visitor should see that it arrived on time, although in no case should she sanction municipal outdoor relief. If the home was not clean enough, the "visitor should . . . endeavor to induce the poor to keep their dwellings in a wholesome, healthy condition." When all of these goals had been accomplished, the visitor "should endeavor to inculcate *provident ideas* and foster *provident habits*." In truth, the visitor was to be at once a sympathetic friend, an official, a teacher, and a spy.[47]

No one in Buffalo could have missed the dose of coercion mixed into charity organization, because as its first agents the COS there used the police, who investigated the homes of everyone on relief and helped draw up a central

76

register of the poor. The police distributed 30,000 forms; within 24 hours, 3,000 had been returned. The COS turned these forms into a central, alphabetical register which showed, despite the imperfections in the early process, that "the same person was in receipt of relief from three or four different societies, from a dozen different individuals, and from one or more churches, besides being on the poor-books. It was a lesson Buffalo will never forget." The cooperation between the COS and the police did not end with the initial survey of relief. Rather, in Buffalo, every applicant for municipal relief was ordered to answer "a printed form of questions, and to swear to it." The form was sent to the superintendent of police, who forwarded it to the captain in the district where the applicant lived. The captain detailed "an officer to make an investigation of the case and then report back in printed form to the Superintendent"; the overseer of the poor was "bound by municipal ordinance to give only in accordance with police recommendations." Clearly, when the stakes were high enough, the boundary that the COS tried at other times to erect between public and private could be ignored. By enlisting the police, the COS underlined the urgency of the problem, highlighted its own quasi-public status, and transmitted a message that Buffalo's poor could not mistake. According to Gurteen, the first year of the COS was a great success. Most of the city's churches and charities cooperated, and, for a mere $6,700 in expenses, the COS saved the city $48,000 and "the benevolent quite as much, by the repressing of imposition and fraud."[48]

Anyone helped by public sources, said Gurteen, should be put in a poorhouse. No public outdoor relief should be given, ever. As for the decisions about relief that charity organization societies had to make, he admitted that distinguishing "between worthy and unworthy cases" was "at times extremely difficult." However, *in all cases . . . let the 'labor axiom' be the test, i.e., whether or not the applicant is willing to do as much work as his condition will allow.*" For this reason, a wood yard or a place to break stone was the most important venture for the central office to organize. Others were savings banks; housing reform; and creches, where working mothers could leave their children during the day.[49]

Like Josephine Shaw Lowell, Gurteen recognized that many women did not work because they had no one to care for their young children. However, Lowell argued that competent, moral women should be helped to stay home with their children. For Gurteen, aid to ablebodied women was not an option, partly because everyone should work, partly because he so distrusted the poor that he believed their children would be better off in a well-run nursery. Gurteen lapsed into mawkish sentimentality when he wrote about home. ("If there is one word in the English language for the unimpaired transmission of which we owe an especial debt of gratitude to our English or Anglo-Saxon ancestors, it is the sacred, the holy word Home.") By contrast, once she had passed beyond her romantic adolescent fascination with war, Lowell never lapsed into such trite sentiment. Still, it was her attempt to assist the mothers of young children in their homes and, later, her advocacy of higher wages and better working conditions for women that followed more consistently from a concern with home, family, and women than Gurteen's recommendation of day care alone as the solution to the problems of single-parent families. Nowhere in his discussion of poverty did Gurteen suggest their problems might also include low wages or, even, the lack of work. Indeed, to the contrary, he believed jobs that paid a living wage were always available for everyone who wanted to work. The real reason for the misery of the poor was their ignorance. "The necessity of almsgiving," he said, "in the large majority of cases, is due to ignorance on the part of the poor as to the economic and provident disposition of their weekly earnings."[50]

Gurteen had one special intellectual problem. Closely attuned to intellectual fashion, he knew that a surface reading of social Darwinism implied that all charity only impeded the evolution of the species by preserving the unfit. Was even scientific charity a retrogressive attempt to interfere with the law of nature? His answer had two parts. His capacity for coordinated, associated activity distinguished man from animals. Therefore, the survival of the unfit represents the fulfillment rather than the negation of a great natural law because only through men acting in concert have the sick and defective been kept alive. In the same way, only through concerted action to deny aid to the undeserving could "these same classes . . . be prevented from becoming a positive burden and a curse to Society." Therefore, "Organization" was "the only scientific method of dealing with Pauperism—the method which Nature itself points out." His other argument also put charity organization at the top of the evolutionary scale. "Nature's great law," Gurteen wrote, was the " 'division' of labor'," and this was "the underlying principle of the [Charity Organization] Society's method of dealing with Poverty and Pauperism."[51]

Gurteen concerned himself with the gender as well as the administrative division of labor within charity organization. Although he hoped that business and professional men would act as friendly visitors, he realized that few of them would have the time, and, for the most part, the job would fall to women. Women, however, were not to be allowed any administrative or policy roles within the COS. The various councils and agents, Gurteen said, all should consist of men. The work of the council and district committees was "man's work; but to perform that higher and more difficult task of visiting the poor, and the pauperized poor, as friends," Gurteen contended, was "no easy task," and "it might well satisfy the ambition of any woman's life to have raised but one family from dependence, idleness and beggary, to self-support, honest labor and independence." Friendly visiting would help not only the poor; it also would discipline, control, and educate well-to-do women. Indeed, "the whole complexion of the habits of thought of our women would undergo a change; life itself would become a more serious matter; it would be seen that our women have duties which they owe to the community and to the nation no less than the men."[52]

Charity organization was more than a way of repressing pauperism. It was a bureaucratic resolution of tension over sex roles among the well-to-do in the Gilded Age. A curious contradiction undercut Gurteen's attempt to define and justify a place for women within the movement. For he began by implying that women sought a more active, directing role than he felt they deserved. Friendly visiting was enough to "satisfy the ambition of any woman." What else did they want? Seats on the council and district committees? Jobs as agents? But he slipped quickly to another and very different implication: women were frivolous, unaware of their social responsibility. They needed the exposure and discipline that work among the poor would provide. By defining women as frivolous, Gurteen could disguise the effect of his scheme, which was not to offer women an exciting new opportunity (after all, they had had decades of experience with voluntary charity, including visiting the poor) but to sharply delimit their sphere of action. Throughout the country, in fact, tensions over sex roles were acted out in local contests over the control of charity. Men removed women from control of the orphanage in Petersburg, Virginia; the Associations for Improving the Condition of the Poor that sprang up in most cities used male visitors; the new charity organization societies tried to confine women to the infantry in the war against pauperism.

As Daniel Calhoun has pointed out, educational reform also was used to resolve sex-role tensions through bureaucratic fiat: women would occupy the lowest ranks within educational systems, which would be run by men.[53] The men who built school systems succeeded better than the architects of charity organization at fixing a place for women at the bottom of their organizations, because women took longer to achieve positions of leadership in education than in charity. Too many active, able women were already involved in the charity organization movement itself, and women played a more active role in the construction of the new organizations than in the elaboration of educational bureaucracies. Even more, the women who worked in charity organization by and large were richer and older than those who taught school; indeed, often they were married. They could look forward to longer careers than schoolteachers (women teachers usually had to resign when they married). They had served apprenticeships in voluntary societies and, during the Civil War, in the Sanitary Commission. They were poised to demand real authority in a way that young, unmarried schoolteachers, fresh out of normal schools, were not.

Any reasonably perceptive observer could not miss the contradictions that debilitated organized charity. In an 1896 article, Josephine Shaw Lowell wrote, "It seems often as if charities were the insult which the rich add to the injuries which they heap upon the poor." Two years later, she complained that the "teaching of charity organization societies" had "been misunderstood, and most grievously misunderstood, by many people who have adopted the perverted opinion that to inquire into the cause of the trouble afflicting a poor man or woman is itself a good thing, no matter what use is made of the knowledge obtained." To the contrary, she argued, "investigation by itself is bad." There was no

> excuse for trespassing upon the privacy of other human beings, for trying to learn facts in their lives which they prefer should not be known, for seeking to discover the weak spots in their characters, for trying to find out what pitiful personal sorrows their nearest and dearest have brought upon them—the only justification, I say, for doing all these painful things which are too often included in the single word [,] investigation, is that the person in distress has asked you to help him, and that you mean to help him, to help his soul and not only to feed his miserable body, and that you cannot help him unless you do know all about him.

Josephine Shaw Lowell resolved the contradictions within organized charity by shifting her efforts to economic reform, organizing women, supporting unions, and fighting for higher wages. Stephen Humphreys Gurteen resolved the tension between the nasty mix of sentimentality and repression in his conception of organized charity by retreating into the mists of Avalon and Camelot.[54]

The Failure of Charity Organization

No city managed to implement a charity organization movement that fit Gurteen's ideal. Despite the brave and optimistic accounts in their early annual reports, most charity organization societies failed to match the template cut by the movement's theorists. The internal contradictions within the theory itself coupled with the realities of local urban politics defeated even the most zealous reformers, and by the early twentieth century it was clear to all but the most doctrinaire that a combination of centralization, investigation, and friendly visiting under private auspices would not reduce dependence in American cities. Within thirty or forty years, charity organization had moved from the vanguard to the backwaters of social policy.

Charity organization failed on every major dimension. Only a few societies did not give material relief, and even they were not able to hold out permanently. Virtually everywhere, individual charity organization societies were unable to overcome completely the suspicion, hostility, and rivalry of churches and local relief organizations. Although charity organization societies emerged fairly quickly in most of the country's largest cities, it took decades before they spread to smaller centers around the country. Aside from Boston and Baltimore, no individual society could find enough volunteers to mount an effective friendly visiting campaign, and paid, full-time agents did more and more of the work. In only ten of the largest cities, did the forces of charity organization manage to persuade local governments to abolish outdoor relief completely, and, by the end of the century, the amount of outdoor relief in one form or another had begun to creep upward again. In most places, existing charity organization societies proved inadequate to cope with the recurrent depressions that made destitution a mass emergency in late nineteenth and early twentieth century cities, and no evidence suggests they softened relations between classes or even began to reduce the great social distances that had disturbed and frightened their founders.[55]

Everywhere, charity organization in practice assumed a distinctive shape molded by its local context. Of all major cities, Boston most closely approximated the model of charity organization, but it, too, failed to match the ideal completely or to privatize relief.[56] Indeed, although its per person charitable contributions ranked highest in the nation, late nineteenth-century private giving in Boston failed to match, let alone exceed, public expenditure for relief. Led by wealthy women, especially Mrs. James T. Fields, in 1879 Bostonians united most of their important charities into the Associated Charities. The Associated Charities cooperated with the overseers of the poor, who were made members of its district conferences. Each district sent three delegates and a secretary to a central council, which also included *ex officio* public officials. The Associated Charities itself, true to the COS model, did not give relief, but was very successful in persuading large numbers of women to serve as friendly visitors. Even though they cooperated with public officials, Boston's charity organizers kept up a steady criticism of outdoor relief and failed to engage the cooperation of one of the city's oldest and largest charities, the Provident Society, which continued to give direct assistance. Indeed, the Provident Society proved a constant critic of the new Associated Charities. Its attack had two themes:

> This newcomer was merely another claimant upon a general charitable fund, which was already too small to go around; and while the usefulness of the system of registration was recognized, it was the only valuable innovation and might cost more than it would be worth. The second objection touched more to the heart of the new method. Application of the new ideas, some believed, would make charity hard. . . . There was too much organization and machinery to permit the natural

'beauty and sweetness of ministering to the poor.' It was the system, the mechanics, that people objected to.[57]

As elsewhere, in Boston the depression of 1893 exposed the bankruptcy of organized charity. When the depression struck, the city's charities responded calmly, confident that careful methods of investigation and a refusal to sanction emergency measures or indiscriminate aid would prove the right course with which to steer the truly needy through hard times. They criticized make-work projects, such as the city's wood yard, where one charity agent found the men "unwilling to take jobs," often "hopeless . . . wholly indifferent to their own welfare, caring only to obtain a shelter for the night and something to eat." Organized charity also fiercely opposed organized labor. "If the laborer lacks the qualities that make the capitalist, it seems to be no reason why he should quarrel with his employers, or with his opportunities." The labor problem, charity leaders claimed, had been caused by the un-American practices of immigrants; "when the workmen were all American . . . strikes and contests were unknown." Unlike Josephine Shaw Lowell, Boston's charity organization leaders failed to move beyond the individual interpretation of poverty. Searching about for a cause of the distress and disorder they saw around them, they retreated to a nasty and "virulent" nativism. "If wages were low or there was unemployment, it was because the labor market was crowded by Chinese and 'paupers from Europe.' " Increasingly irrelevant to the situation of workers in late nineteenth and early twentieth century Boston, the charity organizers were attacked by "labor and settlement people." In 1898, the poet John Boyle O'Reilly wrote of:

> That Organized Charity, scrimped and iced,
> In the name of a cautious, statistical Christ.

Indianapolis probably had the most successful charity organization movement in the country. Smaller, with a more cohesive leadership and less rivalry among charitable societies and churches, in 1879, charity organizers there implemented their plans with minimal compromises. Led by the energetic, zealous Reverend Oscar C. McCullough, one of the leaders in organized charity and author of the well-known "The Tribe of Ishmael: A Study in Social Degradation," which used charity organization records to argue the hereditary basis of crime and pauperism, Indianapolis' civic leaders created a remarkably centralized society. Its offices became headquarters for other voluntary societies, and its district committees had offices "in the same building. Telephonic connection was arranged with all public institutions. Every case of need, accident or begging was reported to the central office, and was referred to the district superintendent to whom it belonged." With its centralized organization, Indianapolis, according

82

to Watson, managed the destitution and unemployment created by the depression of 1893 better than most cities. The COS and the city coordinated their efforts and when the city ran out of money, the COS agreed to pay the wages—in supplies rather than money—of men employed on public works. Still, at the end of the century, public outdoor relief remained almost as large as voluntary aid. Both figures were low for a city with 185,000 people and reflected a level of general prosperity higher than in the larger, Eastern cities. This, certainly, was the major reason why Indianapolis implemented charity organization with greater success. That success, however, was relative. Throughout its history, the Indianapolis COS contended with attacks from a variety of sources. When it was newly organized, a socialist newspaper criticized the COS as "in league with the Township Trustee," and "spending dollar upon dollar for investigation—but not one cent to relieve 'cases' until they have been investigated." The minister of the wealthy Second Presbyterian Church also attacked the COS, as did others who referred to its method as a "system of espionage." A few years later a group of Methodist ministers, joined a Baptist minister, criticized the COS for its connection with McCullough's church, which, they said, "was getting benefits at the expense of other churches by the rental of rooms." Others continued to criticize the proportion of funds spent on organization and investigation rather than relief. One commentator called it the "society for the suppression of benevolence." Another said, "So the poor—the deserving poor, the superlatively, double-distilled, deserving poor—get only fifty cents out of each dollar collected. It is a beautiful work."[58]

In the early twentieth century, charity organization spread from larger to smaller cities and from North to South, but the principles of charity organization no longer reflected the cutting edge of modern social policy. In fact, within the charity organization movement itself a few new leaders tried to move practice in other directions, and large organizations, such as in Philadelphia and New York, expanded their activities to include research, publications, public health, training, and tenement house reform (and, in New York City, active involvement in politics). But these new thrusts hardly could be called charity organization, and the different departments of the New York COS virtually became different organizations.[59]

Early in the second decade of the twentieth century, Edward T. Devine, the secretary of the New York COS, confessed failure: "Our use of relief has been most sparing and timid. I am inclined to believe that we have caused more pauperism by our failure to provide for the necessaries of life, for the education and training of children, and for the care and convalescence of the sick, than we have by excessive relief, even if we include the indiscriminate alms." With even the leading spokesman for the country's largest COS full of doubt, it is not surprising that radical critics were much tougher on charity organization.

83

In 1917, Konrad Bercovici, a journalist, published a fictional expose of organized charity, which he called *Crimes of Charity*. In it, he portrayed organized charity as a harsh, callous, self-serving bureaucracy that supplied scab labor when contributors' employees struck. In an introduction to Bercovici's book, John Reed wrote:

> Every person of intelligence and humanity who has seen the workings of Organised Charity, knows what a deadening and life-sapping thing it is, how unnecessarily cruel, how uncomprehending. Yet it must not be criticised, investigated or attacked. Like patriotism, charity is respectable, an institution of the rich and great—like the high tariff, the open shop, Wall street, and Trinity Church. White slavery recruits itself from charity, industry grows bloated with it, landlords live off it; and it supports an army of officers, investigators, clerks and collectors, whom it systematically debauches. Its giving is made the excuse for lowering the recipients' standard of living, of depriving them of privacy and independence, or subjecting them to the cruelest mental and physical torture, of making them liars, cringers, thieves. The law, the police, the church are the accomplices of charity. And how could it be otherwise, considering those who give, how they give, and the terrible doctrine of the 'deserving poor'? There is nothing of Christ the compassionate in the immense business of Organised Charity; its object is to get efficient results—and that means, in practise, to just keep alive vast numbers of servile, broken-spirited people.[60]

4 The Transformation of
the Poorhouse

The advocates of scientific charity did not oppose all public relief. They wanted to abolish only the outdoor variety and to restrict public assistance to reformed poorhouses. Between 1850 and 1930, according to the depressingly similar portraits painted by most observers, poorhouses appeared the backwaters of social policy, stagnant and festering exceptions to the progressive spirit in American life. Although an occasional county or an unusual superintendent might run a decent poorhouse, most remained dreary, lifeless, and degrading. Yet, this static portrait is only partly valid, for even poorhouses had a history of their own. In fact, by the early twentieth century poorhouses had been transformed from family refuges to old-age homes. The process, which took nearly a century, may be traced in two ways: through official policy and through the actual demography of the institutions themselves. Within policy, the great theme was the attempt to siphon special groups from the poorhouse into separate institutions. The blind and the deaf and dumb were the first to receive separate institutional care, but the three groups that caused the most controversy and the most difficulty were children, the mentally ill, and the ablebodied. In time, their removal from poorhouses produced greatly enlarged orphanages, huge custodial hospitals for the chronic insane, and flophouses for the newly homeless.

Throughout the country, public responsibility for dependence had increased enormously in the decades before the Civil War. State governments were supposed to supervise poor laws, which were administered locally and through county institutions; they had created reform schools, mental hospitals, and new prisons; and they funded nominally private institutions for the deaf and dumb, blind, feebleminded, and other people unable to care for themselves. Every year, it seemed, expenses for dependence grew and state responsibility increased. Yet, every institution had its own charter and board of trustees, and no state even gathered together in one source financial information and other data about its activities, let alone tried to coordinate or control its policies toward dependence. State governments created boards of state charities to bring order to this administrative chaos. The first was Massachusetts, in 1863, follwed by New York, in 1867. By the end of the century, sixteen other states had followed their lead. "All of the new state boards," according to Gerald Grob, "represented a thrust toward the "centralization and rationalization" of state power, which was "strongest in the older and more populous regions of the Northeast and Midwest" and "weakest in the South." Even though they lacked many official powers, everywhere, the investigations and reports of the new boards influenced legislative policy and public opinion by compiling statistics, investigating state institutions, monitoring compliance with state laws, and issuing reports and recommendations. Among other accomplishments, they guided the transformation of poorhouses.[1]

Poorhouse Demography in Fact and Fabrication

In some instances, the new boards of state charities had a national impact. The great example was the survey of poorhouse inmates carried out for New York's board in 1874–75 by its secretary, Dr. Charles S. Hoyt. The board had decided to find out, once and for all, the true causes of pauperism. Its real agenda, however, was not objective social inquiry. Rather, it was the confirmation of scientific charity's image of the unworthy poor. Hoyt claimed his survey supplied irrefutable evidence of the degradation common to poorhouse inmates. In fact, it showed nothing of the sort. Hoyt wrote:

> By far the greater number of paupers have reached that condition by idleness, improvidence, drunkenness, or some form of vicious indulgence. . . . These vices and weaknesses are very frequently, if not universally, the result of tendencies which are to a greater or less degree hereditary. The number of persons in our poorhouses who have been reduced to poverty by causes outside of their own acts is . . . surprisingly small.

Hoyt's sixty-question survey administered to 12,614 inmates became the most influential and widely quoted document on pauperism in the late nineteenth century. Its impact rested partly on its extensive sample and exhaustive questionnaire but, even more, on its conclusions. For Hoyt told people what they wanted to hear. Despite his veneer of empiricism, Hoyt neatly sidestepped the most troublesome facts about poorhouse inmates and fabricated an image that suited the times.[2]

By administering his questionnaire only to the "fixed population" of poor-houses and by lumping together paupers, inmates of insane asylums attached to poorhouses, and some children in orphanages, Hoyt could claim that he had discovered few ablebodied men in poorhouses and that most inmates were long-term residents, helpless people destroyed by their own shiftless, degraded lives. He would concede only that many of them lacked responsibility because they had inherited their distaste for work and their fondness for drink from their pauper parents. In fact, Hoyt knew perfectly well that poorhouses were full of ablebodied men. He even had pointed out the problem forcefully in his fourth report, but the image spread by his survey only a few years later differed dramatically.[3]

Despite his claims, Hoyt's survey failed to show the hereditary basis of pauperism or that most paupers were the drunken offspring of intemperate parents. In fact, his data showed that almost all poorhouse inmates had lived their lives in the most vulnerable sectors of the working class. A very high proportion of the men had been unskilled laborers; only a tiny fraction had worked at white-collar occupations. Most women listed no occupation; those that did usually had been domestic servants. Most, moreover, had received very little public relief before entering the poorhouse. Few had received outdoor relief and most were in a poorhouse for the first time. Because they had not worked for wages, women became dependent earlier than men, especially when they were widowed. Thus, the women in poorhouses had been dependent longer than the men. As well, they were more likely to have received outdoor relief, especially when they had children. Poor men were able to support themselves until relatively late in their lives and avoided the poorhouse longer than women. Although women more often succeeded in avoiding it altogether, when they did enter they usually did so younger than men because of their vulnerability and lack of employment opportunity. Among the insane poor, by contrast, men received less help from relatives and were institutionalized earlier than women, although, overall, many more women than men ended up in insane asylums.

Hoyt failed completely to discuss one of the most remarkable and consistent patterns in the data: the greater number of elderly men than women among the inmates. Children, poorhouse demography underlines, were less willing to take care of their fathers than their mothers. On the basis of her survey of 1,000 homeless men in Chicago, Alice Willard Solenberger wrote, "Their children are the natural and most usual sources of help for the aged, but of these particular [132] old men only 51 had living children. . . . Of the children whom we did find, a number were either unwilling or unable to help their fathers." Four of the children refused to help their fathers because "the men had deserted their families when their children were young and helpless." In several other cases, "similar refusals to aid ... the habitual drunkards came from sons who had suffered much because of their fathers' vices."[4]

According to Mary Roberts Smith, assistant professor of social science at Stanford, women actually were more dependent than men because "domestic occupations" unfitted "women for self support." In her 1892 study she reported that the childbearing that "consumed" the lives of uneducated married women resulted in "lack of ambition, and in a round of small routine duties and petty details of the most unsystematic sort." With their intelligence, energy, and ambition drained away, widows were left with "domestic service" as their only source of work, and even for that their "home life" had "unfitted" them. To the almshouse women Roberts interviewed married life had been an escape from self-dependence, and many mourned their "dead husbands and children chiefly" for the support they had lost. Women less often ended their lives in poorhouses, Roberts said, because the public recognized "the inevitable dependence of women by considering it a most disgraceful thing for relatives or children to allow an old woman to go to the almshouse." But men were thought to "have had their chance to lay up money, and if they have not done so they must take the consequences. This one-sided filial obligation keeps large numbers of women out of the almshouse who are wholly dependent." When it commented on the increasing ratio of men to women in poorhouses, the 1910 Census Bureau report made much the same point. First, dependent women, it observed, were "more than men ... similarly situated to be taken care of by relatives, friends, or even private charities." Even more, "special institutions for the care of indigent women" had developed rapidly; for men they were almost nonexistent.[5]

More than any other characteristic, their lack of children set men and women in poorhouses apart from other poor people. A very high proportion had never married; about three-quarters of the widowed paupers had either no living children or only one. These proportions were far higher than in the population as a whole. Thus, many people entered poorhouses simply because they had no one to give them a home. They did not end their lives in poorhouses because they were especially debauched, idle, or thriftless. Rather, they were so poor that when the death of a spouse or sickness pushed them over the "verge of pauperism," they were unlucky enough to lack grown children to whom they could turn for help.

Hoyt managed to avoid the demography of destitution by excluding the mass of young, temporary poorhouse inmates from his sample, lumping together men, women, the sane, insane, and children into the same analyses, manipulating the categories with which he reported his results, and simply ignoring uncomfortable patterns. Nowhere in his more than 300-page report did he mention the great depression that raged around him.

The registers of poorhouses created under Hoyt's supervision would have shown a picture equally at variance with prevailing images of pauperism if anyone had cared to analyze them. In the late nineteenth century, most inmates of New York's almshouses were literate and had been to school. Most, too, came from working-class families. However, fewer inmates than their fathers had worked in agriculture, and many were men and women caught in the transition from agriculture to industry. Even though their families were working class, few inmates came from pauper backgrounds. Of inmates in one large sample who answered questions about their families, 66 had pauper fathers and 2,671 had fathers who were self-supporting; 83 had pauper brothers and 1,961 brothers who supported themselves. Of all relatives, only 3 percent were known to be paupers. Nor were the majority intemperate, even by the stringent standards used at the time, and only a little over a fifth of fathers were thought to have been intemperate, either.[6]

The demography of dependence shows quite the opposite of what Hoyt intended. It gives a picture of poverty rooted in the conditions of working-class life. Seasonal work, fluctuating demands for labor, and periodic depressions often produced destitution. Thus, many paupers were men on the move in search of work, either by themselves or with their families, in need of short-term help between jobs. Others—victims of industrial accidents, the mentally ill, the chronically sick—unable to care for themselves, landed in poorhouses where they remained for long periods of time. Still other people were casualties of the working-class life cycle. They were widows with young children; young, pregnant women; orphans; and, especially, old people without spouses, kin, or children able or willing to care for them. All of these people crowded into large, nineteenth century poorhouses at the same time. Thus, the lack of classification, the heterogeneous quality of poorhouse populations, about which critics tirelessly complained, was not only the product of bad management. Even more, it mirrored the complex causes of destitution, a structural artifact of working-class life.

Poorhouse populations reflected both the great structural sources of destitution and shifts in public policy. As a result, their demographic history was far more complex than most contemporary commentators admitted. As an example, consider the Erie County, New York, Almshouse, which served Buffalo and the surrounding region. Between its opening in 1829 and the mid-1880s four distinct periods marked its history. From its founding through the early 1840s, many families—parents with children—used the poorhouse, and most inmates had been born in America. The proportion of inmates entering with relatives declined from 38 percent in 1839 to 10 percent in the 1850s and to only 3 or 4 percent late in the century. In the same period, the percentage of native-born inmates shrank from over 55 percent in 1829 to 40 percent in the 1840s and 10 percent between 1853 and 1854. Within poorhouses, in the 1840s Irish immigrants entering without kin replaced the earlier native-born inmates. In these years, fewer families came to the poorhouse together, and most inmates entered by themselves. The third era was the Civil War. Not surprisingly, the proportion of young men in the poorhouse dropped sharply then, and many more young, unmarried women entered. (Throughout most of its history the poorhouse served as a maternity hospital for unmarried women.) The proportion of women among inmates increased from about 30 percent early in the poorhouse's history to 40 percent on the eve of the Civil War and 47 percent during the war. By 1870–74, it had dropped back to 22 percent. When the war ended, the proportion of children as well as women started to decline, and the proportion of elderly inmates, among whom men outnumbered women by a large margin, climbed. The proportion of children less than 14 years old among inmates dropped from about 30 percent before the Civil War to 13 percent in 1870–74 and, after the passage of the Children's Act in 1875, to 3 percent in 1875–79. Conversely, the elderly increased from 9 percent of inmates in 1829 to 15 percent in 1855–59 and 37 percent in 1880–86. By the end of the century, the poorhouse clearly was becoming an old-age home. Nonetheless, at no time in the nineteenth century was the poorhouse a monolithic institution, for it always sheltered many different kinds of people.[7]

The length of time people spent in the poorhouse highlights its dual role as both a short-term refuge for people in trouble and a home for the helpless and elderly. Throughout these years a strikingly high proportion of inmates stayed for only a short time. At least two-fifths of the inmates stayed in the poorhouse for three weeks at most. In fact, nearly three-fifths were there for a maximum of six weeks, and only between one-fifth and one-quarter stayed there for a year or more. For most people the poorhouse was a temporary refuge during crises, not a permanent home. Young men and others who entered during depressions were especially likely to be short-term residents. Those young men who entered during the winter stayed longest, and those who came during the summer remained for the shortest time. Clearly, poorhouses played an important role in tiding men over periods when work was hard to find.

Erie County was not unique. In Newburyport, Massachusetts, between 1815 and 1829, married couples often entered the poorhouse together; almost two-thirds of those admitted eventually left; men outnumbered women by a ratio of two to one; and inmates clustered into two groups: young or middle-aged people who needed short-term help and old people who stayed in the poorhouse until they died. In Franklin County, Ohio, in 1880, many poorhouse inmates were young, temporary residents seeking shelter between periods of work, and men outnumbered women by almost three to one. There, too, the poorhouse population varied by season as departures from the poorhouse peaked in March, April, and May. Throughout the country, the sex ratio of poorhouse inmates (number of males per 100 females) rose between 1880 and 1910 from 116.1 to 210. About one-third of them were less than fifty-five years old; another third between fifty-five and sixty-nine; and the remaining third seventy or older. Although poorhouses increasingly had become old-age homes, their populations were "roughly divisible into two elements—the larger group . . . of temporary inmates, who come in times of misfortune or unemployment, and generally leave within a year, and the smaller one . . . who go to the almshouse to spend their declining days."[8]

Poorhouse demography did not match official images of paupers or the goals of policy very well. Inmates did not come from a degraded culture of poverty marked by illiteracy and intemperance. They were not, by and large, apathetic, unwilling to work, and permanently pauperized. Despite official policy, the poor used the almshouse for their own purposes: early in its history as a short-term residence for native families in crisis, and in later years as a place to stay during harsh seasons, unemployment, or family emergencies. At the same time, it was a hospital where unmarried mothers could have their children and a home of last resort for the sick poor and destitute elderly. Many of its inmates were ablebodied, short-term residents looking for work. To be sure, fewer were children, and increasing numbers were elderly. But the poorhouse remained a complex institution. Indeed, to reformers its complexity signaled an indiscriminate and unjustifiable mixing of categories of dependents, and after the early 1870s they directed most of their effort to siphoning off everyone except the elderly. Although they did not succeed completely, their campaigns did transform poorhouses and stimulate the expansion of other, more specialized institutions. In the end, however, they did not solve the real problems they had identified; they simply displaced them.

From Poorhouse to Flophouse

Of all the varieties of unfortunate people in poorhouses, none proved as troubling as ablebodied men. Despite Hoyt's survey, everybody really knew that healthy, working-age men often stayed in poorhouses for a few weeks or months in the winter, during depressions, or between jobs. Their presence in poorhouses or on outdoor relief aroused passionate responses because it seemed unjust to tax the public to support men perfectly capable of earning their own living. Even more, aiding the ablebodied undercut the incentive to work, inflated wages, and reduced the supply of labor. Attacks on the ablebodied rested on two assumptions: one was the presence of a clear boundary between them and the truly needy or deserving poor. The other was the availability of work for every healthy man willing to labor. As many commentators pointed out, neither of these assumptions was valid. Nonetheless, some reformers tried to purge the ablebodied from relief; others advocated work tests; and many tried to eject them from poorhouses. Most officials and reformers would have agreed that any relief given the ablebodied should be as unpleasant and degrading as possible. Nor should it be offered freely. Only those men willing to break stone or cut wood for their meager supper and spartan bed should be sheltered from the streets.

When officials and reformers attacked apparently healthy young men who asked for relief, *tramp* often became a synonym for ablebodied. Indeed, the noun tramp first came into widespread use in the 1870s as a label with which to denigrate the swelling numbers of young men roaming the nation in search of work. With an obstinate refusal to connect the rise in the number of tramps to the great industrial depression that began in 1873, spokesmen for the respectable classes manufactured an image of a menacing new class. Not until the 1890s, at the earliest, did tramps appear to be a colorful subculture, characters for the folklorist and cartoonist as well as the reformer and policeman. To the contrary, they seemed a threat, prowling the streets of towns and villages, stealing, assaulting women, and fomenting discontent among the working class. Tramps were lazy, dishonest, agitators living off the sentimental generosity of soft-hearted women and the public bounty of poorhouses, where they retreated to spend their winters in warmth and comfort. Ablebodied tramps had absolutely no redeeming qualities, and they should be ejected from poorhouses as surely as they should be cut from outdoor relief.[9]

In its second annual report, The New York Commissioners of State Charities raised the spectre of the ablebodied with fearful clarity.

> Every able-bodied pauper who, after a year's support in a county house, goes out from it into society is an active missionary of a vile propaganda among the poorer classes to depreciate the dignity of labor and to recommend the comfort and ease of a self-assumed dependence. There should be one rule for every poor house: Support the infirm and helpless; hard work for the sturdy and strong.

Two years later the commissioners still were complaining about "the presence of able-bodied vagrants in our various poorhouses, and their retention without occupation therein," and they recommended "the establishment of industrial alms-houses, homes and refuges for the able-bodied paupers, and the limitation of county poor-houses exclusively to the sick, aged or helpless."[10]

However, the commissioners did not persuade counties to create two different types of institutions for poor relief, and in 1880, they tried another tack, advocating a tough policy based on the use of expert medical knowledge to distinguish between the ablebodied and the deserving poor. For the most part, the county superintendents agreed with the attempt to rid poorhouses of the ablebodied, and, in practice, superintendents discouraged tramps in various ways. Some simply refused to admit them; some had them arrested as vagrants; others applied a strict work test. Although unemployment and hard winters prevented the complete ejection of the ablebodied from poorhouses, pressure from state officials, reformers, and many of their colleagues drove most superintendents to try to reduce the number in their care. Slowly, they succeeded.[11]

In 1893, Oscar Craig, president of the Board of State Charities, reported that the ablebodied pauper had "practically . . . been excluded from the poorhouse," and in 1903, Alice Stoneaker, chairman of the Committee on County and Municipal Institutions of the National Conference of Charities and Corrections, asserted "in our best communities, the almshouse today is recognized as an infirmary and hospital, rather than as a place of segregation of the nonproductive elements of society." In New York, by "the end of the [first] World War," according to Schneider and Deutsch, the poorhouse "was being looked upon as an institution mainly for the care of the aged and infirm." To take another example, by the early twentieth century the Philadelphia almshouse had been transformed into the Philadelphia General Hospital.[12]

For the most part, poorhouses became old-age homes, which paid a high price for their origins. Emerging as part of the structure of public relief, they never wholly lost the stigma attached to welfare. They were places of last resort, dreaded by the poor. Writing of homeless old men in Chicago in the early twentieth century, Alice Willard Solenberger observed, "Dread of life in an institution seems to be almost universal among them, although the particular institution most dreaded is, of course, the poorhouse." No one in Chicago needed to beg or starve when the poorhouse always stood "ready to receive him," but many men begged on the street anyway, because "life in a poorhouse would mean the endurance of mental suffering far worse than the disgrace of begging."[13]

Whatever their inclinations, after 1880, ablebodied men encountered much more resistance gaining shelter in poorhouses or persuading public and private agencies to give them outdoor relief. What, then, were they to do? Poor relief reformers would answer in a word: work. For they believed the refusal of relief would force the ablebodied to support themselves. But even in the best of times thousands of men were unemployed, and, of course, during the severe depressions that punctuated late nineteenth and early twentieth century America, many men could not locate work of any kind. The massive immigration from southern and eastern Europe compounded employment problems by flooding the labor market with unskilled young men. Given these conditions, ejecting the ablebodied from almshouses and outdoor relief could not eliminate the problem; it only could displace it.

The ablebodied went first to police stations where they were allowed to sleep on the floor or sometimes in cells. Until the late 1890s, thousands of homeless men (called "lodgers") slept in police stations every night. According to Eric Monkkonen, in depression years or during harsh winters "the number of overnight lodgings provided by a police department exceeded all annual arrests." In 1876, the Cincinnati Police Department sheltered and lodged "75,331 indigent persons without homes." Figures for other cities were comparably large. It is very difficult to estimate just how large a proportion of adult men spent at least a night in a police station, but Monkkonen thinks it might be as high as one in twenty-three in the late nineteenth century. Or, to look at the figures another way, "between 10% and 20% of the U.S. population in the late nineteenth century came from families of which one member had experienced the hospitality of a police station." During the last quarter of the century, police stations sheltered many more men than did poorhouses. For example, between April, 1873, and March, 1874, the Columbus, Ohio, Police Department housed 3,175 people or 50.7 per 1,000 of the population. Admissions to the poorhouse varied from 11.3 per 1,000 in 1874 to .97 in 1881. (These rates were based on the county rather than just the city and should be doubled. On the other hand, they include all poorhouse entrants, not just ablebodied men.)[14]

Conditions within police stations varied greatly. Although some were not too foul, most were crowded, dirty, and uncomfortable. According to Theodore Roosevelt, the lodgings in the New York City police stations were "filthy in the extreme. The casuals slept on planks, of which there were two tiers. The atmosphere was so foul that it made the policemen, who occupied another part of the building, sick." Writing of conditions in Boston, a reformer described men "huddled together in their damp, reeking clothes, no bed but a hard bench, no food if hungry, turned out at day break into the snow of a winter morning." Walter Wyckoff, traveling as an unskilled laborer in 1891, spent a night in a Chicago police station in an "unventilated atmosphere of foulest pollution." The "dark, concrete floor" was "packed with men all lying on their right sides with their legs drawn up, and each man's legs pressed close in behind those of the man in front."[15]

By the late nineteenth century reformers had mounted a sustained attack on police station lodging. Their case rested partly on humanitarian grounds: the unhealthful, filthy, overcrowded conditions in police stations. However, it had other motives as well. For reformers coupled their attempt to end police station lodging with their campaign against outdoor relief. Each was a prong of an attack intended to purge the ablebodied from public assistance. The first great reform victory occurred in New York City in 1896 when the commissioner of police, Theodore Roosevelt, influenced by Jacob Riis, forbid lodging at the station houses and persuaded the Charter Revision Committee "to remove from the organic law of the city the clause giving to the police the care of vagrants, which was the cause of it all." As a way of assuring that homeless, ablebodied men would be cut off from food as well as shelter, New York City also passed the Raines Law, which outlawed the free lunches given out in many bars. These "had been the sustenance for many of the homeless."[16]

Reformers did more than end police station lodging, outlaw free lunches, eject ablebodied men from poorhouses, and cut them off from outdoor relief. They also attacked lodging in private homes, the other major source of shelter for single men living away from their families. Indeed, in the late nineteenth century, reformers launched a major campaign against the "lodger evil," by which they meant the presence of boarders in poor, particularly immigrant, families. Of course, boarding or lodging certainly was not new in the late nineteenth century. However, its social character had changed, because earlier in the century boarders had much more often lived with well-to-do families than with poor families. (The major exception was widows, who often took in boarders as a source of income.) For a complex set of reasons, the conditions that had made boarders a more common addition to affluent than to poor households changed radically after 1850, and by the end of the century the proportion of well-off families with boarders had dropped drastically. Meanwhile, thousands of unmarried immigrant men needed homes, and poor families needed extra income. This newer meaning of boarding—its association with poor immigrant families—was the one reformers attacked as a menace to the health and morality of family life. Worried about the effects of overcrowding—which they believed to be ubiquitous among poor families with boarders—reformers also hinted at the sexual consequences of introducing unmarried men into families with young women. Offended by domestic arrangements that departed from the model of the privatized, bourgeois family, reformers could not even get their facts right. For families with boarders usually were not more crowded than other working-class families, and no one had solid evidence of moral decay or serious sexual problems accompanying boarding. Even though they had no empirical basis for their anxiety, reformers still tried to change local ordinances to prevent poor families from taking in boarders.[17]

Homeless men did not quietly disappear as an issue when they were ejected from their customary sources of shelter. To the contrary, so many of them still needed shelter every night that temporary lodging houses blossomed in the late nineteenth and early twentieth centuries. Writing in the first decade of the twentieth century, Alice Willard Solenberger, of the Chicago Bureau of Charities, observed:

> Twenty or twenty-five years ago there were few if any cheap lodging houses of the types with which we are are now familiar; and today there is no more striking evidence of the rapid and enormous growth in the number of "homeless" men in the country than is shown by the increase both in number and in size of the buildings erected for their accommodation in our cities. Formerly, unattached workingmen in large cities, as a rule, roomed in private houses where they also boarded, or in small cheap hotels somewhere near their places of employment. It was not until the latter eighties and the early nineties that large buildings put up exclusively for the accommodation of homeless men began to make their appearance in Chicago and New York, and it has been only since 1900 that these have also become numerous in the small cities of the country.[18]

Solenberger sidestepped the reason why boarding had ended and why so many more men needed accommodation, but she was right about the trend. In 1903, she described the three major types of lodging houses in Chicago. First were the "cheap lodging houses" which charged from ten to twenty-five cents a night. There were about 200 of these, "some better than others, but all on the same general plan, and all housing a very mixed group of men, so that good men and bad, professional beggars and young boys are all thrown together." Below these were the "barrel-houses," about forty or fifty in number, which housed hundreds of men a night in certain seasons. They were "not lodging houses but saloons of the lowest grade. They have no bar; the liquor is drawn from the barrels about the room and the men sleep on the filthy floors." Police stations had provided the third major source of lodgings, but the city had tried to shift homeless men away from them to a new institution, the Municipal Lodging House, opened in 1902. In its first year, the Municipal Lodging House sheltered 11,097 people, but the police stations still housed 5,740. There were three reasons for the persistence of police lodging: men sought lodging too late to be admitted to the Municipal Lodging House; they applied to "outlying stations many miles" away from it; and the police were largely indifferent "to the order to refer all such men to the Municipal Lodging House."[19]

Chicago's Municipal House was one of a number of similar institutions (sometimes called Wayfarers' Lodges) founded in many cities at around the same time. All of them inherited the mixed goals of the poorhouse: shelter, punishment, and deterrence. For example, one of the early lodges opened in Baltimore during the great depression of 1893 when a group of leading citizens agreed that the strain on poor relief resources would be severe because of both the depression and the way in which "Baltimore had grown into exceptional favor with members of the wandering fraternity" during the preceding 2 years. At the same time an influential member of the police commission wrote to the Charity Organization Society (headed by Daniel Coit Gilman, president of Johns Hopkins University) that the commissioners would "close the station-houses to male lodgers as soon as adequate provision was made elsewhere." As a response, "seven leading charitable organizations and the five largest business associations" organized a conference; its result was the formation of a Central Relief Committee, "typifying the co-operation of business interests with philanthropy."[20]

On the committee's recommendation, the city created a Wayfarer's Lodge in a building previously used as a pencil factory. It cost only $3,000 to equip the building for its new use, excluding running costs, estimated at $2,500 for the season. The lodge could shelter 125 men each evening and no one could spend more than 3 consecutive nights there. "Wood-sawing and splitting was offered as the only means of payment for meals and lodgings. Certain compulsory features, such as a hot bath every evening under the supervision of an attendant, with a liberal use of carbolic soap, and nightly disinfection of wearing-apparel, were regularly exacted. Clean night-gowns and slippers were also furnished." The lodge opened on January 15, 1894, only 3 weeks after the meeting at which it had been proposed. Police immediately started sending lodgers, and on February 3, at the height of the depression, the "police stations were finally closed to male lodgers." Although, undoubtedly as a result of its stringent rules, the new institution never was filled to capacity, a spokesman for the lodge, with no investigation of what actually happened to the homeless—whether they went to cheap lodging houses or found shelter in other communities with less rigorous policies—claimed success.[21]

Others also stressed the importance of strict regulations and a work test in municipal lodging houses. James L. Jackson of Minneapolis expected lodges to return many homeless men to a "normal life"; and in a visionary address to the National Conference on Charities and Corrections in 1904, Raymond Robbins, superintendent of the Chicago Municipal Lodging House, described the model municipal lodging house and its role in reclaiming vagrant and homeless men and boys. Lodging houses, he argued, reached groups that other agencies missed. "The significant fact of the model municipal lodging house is that its hooks will reach clear down to the bottom of the human sewage in the dark channels of the underworld." The hooks set out by other agencies hung "too high to catch many persons that are in direct need." The lodges, according to Alice L. Higgins, general secretary of the Associated Charities of Boston, occupied a strategic place in the network of public welfare that had emerged in the early twentieth century. They were switching points, receiving homeless and vagrant men, sending many out to work, others to hospitals, some to poorhouses, and a few to jail, all the while protecting society from the imposition of tramps and other ablebodied and unworthy poor.[22]

Alice Willard (later Solenberger) remained much more skeptical of Municipal Lodging Houses, which, she observed, failed to "solve the problem of vagrancy in any city" because they did not "reach the lowest and most dangerous class of lodging house men." Men who entered Municipal Lodging Houses came mainly from "the better grades of such men, the unfortunate, and the workingmen out of work." The "parasites" avoided it entirely because they knew the lodging house remained fundamentally a "police institution." (Indeed, superintendents of Municipal Lodging Houses often had police powers.) Moreover, "men of independence and refinement" shrunk from the intrusions that accompanied assistance, the "questions of the officer in charge, however kindly put, and from the publicity of the street-work test." In 1901, Willard pointed out, 92,591 men had been given police lodgings. When the Muncipal Lodging House opened the next year, it provided 11,907 lodgings and the police gave only 5,740, making a total of 16,837, a drop of 75,754. "Where," asked Willard, "were these 75,000 men lodged? These are the men we must reach."[23]

Many of them slept in the cheap lodging houses that she described in her book on homeless men, published posthumously in 1911. There the conditions were as wretched as they had been in the worst poorhouses. Here is an excerpt from her description:

> The cheap lodging houses in Chicago are mainly of two types: the dormitory type, which was the earlier; and the small room type, sometimes known as the "cubicle" or "cell" lodging house, which is more recent and today more generally popular with the men.
>
> For a dormitory lodging house a large building is chosen—usually one not originally built for the purpose—and the ground floor is sub-let for a store or a saloon. In some houses, however, the living room or general assembly room for the lodgers and the office and perhaps the washrooms besides, are found on the ground floor. Each floor above the first is devoted wholly to sleeping purposes.
>
> According to the law in Illinois, there must be a space of two feet horizontally on each side of each cot or bed in lodging house sleeping rooms; but very little attention is paid to this law in the majority of houses. I have seen as many as six cots standing in a row next to each other without any space between them, and dozens of others in the same room standing but a few inches apart. . . . For several reasons the air in these rooms is as a rule very far from pure. . . . the greatest cause of impure air in many of the dormitory lodging houses is the fact that toilet rooms with partition walls not reaching to the ceiling open directly out of the rooms in which the men sleep. The doors of these toilet rooms are usually open—are often fastened back by the men in order that their slamming may not disturb the sleepers— and the odors that pollute the air in some of the houses are intolerably offensive.
>
> However, when all is said that may be regarding the unsanitary conditions and

the impure air in the dormitory lodging houses, they nevertheless have advantages in these regards over the small room or cubicle style of lodging house.

Here in the flophouses of great cities was the legacy of the campaign to purge the ablebodied from poorhouses and outdoor relief.[24]

The Mentally Ill and the Centralization of State Power

Another legacy of the campaign to transform poorhouses was the expansion of state mental hospitals into huge warehouses for their unfortunate inmates. Throughout the nineteenth century, despite the creation of state mental hospitals, most of the mentally ill sent to institutions remained in almshouses, and the treatment of mental illness (like public support of the elderly) continued within the framework of public welfare. For decades reformers, most notably Dorothea Dix, and public officials criticized the inadequate care of the mentally ill in poorhouses. Although Dix's indefatigable campaigns within several states had promoted the creation of state mental hospitals, these new institutions could not accommodate a majority of those in need of care. In larger states, poorhouses near cities often had separate departments for the mentally ill or separate hospitals for the insane poor. But in more rural areas, the mentally ill remained in almshouses, mixed with the other inmates, receiving little if any special treatment.[25]

The first major state attempt to improve the care of mentally ill paupers began in New York in the 1860s and culminated in the State Care Act of 1890, which influenced policy throughout the country. In 1864, Dr. Sylvester D. Willard, secretary of the Medical Society of the State of New York, acting for the state legislature, investigated the condition of the state's insane poor. His report stressed the "gross want of provision for the common necessities of physical health and comfort, in a large majority of the poor houses where pauper lunatics were kept." Many of the attendants were themselves paupers, often "depraved by vice—cold, sordid, selfish from poverty—utterly incapable of taking care of themselves; these are employed to oversee and apply moral and physical means of restraint for the insane!" Willard urged the state to create a hospital for the incurably insane that would take chronically mentally ill paupers out of the almshouses. In 1865, the legislature authorized the new institution, and in 1869, the Willard Asylum for the Insane opened. (Its purpose also was to free the state asylum at Utica to deal only with the potentially curable or acute insane.) Willard was the first of a new kind of asylum. "The early State asylums," commented Warner, "had been comparatively small, designed for not more than 300 persons. In the later sixties and seventies, the agitation for the removal of the insane from county to State care resulted in the building of mammoth institutions, capable of accommodating in some case as many as 2,000 patients."[26]

Public criticism of the new institutions often focused on their cost. Extraordinarily expensive, they sometimes featured luxurious quarters for the superintendent and his family as well as imposing architectural details. These new asylums co t between $1,000 and $3,000 or more per capita for building and plant at a time when the per capita cost of constructing a luxurious hotel was not more than $1,500. Even more, they did not reduce the burden on the counties. When Willard opened, there were 1,500 insane persons in county care in New York State; 6 years later Willard was full and 1,300 mentally ill people still remained in county institutions. Indeed, county almshouses continued to house a majority of the state's insane.[27]

By the 1880s, a coalition of reform forces in the state—Dr. Stephen Smith, appointed State Commissioner in Lunacy in 1882; the State Charities Aid Association; the State Medical Society; and the New York Neurological Society—had accumulated the experience and political influence necessary to launch a major attack on the care of the mentally-ill poor in county almshouses. In 1890, the coalition finally persuaded the legislature to pass the State Care Act, under which the state, except for three large counties, assumed the complete care and expense of all the insane poor. All the mentally ill in county institutions were to be moved to state hospitals as soon as possible.[28]

Most histories herald the State Care Act as a major triumph of nineteenth century reform, a great step forward in the treatment of the mentally ill. Almost everywhere, progressive opinion supported removing the insane poor from county almshouses to state hospitals, and other states followed New York's example. Nonetheless, like the removal of children from poorhouses, the other great accomplishment of the period, the removal of the insane from county almshouses was not as unambiguous as its champions declared.[29]

Consider the case advanced in New York by the County Superintendents of the Poor, who bitterly opposed the State Care Act. Of course, they had a great deal to lose because the act cut their power and authority. Still, because of its uneasy, often hostile relations with the county superintendents and its drive for greater authority over the state's charities, the State Charities Aid Association did not have unsullied motives, either.[30]

The county superintendents criticized the reports that the State Charities Aid Association released to the public. The superintendents claimed that the reports were gross, ignorant distortions of the actual situation with poorhouses and vicious, political fabrications. Contrary to the charges leveled against them, the superintendents asserted that their almshouses by and large gave mentally ill paupers decent and humane care. However, they rested their case on more than the quality of the care they provided. First was the inexperience and incompetence of the staff in state institutions. Even more, the very size of the state institutions militated against kindly care. "I don't believe that the machinery of a large State institution is calculated to give as good care as a small institution which is overlooked by a kind-hearted Superintendent and his wife." Then, too, the great expense of state institutions imposed an unjust burden on taxpayers, especially when the money did not appear to directly benefit the insane. The superintendents were impatient with the testimony or recommendations of experts, and they claimed recovery rates were higher in the small county institutions than in the large state hospitals.[31]

The superintendents stressed the importance of friends and familiar surroundings. In local institutions, "these poor unfortunates are located near their friends, and are under the care of those who are personally well known in the community . . . it is a great thing for their friends to have them to care for within easy reach and to be personally acquainted with those to whom their afflicted relatives are committed." By monitoring the quality of care, friends could assure that attendants did their job well. Their vigilance would prevent the abuses alleged to have infected the large state asylums. Even Charles Hoyt, secretary of the State Board of Charities, admitted that most county attendants were equal to those in state institutions "and, in many instances, superior." A superintendent spoke of the "relations of the attendants to the patients . . . such that they work together harmoniously, very often being former neighbors, friends and acquaintances, and belonging to the same social classes." Proximity to friends and familiar surroundings, moreover, would comfort the patients. "We believe," claimed one superintendent, "that the mind feeds on impressions which reach the brain through special senses . . . immeasurably more powerful under a home-like method of living near their friends who can see them at will, than they would be far removed from home, shut up in a crowded asylum, where the wild wailing of the terribly insane never ceases."[32]

Within small institutions among "a farming population, where daily labor is performed by all the able-bodied members of a household," the mentally ill could more easily be involved in useful work. There the attendants worked along with the patients in contrast to the large state hospitals where attendants merely "set tasks for the patients without participating in them." Above all, the "domestic character" of the county institutions, their small size, stamped them with their distinct virtues. Indeed, size itself was the critical factor. "Under the present system the treatment of these unfortunates is more humane than it can possibly be in large and crowded State Asylums."[33]

The accuracy of the charges and countercharges hurled back and forth between the county superintendents and the State Charities Aid Association is far from clear. It is hard to believe that county poorhouses offered warm, supportive care for the insane, as their defenders claimed. Yet, the large state asylums for the chronic insane certainly were cold, impersonal, and often brutal bins for warehousing the mentally ill. Whatever the accuracy of specific claims, the controversy illustrates the variation in social values embedded in policy issues. The superintendents stressed the importance of localism, warmth, and intimacy. The oversight of local people combined with the small size of county institutions assured humane care. Good institutions existed in a close, symbiotic relation with their communities. Cut off from their local roots, allowed to grow without restraint, institutions became huge, impersonal, and ineffective bureaucracies. Mental illness, moreover, required little expert care. Experts did as much harm as good. The mentally ill needed their friends, familiar surroundings, and a kind, domestic setting. The State Care Act, by contrast, reflected a faith in experts, a distrust of localism, a commitment to economies of scale, and an equation of progress with centralization and the growth of state power.[34]

Even if the criticisms of county care were accurate, moving the insane to large state institutions did not follow ineluctably. One alternative was to improve the smaller, local institutions by better management and, perhaps, more state supervision. This is what happened in Wisconsin. Under an 1881 law, counties could request permission to build "facilities for chronic insane patients." The state supervised the plans and funded the new asylums, which were managed by lay boards monitored by local physicians. Sixteen asylums had been built by 1888, most of them on small farms. The county system reduced the number of mentally ill in jails and poorhouses. Although opposed fiercely by champions of state authority elsewhere in the country, for instance, Charles Hoyt in New York and Franklin Sanborn in Massachusetts, and state superintendents of mental hospitals, the Wisconsin plan, as it became known, influenced policy in New Jersey, Maryland, and Pennsylvania.[35]

The controversy over state care was about the centralization of state power as well as about the care of mentally ill paupers. It acquired its momentum not only from the abuses documented by promoters of state care but from the drive to extend the reach of the state. In the last quarter of the century, the extension of state authority accelerated powerfully. State governments, like business corporations, sought monopolies as they attempted to consolidate and rationalize their control over welfare, social services, and education, and, as with the State Care Act in New York, they were remarkably successful. The question is what did they accomplish.

According to Grob, in New York centralization helped "promote uniform standards of care and administration throughout the system," including the appointment of a female physician to the staff of every hospital and "autonomous institutes . . . devoted primarily to medical and scientific research." The act also enhanced the role of psychiatrists "within the state hospital systems in New York and Massachusetts [more] than . . . in many other parts of the country." Their influence on public policy was reflected in a growing "emphasis on disease per se rather than on the mentally ill as a dependent group." One other outcome was ironic, given reformers' goal of separating mental illness from dependence. The population of state mental hospitals changed dramatically when the state assumed the costs of their care. County almshouses, funded by local taxes, "reclassified many aged senile persons" to facilitate their transfer to mental hospitals, where the state would pay the cost of their care. As a result, "the care of aged, senile persons became an implicit function of mental hospitals during the early 1900s." The influx of aged people from poorhouses changed the age structure of mental hospitals and swelled their size. (Between 1900 and 1910, the hospital population of New York grew from 5,402 to 21,815.) In the end, the state had neither moved mental illness from under the mantle of welfare nor transformed the quality of care. Rather, it had shifted its location and perhaps its style. In the process, the centralization of state power and the growth of large institutions built the model of care whose abuses and limits other reformers have documented for more than a century.[36]

Children, Poorhouses, and Family Breakup

Reformers succeeded best at removing children from poorhouses. The results, however, hardly matched their predictions. According to their founders, poorhouses would educate and redeem destitute children. For a number of reasons these early expectations soon proved illusory. Poor relief policy did not intervene sharply enough between paupers and their children; outdoor relief subsidized families; other families entered poorhouses together. In these ways, poor relief practice reinforced the influence of parents when, it was thought by many reformers, families should be broken up so that pauper parents could not pass on their lax morality and distaste for work to their children. Although family breakup surfaced as a reform strategy in Philadelphia as early as the 1820s, it wielded greatest influence during the 1870s and 1880s as part of the campaign to move children out of poorhouses.[37]

By the last quarter of the nineteenth century a broad consensus across the country urged the removal of children from poorhouses. In its Seventh Annual Report (1874) the New York State Commissioners of Public Charities asserted,

"There can be no question that the county poor-house is an entirely unsuitable place in which to rear and educate children." The board elaborated the fate of children in poorhouses:

> Degrading and vicious influences surround them in these institutions, corrupting to both body and soul. They quickly fall into ineradicable habits of idleness, which prepare them for a life of pauperism and crime. Their moral and religious training is, in most cases, entirely neglected, and their secular education is of the scantiest and most superficial kind. Self-respect is, in time, almost extinguished, and a prolonged residence in a poorhouse leaves upon them a stigma which clings to them in after years, and carries its unhappy influences through life.[38]

Individual counties already had begun to move children out of poorhouses into orphan asylums or, less frequently, foster homes. As a consequence, the number of children in poorhouses dropped from 1,222 in 1868, when the commissioners first investigated the problem; to 920 in 1869; 792 in 1870; 675 in 1871; 644 in 1872; and 579 in 1873. Still, the number was too large, and in 1875 the New York State Legislature passed the Children's Act, which ordered the removal of all children between two and sixteen from poorhouses. Other states also took action in the same period. Pennsylvania passed a similar law in 1883, as did Indiana in 1881. In 1871, as part of a movement to take children out of poorhouses, Michigan founded a state public school for the care of dependent children, and private and public agencies, motivated by the same concerns, created new institutions for children in Minnesota and North Carolina, to take two other examples. By 1924, North Carolina had twenty-three orphanages with 3,719 children. (In Kansas, for some reason an exception to the trend, efforts to move children off the poorfarms were at best "spasmodic".)[39]

The New York Children's Act had ambiguous consequences because the number of children in orphanages mushroomed, far exceeding the number transferred from poorhouses. After they had investigated the problem in 1877, the Kings County (Brooklyn) Committee on Homes and Asylums of the County Board of Supervisors blamed legislative weaknesses and indicted poor parents for their cupidity. As passed in 1875, the Children's Act ordered children placed in institutions "governed or controlled by officers or persons of the same religious faith as the parents of the child, as far as practicable." This, of course, boosted the enrollment of Catholic asylums and orphanages. Of the original 348 children who had been moved from the almshouse to orphanages in 1875, all but seventeen went to Catholic institutions. In effect, the new law had transferred large amounts of money to Catholics, a very sore point with Protestant public officials. Even more of a problem was the increase in the number of children in institutional care. Within fourteen months, the number of children in asylums and orphanages had nearly doubled (from 408 to 756), and in one institution, the

1876 population exceeded the entire number for the past twenty-five years. The per capita cost of care had risen alarmingly as well.[40]

Most of the children now flooding into the homes and asylums did have living parents. Of the 348 children removed from the old almshouse nursery to the asylum in 1875, only about 31 percent had both parents living. By contrast, 63 percent of the 483 who entered during the next year had two living parents. In fact, 69.2 percent of the children who left the homes and asylums during the year had been taken out by their parents. "It was never intended," complained the committee, "that children having homes or parents able to support them would be sent to these Orphan Asylums as paupers and maintained at the County's Expense." Previously, poor parents had been reluctant to send their children to poorhouses, knowing how wretchedly they would fare. Now, the poor thought of orphanages "more as free boarding schools than as charitable shelters for destitute children—temporary resting places until they could be adopted into families or bound out as clerks, apprentices, or servants." Not only an expensive practice, it was bad for the children as well. For "it sows the seed of pauper poison in the most effective manner." Asylum managers compounded the problem because they often preferred to retain children "in their institutions rather than to put them out into families of their own faith even. Institutions pride themselves on the number of their inmates, boast of the good they are doing, and at times seem not over anxious to find homes for the children."[41]

One member of the committee, John T. Moran (undoubtedly a Catholic), dissented vigorously from both the majority's analysis of the problem and its recommendations. Moran did not deny the majority's statistics or the existence of abuses. However, he argued that the large increase in the number of children in institutions was "a natural and an inevitable consequence of the hard times" that had "so impoverished the homes of our laborers and mechanics." Men and women "who had managed in years gone by to maintain themselves and their families have been forced by the hard times to break up the home circle, committing their children to the care of private institutions, and going themselves to the poorhouse."[42]

No policy could seem more humane and less controversial than taking children out of poorhouses, but one of its consequences—as Moran pointed out—was family breakup, because parents who entered poorhouses now had to surrender their children. Given conditions in most poorhouses, children probably did receive better care elsewhere, even without their parents. Nonetheless, and this is the crucial point, other alternatives did exist. One was an adequate standard of outdoor relief. The other was to create decent family quarters within poorhouses. Neither was impossible to implement or substantially more expensive. Rather, they were unacceptable for two reasons: first, it was thought they would encourage pauperism; second, family breakup was one goal of policy.

105

Whatever the majority report in Kings County said, most officials and legislators who sponsored the Children's Act would not have been dismayed to learn that they had precipitated the breakup of poor families. Indeed, by the 1870s, many charity reformers had decided that only by snapping the bonds between pauper parents and their children could they prevent the transmission of dependence from one generation to another. Although adults often proved impossible to reform, their children remained malleable. If only they could be placed early enough in a better environment, even the children of paupers could aspire to independence and self-support.

The story of family disruption as acceptable policy begins in a serious way with Charles Loring Brace, who also was the first major reformer to formulate an antiinstitutional strategy of child rescue. After his graduation from Yale in 1848, Brace studied at Union Theological Seminary and then drifted into work with Reverend Louis Morris Pease in New York's notorious "Five Points" district, where he found that distributing religious tracts and organizing meetings for young men made little impact on the great social problems he encountered. At the age of 27, in 1853, dissatisfied with conventional approaches to reform, he created his own organization, the New York Children's Aid Society. Supported by an eminent board of trustees, Brace in time developed a series of strategies that seemed to work: lodging houses for newsboys and other street children; industrial schools that offered instruction to both boys and girls in a variety of trades; and emigration, the technique for which Brace became most famous. Because Brace saw crime primarily as an ecological problem, that is, a consequence of overcrowding, he looked for ways to reduce the population of New York's densest sections. His solution was to send thousands of children to homes outside the city, preferably in the West. By the mid-1890s, Brace has placed at least 90,000 children in homes outside New York City, and every one of his surveys showed how well his strategy had worked. Most children, he reported, pleased their new families, adapted to farm life, and grew into healthy, independent adults. Despite Brace's euphoric reports, the actual situation was more complex: a great many children bounced from one placement to another; a very high proportion found their way back to New York City; and in many instances the family ties that Brace had hoped to snap remained unbroken as children sent West often managed to reestablish relations with their families.[43]

Although many other antebellum reformers shared Brace's reservations about the family life of the poor and the importance of environment, most of them had chosen a different strategy: institutions. Throughout the early decades of the century, reformers had built houses of refuge, orphanages, and reform schools. The early houses of refuge usually made no distinctions between children whose parents were paupers or criminals and those who had been convicted of crime. All of them were potentially dependent. Crime, poverty, and ignorance (as Brace also agreed) all stemmed from the same underlying conditions; it was a matter of circumstance which character defect appeared dominant at any one time.[44]

Nonetheless, Brace and a few of his contemporaries broke ranks with the reformers who supported institutions. Although Brace's arguments against institutions had little impact on policy until the 1890s (see chapter 5), state and local governments elsewhere adopted some of his actual strategies and created their own Children's Aid Societies. In fact, Brace soon collected more than half his operating expenses from public sources, which made the CAS an early, successful public/private venture. In 1870, for instance, the CAS had an income of about $200,000. Of this amount, $60,000 came from county taxes; $20,000 from an excise fund; $20,000 from the Board of Education; and $9,000 from the state. In other words, $109,000, over half the society's income, had come from public sources.[45]

In his reports and major book, Brace avoided any direct suggestion that the families of paupers should be broken up, although the implication was clear. However, when he addressed the county superintendents of the poor in 1873, he was less restrained. "The greatest evil that I have experienced in the whole course of twenty years' experience, and the one that requires the most difficult handling," Brace told the superintendents to whom he offered the services of the CAS, "is 'hereditary pauperism.' " Two things, he said, stood in the way of solving the problem by sending children away. "First. The want of machinery, and, secondly, a supposed want of charitable feeling; for it is an absurd opinion that the proceeding is cruel and unfeeling."[46]

In the next few years, other experts drummed up support among the superintendents for the 1875 Children's Act and its consequences. Influenced by a new literature on the heritability of crime, poverty, insanity, and drunkenness, they also supported breaking up families. William Pryor Letchworth, the most famous advocate of children's causes of the day, told the superintendents in 1874:

> In some poorhouses I find that the children have one or both parents with them, and the kind heart of the keeper, or mayhap, of his amiable wife, who is a mother herself, protests against the separation of the child from the parent. But in every case that has come to my notice . . . the antecedents of the parent were such as to make it evident that the only hope of rescuing the child from a life of pauperism was to separate it from its parent or parents.

This was, said Letchworth, the "surest way of correcting the great evil of hereditary pauperism now growing rapidly in our state." Three years later he continued to hammer away at the same point.

If you want to break up pauperism, you must transplant. . . . I think we sometimes forget, out of the kindness of our hearts, and the sympathy that we feel for the parent, the rights of the child. When parents cannot protect their child, cannot feed, cannot clothe it, cannot keep it from evil influence, and are perhaps degrading it by their own example, it is the duty of every true man to step forward to save it.[47]

No longer did parents need to commit a crime, act immorally, or abuse their offspring before reformers urged authorities to step in and remove their children. Extreme poverty itself had become evidence of their incompetence and adequate grounds on which to break up their families. As the famous R. L. Dugdale himself, author of the study of the Jukes family that allegedly proved how degradation and pauperism transmitted themselves from one generation to another, told the superintendents: "I would make Alms-houses in which there should be a separation of families. I would say to a man and woman, if you cannot support your family you must be kept separate, that there shall be no more children born." In 1881, Charles Hoyt reinforced the same point by arguing that when parents asked for relief, they should cede their natural rights to the state. "Imprudent and indolent parents often make their large family the pretext for out-door aid. When such parents fail to discharge their duty to their children, their right of possession terminates and the children become the wards of the state."[48]

The county superintendents did not need much persuasion. When he referred to the problems arising from the administration of the Children's Act, Superintendent Mcgonegal of Monroe County told his colleagues, "They will think it is hard to separate the mother from the child. It is hard; but in cases where the parents have become demoralized, it is not only right, but it is the duty of the Overseer to take the children away from such parents and to place them where they will receive proper instruction." Support for family breakup peaked among the superintendents in 1881 when they unanimously accepted a motion proposed by Superintendent Dennis Sullivan of Queens County:

> RESOLVED. That this Convention recommend to Superintendents and Overseers of the Poor that whenever families of children are likely to become pauperized by the dissipated habits of their parents, that they use their best endeavors to have the children removed from those pernicious influences and placed in good, respectable families.[49]

The aggressive style of Gilded Age family reform inspired another new society—the Society for the Prevention of Cruelty to Children (SPCC)—founded by leading citizens in large cities. Again, in 1874, New York led the way, but others soon followed. Unlike other societies that assisted children, the SPCC did not operate institutions or find placements. Instead, it devoted itself solely to enforcing existing laws by searching out child neglect and abuse, prosecuting parents, and turning children over to the appropriate agency. Although it found ways to settle many cases out of court, the SPCC did not hesitate to press charges against parents. The precise powers of SPCCs in different states varied, but they could command the assistance of the police, and they had standing in court. (In Philadelphia, the SPCC asked for 3-month sentences to give other agencies time to move children where their parents could neither find nor reach them.) The SPCC represented more than another intrusion into the lives of the very poor. It embodied a prevailing consensus that the most effective manner to root out pauperism was to break up families. At the same time, it fomented suspicion, hostility, and disunity among the poor of great cities by encouraging neighbors to spy on and accuse one another. It was appropriate that Philadelphia's poor, afraid of the SPCC, dubbed it "the Cruelty."[50]

Although no one could deny that almshouses were awful places for children or that many poor children were neglected and mistreated, the removal of children from almshouses, like the attack on outdoor relief and the breakup of poor families, reflected the brittle hostility and anger of the respectable classes and their horror at the prospect of a united, militant working class. Whether by rekindling cross-class allegiances through friendly visiting, destroying the working-class political base of urban machines, smashing trade unions, driving the destitute into poorhouses and taking away their children, public/private policies tended in the same direction. With far fewer euphemisms than would become tasteful in later decades, authorities scarcely bothered to disguise their contempt or the blunt instruments they wielded.

By the late nineteenth century, public officials and private reformers—categories with shifting, overlapping membership—had transformed the relief of dependence. Outdoor relief had been reduced radically; state authority had expanded; and special institutions had drawn children and the mentally ill out of poorhouses. At the same time, public hostility finally had forced out the ablebodied, too, and then attacked their use of police stations, and, even, private lodgings. As a result, more and more homeless men could turn for shelter only to the foul, cheap hotels and flophouses that recently had sprouted in American cities. A harsh new doctrine, scientific charity, and its organizational embodiment, charity organization, justified and helped implement the emerging structure of relief. Allegedly supported by theory and data, not to mention raw political and economic power, the new organization of relief exuded such self-righteous confidence that few guessed its fragility. Nonetheless, within less than two decades, most public officials and social welfare professionals, knew that family breakup, poorhouse reform, and scientific charity all had failed, and in the 1890s, under the guise of child-saving, Progressive era reformers suddenly switched strategies.

PART II

BUILDING THE SEMIWELFARE STATE

5 Saving Children

The 1890s mark the start of a new era in the history of social welfare. Twenty years earlier, in the 1870s, fears about the isolation of the poor in great cities, the spread of socialism, and the rise of organized labor had impelled reformers to devise new strategies for reaching into the lives of the poor, but their major innovations, scientific charity and family breakup, had failed miserably and even exacerbated class antagonisms. By the 1890s, the human misery and utter inadequacy of both private and public relief exposed by the depression of 1893, the explosive growth of cities, the new immigration, the emergence of a militant labor movement, and the currency of radical ideas all made a new strategy imperative. The first major alternative was child-saving. Child-saving not only shifted the focus of social welfare; even more, it rested on a new psychology, a series of major strategic innovations, an enhanced role for government, and a reordered set of relations between families and the state. For these reasons, child-saving heralded a new departure in welfare history.

The president of the 1893 convention of New York's County Superintendents of the Poor told his colleagues that "child-saving work . . . alone is the foundation of prosperity, happiness, and heaven."[1] Few would have disagreed, or even expressed surprise. Throughout the country, by the 1890s children had captured the energy and attention of social reformers with an intensity never matched in other periods of American history. Indeed, until about World War I, the welfare of children unified social reformers around campaigns to which contemporaries were more likely to refer as "child-saving" than "Progressivism." Almost overnight, it seemed, children became the symbol of a resurgent reform spirit, the magnet that pulled together a diverse collection of causes and their champions into a new, loose, informal—but very effective—coalition.[2]

113

Child-saving embraced a wide variety of causes (some of which have been discussed in earlier chapters): the removal of children from almshouses; the creation of Societies for the Prevention of Cruelty to Children and Children's Aid Societies; the attempt to replace institutional care with foster homes; the reformation of juvenile justice through the introduction of probation and juvenile courts; the playground movement; compulsory education; day care and kindergartens; educational reform; the campaign against child labor; the advocacy of mothers' pensions; and public health measures to reduce infant mortality and tuberculosis and alter the delivery of health care. These goals of child-saving seemed faultless. Who could possibly defend the gruesome conditions under which children labored in factories, fields, and sweatshops? The harsh, punitive, ineffective institutions of justice that helped turn young offenders into criminals? The massive, regimented institutions into which homeless and dependent children too often were shunted? Or the crowded, unsanitary streets and tenements that killed infants and young children? Still, child-saving had its ambiguities. The intrusion of the state into family life, the extension of professional influence, and the elaboration of social service bureaucracies have had, to say the least, mixed consequences. Christopher Lasch, for example, has argued that the "socialization of reproduction" that began in the Progressive era has undermined the family structure essential for strong, independent personality development. Whatever its long-range effects on personality, the "socialization of reproduction" had an urgent, contemporary purpose. Deployed in a time of great conflict in American life, child-saving was one key strategy for stemming the slide of the poor in great cities into savagery, hostility, and socialism.[3]

Child-saving inherited a complex legacy. In part, the legacy was human and organizational. Especially in its early years, child-saving drew on the personnel and resources of the charity organization societies, child welfare agencies, and public authorities that had dominated relief in the era of scientific charity. Impatient young reformers, critical of past policies, eager to put new ideas about child development and state responsibility into practice, had to work out compromises with an older generation suspicious of government, jealous of the line between charity and entitlement, and attuned most closely to individual responsibility for dependence.

Child-saving also inherited the contradiction between privatism and public responsibility embedded in the nineteenth century liberal state. As economist W. Norton Grubb and historian Marvin Lazerson show, within liberal thought a sharp boundary separated economic and family decisions from the state. In practice, the boundary always has been a fiction, because government decisions have shaped both the structure of economic life and the organization of family experience throughout American history. How to implement public responsibility

114

in a setting where economic and family decisions are considered private is a dilemma that has undermined almost every effort to use the resources of government to ameliorate or eradicate the hunger, disease, poverty, discrimination, and exploitation which always have formed the soft, embarrassing underbelly of this land of prosperity and opportunity.[4]

Three debates ran through the child-saving movement. The first concerned the relative merits of institutions and families as settings for dependent children. The second focused on the appropriate role of government, and the third asked whether children of destitute parents should be taken from their families. By 1909, a rough consensus, shared by the leaders of most public and private agencies and institutions, had been reached on each issue. Institutions, most people thought, were bad for children, who should be placed as soon as possible in foster homes. On the role of government, the two sides reached a compromise that stressed the importance of both public and private action but extended the administrative and supervisory authority of the state. As a result of the child-saving movement, governments gained unprecedented powers to intervene in and regulate relations between parents and their children. Nonetheless, despite the augmented role of government, almost no one defended the disruption of families anymore. Instead, the preservation of the family became a ritual incantation performed by almost every commentator on family issues, and in 1909, resolutions embodying these principles were adopted unanimously by the delegates to the first White House Conference on Children.

New Concepts of Childhood

New concepts of childhood underpinned the fragile consensus on social policy. For in the late nineteenth and early twentieth centuries, the influence of Darwin and evolutionary biology reshaped the way in which informed people thought about childhood. No longer simply a quantitative stage—children as miniature adults—childhood became a qualitatively distinct phase in the life course. G. Stanley Hall, president of Clark University and the most influential child psychologist in the country, argued that the development of children recapitulated the evolution of the human race. Each developmental stage had an integrity of its own, which should be studied and respected by parents and teachers. Puberty marked the great divide in the human life course; youngsters

115

who stood on either side had a wholly different psychology which called for radically different educational methods. To advance knowledge of children, Hall not only wrote the first major text on adolescence; he also founded the child-study movement, which stimulated eager scientific acolytes across the country to record the countless observations about children out of which Hall expected to build an inductive science.[5]

A seismic shift in the perceived value of children underlay the new child psychology and the rise of the most important child-saving strategies. Viviana Zelizer refers to the shift as "the profound transformation in the economic and sentimental value of children—fourteen years of age or younger—between the 1870s and the 1930s," that is, "the emergence" of the "economically 'worthless' but emotionally 'priceless' child." This transformation, she contends, occurred among all classes, although at different rates. By the mid-nineteenth century, middle-class children had lost their economic utility; they were kept longer in school and no more thought of as insurance for old age. By contrast, "the economic value of the working-class child increased, rather than decreased in the nineteenth century" because industrialization created many new jobs that children could perform, and "working-class urban families in the late nineteenth century depended on the wages of older children and the household assistance of younger ones." However, by the 1930s a combination of compulsory education and child labor laws had removed them, too, from the labor force. Thus, "in the first three decades of the twentieth century, the economically useful child became both numerically and culturally an exception."[6]

According to strict economic logic, as children became less useful, as their economic contribution decreased and their costs rose, they should have become less valuable. But, with overwhelming evidence from the debates over compensation for children's death, child insurance, child labor, and adoption, Zelizer shows that precisely the opposite happened. In this case, value shaped price, "investing it with social, religious, or sentimental meaning." Earlier in the century, couples who wanted to adopt a child frankly admitted they could use help, most often around the farm, and the need to augment their household labor supply was a perfectly acceptable motive, as long as it did not suggest that the child would be overworked or badly treated. By the early twentieth century, the need for extra household labor had become an illegitimate motive for adoption, for which the only acceptable reason had become a selfless desire for a child. Couples by and large no longer asked for strong, older children; they wanted babies, and they were willing to pay handsomely. In the process, the social class of adopting parents, of course, shifted dramatically upward.[7]

A number of factors had intersected to transform the value of children. One was the new child psychology. Another was the combination of technological innovation with cheap immigrant labor that reshaped the youth labor market by dramatically lessening the need for young workers, who, unable to find industrial jobs, stayed longer at school and at home. At the same time, a variety of developments promoted anxiety about family stability, especially among middle-class male social critics. The falling birth rate, particularly among more highly educated native-born whites, made children a scarcer commodity and provoked fears of race suicide that led some observers, such as G. Stanley Hall, to look for ways to elevate the sentimental attractiveness of children, which, Hall predicted, would be one outcome of child study. Certainly, the new, noninstrumental appreciation of children meshed with the "increasing domestication of middle class women," that had promoted a sentimental elevation of family life as a moral crucible rather than an economic system. The family, however, suddenly appeared threatened by rising divorce rates, the increased participation of women in the workforce, the suffrage movement, and the remarkably low marriage rate among the first generation of college-educated women. Still another factor fueled anxiety about the future of America and its families: the massive immigration of southern and eastern Europeans who, it was feared, threatened to break the country apart into squalid ethnic and linguistic enclaves that bred crime, disease, and pauperism; solidified corrupt political machines; and nurtured radical and subversive ideas. Moving the immigrant child out of the workforce, back home, and into school would teach newcomers American family values and insure, at the least, the Americanization of the second generation.[8]

This fear of family disintegration can hardly be overstated. The president of the Catholic Home Bureau for Dependent Children in New York told the White House Conference in 1909 that "a recent writer on the social question" had identified "an uncompromising and undisguised attack upon the modern family by at least some of the scientific socialists and those who would substitute common ownership for individual liberty," and he warned his colleagues that "there is really a battle on between those who would preserve the family and those who would destroy it." What position should charity take? he asked rhetorically. "Should charitable workers range themselves on the side of those who would destroy modern civilization or on the side of those who believe in it and would preserve it, because it seems to be admitted by both the friends and the enemies of our modern society that the family is the great bulwark of our civilization?" Some way had to be found to shore up families, promote the value of children, and civilize the new immigrants. For many reformers, reeling from the failure of scientific charity, poorhouses and prisons, the temperance movement, or evangelical Protestantism to reshape adult character and reduce the great moral and social problems of the age, the agent became the child herself, whose role flipped from victim to redeemer.[9]

Children and Institutions

Institutions offended promoters of the priceless child. They shuddered at the fate of precious children denied a home and worried about the impact of early incarceration on their adult personalities. Most critics of institutions made the same points: the regimented monotony of institutional life dulled children's personalities and destroyed their capacity for independence; institutionalized children, unable to make a gradual transition from dependence to independence, were hurled abruptly and without preparation into the world; once on their own, ex-inmates knew nothing of money or worldly skills acquired by most children in families; they lacked a network of local friends and acquaintances to help launch them on careers; and, to many commentators, most sadly, their emotional development had been stunted by a lack of affection in childhood. "The child," said Homer Folks, "is so constituted that the relations and associations of the home are just those which are suited to its most perfect development."[10]

Institutional critics reflected the emphasis on individual treatment that underpinned Progressive era reform movements in mental health, penology, and other areas, as well as child-saving. Rehabilitation could result only from policies that respected the unique personality and circumstances of each individual. Institutions had failed because they applied uniform standards to individual cases. In fact, by denying and then destroying individuality, they stunted human development and prevented the growth of children into strong, autonomous adults.[11]

Earlier models of reformation and rehabilitation also had stressed individualism. In the decades before the Civil War, even secular Unitarian reformers, such as Horace Mann, had borrowed evangelical models of individual salvation. Public schools, reform schools, prisons, and mental hospitals: all were to regenerate society by transforming individual personalities. Learning, a return to mental health, and a new capacity for honest and upright living all rested on a profound inner commitment engineered by teachers, psychiatrists, or reform school superintendents who constructed appropriate settings, offered role models, and controlled experiences as carefully as the mid-nineteenth-century evangelical preacher, Charles Grandison Finney, set the stage for a great revival. Evangelical Protestant individualism complemented the individualism inherent in liberal economics, whose stress on rational actors freely making decisions in their own self-interest reinforced the idea that every person was responsible for his economic fate.

In antebellum America, the evangelical model remained more a rhetorical justification for the creation of new institutions than a guide to their actual operation. In practice, with few exceptions, their highly regimented regimes soon turned brutal and custodial, and, in the Gilded Age, the individualism of scientific charity proved a dead end, unable to inspire a movement that cared adequately for the poor without state intervention or to have any transforming effect on the characters of its clients. For these reasons, the individualism that inspired child-savers, although drawing on the evangelical and liberal strands in American culture, seemed to owe as much to new movements in psychology and a rekindled commitment to the possibility of social change as it did to the past.

Institutions posed a critical problem because they had increased dramatically in number and size. In New York City, the number of orphanages grew 300 percent between 1860 and 1895.[12] The *New York Charities Directory* for 1890 listed forty-nine "Homes for Children." These included the Colored Orphan Asylum, which cared for 367 in 1889; the Hebrew Benevolent and Orphan Asylum with a capacity of 560; the Institution of Mercy, which housed 1,010; the Roman Catholic Orphan Asylum with 802 inmates; St. Joseph's Asylum, capacity 750; and, the largest in the country (perhaps the world), the New York Catholic Protectory, which had cared for 3,220 children in the previous year. Reliable national figures are almost impossible to reconstruct. However, in 1910, a special report of the census claimed that more than 110,000 "dependent, neglected, and delinquent children" lived in 1,151 institutions across the country.[13]

Large institutions had a few defenders, notably representatives of Catholic asylums, who pointed out that many parents sent children to them during times of family hardship and crisis. To place these children with foster families would be cruel. Instead, the supporters of these Catholic institutions argued that they tried to strengthen the ties between parents and children by encouraging visits and in other ways assuring that family members kept in close touch with each other.[14] A brave Catholic speaker from New York City told the White House Conference on Children in 1909 that his institution compensated for the loss of the home "by a system of 'mothers' in charge of small bands of children who come to them with their tales of joy and woe." Those "parts that go together to mold the character," he said, "are welded together as well as in the family." At any rate, the average time children spent in the institution was only 18 months and 75 percent were returned to their parents or close relatives.[15]

Still, most of the old congregate institutions probably were grim. As Ashby says, "the physical confinements of the buildings and crowded conditions all too often severely limited what even gentle, well-meaning matrons and super- intendents could accomplish."[16] In fact, by the time of the White House Con- ference in 1909 almost no one defended large congregate institutions in principle.

119

The most their supporters would claim is that they were unavoidable, because all children could not be placed with foster families. Some had living parents to whom they should return when family circumstances changed; others were ill, handicapped, or incorrigible. For these, and their numbers were not negligible, institutions remained the only solution. Even so, most child-savers argued, institutions should be made as much like families as possible, which meant dividing them into "cottages" presided over by surrogate parents.

The questions for debate, therefore, remained primarily administrative. How many children could a cottage house and still be like a home? At what point should children be placed in foster homes? Did they need some prior education and observation? How should foster homes be selected and supervised? Were homes that took children without charge and those that asked for reimbursement equally acceptable? These administrative details shaded into questions of social policy as child-savers argued over the different systems that had developed throughout the country. The oldest and least innovative was New York's, which essentially delegated the care of dependent children to private institutions that collected a per capita fee from the state. No one disagreed that New York's system offered the fewest incentives to deinstitutionalization, and only New Yorkers, (and presumably California, Maryland, and the District of Columbia, which had copied it) defended the state's practice. Michigan, by contrast, gathered all dependent children into one state institution, called a State School, where they stayed for a very short time before they were placed with families. The state claimed the practice had reduced radically the number and cost of dependent children, and its policy was followed in Wisconsin, Rhode Island, Minnesota, Kansas, Colorado, Nebraska, Montana, Nevada, and Texas. The third system was Ohio's, which placed dependent children in county institutions from which they were supposed to be sent quickly to families. Observers felt the standards in the county homes were not as high as in Michigan's State School and that placement was neither as quick nor as well supervised. Connecticut and Indiana adopted the same practice as Ohio. Massachusetts had the most progressive policy in the country. It simply abolished institutional care for almost all dependent children, who were placed immediately with families, most of which received payment for the child's board. The effect had been dramatic. Between 1876 and 1900, the proportion of all Massachusetts's "juvenile state charges" in institutions had dropped from 51 percent to 15 percent.[17]

Despite the antiinstitutional sentiment of the period, Ashby reports, "The number of institutions for dependent children . . . rose dramatically. The 1890s may in fact have been more prolific in this respect than any other decade in American history. At least 247 institutions were incorporated during those ten years." Various other agencies that served children—"Humane Societies, Children's Home Societies" and others—also proliferated; twenty-two were organized in the 1870s, twenty-three in the 1880s; and forty-nine in the 1890s.[18] Most of the new institutions and organizations, however, reflected the priority that child-savers assigned to family life. Organized into cottages, they tried to find foster or boarding homes for the children in their care. Still, they composed a varied collection with many different sorts of sponsors, as were the new agencies that tried to rescue or place dependent and delinquent—the line between the two remained thoroughly blurred—children with families. Indeed, the intensity and variety of innovations show how the "variety and diversity of Protestant voluntary activity" remained a major theme in the child-saving movement.[19]

The Role of Government

Child-savers reached less consensus about the role of government than about the problems of institutions and the importance of family life. Some of the disagreement surfaced in arguments about rival state systems. New Yorkers who supported their state's subsidy of private institutions distrusted the public near-monopolies in other states. They remained suspicious that public institutions could ever avoid the corrupting embrace of the spoils system. Feigning a political innocence, (in fact, they played political hardball), they said that children's institutions should be kept out of politics. Midwesterners, by and large, had fewer reservations about the state. They saw no reason why the state could not run institutions honestly and efficiently, and they were proud of their accomplishments. The other issue concerned state supervision. Should the state supervise all children's institutions, even those it did not fund? Most child-savers answered affirmatively, although in New York the Society for the Prevention of Cruelty to Children had waged a successful campaign for the exemption of all agencies and institutions that did not receive state funds.[20]

By the early twentieth century, the public's role in "the care and protection of dependent and neglected children" had increased dramatically. Between 1900 and 1904, the proportion of children in public institutions doubled from 10 percent to between 18 and 21 percent. County boards of child welfare, first started in Indiana in 1891, also spread in this period. By 1923, Indiana had sixty-five county boards that supervised 1,561 children. Some states, such as West Virginia, replaced their private humane societies with a State Board of Children's Guardians, and by "1929 the majority of states had passed legislation regulating the activities of children's institutions and placing agencies."[21]

Even the federal government assumed new responsibilities for children. For years, leading reformers, especially Florence Kelly, for many years head of the National Consumers' League, had argued for the creation of a federal bureau to gather and disseminate material on child welfare. After Theodore Roosevelt had been elected, she, Lillian Wald of the Henry Street Settlement, and Edward T. Devine of the New York Charity Organization Society took a plan for a children's bureau to the president. Despite Roosevelt's support and a national campaign waged by the National Child Labor Committee, the bill calling for the creation of a federal children's agency never left the congressional committee. However, Roosevelt did call a national conference on the care of dependent children: the first White House Conference on Children, which met for two days in January, 1909. Although the White House conference vigorously recommended the creation of a federal children's agency, three more years elapsed before Congress created the Children's Bureau early in 1912. The bureau had no authority, and its initial budget was only $25,640. Nonetheless, led by its first director, Julia Lathrop, an ex-Hull House resident and member of the Illinois State Board of Charities, the Children's Bureau quickly became the "source of authoritative information about the welfare of children and their families" throughout the country and the institutional leader of the child-saving movement.[22]

State and sometimes local governments extended their responsibilities for children in four major areas: education, labor, juvenile justice, and public health. In each area, innovations often required a faith in the disinterested benevolence of the state. For example, juvenile courts did not simply provide a new and less formal forum in which to consider the misbehavior of young people. By dispensing with customary rules of evidence, the right to jury trials, and restraints on judicial behavior, they suspended the civil rights of children and their parents. Brought before a juvenile court, a youngster had few procedural or constitutional protections, for juvenile courts invested judges with awesome peacetime powers. (There was, after all, little precedent for suspending civil liberties other than in war or national emergencies.) The slight attention juvenile justice reformers accorded questions of civil rights did not reflect a callous disregard for constitutional principles. Rather, it rested on a faith—from the vantage point of eight decades later both touching and naive—in the decency of the state.[23]

Faith in the disinterested benevolence of the state also had roots in antebellum reform. Over and over again, the early promoters of schools, reformatories, and mental hospitals had used the metaphor of the state as a parent to justify the extension of government responsibility for the young, the delinquent, and the sick. The bureaucratic, custodial institutions that soon dominated urban education, criminal justice, and health care contradicted the warm, parental images used by their founders. Especially in the East, as already observed, reformers revolted by the corruption of politics found little parental or trustworthy in the state and remained most skeptical of public social responsibility. But in the West and Midwest, myths of frontier individualism notwithstanding, government seemed much less threatening. There, in the absence of old private institutions and old private money, governments had to provide social services and promote economic development. To midwestern reformers government was an engine of progress they were eager to harness to their projects. Even midwestern reformers who worked in the private sector, for instance, Jane Addams and Edith Abbott, used their positions to advocate increased state responsibility.[24]

A mix of European examples and professional aspirations also promoted faith in the state. Many of the leading reform advocates, educated in the new American graduate schools, had studied or visited England and the Continent, where they observed the more extensive role played by experts and government. Impressed by the capacity of government for social action, with faith in their own ability to apply expert knowledge to social problems, eager for professional recognition, they became the first generation of modern American social scientists. Founders of professional associations, such as the American Economic Association, 1885; the American Political Science Association, 1903; the American Sociological Association, 1905, and aggressive academic entrepreneurs, they assumed they would advise and staff new government agencies with disinterested expertise.[25]

Buoyed by their faith in the potential of disinterested expertise, advocates of expanded state responsibility saw little potential conflict among the parties involved in juvenile justice, child labor, or education. They thought that informed, rational people could reach agreements about the great questions of social policy, and they expected new policies to serve all interested parties equally well. In restrospect, this seems an extraordinary assumption. Aside from the Civil War, America had never been so riven by class conflict, so bewildered by cultural diversity, as in the years between the Gilded Age and World War I. In no other period were labor conflicts so bloody and so frequent; at no other time was there as much discourse about class and the opposition of Capital and Labor; in no other era did the Socialist party gain such electoral strength; in no span of years did the population of cities grow and diversify so greatly through the immigration of ethnic groups with their own languages and customs.[26]

Nonetheless, social scientists and social reformers—often, of course, the same individuals—rejected theories of social development based on class and conflict. Indeed, as corporate interests reached for control of the state, whether to retain the gold standard, insure high tariffs, or to send in the army to break up strikes, American social reform and social science turned away from theories that stressed the interpenetration of the state and economy. Instead, they reinforced the fictive separation between state and economy that has been a hallmark of American political culture. How reformers and social scientists managed to retain their faith in the neutral, benign, classless state is a great question. Here, however, the faith itself is critical, for it legitimated an unprecedented, often constitutionally questionable, intrusion of the state into the relations between children and their parents.[27]

The Strategy of Family Preservation

By the early 1890s, child-saving strategies had changed radically. Not only did most reformers reject large institutions and advocate placing children with foster parents; not only did they urge an expanded role for government; they also rejected the notion that children should be taken from their families simply on account of poverty. In fact, in 1909, the preservation of families ranked first among the recommendations of the White House Conference on Children. "Children of worthy parents or deserving mothers should, as a rule, be kept with their parents at home." Quotations expressing the same sentiment could be multiplied endlessly from a wide variety of sources: county superintendents of the poor, social workers, settlement house leaders, and virtually all serious commentators on children's issues.[28]

This emphasis on family preservation reflected a major shift in reform thought. Recall that only a couple of decades earlier, the same sorts of people advocated family breakup not just when parents drank, stole, or seemed otherwise immoral and neglectful but, even more, when they were so poor that they had to ask for relief. Extreme poverty itself, many of the leading authorities of the time had argued, was reason enough to break up a family; only misguided sentimentalism and misplaced sympathy for mothers prevented poor law officials from acting as they should to find better homes for children. Within less than 20 years, family breakup had virtually disappeared as the strategy of first resort.

If children were to remain with their parents, then someone would have to support poor families. Once family breakup was rejected, the campaign against outdoor relief, which already had run out of steam, was doomed, and, even more, some sort of mothers' pensions had to follow. Miss Frances Greely Curtin, a member of the Massachusetts State Board of Charities, told the White House conference delegates, "The removal of children, even temporarily, in my mind, is not to be compared with the advantages of the payment to the parent of a certain amount of money by a friend at regular intervals, and a stated income, with no question of doubt or uncertainty."[29] It remained only to decide whether that friend should be a private agency or the state treasury.

More than a strategy, family preservation became the mainspring of child-saving activity in the Progressive era. The question is, why? Most advocates at the time were not very precise about their reasons. They simply asserted that families were the natural setting for childhood, that no foster parent could replace a natural parent, and that the family was the fundamental unit of social organization. Beneath this lack of specificity, however, lurked a complex set of relations between family preservation, the rejection of institutions, and the expanded role of the state.

Recent developments in child psychology, the newly sentimentalized ideal of the economically useless child, and the fear of family disintegration, all discussed already, played an important role in the new strategy of family preservation. Indeed, hostility to women's work gave some men a reason to support family preservation, for it was a policy designed to keep women at home as well as to keep parents and children together. In July, 1918, an official of the United States Children's Bureau, Nila Allen, wrote her chief, Julia Lathrop:

> In the early days of agitation on the subject, it is true that it was frequently said that widows' pensions would be a means of keeping children out of institutions, but of late the dominant idea has been that they would keep the mother in the home, preventing her from going away to work. While earning the means to keep the family together, the children were growing up hap-hazardly, without her restraining influence and care during her working hours. This situation far more than keeping the child out of institutions, I understand to be the aim of widows' pensions.[30]

Earlier in the nineteenth century, the doctrine of separate spheres and domesticity had justified the exclusion of women from the workforce and public life with a sentimental exaltation of their moral sensibility and natural responsibilities. Cast as it was in a sentimental naturalism, family preservation extended the ideology of domesticity and separate spheres from women to children. The doctrine of family preservation moved children out of the labor force, where they had become a nuisance, and back into the house with their mothers, where they needed supervision. Therefore, for both women and children, the flip side of pricelessness was powerlessness.

Psychology, sentiment, anxiety, and male backlash reinforced a more mundane set of policy considerations that made family preservation the child-saving strategy of choice. Consider reformers' dilemma. First, institutions worked badly. Very few people could pretend any more that they gave children the love, attention, and education they needed. Even the cottage system was a decidedly second-best alternative. What was more, parents abused institutions, because too many used them as boarding schools in times of family trouble or, some reformers said, when children became inconvenient. In 1910, about half the children in New York State institutions had one living parent; only 17 percent were orphans. These figures were typical of those throughout the country. "Do not many parents of their own volition send their children to boarding schools and thus remove them from the immediate contact with the family?" asked the Right Reverend D. J. McMahon, supervisor of Catholic Charities in New York City. "This they do because they feel that the influence of companions, social class, and good teachers will be more beneficial for the child than even their own family circle." Other parents gave up their children simply because they could not support them. As an example, take the case of Mrs. G., twenty-four years old in 1908 with three children, age six, three, and one:

> Mr. G., who was a driver, died of stomach trouble in 1908, leaving no insurance and but small savings. For six months before his death the family had been aided by the C.O.S. and the widow turned immediately to that Society for help and advice. Her father and mother were living with her, both being at that time without employment. She was given some assistance by the Society and by an agency for the relief of widows, and with the help of the former secured work in a factory, earning from $2 to $6 a week. Her father also secured work and her mother later went out to service. Up to that time the grandmother had cared for the children while their mother was at work. The family was for a time self-supporting. Nine months later, when the father lost his position and Mrs. G.'s work was very slack, she decided to commit the children to an institution. The Society disapproved of this plan and offered to give $2 a week and tickets for work in a woodyard to her father until he should get work again, and to arrange for her to put her children in a day nursery. Mrs. G. refused to accept this plan, and contrary to the advice of the Society, placed two of the children in an institution. The material relief recorded was $48.[31]

Without the civilizing influence of their children, increased numbers of parents, child-savers feared, would slide into immorality and degradation, hastening the ominous and progressive unraveling of families that threatened the social foundations of American society. Julian Mack, judge of the circuit court, Cook County, made the connection between the preservation of the child in the home and the moral salvation of its parent. Nothing was "sadder," he said, than children taken from their parents or parents who came to the juvenile court to surrender their children on account of poverty. In these cases, Judge Mack saw a "twofold danger": first, no foster home, no matter how good, could substitute for the "mother's love and companionship." Second, he "saw . . . time after time, the terrible danger that confronted the young mother without proper stay in the world except that child's love, forced to go out and fight the battle alone in the big cities." Judge Mack wanted to extend his definition of a worthy parent to the "mother of an illegitimate child, because if we can stop that mother from giving away her child . . . we are going to save not only the child but the mother too."[32]

Of course, institutions were very expensive, and it cost a lot more to keep a child in an institution than to board it in a private home. But boarding itself was not a general solution to the massive problem of dependent children in America. Although some agencies chose foster families with care and supervised the children they placed, far too many placed them carelessly. Investigations in large cities turned up horrible baby farms masquerading as family homes and receiving large public subsidies. Indeed, the fear that many families would turn child care into a profitmaking business haunted the advocates of child placement. Irresponsible public officials, Robert Hebberd told the National Conference of Charities, sometimes "joined hands with more or less irresponsible persons, pretending to be charitably disposed, who carry on for their own emolument a work closely akin to that form of industry known as 'baby farming.' " When the New York State Board of Charities asked a charity organization society to investigate public child placement in one of the state's "leading counties," the agent in charge reported, "I have found children dead who were reported living; false addresses; children placed in immoral homes and in immoral localities; and children placed with so slight an investigation of the homes, and receiving so little supervision in these homes, that a state of affairs exists which calls for a radical change." Even with supervision, it was doubtful that enough good homes could be found to accommodate all needy children. Indeed, the complete abandonment of institutions threatened to overwhelm the administrative capacities of state and local governments as well as private agencies.[33]

One alternative remained: the child's own home. A small stipend would be enough to keep most children with their parents, and the cost almost certainly would be far less than an institution or even board in a private home. Most of the parents eligible for pensions, everyone assumed, would be widowed mothers, which meant that the stipend would have to be large enough to permit women to stay out of the workforce, or at least to work only part time.

Mothers' pensions had been advocated by the same sort of coalition that supported laws against child labor, the creation of juvenile courts, and the expansion of compulsory education. Western and midwestern juvenile court judges, whose work made them experts in problems of family dependence, played an active role as did many settlement workers, women who led Jewish charities in New York City, women's organizations—at the national level, the General Federation of Women's Clubs and the National Congress of Mothers; public welfare officials; the more progressive representatives of private charity; and, after its creation in 1912, the United States Children's Bureau, which had authority to investigate and report on "all matters pertaining to the welfare of children and child life among all classes of our people." For the most part, charity organization societies and eastern philanthropic organizations led the opposition to mothers' pensions, which they correctly saw as the entering wedge in the transformation of charity into entitlement. Nonetheless, the experience of charity organization proved how useful mothers' pensions could be. For charity organization had shown that regular assistance could help keep families together and facilitate their return to independence. Here is an example offered by Mary E. Richmond and Fred S. Hall, director and associate director of the New York Charity Organization Society, in their 1913 national study of widows:

> No. 2—Irish, aged thirty-six in 1896; children nine, eight, five, three, one year.
> Mr. A. was a hostler, earning $14 a week, who died in 1896 of suffocation, leaving no resources. For three months his wife managed to get on with her earnings and some help from relatives, then applied to the city and received $2 worth of groceries a week and a quarter of a ton of coal. Her application to the C.O.S. was made a little later. The Society replaced the city aid by a regular allowance of $2 a week (later increased to $3) with extra relief in emergencies; the church gave $1 a week besides. Mrs. A. took as lodgers her brother and cousin; this, with sewing at home, brought her total weekly income up to $6 or $7, exclusive of relief. When the children got older and went to school, she went out cleaning for part of the day. Her own health was good, but the children were sickly. One had kidney trouble, another tubercular glands, and the youngest was very nervous for a time, though better now. The tubercular child was sent to the country for months, later to Ireland for a holiday, and has entirely recovered.
> The family was a satisfactory one in every way. A volunteer has visited them from the very beginning who has been able to help in securing needed medical care, and in meeting emergencies. The boy with kidney trouble was musical; she secured a violin for him and his mother earned enough to pay for his music lessons by cleaning at an institutional church. The lad's disease proved incurable; he died in 1909. All the other children have grown stronger, and all reached the ninth grade in school before the age of fourteen. The oldest girl continued her studies in an evening school so that she now earns $12 a week; one boy is a teamster at $10; the youngest, fifteen, is still in school, but earns $2 weekly in a store out of school hours. The regular allowance was first decreased, then discontinued altogether in 1908, although occasional help in emergencies has sometimes been needed since.[34]

Missouri and Illinois passed the first mothers' pension legislation in 1911, and a number of states quickly followed. By the end of 1913, twenty states, mainly Western and Central, had authorized mothers' pensions; by 1919, the number had increased to thirty-nine states, and the territories of Alaska and Hawaii. In 1931, 200,000 children in every state except Georgia and South Carolina lived in homes supported in part by mothers' pensions. Most pensions went, as expected, to widows—in Massachusetts 82 percent; they were small and inadequate; they were granted only to a fraction of eligible recipients; and they carried very restrictive clauses (such as the 1913 amendment to the Illinois legislation that made divorced women ineligible for help); demanded strict behavioral standards; long residence; sometimes citizenship; and proof of utter destitution. Nonetheless, mothers' pensions helped families stay together, and they offered many women a modest independence they otherwise would have lacked. For once certified as eligible, women received a regular income without repeated investigations. They remained at liberty to supplement their pensions with work and to conduct their lives without the regular intrusion of friendly visitors. Even more, mothers' pensions were a small, halting, but consequential step away from charity and toward entitlement. They were the precedent for the Aid to Dependent Children title of the 1935 Economic Security Act (the foundation of Social Security), which, in turn, in a completely unanticipated way, became the foundation of the federal government's only mass program of public assistance (AFDC).[35]

The strategy of family preservation not only fostered government support for women with children; it also prompted them to develop an apparatus for supervising families. As Judge Ben Lindsay observed, "we can never keep" a child in its home "until we have to the full extent of the powers of government protected that home and the parent in the home."[36]

Reformers and public officials lacked faith in the families with whom they left children, and they quickly deployed strategies to shore them up. The opportunity to more closely monitor children, in fact, was another benefit of the family preservation strategy. "So long as the child remains in his own home," said Frank D. Loomis, secretary of the Children's Bureau in Newark, New Jersey, "the State supervises him in many ways which are discontinued if the child is removed to an institution."[37] Public health officials tried to change sanitary and child-rearing practices in poor neighborhoods. Juvenile court judges not only probed into family circumstances but deployed social workers and probation officers to watch and advise families, not just single young offenders. Child labor laws tried to assure that parents could not exploit their children either through work at home or by sending them out to earn money, and compulsory education kept children under public scrutiny during most of their childhood and early adolescence. Family preservation, therefore, sanctioned rather than challenged the state's intrusion into the relations between parents and children. Only through careful supervision, only by surrounding families with a network of specialists and regulations, and, ultimately, only by assuring them a regular, if meager, income, could child-savers reject the old strategy of family breakup, the unsatisfactory and expensive combination of institutions and foster care.

129

The Achievements of Child-Saving

Child-savers lost one major battle: child labor. Otherwise, to a remarkable degree, child-savers won their campaigns in the areas of education, juvenile justice, and public health. The question is what their victories accomplished.

Education

Child-savers made compulsory education a key component of their reform campaigns. In the late nineteenth century, compulsory education hardly was a new concept. Massachusetts had passed the first law in 1852, but most other states followed slowly, and, indeed, the early laws were weak and difficult to enforce. To its sponsors, compulsory education started as a mop-up operation. In Massachusetts, educational promoters at first thought that everyone would take advantage of the improved schools and lengthened school year that resulted from the intense educational reform movement which began around 1830. Nonetheless, not all youngsters attended school, and many—educational promoters believed the nonattenders—loitered on street corners, slept out at night, and contributed to the epidemic of juvenile crime that contemporaries thought they saw around them. School promoters and the state legislature responded in 1848 by creating the first state reform school for boys, which they saw, explicitly, as an extension of the public school system designed for those relatively few youngsters who had to be compelled to attend. Quickly, though, they realized that the reform school by itself could not solve the problem, and their next major response was the 1852 compulsory education law.[38]

The logic of compulsion was straightforward. Taxpayers who supported schools had a right to expect children to attend. The duty of taxpayers implied a correlative duty on the part of children. The issue involved not simply the welfare of children or their future social mobility. It bore directly on the highest interests of society and the state, because school promoters had defended the expensive expansion of public education by predicting it would reduce crime and poverty, heal social antagonisms, promote upward mobility, improve social morals, and create wealth. By mid-century, in fact, the familiar American faith in schooling as the solution for virtually all social problems had diffused widely throughout the country. Even so, compulsion, which, after all, brought with it a major intrusion of government into the relations between parents and children, was an idea that took a long time to sell. By 1900, thirty-two states had compulsory education laws that demanded "attendance, generally for the entire school session," fixed "stiff penalties for parents who failed to comply," and set up "facilities for inspection and prosecution." Most of the states that passed compulsory education laws in the nineteenth century were in the North and West. Later, and with some irony, racial fears helped spur the passage of compulsory education in the South. In North Carolina, according to Louis Harlan, white politicians observed blacks crowded into schools that whites attended much more haphazardly. Without compulsion, they feared, black educational achievement would outstrip white, with disastrous consequences for competition between the races. In 1918, Mississippi became the last state in the nation to make education compulsory.[39]

All but a relatively small proportion of parents sent their children to school without compulsion. Indeed, modern attempts to measure the impact of the new legislation have concluded that the rate of school attendance went up very little after the introduction of compulsion. The reason, of course, is that it was high already. Compulsory education only passed state legislatures after most parents had started to send their children to school with reasonable regularity. In effect, compulsory education ratified the importance of schooling in America and drew the stragglers into school. With their limited resources and small staffs of truant officers, local governments, which had to enforce compulsory education, could not have coped with massive noncompliance. In fact, some big cities had a rather different problem: too few school places for all the eligible children. Indeed, the major practical problem confronting educational administrators was not persuading children to attend school. Rather, it was accommodating a massive increase in school enrollment, especially among adolescents. No longer the preserve of the middle classes, high schools had to decide what to do with huge numbers of children from immigrant and working-class families headed neither for college nor commerce. Indeed, how to wrench city schools into the industrial age became the theme of progressive reforms in curriculum and pedagogy.[40]

Child Labor

More than compulsory education, the child labor question brought competing family strategies into sometimes open conflict. Working-class strategies that used children's wages to advance the collective welfare of families appalled child-savers committed to the individual self-development of priceless children. Child labor was a four-cornered issue. In one corner were industrialists and other employers who did not want to give up cheap help. With the largest resources and the easiest access to legislators, they formed the most powerful opposition to child labor legislation. In the second corner, organized labor sometimes joined the opposition to child labor for protectionist as well as humanitarian reasons. In the other corners were working-class families and reformers. For many working-class families, the logic of survival called for shared contributions, and individual mobility remained subordinate to the family's collective welfare and advancement. If a family was lucky, it could use children's wages to buy a house; if it wasn't, children's wages still could make the difference between independence and the poorhouse. Reform logic was individual. For the most part, reformers did not combine their early campaigns against child labor with an attempt to raise the real wages of adult workers, improve occupational health and safety, or otherwise remove the conditions that made children's wages a critical part of so many family economies. Instead, they argued that selfish parents exaggerated their reliance on children's wages and overlooked their gruesome working conditions, stunted health, and abbreviated education.

Families always had been miniature economies. Farming and artisan households had combined workplace and residence, and all members had been expected to contribute in ways appropriate to their age and gender. Parents looked forward to the extra labor that children would provide and to the insurance they offered in old age. When working-class parents in cities expected their children to contribute to family welfare by working for wages outside the home, when mothers, as they almost always did, took their children's pay packets and returned a small allowance for expenses, they no doubt felt neither greedy nor exploitative. For many of them, their children's wages made the difference between destitution and independence, at least when fathers were unemployed. Family budget studies from the nineteenth and early twentieth century show how close to the margin most working-class people lived. Very few men could expect to earn enough themselves to pay the rent on time or buy sufficient food, clothing, and fuel for their families. Haunted by periodic unemployment and badly paid, most working-class men needed another income. Sometimes, their wives took in lodgers, sewed, or washed clothes at home, but they rarely worked outside for wages. In these circumstances, for a great many families, children's wages were essential.[41]

Nonetheless, whether in a factory, mine, sweatshop, or, even, on a farm, most children worked in hideous conditions. Take the glass industry as an example. Walter Trattner claims that 98 percent of the boys employed worked in furnace rooms:

> Most worked as blowers' assistants. "Mold" boys either had to squat in an awkward, cramped position or, if they stood, had to stoop to their work in order to get close to the mold which was kept near the hot furnace. "Carrying-in" boys were required to remain on their feet for hours at a time, while "snapping-up" boys were forced to endure intense heat and the bright, glaring light of the glory hole which kept the glass molten.
>
> The heat was intense all over. The temperature of the molten glass was 2,500

degrees Fahrenheit; the temperature in the factories (which had to close during July and August) usually ranged between 100 and 130 degrees. Stiff necks, colds, pneumonia, rheumatism, and other throat and lung ailments were common. So were heat prostration, headaches, sleeplessness, and exhaustion, especially in warmer weather.

Because of heavy fumes and dust, many glass-house employees also suffered from injury to the tracheal passages, which induced respiratory diseases. Tuberculosis was common and skin irritation frequent, as was eye trouble, caused by the intense glare. The most common injuries, however, were cuts and burns, for the floors were always littered with broken glass.

Even more, most of the boys had to work frequent night shifts, which meant they finished at 3 A.M., when there was no transportation available. Either they had to walk home or sleep on the factory floor. Similarly awful accounts could be given of child labor in coal mines, tenement house sweat shops, or on large farms.[42]

Some forms of child labor appeared less harmful. One was child-acting. Although child actors led irregular lives, they worked at jobs they enjoyed and, often, made quite a lot of money. Was this really work? Were child actors harmed? Child-savers had no clear answer. Newsboys were another ambiguous group. Critics argued that most young criminals had graduated from their wild, unschooled, exploited ranks. Others, though, thought of newsboys as plucky, independent entrepreneurs on the road to commercial success. In Toledo, John Gunckel built a large, vibrant, largely self-governing organization of newsboys, whom he regarded as little merchants. Despite his success, although he became a revered figure in Toledo, Gunckel met stiff criticism from reformers who blamed him for encouraging child labor. In fact, the evidence there was mixed. Toledo had about the lowest youth crime rate among large cities—which many observers attributed in large measure to Gunckel's efforts—but it also was one of the last to pass a law regulating child labor, and when it did, the legislation was very weak.[43]

The earliest child labor legislation was the factory inspection begun in Massachusetts in 1867 and followed two years later by Connecticut. "Between 1885 and 1889 ten states passed minimum-age laws, while six prescribed maximum hours for child workers." In 1888, Massachusetts became the first to prohibit night work, although New York passed a similar law during the next year. Minnesota passed legislation regulating the age and hours of work in 1875, as did Ohio in 1898, and Michigan and Wisconsin in 1899. Seven other states also passed child labor laws in the 1890s. Nonetheless, reports Trattner, this legislation "failed to stem the tide of child labor. In fact, the number of children at work continued to increase."[44]

Around the turn of the century, opponents of child labor—led by Southerners who faced the worst problem—began to organize seriously. Living in New York as secretary of the Southern Education Board, Edgar Garner Murphy, an Episcopal clergyman who in 1903 won a long campaign for a tougher child labor bill in Alabama, soon joined forces with settlement house workers and Felix Adler, a Columbia professor who founded the Ethical Culture movement, to organize a committee to investigate child labor in New York. The New York Committee, in turn, sponsored the formation of a National Child Labor Committee in 1904, whose research, publications, and agitation resulted in a remarkable national coalition that included the country's most important settlement house leaders, juvenile court judges, clergymen, representatives of organized labor, former President Grover Cleveland, Harvard president Charles William Eliot, the publisher of the *New York Times*, and even some important industrialists. Its greatest triumphs were the creation of the U.S. Children's Bureau, for which it had lobbied hard, and federal legislation, the Wick's Bill, passed in 1916 and administered by the Children's Bureau, which outlawed some forms of child labor used in interstate commerce. However, within about 18 months the Supreme Court declared the Wick's Bill unconstitutional, and no more federal child legislation both passed Congress and withstood judicial review until the New Deal. In fact, by 1955, only twenty-five states had legislation that met the standards of the National Child Labor Committee. Despite a rash of new state laws, the failure to abolish child labor was the Progressive era child-savers' major defeat. When child labor finally began to lessen, the reason was not so much reform rhetoric as the uselessness of children to industry, the rising real wages of their parents, and, in the Great Depression, their competition for jobs with unemployed adults.[45]

Juvenile Justice

Probation and juvenile courts were child-saving's major contributions to juvenile justice. They, too, had mixed results. Indeed, innovations in juvenile justice showed how, despite the new emphasis on individuation, Progressive era reformers still confounded crime and poverty. For, by compounding dependency with delinquency, they erected a new institution with unprecedented power to intrude into the lives of children and their families.

Juvenile justice reform, like the opposition to child labor, responded to real abuses. Everyone could see that the reform schools inaugurated with high expectations earlier in the nineteenth century had failed miserably. Few of their inmates had reformed, and most of the institutions had degenerated into custodial warehouses that often turned their young inmates into real criminals. Nor were the courts very much help. Children charged with offenses faced the same legal process as adults. Judges had no authority to apply different rules, to suspend adversarial proceedings, to investigate family situations, or to devise special sanctions suited to individual circumstances. Even if they did create some sort of special, noninstitutional sentence, no one was responsible for supervising its application. Judges really had two alternatives: a punitive sanction or dismissal. Given the degradation of reform schools, a rehabilitative option was neither a legal nor a practical possibility.[46]

Cook County, Illinois, established the first juvenile court, in 1899, after years of agitation by the Chicago Women's Club, the Illinois Board of Public Charities, the Illinois Conference of Charities and Corrections, and the Chicago Bar Association. Denver Judge Ben Lindsay, who led an independent campaign for a juvenile court in his city, succeeded in 1901. Eight years later, there were courts in the District of Columbia and ten states. By 1925, every state except Maine and Wyoming had passed laws authorizing their establishment. Juvenile courts did not restrict their activities to children charged with breaking laws. To the contrary, they had wide discretion over dependent, neglected, and delinquent youngsters. In this way, they muddied the blurred boundary between criminality and dependence, which long had been a feature of American social thought. As one writer claimed, "a child who today is simply neglected may be dependent tomorrow, truant the next day and delinquent the day after that." In fact, dependent and neglected children made up a large part of the juvenile court's case load. In 1915, for instance, in Chicago, 1,886 cases of dependence and 3,202 charges of delinquency came before the juvenile court. In eighteen states, juvenile courts even administered mothers' pensions. As juvenile courts expanded their vaguely defined authority, they set themselves up "as the premier child-saving institution" and, by the 1920s, encountered criticism from social workers for their "excursions into the general field of welfare." New, more specialized agencies, social workers and other critics argued, should handle cases of neglect and family problems. Others pointed to the crowded dockets, the delays, and the short time allotted to each case.[47]

Juvenile courts depended on a new professional: the probation officer. According to Homer Folks, the probation system involved "a suspension of sentence, the child being permitted to return to his own home, there to remain under the oversight of a probation officer, and subject to further court proceedings in the case of misconduct. The probation officer is to keep informed of the child's conduct, to aid him if necessary in securing and keeping employment, and to act in general as an adviser, friend, and protector." Folks traced the origins of probation to a "state visiting agency" in Massachusetts in 1869. In 1880, a state law authorized officials in every city and town to appoint probation officers. In Chicago, probation officers were appointed in 1899 when the nation's first juvenile court was created there. By 1901, probation systems existed in fifteen of the country's twenty-five largest cities.

Probation officers had varied responsibilities. They responded to complaints of child dependence and neglect and decided which ones to prosecute. They investigated charges of delinquent behavior and made recommendations to the juvenile court judges, who, in practice, usually followed their advice. Then, of course, they had to supervise the activities of children sentenced to probation. Between 1915 and 1919, Chicago juvenile court judges sent 40 percent of the children whose cases they heard to one of four industrial training schools in the city. Slightly more than a quarter went back to their homes under court supervision. Probation, its advocates expected, would help the families of these youngsters as well as the children themselves. As one of them said, "the use of the probation officer to guard the interests of the child brought in as a dependent and allowed to remain with the parents is just as valuable for the dependent as it is for the delinquent child." Homer Folks thought of probation as an especially powerful way "to reach the parents [of neglected children] and change their attitude toward their children." Nonetheless, from its beginning, an intractable dilemma plagued probation work. Entering families as helpers or friends, probation officers backed up their advice with the authority of the state. No more than the agents of charity organization could they separate friendship from power.[48]

Working-class people long had used the courts to settle disputes among neighbors, friends, and families, or to mediate quarrels with landlords and creditors. Neither terrifying nor strange, courts, especially magistrates' courts, often had remained close to popular life. There, relatives frequently brought charges against each other and parents against children. With the advent of aggressive child rescue, lower level courts also had become the forum in which Societies for the Prevention of Cruelty to Children tried to remove children from their parents, although with mixed success. At least sometimes, judges obviously listened carefully to the evidence, because the agents of child rescue by no means always won. Courts had played so important a part in popular domestic life that the resolution of personal problems before juvenile court judges probably struck working-class families as neither especially threatening or novel. Nonetheless, with the advent of juvenile courts, initiative passed to the state, which, operating under new, unfamiliar, and less restrictive rules, had at its disposal an unprecedented array of sanctions with which it could intrude into families.[49]

Neither probation nor juvenile courts worked in the ways their advocates had predicted. Public authorities never provided enough funds to prove whether in fact probation could be effective, and, with a few exceptions, notably Ben Lindsay's court in Denver, juvenile courts in practice strayed far from their ideal. (For one thing, they often treated black youngsters more harshly than whites.) Although, according to Steven Schlossman, juvenile courts were supposed to use an "affectional mode of treatment" to bring "parents, children, and court officials amiably" together around "mutually agreed solutions," in no way did the actual practice of the Milwaukee Juvenile Court, which Schlossman studied in detail, match these hopes. Instead, "it functioned more often than not as a source of arbitrary punitive authority, and an arena for the evocation of hostile emotions on all sides."[50]

The Health of Children and Women

Of all child-saving reform movements, public health had the greatest success. Within a remarkably short time, it reduced the incidence of smallpox, diphtheria, and tuberculosis and lowered the staggering infant and early childhood mortality rates within America's cities. For a time, it even seemed as though public health reformers, led by the U.S. Children's Bureau, were about to make a radical change in the way health care was delivered to women and children. Here is where it met defeat. The organized, largely male medical profession blocked innovations that lessened its control, just as, in the same years, it began its continued and successful obstruction of national health insurance.

Dr. S. Josephine Baker, first chief of the world's first Bureau of Child Hygiene, created in New York City in 1908, observed, "The infant mortality rate is the most sensitive index of municipal housekeeping of a community. It is more than that; it is an index of civic interest, cooperation, consciousness, and worth."[51] By this measure, American cities were slovenly and neglected. In the late nineteenth century, about 20 of every thousand of the nation's residents died. In cities, the number averaged more than 25, and, in the poorest districts, 30 or 40. Even more, among children it was staggering, and in the poor sections of most large cities, it ranged as high as 135. A variety of conditions sustained these awful death rates: a lack of scientific knowledge about the causes of disease; malnourishment; polluted water supplies; contaminated milk; primitive sanitation; and racial discrimination. (In 1900, the death rate from tuberculosis was three times higher for blacks than for whites.)[52]

Nor were the many hospitals opened in the nineteenth century any help. Until very late in the nineteenth century, hospitals were charities. Often attached to almshouses, everyone understood that they were places for the sick poor, especially those who lacked relatives to care for them at home. Even the early major independent hospitals, such as Massachusetts General in Boston or New York Hospital, served the poor almost exclusively. The sick poor gained no advantage from their monopoly of hospital care. Indeed, hospitals were dangerous places, best avoided. Nor did the poor lose very much, if anything, when they could not afford the fee of a regular physician. For regular medicine still was unscientific, harsh, and often harmful. Until late in the nineteenth century, women attended by midwives were at least as well off, if not much safer, than those in the care of a young doctor, fresh from medical school, who had learned obstetrics from lectures without ever witnessing a live birth. (Not until the 1850s, did medical students actually witness a live birth as part of their training. Even then, the practice remained controversial and spread slowly.) Hospitals and medical practice began to change late in the nineteenth century. A com-bination of factors—scientific discoveries, the ambitions of physicians, the growth of a middle-class urban population without families to care for them—all en-couraged a shift in the social class of hospital patients. Indeed, hospitals suc-cessfully campaigned to attract affluent patients. As social stratification within and between hospitals increased, the sick poor were shunted to city hospitals or special wards in the great private hospitals that prided themselves on the modern, expensive care they offered those who could pay.[53]

In nineteenth and early twentieth century American cities, dispensaries rather than hospitals delivered the bulk of free or very cheap health care. Invented in England in the late eighteenth century, the dispensary "was an autonomous, free-standing institution" created to provide an alternative to the hospital for the "urban poor." Usually, dispensaries had their own building and at least one full-time house physician. Most also hired young physicians to visit patients too sick to leave home. Almost all the dispensaries operated on very low budgets and depended on "private contributions and the often-voluntary services of local physicians." Although the first dispensaries established before 1800 in Phila-delphia, New York, Boston, and Baltimore grew slowly, by the end of the second decade of the nineteenth century, new ones had opened to serve the developing areas on the outskirts of cities, and their number increased rapidly during the next several decades.[54]

In fact, by the late nineteenth century, big city dispensaries had grown large enough either to specialize or reorganize internally into distinct departments. Despite their popularity and importance, dispensaries quietly disappeared in the early twentieth century. For one thing, physicians preferred posts in the newly reorganized hospitals, and interns and residents no longer needed dispensaries as sites for clinical training. Moreover, scientific and technological advances made medical care more expensive, and dispensaries could not afford x-ray machines and the other new, costly equipment found in hospitals. Nor were physicians supportive. In fact, many had long resented dispensaries as competitors for patients. Indeed, many people simply could not believe that the "vast numbers who utilized dispensary services" were all too poor to afford private physicians,

138

and they suspected that many patients only pretended poverty. Nor did organized charity rally to defend dispensaries. To the contrary, charity organization societies disapproved of dispensaries as a form of indiscriminate outdoor relief that bred dependence. With so many forces lined up against them and only a very "shaky" defense by their supporters, "Even the oldest dispensaries did not survive as independent institutions past the early 1920s." The outpatient departments of general hospitals, which assumed some of their functions, were by no means "an unqualified success" or an adequate replacement. Despite their imperfections—and they were many—the dispensaries had provided poor people with free, local access to medical care. No other institution has been able to make the same claim on such a large scale.[55]

Child welfare clinics filled some of the void left by the decline of dispensaries. In New York, the Bureau of Child Hygiene, created in 1908, offered services and education to children and their families. The bureau worked through Baby Health Stations, of which there were 68 in the city by 1920, administered by "women trained in the care of children." They sold pasteurized Grade-A milk to mothers at below market price; taught mothers about hygiene, child care, and nutrition; referred sick children to the right medical services and poor parents to the appropriate charity or welfare agencies; and sent municipal public health nurses to "the homes of expectant mothers before, during, and after childbirth."[56]

In other ways, city governments periodically had tried to improve health conditions. Before the discovery of the bacterial origins of infections, most informed people thought that disease came from dirt and usually blamed foreign ships and immigrants for importing the smallpox, cholera, and typhus plagues that periodically devastated city populations. However, the various boards of health created before the late nineteenth century usually lacked power as well as scientific knowledge. Especially during epidemics, they focused primarily on ports, where, with very mixed success, they tried to quarantine and inspect incoming ships, crews, passengers, and cargo. Unfortunately, they had little impact on disease or mortality. The Civil War, especially through the "massive effort" of the United States Sanitary Commission, transformed this laconic concern with public health. The commission not only demonstrated the effectiveness of sanitary reform; it also unleashed the ambition of energetic women, who, after the war, with their work for the commission as a precedent, turned to the reform of urban charities. The commission's example also helped stir sluggish legislatures to create state boards of public health, first in Massachusetts in 1869, but followed soon afterward in other states. The new state boards varied greatly in their legal authority and practical effectiveness. At their best, they enforced regulations against slaughterhouses, tested and inspected drinking water, fought to purify food and milk supplies, promoted vaccination against infectious disease, and led campaigns to raise the qualifications of doctors. Even at their weakest, they collected the statistics essential to monitor public health and broadcast information about the origins and prevention of disease.[57]

Advances in public health needed more than dedicated reformers, reorganized and strengthened administration, and an aroused public. They depended, as well, on scientific knowledge. The great breakthrough came in the 1870s when Pasteur and Koch showed how microorganisms caused disease. Within 20 years, the specific bacteria responsible for the most dreaded killers were identified: typhoid, leprosy, and malaria in 1880; tuberculosis, 1882; cholera, 1883; diphtheria and tetanus, 1884; plague, 1894; dysentery, 1898. With good reason, historians have labeled the period 1890–1910 "the golden age of public health."[58]

By the early twentieth century, the results of the national, as well as state and local, campaign against infant death showed most dramatically in declining mortality rates and rising life expectancy. In Philadelphia, life expectancy at birth rose from forty in 1870 to fifty-eight in 1930. Most of the improvement reflected the great decline in infant deaths. In 1870, 175 of every thousand infants died in their first year of life; by 1930, the number had dropped 175 percent to 75. More than a third of all children died before they were ten years old in 1870; by 1930, only about 10 percent did not reach their tenth birthday. As for young adults, in 1870, 114 of every thousand who reached age twenty died in the next ten years; sixty years later the number had dropped to less than twenty. Unlike the mortality rate among infants and young adults, the maternal death rate did not begin to fall until the 1930s. Between 1920 and 1933, the number of deaths per live births in New York City declined from 85.4 to 50.9, but the rate at which mothers died in childbirth increased from 5.33 to 5.98 between 1921 and 1932. In fact, in America the maternal death rate was higher than in any other developed country.[59]

Most of the improvement in life expectancy came from the "spectacular decline" in infectious diseases. In 1870, 600 of every 1,000 Philadelphians died from infectious diseases for which diagnostic procedures were quite accurate: diphtheria and croup, erysipelas, malaria, measles, scarlet fever, smallpox, tuberculosis, typhoid, and whooping cough. In 1930, fewer than 80 in 100,000 died from these infections. Improved city services accounted for most of the decline. For example, the city reduced the incidence of typhoid by cleaning up and filtering its water supply. At the same time, the Philadelphia Bureau of Public Health issued pamphlets "on the care and feeding of children"; created a Child Hygiene Bureau that organized clinics in eight wards, whose infant diarrheal death rates subsequently declined more than in wards without clinics; and worked to improve the quality of milk. Other factors in the city's history— a general improvement in living standards and impressive economic growth—

also speeded the mortality decline. To be sure, special interest groups, infighting among city agencies, and the limited knowledge of many public officials retarded civic action. Nonetheless, its most recent and thorough students argue, by the most conservative estimate, government intervention accounted for at least a third of the decline in Philadelphia's death rate.[60]

Elsewhere, gains were equally impressive. In New York City, Dr. S. Josephine Baker reported that the infant death rate had dropped from 144 per thousand births when she started her work in 1890 to less than 50 per thousand by 1939, when she published her remarkable autobiography. In 1897, Nathan Strauss demonstrated the effect of pasteurization on milk by halving the death rate in the city's infant asylum on Randall's Island. In New York State, the mortality rate from tuberculosis dropped 61 percent between 1907 and 1917, and with the advent of immunization the death rate from diphtheria declined a similar amount between 1925 and 1930. Milwaukee deployed public health measures with unusual thoroughness. In the process, it transformed its reputation as one of the country's unhealthiest cities so dramatically that in 1930 it took top place in the Class I division of the first national Health Conservation Contest. Throughout the city, child mortality dropped and life expectancy rose. In the ward with the highest mortality, the death rate dropped from 25.1 to 15.7 per thousand in only twenty years.[61]

Everywhere, public health reform came through struggle. In Milwaukee, for instance, it was the great fear of cholera in the early 1890s that finally pushed municipal authorities to support public health measures. Physicians, at first skeptical, often resisted even scientific innovations longer than the public. In New York, according to Josephine Baker, they feared that dramatic improvements in public health would lessen their incomes. Vested interests, especially milk producers, tried to block changes that would raise their costs and increase their responsibilities. Immigrants often resented the intrusion of public health officials, who tried to convince them to change long-standing housekeeping and child-care practices. They knew that Baby Health Stations, as S. Josephine Baker said, were "a way of coming into contact with mothers in order to educate them in scientific child care," as well as a source of free or cheap milk and medicine. The motto of Baker's Bureau of Child Hygiene was, "Better babies, better mothers, better homes." Compulsory vaccination also remained an emotional issue, resisted fiercely in many immigrant neighborhoods.[62]

What accounts for the relative success of public health reform? Why did it meet its goals better than other child-saving campaigns? In Milwaukee, a socialist mayor and a German population accustomed to a more active government facilitated reform. Nonetheless, it took a conjunction of other factors to overcome the resistance of interest groups, skeptical politicians, and suspicious ethnic communities:

Municipal responsibility developed most readily when the health problem was acute, when medicine understood the crisis and could solve it, when business interests could profit from the changes, when at least one major political party accepted the reforms, when a strong but sensitive individual emerged to guide the reforms through the system, and when the different cultural groups agreed on a medical solution.[63]

Public health had four great assets shared by no other reform movement. First, it had a clear, measurable goal: the reduction of death and disease. Second, after the discovery of the bacterial origins of infectious disease, it had a scientific basis. Third, it could draw most of its authority and resources locally. By and large, cities on their own could reduce disease and lower mortality without improvements in macroeconomic conditions, such as unemployment, or structural changes in the distribution of wealth and power. Fourth, public health was not class-specific. Unlike any other major aspect of child-saving, it served everyone. In this way, it sidestepped the contradictions between public responsibility and privatism by extending the reach of the state without singling out any group as inferior or degraded. In the process, public health acquired a constituency that included urban political and business leaders as well as reformers. In this way, its success confirmed rather than challenged the contradictions that undercut the other child-saving innovations in Progressive America.

Ambitious child-savers wanted to extend their success with mothers' pensions and the reduction of infant and early childhood mortality by reshaping health care delivery for women and children. In the 1920s, with the support of the Children's Bureau, they nearly succeeded. However, within a decade, the male medical establishment destroyed their innovative and popular new clinics.

Class and gender have always shaped health care delivery, and men, by and large, have controlled official medicine. However, in the nineteenth and early twentieth century, male dominance of the most powerful and lucrative medical roles did not mean that women played only a marginal part in health care. Rather, they developed specialties outside the mainstream of regular medical practice. Women midwives delivered more babies than regular physicians until late in the nineteenth century; others (such as the famous Madame Restell in New York) ran abortion clinics; the first women physicians, unable to practice in most hospitals, turned to the branches of medicine least attractive to male physicians, such as public health; and, of course, as nurses, women did the routine work of caring for the sick by tending them within hospitals, visiting their homes, and staffing the new clinics that opened in the early twentieth century.

Women by and large staffed the Baby Health Stations created in the 1920s, which served as models for the Sheppard-Towner Act, passed by Congress in 1921. The act created "the first federally funded health care program to be implemented in the United States." According to Sheila Rothman, it had a clear purpose—"to reduce the infant and maternal mortality rate"—and a straightforward strategy:

> to provide states with matching federal funds in order to establish prenatal and child health centers. In these centers, women trained in the scientific care of children would teach expectant mothers the rules of personal hygiene and offer advice on how to maintain and improve the health of their children.

Reformers had tried to persuade Congress to pass infant and maternal health legislation since 1917. They finally succeeded in 1921 because four factors coalesced. One was the irrefutable data on mortality in the reports of the Children's Bureau. A second was the obvious success of child welfare clinics in reducing infant mortality and improving health. (Although the New York Bureau of Child Hygiene served in many ways as a model, Sheppard-Towner had a different focus: families in rural areas and small towns.) Third was the experience of World War I when thousands of men had to be rejected for the draft for physical conditions that could have been prevented by adequate child care. Fourth was women's suffrage. After the passage of the nineteenth amendment, in 1919, Congress feared the backlash from newly enfranchised women if they failed once again to pass legislation promoting child and maternal health.[64]

The Sheppard-Towner Act tried to draw a clear distinction between the activities funded by the act and the activities of physicians. Physicians cured people already sick. They did not conduct regular, preventive health examinations. The new clinics, by contrast, would concentrate on prevention, and sick children would be sent to physicians. At the same time, the act tried to improve health care administration by requiring each state "not only to approve matching funds, but also to establish a state agency that would coordinate its health programs with the Children's Bureau." The American Medical Association (AMA), reluctant to endorse any government expansion in health care, at first opposed Sheppard-Towner, but not very vigorously. Most physicians simply lacked much interest in the new program because it seemed to pose no threat to their relations with private patients. "This was a public health program that belonged to women and the state, and hence it was not their concern." Public health nurses and female physicians were the program's principal staff. The former, whose role combined nursing with social work, had trained in social work schools and worked in a "settlement house, municipal department of child hygiene, or a public school," but not as "a member of a hospital team." Although female physicians had no special training, they were available and willing to pioneer new roles in public medicine because they often were excluded from hospitals and had difficulty building up private practices.[65]

Despite its popularity and the enthusiasm of its supporters, by 1929 Sheppard-Towner was dead. Congress killed the program by failing to renew its appropriation. The immediate reason was a virulent campaign mounted by the medical profession. In the years after the passage of Sheppard-Towner, the medical profession began to invade the domain that had been left to women and children: that is, preventive medicine. Worried about competition from clinics, family physicians for the first time began to keep patient histories and give regular physical examinations. Indeed, many physicians felt the clinics offered free, public services they could provide just as well. Medical specialists also attacked Sheppard-Towner and tried to seize control of child and maternal health care from women. To win back the field, they reorganized health care delivery by turning "the supervision of pregnancy [which they defined as an illness] into a physician's job, preferably an obstetrician's" and denigrating the care given by women who ran clinics. While specialists attacked women's abilities, "the American Medical Association [which wanted to move the government out of health care], along with other 'liberty-minded' organizations, discredited their politics" through a "vicious smear campaign." The White House Conference on Children convened by President Hoover in 1930 symbolized the male physicians' victory. Even Grace Abbott, head of the Children's Bureau, which administered Sheppard-Towner, played only a small role in the conference, which was dominated by male medical specialists without sympathy for public child and maternal health clinics staffed by nurses and female physicians. The defeat of Sheppard-Towner—which Lela Costan calls the "first round in what was to become a recurring confrontation between women and physicians"— had lasting consequences for the delivery of health care. As Rothman observes, it simultaneously "marked the end of female expertise in the field of health care and . . . shifted the provision of preventive health services from the public to the private sector."[66]

Sheppard-Towner had tested the limits of reform in America. Unlike vaccination, better nutrition, pasteurized milk, or improved sanitation, its potential invasion of physicians' prerogatives and incomes had violated the fictive boundaries between public and private. Its defeat illustrates once again the barriers to the extension of public responsibility where economic decisions remain officially private. Sheppard-Towner's opponents had three weapons: (1) the plausibility of arguments based on the skill of the specialist; (2) the problem of financing public health care in the depression; (3) the fear of socialism that swept through America in the wake of the Russian revolution. In fact, with the hysterical Red Scare of the 1920s as a rhetorical weapon, the AMA could dredge up the pieties of economic liberalism to cover its straightforward attempt to wrest the control of infant and maternal health from women-run public clinics and put it where it belonged, under the supervision and care of private, male physicians. Nothing could be more American.

By 1930, with the exception of the campaign against infant and early childhood mortality, none of the child-savers' innovations had met the expectations of their advocates. Early attempts to save children by moving them out of poorhouses or by rescuing them from their parents had only shifted them to institutions, where they fared little better. Efforts to improve congregate institutions by dividing them into pseudo households or cottages failed to create model families, and the first attempts to shift children from institutions to foster families foundered, because neither public nor private placement agencies had the resources to select families with much care or to supervise the children sent to them. With the exception of a few states, the number of children in institutions or in foster care continued to grow, despite the new efforts to preserve families, and mothers' pensions remained so hedged with restrictions and so inadequately funded they hardly dented the problem. Advocates of child labor did persuade a number of states to pass restrictive legislation, but the laws remained weak and inadequately enforced, and it proved impossible to pass federal legislation that the Supreme Court considered constitutional.

Although inadequate funding crippled every innovation from the start, inherent contradictions would have undermined even adequate appropriations. One of them was the irreconcilable conflict between punishment and rehabilitation. No prison or reformatory regime, no matter how well intentioned, could hide the authority to incarcerate and coerce vested in it by the state. No probation officer or juvenile court judge could veil the power to punish with informality or kind advice. Nor could any policy transcend the great divisions between classes and cultures or harmonize the tensions between the goals of reform and administrative convenience. In the end, reform foundered on the conflict between privatism and public responsibility that created fictive boundaries between family, economy, and state, which government could cross only as a last resort. As long as the objects of public assistance have been, by definition, incompetent, they have also been inferior, and, sentimental rhetoric aside, their welfare has deserved the half-hearted attention and mean-spirited response it has elicited. Meanwhile, a related fiction—the benevolent, disinterested, and classless state—has masked the less appealing uses to which charity, relief, welfare, and reform have been put.

6   Reorganizing Cities

In the first two decades of the twentieth century, America's most forward-looking and progressive cities reorganized their governments. They also expanded their responsibilities for relief—which they began to call welfare—and transformed its administration. Several powerful forces tugged American charity into the era of social welfare. The new urban wilderness, the attractions of socialism and the spectre of bolshevism, the growth of the labor movement, the problems of a transient and accident-prone labor force, the cost of public relief, the inefficiency of both private and public administration, professional aspirations and the lure of expertise: these were the complex, interconnected, dynamic influences that persuaded business and municipal leaders to join public welfare officials, settlement workers, and other urban professionals in a successful campaign to reorganize cities, labor markets, and social welfare in early twentieth century America. Although America's "devices for minimizing dependencies"—to use a phrase of Jane Addams's—looked a lot more modern by the 1930s, none of the innovations proved adequate to their tasks. All of them remained crippled by the fictive boundaries between private and public that left governments reluctant to intervene in economic decisions and hobbled by the decentralized political structures that made the mobilization of resources difficult, if not impossible, even in times of crisis.[1]

146

Cities and the Shock of 1893

With a mighty jolt, the depression that began in 1893 dislocated the frail mechanisms of relief throughout urban America and exposed the utter inadequacy of the ideas on which they rested. The plausibility of scientific charity had floated on nearly 15 years of prosperity. With demand for relief steady or declining, its definition of reform as administrative efficiency and retrenchment, its assertions of individual responsibility for dependence, and its dismissal of the need for public relief still could persuade someone not very familiar with the daily struggles of the poor. No longer. After 1893, doctrinaire adherents to scientific charity increasingly retreated into a rigid and reactionary defensiveness that left them outside the dynamic currents of social action. The shock of 1893 reshaped political alignments, escalated the war between capital and labor, and changed the direction of social reform.

The depression began as a financial panic in May, 1893, when the stock market tumbled, a major railroad filed for bankruptcy, banks began to fail, and fears of a currency shortage swept through the country. By the fall, more banks and railroads had failed, industrial production had dropped, and unemployment soared. Although hard times lasted until 1897, the worst months were in the winter of 1893–94. No one could say exactly how many people were unemployed. Statistics remained far too primitive. The best modern estimate is between 17 and 19 percent of the workforce, or between 2.4 and 2.7 million people at the worst point. Gross figures, however, are misleading. Unemployment varied by region and by industry; manufacturing and mining areas suffered most. In 1893, for instance, *Dun's Review* estimated unemployment at 40 percent of the labor force in the iron industry and over 50 percent in woolens. In Massachusetts, 62 percent of the workforce in carpets, 30.9 percent in woolens, 14 percent in paper and paper goods, and 16 percent in metals and metallic goods lacked work. At different points in 1893 and 1894, the unemployment rate was 35 percent in New York, 25 percent in Pennsylvania, 22.3 percent in Massachusetts, 11 percent in Ohio, and 43.6 percent in Michigan. Clearly, even allowing for inaccuracy, unemployment rates were staggeringly high.[2]

The distress overwhelmed local agencies. Both private and public relief mechanisms already in place buckled under vastly increased demands for help. Throughout the country, a variety of expedients quickly emerged. One set aimed simply at increasing the amount of available relief. New central relief committees solicited funds, which they either dispensed themselves or distributed among existing agencies. Soup kitchens and cheap or free lodging houses opened;

newspapers created special relief funds and distributed food and fuel; even charity organization societies and settlement houses were pushed into the direct distribution of relief with only cursory, minimal investigations. Work relief was the other, and more novel, expedient. Both public and private groups tried to create jobs other than the traditional stone breaking or wood chopping used by scientific philanthropists to test an applicant's work ethic. For the first time on a large scale, cities used public works projects as a principal method of relief. (Projects included street sweeping, sewer construction, street paving, and sometimes construction.) For the first time, too, private associations collected money for use in work relief, which they turned over to city governments to spend. All public works projects, it should be pointed out, were municipal; none were started by either state or federal government. Mayor Hazen Pingree of Detroit introduced one of the most widely publicized, if strictly limited, schemes when he offered small plots of land, seeds, and advice to poor families who wanted to grow their own vegetables. "Potato patches," not surprisingly, struck a responsive chord and spread briefly to several other cities. For the first time, too, labor unions supported unemployed members, and at its 1893 convention, the American Federation of Labor (AFL) argued for "immediate and adequate relief" by public authorities. "When the private employer cannot or will not give work, the municipality, state, or nation must."[3]

Unable to draw lines between the worthy and unworthy poor among their citizens, relief efforts displaced the old boundary to a newly hardened wall between residents and strangers. As the number of unemployed men on the road looking for work swelled, municipal authorities and relief agencies across the country defined the limits of their responsibilities ever more narrowly and devised various stratagems for discouraging needy strangers. One was ideological: the indiscriminate expansion of the despised category "tramp" to embrace everyone on the road. By labeling men tramps, relief authorities automatically justified both their refusal to help and the vagrancy laws under which officials could toss poor strangers into jail. Virtually alone among mean-spirited public officials, the Populist governor of Kansas, Lorenzo D. Lewelling, declared the state's vagrancy law unconstitutional:

> Kansas has her share of the 3,000,000 unemployed workmen in the United States, and these men should not be put in jail and made to suffer degradation for no other reason than that they are out of money. It is no crime to be without visible means of support. I was in that condition once, in 1865, in Chicago. I was no thief, but I was a tramp, in the present acceptation of the term; and, had I been picked up by the police, I could not have found honest work. My circular only applies to men who are in enforced idleness. To that class the rock-pile shall be abolished in Kansas as long as I am governor.

Lewelling's refusal to equate poverty with crime sent chills as far east as New York. One critical observer reported that tramps were flocking to Kansas from across the country and increasing its crime rate.[4]

Tramps were not the only source of fear among the respectable classes. Coxey's Army and other ragged bands of unemployed workers staggered toward Washington to demand help. In 1894, about 750,000 workers went on strike, mainly to protest wage cuts. Socialists and other radicals used the hard times to advance their case among newly sympathetic audiences. In politics, the Populist party emerged out of the dust of discontent, and William Jennings Bryan's capture of the Democratic nomination injected issues of fundamental significance into presidential politics for the first time since 1860. Respectable America countered by crushing strikes with state sanctioned or supported violence and by regrouping around the Republican party.[5]

Even conservatives had to admit the structural roots of unemployment. With millions of people out of work, no one could pretend that most of the unemployed simply did not want to work. Indeed, one lasting effect of the depression was "the discovery of unemployment." For the first time, unemployment received serious, official study, most notably the long, detailed analysis published by the state of Massachusetts. Still, most analysts refused to connect unemployment with capital's need for a reserve army of labor and its wasteful personnel policies. Instead, they defined unemployment as a consequence of faulty distribution. Workers lacked information about job availability, and employers in areas where labor was scarce had no efficient, reliable way to reach potential employees. The answer, it followed, was employment agencies, a number of which were created in the 1890s. None of them worked very well. Indeed, private agencies sometimes exploited their clients or served as covers for the white slave trade. Public agencies were too small, too limited in geographic scope, and too inexperienced to offer effective service. The most that can be said is that their failure stimulated both the campaign for professional public employment bureaus and unemployment insurance.[6]

The experience of depression also forced organized charity to develop more complex, less rigid views of dependence. In part, the change came about as charity workers confronted mass poverty that could not be attributed to individual weakness. It also was forced on them by hostile critics who began to argue that charity organization was, in fact, part of the problem. Stanton Coit, one of the early settlement house leaders, attacked the intellectual roots of charity organization and argued that only governments could provide adequate relief. "It is deeply to be deplored," he said, that "the people who started the Charity Organization Society were tainted with laissez-faire doctrines and extreme individualistic theories." They did not realize that one private agency could not unify all the relief in a great city. "Scientific philanthropists will some day learn that charity organization is a distinctive municipal function." The Massachusetts unemployment commission was even more blunt:

> The ordinary charitable institution as now constituted is not in touch with industrial conditions. . . . They are so well accustomed to deal with the degraded or particularly unfortunate class that they necessarily lose a certain sort of tact and a generous discrimination which is needed in dealing with men and women, who, under ordinary conditions, are steady wage-earners. . . . the inquisitorial and repellant attitude assumed by those who apparently regard the chief duty of a relief body to detect imposition reflects unfortunately upon the work of a relief association as a whole.[7]

By the early twentieth century, charity organization's defensiveness showed in the sleazy tactics to which it resorted. In New York, when the social secretary of a municipal lodging house supported government ownership of railroads to ease seasonal unemployment, Johnston Deforest of the COS circulated a critical and confidential letter to his colleagues. The social secretary's contract was not renewed. When studies it secretly sponsored "revealed too strikingly the industrial causes of poverty," claimed one writer, the Russell Sage Foundation, which had its own Bureau of Charity Organization, suppressed them. Of course, the COS had good reason to be defensive. Its day had passed, for as no other event before it, the depression of 1893 had shown that only government had the resources and authority to alleviate the misery endemic to modern industrial civilization. But state government did not dispense relief, and city governments, the depression underscored, lacked the administrative capacity to respond effectively to economic crisis. Small, weak, lacking effective central direction, city government nearly collapsed under the urban explosion that transformed America.[8]

Welfare and Municipal Reform

Between 1880 and World War I, great forces expanded, reshaped, and rebuilt American cities as they propelled them into the industrial age. First consider the sheer magnitude of population growth: in the half century after 1860, the number of urban residents leaped from 6.2 million to 42 million. By 1920, half of the American population lived in urban areas. Many city dwellers (about a third in 1910) had migrated from rural areas, and, after 1880, from southern and eastern Europe. In 1910, about 10 million foreign-born and over 12 million native-born children of immigrants lived in American cities. In most cities with more than 100,000 people, the native-born children of foreign parents outnumbered the children of natives. In the South, blacks migrated toward cities, and by 1900, amounting to nearly 43 percent of the southern urban population, they had begun to migrate north.[9]

In the late nineteenth and early twentieth century, American industrialization took place in cities, and industry replaced commerce as the economic base of most cities. Indeed, more than 90 percent of factory output was produced in urban areas. At the same time, technology at once integrated and splintered cities. Elevators and, even more, cast-iron metal frame structures made possible the construction of tall buildings, which drew throngs of workers to reconstructed city centers. They came there on steam railroads and electric trolleys, introduced after 1887, which replaced the slow, horse-drawn trams in use since the 1850s. Within one decade, 48,000 cars belonging to 909 trolley companies, crossed 15,000 miles of tracks. Although steam railroads carried 5 million commuters a year in 1890, within a decade, electric trolleys took twice as many people to work as the railroads. The same technology that brought people to work downtown took them home to the cities' outskirts and suburbs. Better-paid workers, business, and professional people deserted the old sections of cities, which filled rapidly with factories and immigrants. As immigrants moved into the old housing, cities increasingly fragmented into social and ethnic enclaves. These isolated, poor tracts within great cities became the new American wilderness, untamed, unknown, subversive. Plagued by poverty, congestion, disease, and wretched housing, they sustained the shadow government of political machines that tinged urban service delivery with its peculiarly American, localized, personalized, and corrupt style.[10]

Whatever its detractors said then and afterward, late nineteenth century American city governments could boast of remarkable accomplishments. New York built Central Park, and other cities hired its architect, Frederick Law Olmstead, to "design the first public park system in human history." Brooklyn constructed its magnificent bridge, "a brilliant synthesis of art and engineering." Other monuments to the era include San Francisco's Golden State Park, Boston's Public Library, and the huge "nineteenth-century water and drainage schemes that still serve the cities." With vastly increased populations spread out over larger areas, cities had to expand their services and finance sewers, water mains, police and fire protection, street paving, lighting, and schools. All of the cities managed to pay for these new or expanded services without going bankrupt. By the end of the century, claims Teaford, "American city dwellers enjoyed, on the average, as high a standard of public services as any urban residents in the world." Unfortunately, despite their other successes, urban governments did not find better ways to mitigate or prevent the poverty that disfigured the lives of so many of their citizens.[11]

In the late nineteenth century, foreign observers, (such as James Bryce), muckrakers, and a legion of municipal reformers united to condemn urban government as hopelessly corrupt, inefficient, and boss ridden. It was, they said, America's great political failure. In fact, they were only partly right; American cities had developed complex, distinctive political structures that reflected the local focus of most city life, and the narrow definition of public responsibility retarded the development of city services. City governments were confederations of neighborhoods that advanced and protected their interests by sending alder-men, usually small businessmen or local professionals, to large city councils, where they dominated weak, mostly powerless mayors. "Page after page of council minutes in America's major cities," writes Teaford, "reveal the alderman not as a figure dedicated to molding city government but as a neighborhood envoy who sought to secure as many services and favors as possible from the city government and to make certain that the city served his constituents." With mayors largely impotent and councils preoccupied with neighborhood interests, state legislatures retained the only effective central authority over the structure of city governments. Indeed, urban reformers usually turned first to state leg-islatures rather than to city councils or mayors when they wanted to initiate major, city-wide change. Within city wards, local political machines often supplied the jobs, relief, and other favors that weak city governments failed to provide, but very few machines transcended ward boundaries to extend their influence over entire cities. For the most part, they, too, reflected the neighborhood base of city politics. As long as cities remained small, demands for services relatively simple, and the need for functional integration minimal, urban governments could limp along, by and large without disaster, if without distinction.[12]

By the late nineteenth century, urban growth and transformation had over-whelmed the capacity of city governments. Demands for sewers, water, electric lights, street paving, and better transportation; problems of overcrowding, high rates of disease and mortality, crime, threats to social order, education, and welfare: none of these respected ward boundaries. All required a strong, coor-dinated, central response, which neither city governments nor political machines could deliver. The first serious attempt to crack the power of ward machines and improve the quality of urban government was civil service reform, cham-pioned, especially, by business and professional groups. Although civil service advocates did win important victories in the 1880s, they soon learned the limits of improved personnel procedure as a strategy of administrative reform. For one thing, the loopholes in early civil service laws allowed local politicians to slip their friends into city jobs. Even more, the roots of the problem were sunk in the structure of urban management as much as in its personnel; by themselves, new faces without new power could accomplish very little.[13]

When the limits of civil service became clear, municipal reformers throughout the country, led again by business, devised a strategy of structural reform with several components. (As with the abolition of outdoor relief, Brooklyn, led by Mayor Seth Low, pioneered the innovations in city government, in 1881.) Municipal autonomy headed the list. State legislatures dominated by rural interests, argued reformers, made structural change slow, difficult, and uncertain. Cities needed the capacity to govern themselves. Next came a strong mayor with the power to appoint top city officials and veto budget items. A smaller, unicameral city council elected at large would lift the focus of city politics above ward boundaries and, at the same time, assure the continuation of representative democracy in the newly strengthened and centralized government. The government itself would be reorganized into a series of specialized departments staffed by experts. For smaller cities, reformers recommended government run by special commissions—an innovation which did not take hold— or by city managers—one which did. Whether led by a mayor or an appointed city manager, the spirit of the new, ideal urban government could be summed up in one word: efficiency. Reformers expected to make city government both better and cheaper.[14]

Reformers applied the same strategy to cities that industrialists did to corporations. For both, the key problem was devising ways to manage structures that had outgrown their means of administration. In each case, reform proposals favored a strong executive leading a series of functional departments staffed by experts. Nonetheless, neither industrial nor urban reorganization were neutral attempts to improve quality and administration. (Indeed, every administrative reorganization reflects social values and tilts power relations. Organizational neutrality is a theoretical fiction.) In neither industry nor city was technology the real problem. For all its managerial inefficiencies, American industry dominated the world, and unreformed cities built bridges, parks, water works, and major new institutions. Rather, the issues were coordination and control. Industrial reorganization extended management's control of work processes and reduced the autonomy of skilled workers and foremen. In cities, reorganization increased executive control of city services and curbed the power of local aldermen and political bosses. In both industry and city, power shifted upward, away from workers toward management, and away from working-class spokesmen toward the business and professional class and its proxies.[15]

Across the country, municipal reformers altered the structure of city government. Details differed from place to place, but throughout the country cities won increased autonomy from states, strengthened their executives, regrouped functions into departments, and hired experts. Civil engineers, city planners, landscape architects, accountants, school superintendents, social welfare specialists, public health physicians, housing experts, even fire and police chiefs injected professional standards into urban administration. The results, however, were not wholly what reformers had expected. As interested in the quality of service as its cost, with the help of the U.S. Census Bureau, the new urban professionals shifted the criterion of efficiency away from cheapness and toward results. Because wide variation in city accounting practices hampered attempts to compare the way cities spent their money or to develop standards with which to assess their effort, the Census Bureau devised a standard set of categories into which it reaggregated city budgets. When the Census Bureau published its major report in 1913, city professionals at last had one objective standard, and they used it to persuade cities to adopt the bureau's categories and increase the amount of money they spent on city services. The strategy worked; cities throughout the country adopted the Census Bureau categories. Even more, in most cases they increased the amounts they spent on city services.[16]

The mean per capita expenditure of large cities increased, in constant dollars, only 3 percent between 1904 and 1912 and then soared 59 percent between 1912 and 1930. Public spending on charities, which actually had declined 8 percent during the first period, rose 79 percent in the second. Only expenses for schools (103 percent) and health (87 percent) increased more. In fact, by the late 1920s, most cities spent three times more money than private agencies on outdoor relief. Despite the difficulty of translating dollars into quality, these trends almost certainly mean that city services had improved. For instance, although mothers' pensions added many women and children to municipal welfare roles, higher per capita spending reflected a solid increase in the amount of assistance given each family.[17]

In most cities, new municipal departments administered the escalating amounts spent on public welfare. In 1913, Kansas City was the first to reorganize by creating a Board of Public Welfare. Its general superintendent, L. A. Halbert, proudly told the National Conference of Charities and Corrections what the city hoped to accomplish, summarized its early accomplishments, and explained the principles on which the new board rested:

1   Government care for the unfortunate classes.
2   Government control of the conditions of living.
3   The centralization of all the government's social agencies into one system [in the interests of efficiency, which is the watchword of our times].
4   The establishment of social action on a scientific basis.

As he explained each principle, Halbert turned the key assumptions of scientific charity on their heads. The impersonality of municipal relief was, precisely, its virtue; "relief becomes merely a business transaction and the element of charity is entirely eliminated." Nor was most dependence the fault of individuals. "We are fully convinced that no people born with normal faculties should be either led or driven into pauperism or crime and the ranks of the poor and the delinquent are filled with people who began life as normal individuals." To improve living conditions, the board inspected housing and factories; ran an employment agency, municipal quarry, legal aid bureau, loan agency, and vacant lot gardening scheme; and supervised dance halls and "other forms of commercial recreation." This *"comprehensiveness,"* stressed Halbert, was the board's "most marked characteristic." Nothing it did was "not being done elsewhere by some social agency, but there is no other place, that I know of, where a government agency has so many lines of activity correlated under one authority." The collection of detailed sociological data, said Halbert, was the way to build a scientific basis for social action, which was the board's fourth principle. "All you need to correct many evils is to turn on the light. The process of recording data and analyzing them would do that."[18]

Halbert's exposition highlighted the principles of urban reorganization and welfare reform: centralization, efficiency, and science. His aggressive pride in the board pointed to a renewed faith in the capacity of urban governments, and his disdain for charity and thoroughgoing environmentalism show that the era of scientific charity had ended. His notion of science as data collection reflected the liberal faith in the power of facts to dissolve social conflicts with the inescapable force of objective truth. Neutral experts would not so much mediate as transcend class conflict by discovering social policy in a mass of empirical data. Although boards of public welfare usually failed to capture the citadel of urban data collection, in cities throughout the country municipal research bureaus—the first, in 1907, was New York City's—embodied the new gospel of social science. Only partly funded by city governments, they received generous support from business and foundations. In fact, business had expectations that Halbert did not mention. When the director of Philadelphia's Department of Public Welfare visited St. Louis, a friend told him, "We have no extreme Bolsheviks, and we have no extreme radicals in the City of St. Louis. . . . Because we have a department of public welfare here that has been functioning for the last ten years."[19]

In 1916, city boards of public welfare combined to form the National Public Welfare League, headquartered in Kansas City. Two years later, Halbert reported that "About fifty boards have been promoted by the National Public Welfare League in Kansas, Oklahoma, Colorado, and Nebraska." After the war, eastern cities, where private charity interests remained stronger, finally joined the trend. In the 1870s and 1880s, almost all charity workers and municipal reformers had condemned public relief; by 1915, most either welcomed it or, at least, accepted it grudgingly.[20]

In Philadelphia, to take one instance, when the business interests that long had dominated private charity proposed a Department of Public Welfare in 1919 as part of their attempt to reorganize the city's government, private social agencies did not object. Two major factors account for this new acceptance of public welfare by private social agencies. One was the enormous, intractable problem of poverty. Starting with the depression of 1893, private charity learned that it simply could not cope by itself with urban dependence. Neither its resources nor methods could do more than dent the problem. Even more, the distribution of relief distracted social workers from their primary role as counselors and therapists. Second, as social workers became more self-consciously professional, they argued that the source of funds mattered less than their management, and they redefined outdoor relief as a problem of administration rather than a matter of principle. With the poor subdivided into appropriate categories, public officials could hand out relief while private agencies concentrated on casework. Departments of public welfare, they realized, promised to relieve them of the most unpleasant and least professional part of their job.[21]

Although business could raise the fictive boundary between public and private to the level of sacred principle whenever it felt threatened, in practice its representatives moved between both spheres as they spearheaded the subordination of municipal government to the principles of centralization, efficiency, and science. Within the nominally private sphere, their major achievement was the financial federation, better known as the community chest. "Financial federation," writes Lubove, "captured the imagination of businessmen" because it promised "efficient coordination and organization of the community welfare machinery, immunity from multiple solicitation, economical collection and distribution of funds, and the development of a broad base of support which would relieve the pressure on the small circle of large givers." Executives and board members of large agencies had a much more "ambiguous" attitude. Although they "feared and resented a potential threat to autonomy," they also "welcomed liberation from the time-consuming, often frustrating, burdens of fund raising." In the end, the "allure of financial security outweighed the fear of centralized control."[22]

A number of cities—most notably Cleveland—started financial federations early in the twentieth century, but the movement languished until after World War I when, inspired by the success of the Red Cross and War Chests, civic leaders organized federations throughout the country. In most cities, Chambers of Commerce spearheaded the drive for federation. In 1914, there was only one community chest. By 1919, there were 12; by 1924, 180; and by 1929, 329. In the early 1930s, among the country's largest cities, only New York, Chicago, and Boston failed to organize one. Community chests developed most rapidly in the West and Midwest where cities lacked "charitable endowments." In the early 1930s, 61 percent of all American city dwellers lived in a city with a community chest, compared to less than half in New England and more than three-quarters in larger cities in the West, North Central, and Pacific states.

Despite their rhetoric, community chests excluded many private agencies: "reform and radical organizations, civic, labor and propaganda organizations, and cultural enterprises of a luxury nature—orchestras, art museums, and little theaters." Other agencies with "well developed sources of local support" also remained outside federations.[23]

Community chests succeeded, in part, because they drew on the skills and experience of a new group of experts: professional fundraisers, who, after World War I, helped change charity into philanthropy, stimulate large-scale corporate contributions, and broaden the base of giving outward from the wealthy to a cross-section of the social structure. Thus, chests did more than coordinate fund drives. They escalated the bureaucratization of private charity and hastened the redefinition of the volunteer from friendly visitor to fundraiser. Indeed, as they smudged the line between public and private, community chests hardened the newer and now more important distinction between volunteer and professional. Federation also reinforced the forces of convention and social order. With the authority to define legitimate charity, community chests solidified the distribution of power and resources within urban philanthropy. Because they depended heavily on corporate and other large contributions (in 1923, in Philadelphia, 440 contributors gave 46.4 percent of the total collected; in Buffalo, 385 gave 50.5 percent; in Nashville, 225 gave 53.0 percent), community chests tightened the links between wealth and philanthropy and effectively, if implicitly, restrained the individual agencies within the federation. They also heightened the financial difficulties of small, innovative, or dissident organizations by leaving them outside the bounds of respectability, where they have remained ever since.[24]

Three final observations about the relations between welfare and municipal reform: first, the expansion of relief, the creation of city welfare departments, and the organization of financial federations did not sharpen the boundary between public and private or insulate welfare and philanthropy from business influence. To the contrary, they signified the coordination of public welfare and private philanthropy under the watchful supervision of their corporate sponsors. Second, for the last time in American history municipal reformers did not want either state or federal aid. To the contrary, they wanted autonomy, because they assumed, incorrectly, that local governments had the resources and competence to solve their own problems. As the lessons of the Great Depression became clear in the 1930s, their illusion of self-sufficiency shattered forever. Third, a new corps of urban experts guided municipal reform and administered its results. Although they all led to a self-conscious professionalism, the paths followed by the major clusters of new urban experts emerged from different starting points and remained remarkably distinct. The first one began in the settlement houses.

Urban Experts

Settlements and the City Wilderness

In 1898, William I. Cole captured contemporary anxieties about cities with his opening sentence in *The City Wilderness*, a collection of essays by settlement workers attached to Boston's South End House. "Isolated and congested working-class quarters with all the dangers to moral and material well-being that they present," he wrote, "grow along with the growth of all our great cities." Isolation and congestion worried observers most: isolation because the estrangement of classes from each other broke the bonds of sympathy and understanding essential if cities were not to deteriorate into hostile, warring, resentful camps; congestion not only because overcrowding bred filth and disease but also because it destroyed the conditions of modesty, removed the veils from sexuality, and threw boys and girls, men and women, into inescapably dangerous proximity.[25]

Settlements, said Robert Woods, had been founded to reunite newly fragmented urban spaces and to tame the city wilderness. It could not be put "too decisively," said Woods, "that philanthropy, however well devised, is not their final end and aim. Their real use in the world is to reestablish on a natural basis those social relations which modern city life has thrown into confusion, and to develop such new forms of cooperative and public action as the changed situation may demand." How were settlements to reintegrate the city wilderness? Their goals spanned every facet of urban life from housing to politics, from culture to labor relations, from research to sanitation. Settlements were not exercises in social nostalgia. Their leaders accepted cities and appreciated the dynamism and energy of city life. At the same time, they were appalled at the estrangement between classes, the corruption, and the poverty they saw around them. Out of this ambivalence, they fashioned their distinctive mission into the city wilderness.[26]

Settlements originated in England in 1884 when an Anglican clergyman, Samuel Barnett, influenced by John Ruskin, William Morris, the Christian socialism of Charles Kingsley, and the example of Arnold Toynbee, founded Toynbee Hall in East London to "bridge the gulf that industrialism had created between rich and poor, to reduce the mutual suspicion and ignorance of one class for the other, and to do something more than give charity." By living in the poor neighborhoods of London, university men would "make their settlement in the slums an outpost of education and culture." Others followed Barnett; by

1911, forty-six settlements had been founded in Great Britain. Young, college-educated Americans visited the English settlements and came away inspired. At first, independently of each other they began to found settlements in American cities. The first was Stanton Coit, who moved to the Lower East Side of New York, where the settlement he started became the Neighborhood Guild and then the University Settlement. In 1889, Vidda Scudder and other young graduates from the leading women's colleges founded the first women's settlement, the College Settlement, also in New York. Another New York settlement, Henry Street, led by Lillian Wald, became a major source of social reform. The most famous of all was Hull House, Jane Addams's settlement on Halstead St. in Chicago. Never a mass movement, most settlements were in the Northeast and Midwest. By 1891, there were 6; by 1897, 74; in 1900, more than 100; and in 1910, more than 400.[27]

American settlements differed from their English counterparts in important ways. Although deeply influenced by social Christianity, they were nonsectarian; they had to deal with immigrants; and they quickly transformed Barnett's concern with personal redemption into a serious commitment to social reconstruction. Their focus on the environmental and political origins of social problems led to an emphasis on both research and activism. Everyone in the settlement houses, it sometimes seemed, was working on a book or an article. Indeed, one historian has called them "ad hoc graduate schools." Impressed by Charles Booth's *Life and Labours of the People of London*, American settlement workers began the meticulous empirical reconstruction of the ethnic, occupational, industrial, and housing patterns within city neighborhoods. In their books, such as *The City Wilderness* or *Hull House Maps and Papers*, are the theoretical, methodological, even personal origins of the Chicago school of urban sociology, which dominated American urban research for decades. Although settlement workers strongly supported environmental explanations of behavior, by no means did all of them shed the ethnic stereotypes of their age, and, even though they tried to assist blacks, few apparently discarded the racist assumptions that disfigured American life.[28]

Their activism set the settlement workers apart from the charity organization societies. In the 1870s, alarmed by the early stages of the same spatial and social fragmentation of cities that appalled the settlement workers, the advocates of scientific charity had parachuted Friendly Visitors into the slums to reestablish relations between classes and stem the tide of degeneration that threatened to overwhelm the poor. But Friendly Visitors were just that: visitors. They called on families, and then went home. By contrast, the "one indispensable requirement" of settlement work "was residence in a poor section of a great city." Charity organization defined the problem of the poor in personal terms. Friendly Visitors helped worthy families negotiate the maze of relief and social services

159

and learn to make do with what they had. By contrast, settlements started with no very clear theories and not much commitment to political or social reform. Indeed, at first, they emphasized culture and education. However, the depression of 1893, more than any single event, disabused them of any lingering idea that cultural uplift could improve the condition of the people among whom they lived and worked, and after 1893, settlements tried to attack the roots of dependence through a combination of educational, cultural, and political activity. At first, the settlement workers and charity organizers sniped at each other, and tensions between them erupted at conferences and in print. However, by the early twentieth century, younger charity organization staff often had attended the same schools, read the same literature, and realized that over three decades of experience with scientific charity had shown its utter inadequacy. Increasingly, then, they turned to the same reforms as the settlements. In 1905, two events symbolized the convergence of the two camps: the merging of the more or less official journals of charity organization and the settlement movement into one, *Charity and the Commons,* and the election of Jane Addams as president of the National Conference on Charities and Corrections.[29]

It would be wrong to give the settlement movement more unity than it had in the eyes of its participants. In 1898, a group of Chicago settlement workers who met to draft a statement of goals "gave up after several hours: all that the most important settlement workers could agree on was that the settlement ought to become a 'Social Center for Civic Cooperation' and a rallying point for reform in the city." Still, there were some remarkable demographic uniformities among settlement participants and they shared a wide range of common activities. Settlement residents were young: their median age was twenty-five. Most did not live very long in the settlement: the median tenure was 3 years. They were exceptionally well educated: over 90 percent had attended college and 50 percent graduate school. Mostly unmarried, they grew up in moderately well-off, old stock American families, in or near cities, although far from slums. Nearly half of them had moved directly from college to settlement.[30]

Settlements attracted the young college graduate partly because they recreated treasured aspects of collegiate life. Indeed, they resembled no other institution as much as a dormitory at a private college. In no other setting could these young people recapture the special combination of fellowship and stimulation of their undergraduate years. The settlements (like the new graduate schools created in the same years) also responded to the career crises that afflicted young men and women who came of age in late nineteenth century America. Although a host of factors, including the new courses in social ethics increasingly taught on college campuses, inspired some young men to reject a career in business or the conventional professions, they had no real alternative to the ministry, which itself more often became an untenable choice in a more secular age. Graduate school, an academic career, or a settlement house now offered welcome alternatives. Young women college graduates eager to apply their intelligence, education, and energy faced even bleaker prospects. Largely excluded from law, medicine, business, and the ministry, only schoolteaching, nursing, perhaps working in a library, or charity remained as occupations suitable for respectable young women. Settlements offered an exciting option: an unparalleled chance to work for worthwhile ends in the company of other educated, sympathetic women.[31]

Settlement houses were pragmatic. No master plan guided the development of their activities. They responded to the needs they saw around them, to the frustrations they experienced, and to what they learned about the politics of reform. Usually, they offered educational, cultural, and vocational activities. They taught English, sponsored art exhibits, fostered ethnic crafts, and tried to teach occupational and domestic skills. They opened day care facilities for working mothers and tried to improve local public schools. As they learned more about the forces that shaped their neighborhoods, settlement leaders pressed for municipal reform, sometimes working for a single issue, such as a neighborhood public bath or better garbage pick-up. On occasion, (usually unsuccessfully) they tried to unseat machine politicians. They battled for statewide tenement house reform, child labor laws, regulations governing the working conditions of women, factory inspection, and women's suffrage. Although their record on strikes was uneven, they usually supported labor unions in principle and tried to mediate disputes between capital and labor.

Usually, their direct victories were local: a cleaner neighborhood, expanded community services in a local public school, a seat on a school board, or appointment to a civic office. More often, they helped individuals by teaching them English, caring for their children, or responding to the myriad crises of daily life, even, on occasion, delivering a baby. Still, settlements never attracted the majority of neighborhood residents to their activities; they did not end corruption in any city; they did not achieve any very great improvements in housing, schools, or working conditions. More than most reformers, settlement residents wanted to extend the limits of public responsibility. Some were socialists; most favored increased municipal and state action. But when they bumped up against the structure of urban politics, the interests of capital, or the ideological boundaries of privatism, they were, after all, only a small, powerless, and loosely organized band of young college graduates.[32]

It would be wrong to dismiss the efforts of settlements to tame the city wilderness because their concrete achievements seem so modest. As one reviewer of *Hull House Maps and Papers* wrote, "it has never been claimed that the settlements could provide the final solution to any problem. It has only been hoped that, by gaining knowledge at first hand, they might enable men to see

161

more clearly, to bring about a better understanding between each class and every other." Jane Addams's prominence illustrates the settlements' visibility and the broad, national support they elicited. In every early twentieth century public opinion poll before World War I, Jane Addams ranked as the most admired American woman, often as the most admired American. For people across the country, she embodied the transcendence of stale political divisions, the reconciliation of social divisions, the active service in the public interest central to the ideals of grass-roots progressivism.[33]

Settlements did more than reassure middle-class Americans that somebody was trying to recreate the country they had lost. For settlements, as others have said, had their greatest impact on the stream of young men and women who passed through them. Think only of some of the most famous: Julia Lathrop, first chief of the U.S. Children's Bureau; Grace Abbott, her successor; Edith Abbott, founding dean of the University of Chicago School of Social Service Administration; Florence Kelley, long head of the National Consumers' League; John Dewey; Gerard Swope, future president of General Electric and pioneer in welfare capitalism; Frances Perkins, secretary of labor in the New Deal; Harry Hopkins, architect of the federal relief program; and many, many others who went on to careers in politics, research, public service, teaching, and the professions.

The settlement movement and progressivism both reached the pinnacle of their power at the same moment. In 1912, settlement leaders drafted the proposals for social legislation that Theodore Roosevelt incorporated, almost unchanged, into the platform of his Progressive party. When Jane Addams seconded his nomination, she received an ovation as loud as the candidate's. Still, the strains that would enervate the reform energies of progressivism and the settlement movement shadowed the convention, even at its high point. Jane Addams and her colleagues decided to swallow their liberal convictions and accepted the convention's refusal to seat black delegates, and they set aside their pacifism when they failed to protest the platform's calls for rearmament. Within a few years, it was clear that the forces they had hoped would fade away—racism and militarism—proved more popular, powerful, and enduring than the limited vision of social justice on which they had campaigned.[34]

When Jane Addams failed to compromise her antimilitarism by supporting World War I, she swiftly lost her national popularity. By the 1920s, she was, to many, a dangerous radical, as were other settlement leaders who resisted immigration restriction, criticized the harsh terms imposed on Germany, and refused to abandon their commitment to social causes. "Enthusiasm for social reform," writes Chambers, "was squelched by the 'paralyzing fear' that the Bolshevik Revolution had created throughout the Western World." Even proposed reforms that had seemed "praiseworthy before the war," said Jane Addams, were "suspect," and "social workers ... with a protective instinct carefully avoided any identification with the phraseology of social reform." (In 1928, I. M. Rubinow, executive director of the Jewish Welfare League of Philadelphia and one of the nation's leading social insurance advocates, submitted to *The Survey* an article pointing out the inadequacy of private charity and urging expanded government responsibility. The managing editor of the journal, Arthur Kellogg, after consultation with representatives of private charity and correspondence with Rubinow that extended nearly a year, rejected the essay.) As young men and women found careers more easily in expanding universities, public bureaucracies, and new professions, they no longer needed the moratorium, companionship, and alternative that settlements offered. With its most committed leadership discredited, its major source of idealistic recruits dried up, and its favorite causes suspect, the settlement movement exchanged social passion for professionalism. As living in the neighborhood she served no longer seemed very important, the settlement resident became just another social worker and the settlement house a community center. In 1932, even Jane Addams voted for Herbert Hoover.[35]

Paths to Professionalization

Poverty never has been an exclusively urban problem. The depleted soil on early nineteenth century New England farms, the dust bowls of the Southwest, the hidden misery of Appalachian hamlets rediscovered in the early 1960s by Michael Harrington: all testify to the hard, grinding poverty obscured by romantic myths of rural abundance. Nonetheless, because urban poverty has been more visible, and more threatening, most organized efforts to soften the effects of poverty have focused primarily on towns and cities. With no special training, distinctive skills, or proven tactics, the early fighters in America's periodic wars on the consequences of urban poverty soon learned that enthusiasm and outrage by themselves were not very powerful weapons. Battle-scarred, more experienced, they realized that a poverty war was not a fight for amateurs, and by the late nineteenth century they had begun to unite in new associations, publish their own journals, define special skills, organize training programs, and regulate entry into their ranks. With mixed success, these early urban experts tried to turn charity, relief, and reform into new professions.

The new urban experts worked in a wide variety of occupations whose practitioners confronted urban dependence every day: for instance, physicians, nurses, psychiatrists, and school superintendents. Three groups, however, specialized in one or another aspect of social welfare: social workers, public welfare officials, and professional reformers. Despite their mutual concern with many of the same problems, although some people moved from one group to another, each followed a different path toward professional status.[36]

Social Workers. Social workers descended from the paid agents and volunteer friendly visitors of charity organization societies. Although in the ideal charity organization society paid agents investigated cases and volunteer friendly visitors counseled them, no city managed to match the model with practice, and, by the late nineteenth century, with volunteer friendly visitors in short supply nearly everywhere, agents had to carry out both tasks. By and large, agents lacked any formal training for their work. In fact, with only a primitive body of theory and no history of experience with scientific charity, there was very little they could have been taught. By the end of the century, however, charity organization leaders could transmit almost three decades of codified practical experience, and the first generation of professional social scientists could lecture about the causes and consequences of poverty and other forms of dependence. Concerned about the quality of untrained agents' work, armed with the material for a curriculum, charity organization leaders began to create special schools. In 1898, the New York Charity Organization Society first opened its Summer School of Philanthropy, which expanded to a full academic year in the fall, 1903. Soon afterward similar schools opened in Boston, Baltimore, Philadelphia, Chicago, and St. Louis.[37]

In the same years, charity workers formed their first national associations. The first major professional association, the National Conference of Charities and Corrections (NCCC), emerged in 1879 from the Conference of Boards of Public Charities, which, itself, had started as part of the American Social Science Association, organized by the Massachusetts State Board of Charities, in 1865. Officially, the NCCC united representatives of state boards, local public welfare officials, and private agencies. In practice, the private agencies, especially the charity organization societies, dominated the conference, which became the major voice of private social welfare. (In 1917 it changed its name to the National Conference of Social Work and in 1956 to the National Conference on Social Welfare.) Even more narrowly professional in its focus was the American Association of Social Workers, formed in 1921 from the National Social Workers' Exchange, a professional placement organization with its own journal, *Compass*.[38]

In its drive toward professional standing, social work faced two major problems. One was defining exactly what it did. What special skills earned social workers the badge of professional authority? The other was redefining the role of volunteers. Although volunteers could not be allowed to exercise the special skill that defined social work, their financial support and their mobilization of public opinion remained critical. How could they be exploited but contained? By the 1920s, social work leaders had solved both problems. In the process, they narrowed their role and bureaucratized their occupation.[39]

At their best, charity organization agents had mediated between their clients and the sources of help available in every city. They interceded with churches, relief agencies, and relatives. They accompanied clients to doctors, hospitals, and courts. They helped them find housing and jobs. In short, they became experts on urban survival. Not part of the original theory of charity organization, or a role discussed very much by its leaders, mediation or urban survival strategy also was not an expert skill that led toward professional standing, as understood in late nineteenth and early twentieth century America. It lacked any scientific basis; it required no theoretical training. Common sense, experience, and a working knowledge of a city's resources might be useful, but they did not constitute the basis of a profession. Nor did a second direction that social work might have followed, namely, social reform. The incipient integration of charity organization with the settlement movement might have moved the whole occupation leftward, away from a preoccupation with individual causes of dependence and toward their structural origins. For a moment, this is what seemed to be happening in 1912 as reform enthusiasm peaked in Theodore Roosevelt's Bull Moose presidential campaign.[40]

Ultimately, social work followed neither urban mediation nor social activism as its path to professional standing. Indeed, by the second decade of the twentieth century, a third possibility—casework—became the "nuclear skill" on which social work rested its claim to expert authority. Casework followed much more directly than mediation from the theory of charity organization, for the caseworker was a trained, professional friendly visitor. Equally important, the first social work specialties to develop in the early twentieth century—medical social work, school social work, and psychiatric social work—pushed casework to the forefront of the occupation. Attached as caseworkers to hospitals, schools, and new psychiatric clinics, social workers could claim a unique capacity to meet needs generated by recent developments in medicine, education, and psychiatry. In *Social Diagnosis* (1917) and *What is Case Work?* (1922). Mary Richmond developed the first major theoretical statement of social work's new direction. Casework, she wrote, consisted of *"those processes which develop personality through adjustments consciously effected, individual by individual, between men and their social environment.''* Unlike friendly visiting, casework was an impersonal, professional skill. "The friendly visitor's personality," writes Lubove, "had been the essence of her contribution. She had been dispatched not as an expert in investigation or the handling of relief, but as the representative of a middle class." In sharp contrast, one social work authority wrote in 1922, "we believe the best results come from teaching the patient to look upon the social agency or the hospital as the source of help and direction, medical and social. . . . We have found the point of view to be of more importance than the personality of the worker." As the impersonal caseworker replaced the friendly visitor, social workers joined other contemporary experts who tried to teach people to adjust to their environment, not to change it.[41]

In the 1920s, Freudian psychology moved casework away from Richmond's concern with environment and toward a focus on personality. With Freudian psychology, social work could bypass the new social and economic theories that had undercut scientific charity and return with scientific authority to individual explanations for dependence; it needed only to substitute personality for character and to add sex to drink. Needless to say, any passion for social reform vanished in the process.[42]

Social work solved the problem of the volunteer through bureaucratization. Social agencies grew enormously in the early decades of the twentieth century. As they developed internal hierarchies and formal operating procedures, their administrators made efficiency their operational goal and tried to adopt the best managerial practices of modern business. Within newly formal structures, volunteers could be assigned appropriate, marginal roles, and their major task became service on the boards of directors that governed social agencies. What agency directors wanted from them, of course, was help with raising money and interpreting agency goals to the public. The agencies' real work—casework, program development, administration—was done by paid professionals.[43]

Still, one major problem remained: the discrepancy between the theory and practice of social work. With large caseloads, social workers could not practice social diagnosis or therapy, and, even if they had the time, most of them still lacked the training. For there were far too few trained social workers to fill existing jobs. Indeed, even the American Association of Social Workers (AASW) had to create a category of junior membership that did not require formal training or else exclude the great bulk of social workers from its ranks. In 1916, one survey in New York City found 3,968 social workers in 368 organizations; 1,111 were men and 2,857 women. Only 34 percent of the women and 60 percent of the men had graduated from college and a mere 162 had any training in a school of social work. Other surveys usually found similar patterns.[44]

Social work never managed to limit entry as successfully as other occupations. Nor has it successfully established its claim to professional standing. One reason is that it chose the wrong alternative. As social workers rejected urban mediation and abandoned social reform, they became second-class therapists, inferior in standing, if not in competence, to psychologists and psychiatrists. No other group, Lubove points out, picked up the task that social work abandoned early in the twentieth century. None claimed a "generalized mandate" to integrate individuals, institutions, and groups; to help individuals negotiate their way through the thickening maze of social services and bureaucracies; or to stimulate "social legislation." As social work abandoned these "indispensable functions," it "created a vacuum which remains unfilled." With some irony,

166

social workers did not in fact become either therapists or professionals. Instead, they became badly paid servants of bureaucracies and the state.[45]

Public Welfare Officials.   Although private charity workers thought that public welfare officials were corrupt, shadowy, and incompetent, doling out too much outdoor relief, and running miserable poorhouses, nonetheless, there was at least as much activity in the public sector as in the private sector. In the late nineteenth and early twentieth century, state governments not only built new institutions but increased their supervisory authority over private agencies and facilities, and local officials continued to distribute outdoor relief and operate poorhouses. Although their tasks did not change very much, their responsibilities increased because both poorhouse populations and the number of people asking for outdoor relief rose. In fact, in most towns and cities local public officials cared for more dependent people than private charity.[46]

As the complaints of New York's county superintendents of the poor made clear, local poor relief officials found themselves buffeted by powerful forces. The state government threatened their authority, took away some of their responsibilities, and demanded more and more paperwork; private charities criticized the way they ran their institutions, castigated them in public, and judged them by impossibly high standards. As elected officials, they were trapped between county boards of supervisors who wanted to keep expenses as low as possible, constituents who wanted more relief for their friends and relatives, and reformers who attacked their competence and integrity. The superintendents' first defense was democracy. In contrast to power-hungry, meddlesome experts, they pictured themselves elected champions of the people, resisting encroaching state power. In 1906, one county superintendent wrote that he and his colleagues

> constitute the chief bulwark of the people against the ever-increasing concentration of local administrative details in the hands of the different Boards and Commissions at Albany. . . . Particularly in the operations of charity is the trend towards vesting administrative details in the hands of distant Boards, who are only familiar with the clerical and academic aspects of the business and who are out of touch and sympathy with the individuals requiring relief.[47]

Nonetheless, in an age of experts, democracy proved a fragile and not very convincing defense. In fact, with neither special skills nor training, local superintendents had only one alternative: to build a strong organization and control its membership. In its early years, the county superintendents' conventions had been loose affairs. Anyone interested in the issues could come, speak, and even vote. Sometimes, representatives from private agencies and the state dominated the agenda. In 1904, the superintendents officially recognized the problem by renaming their organization The Association of County Superintendents of the Poor and restricting voting rights to county superintendents. The next year, the association appointed a full-time secretary; the year after that it created a committee on finance. The secretary, C. E. Weisz, spoke for the superintendents' interests when he reflected, "Not many years ago the rights of members were fully usurped by private associations. . . . I want to retain the identity of this organization which has withstood all storms in attempts to absorb it by private organizations who may . . . have been seeking glory at our expense."[48]

Increased control of their own organization did not stimulate the superintendents to more profound or thoughtful debate. They avoided abstract, theoretical questions and focused instead on concrete administrative details, such as forestry and county farm administration. When possible, they avoided sessions altogether and used the conventions as a time for picnics and trips to the beach. In 1911, at Weisz's urging, they began to hold a midwinter conference, too, to lobby the state legislature about their concerns. Not immune to the associations that clung to their name, they signaled their heightened professional aspirations by changing the title of their association to the New York State Association of Public Welfare Officials. By 1913, they even identified strongly enough as professionals not to object very much to the periodic proposals to make their office appointive and cover it with civil service regulations. Like so many others, in bureaucracy they found strength and security.[49]

Public relief officials took nearly a decade longer than private social workers to form a national organization. Around the country, the same circumstances as in New York retarded professionalization. As elected officials with no special training or expert knowledge, they needed more time to develop the collegial ties, the sense of occupational identity, and the organizational energy essential for a drive toward professional status. In fact, only the Great Depression finally pushed them into national organization. Faced suddenly with vastly expanded demands for relief, their funds depleted, unable to cope administratively with the emergency around them, in 1930 they formed the American Association of Public Welfare Officials and lobbied for federal relief. In 1933, when Harry Hopkins ordered that only public employees could dispense federal funds, public welfare officials suddenly assumed unprecedented importance. Indeed, the few years during which they served as field officers for the federal government's brief—and unrepeated—foray into general relief have remained the high point in their history. When the dust settled, they reverted, after all, to state and local bureaucrats handing out welfare, eclipsed by the private social workers who adjusted personalities and dispensed services, not money. Tainted by their association with both their clients and public assistance, public welfare officials are still second-class citizens within the field of social work.[50]

Professional Reformers. Professional reformers traveled a different path to professionalization than either social workers or public welfare officials. For many of them, the route led first from college to a settlement house. After the settlement house, these newly minted experts usually worked for national reform organizations, government regulatory agencies, or foundations. Often, they moved in and out of public service, although usually they remained closely identified with a particular interest or cluster of concerns. In fact, by nurturing these urban experts, by teaching them the techniques of social investigation, by giving them the best available education in urban studies, settlement houses made their most profound impact on the development of the social welfare professions, public policy, and, even, social structure. For the settlements became an important crucible for the formation of the aggressive "new middle class" of experts that tried to transform virtually every facet of American life.[51]

Consider some examples: Julia Lathrop, a Vassar graduate, moved from Hull House, membership on the Illinois Board of Public Charities, and the presidency of Chicago's Juvenile Court Committee to become the first director of the U.S. Children's Bureau. Grace Abbott also went from college to Hull House; from there to the Immigrant Protective League; and, finally, to the Children's Bureau, where she assisted and then succeeded Lathrop. Edith Abbott, who lived at Hull House, helped Graham Taylor run his independent social work school in Chicago. When Taylor was absent on a trip, she and Sophonisba Breckenridge engineered the merger of the school with the University of Chicago, which Taylor had opposed, and became its first dean. With a clear commitment to scholarship and social action, she resisted the translation of social work into casework, even though it meant losing her Russell Sage Foundation funding. Florence Kelley became a factory inspector for Illinois while she lived at Hull House. She then moved to New York, where she lived at the Henry Street Settlement, ran the Consumers' League, and lobbied tirelessly against child labor. Harry Hopkins lived for a while at a settlement before he worked for the New York Association for Improving the Condition of the Poor. For a time, he directed the National Tuberculosis Association and, in the depression, headed Franklin D. Roosevelt's pioneer relief effort in New York State. From there he accompanied FDR to the White House, where he organized and directed the first federal relief program.[52]

The multiplication of these examples would only underscore the central point: the emergence of a group of expert reformers at home in both public and private service. Several observations about these new experts are important. First, they kept alive the reform tradition that social work abandoned. Their agitation made child labor, tenement house reform, and public health, to name three key areas, national causes. Second, they played an influential part in the women's movement. Professional reform proved one of the few areas where women could carve out independent careers, and women reformers helped lead the drive for women's suffrage that culminated in the nineteenth amendment. Together, they formed a national women reformers' network that, little more than a decade later, played a vital role in the New Deal. Third, they bridged the distance between universities and public policy. Coupling zeal with technical competence and a passion for hard data, they brought the new methods of social science to bear on public issues. Fourth, they helped replace the predominantly local basis of American social organization with national institutions linked together by new networks of professional associations, large voluntary agencies, and giant corporations.[53]

Because they were so articulate and intelligent, it is easy to overestimate the influence of the new urban experts and to forget they faced implacable constraints that blunted their impact. One set was political; child-labor reformers, to take one example, worked hard to persuade Congress to pass child labor legislation, which the Supreme Court found unconstitutional in fairly short order. Other constraints were financial. Professional experts depended on funding, usually from private sources, and, after their creation, the great foundations. Most important was the Russell Sage Foundation, chartered in 1907 to spend its income on "the improvement of the social and living conditions in the United States of America." In practice, the bulk of the foundation's support "took the form of long term grants or subsidies" to organizations and activities dear to its affluent board members. These, of course, were hardly coterminous with reformers' agenda, and reformers seeking funds had to tread delicately, careful not to offend the foundation's officers and wealthy, conservative board.[54]

World War I gave the new reformer-experts their first great opportunity. By increasing the "scope of governmental activity," it opened "new sources of support and a new arena in which to campaign." It also transformed some of their interests, such as Americanization, into "burning questions of public policy." Nonetheless, the war and its aftermath only underlined the impotence of reformer-experts before the forces of political and economic power. None of their plans for orderly, phased demobilization or a relatively humane, unaggressive approach to Americanization, for instance, made any dent on public policy, and, in the Red Scare, even the experts found their loyalty questioned. The infamous Lusk Committee in New York, to take one example, attacked reformer-experts and social workers as "apologetic" and "without any actual convictions with respect to the value of American ideals and institutions." It comes, then, as no surprise to learn that for the most part reformer-experts traded their commitment to social reform for accommodation. Many of them "all too faithfully mirrored both the concerns and the tactics of the politicians. This was true even in cases where accommodation to the prevailing political pressures" vitiated "expert programs." Experts had learned the price of bureaucratic survival.[55]

Like social workers, urban reformer-experts developed a "nuclear skill": in their case, the social survey. Always, "their first recommendation, no matter what the issue, was . . . the collection of information." The facts, they assumed, would speak for themselves. But facts, as C. Wright Mills pointed out, piled one on top of another with no theory or viewpoint, paralyze reform and only reinforce the status quo. In the end, the reformers' path to professionalism tied the management of social change to the development of their own careers. Along with university-based social scientists, who had faced similar career problems a few decades earlier, they made the trip from "advocacy to objectivity" by resting the case for their authority and importance on the capacity of neutral experts to find technical solutions to complex problems. Somehow, those neutral technical solutions usually supported whomever it was that paid the bill.[56]

The Limits of Urban Reform:
New York's Tenements and Chicago's Ghetto

Early in the twentieth century, housing reform finally emerged as an important national urban campaign. Because it enlisted every variety of urban expert, housing reform, even though it failed, illustrates both the style and limits of urban reform. Like health care delivery, housing reform bumped up against the boundaries between public responsibility and private prerogative; neither state legislatures, municipal governments, nor the activists who organized the national housing reform movement were willing to enter directly into the housing market. With only regulation and inspection as tools, housing reformers could not assure an adequate supply of low-cost housing to the urban poor or renovate the slums. Indeed, housing reformers, including major settlement house leaders, not only capitulated before the market; they shared the racism of their times. As a consequence, they not only failed to eradicate the slum; they helped build the ghetto.

New York City, which had the worst housing problem in the country, housed its poor primarily in tenements.[57] In other cities, where land was cheaper and population less congested, more of the poor still lived in small frame houses. Though often flimsy, crowded, and unsanitary, these houses were considered distinctly better than the tenements into which perhaps half of New York's population had been packed. Even though New York's housing problems were unique, the story of tenement house reform there is instructive. New Yorkers took the initial active interest in housing reform in America. They gave intellectual definition to the movement and sponsored a national campaign, headquartered in the city and led by Lawrence Veiller, the most important housing reformer in the country. New Yorkers also pioneered the strategies of housing reform adopted by other cities—model tenements and restrictive legislation—until the New Deal. Its practical influence, therefore, was very great. The reasons New York's housing reform failed, however, were not indigenous to the city. To the contrary, with special clarity, they showed how the contradictions between public responsibility and privatism played themselves out in the attempt to renovate the slums, guide the development of the city, and improve workers' housing.[58]

As in New York, revelations of Chicago's appalling housing conditions stimulated a housing reform movement. Two of its features are especially noteworthy. First, none of the discussions of housing problems mentioned living conditions among the city's black population, whose housing, by and large, was the worst in the city. Indeed, only the race riot of 1919 aroused any interest in black housing. Second, in Chicago, housing reform adopted the same tactics as in New York: a reliance on model housing and restrictive legislation.

New York had a serious housing problem as early as the 1840s when Irish immigrants crowded into the sections of Manhattan near the docks where they worked. Landlords subdivided houses and built tall new tenements wherever they chose, for the city had no regulations governing housing or land use. Appalled by the conditions it discovered, the Association for Improving the Condition of the Poor, the first organization to respond to the city's housing problem, constructed a model tenement in the 1850s. Because model tenements were supposed to demonstrate how decent working-class housing could be built and run at a profit, they represented, as Lubove points out, "less a solution to the housing problem than an evasion." Although in New York and elsewhere model tenements remained a favorite reform strategy throughout the nineteenth century, they never even dented urban housing problems. For one thing, the scale of the experiments was too small. For another, they never provided houses inexpensive enough for the very poorest people who needed help most. It simply remained impossible to construct housing that was cheap, decent, and profitable. Profit remained critical because model housing definitely was not a philanthropy. Rather, it was supposed to show how to improve the living conditions of the poor and still make money. It was, of course, an illusion.[59]

In 1879, an amendment to New York City's weak 1867 Tenement House Act permitted construction of the notoriously wretched dumbbell tenements which housed most of New York City's poor for the rest of the century. Within these six-story tenements crammed onto tiny lots, two dozen families crowded into small four-room apartments with a living room and kitchen, each about 10×11 feet and two bedrooms, perhaps 7×8, hardly more than closets. Only the living room had any direct light from the street. On each floor, two families usually shared each toilet, which was located in the hall, lighted and ventilated by the "air shaft."[60]

Housing reform drew its energy from the threat of moral collapse and social disorder. Although housing reformers had mixed moralism and fear with compassion since the 1840s, by the 1890s, their fears had escalated. Manhattan, after all, had become the most congested place in the world. Reformers observed with horror the growth of prostitution in the tenements; they had no idea how families could survive amid the dirt, smell, noise, and crowding in the slums. Nor did they forget the way the poor had exploded in the great draft riots of 1863. Jacob Riis warned, "the sea of a mighty population, held in galling fetters, heaves uneasily in the tenements." After 1890, housing reformers capitalized on the sentiment aroused by the publication of Jacob Riis's *How the Other Half Lives* to orchestrate a national housing reform movement, led by Lawrence Veiller, secretary of the COS Tenement House Committee. They also persuaded the state to appoint still another housing commission and to pass another weak tenement law.[61]

In 1900, Veiller's agitation culminated in a masterful tenement house exhibition, complete with models of tenement blocks and maps showing the correlation between high rates of disease, mortality, and bad housing. Within a year, the state had appointed yet another commission, this time with Veiller as its secretary. Its recommendations, most of which became law, outlawed the dumbbell tenement, created a municipal housing department with a staff of inspectors, and developed regulations designed to improve new buildings and encourage the renovation of old ones. Without doubt, the new law tenements were an improvement on the old dumbbells, and within two decades, many tenements had been "swept, garnished, and repaired," according to Edith Elmer Wood, a "well-informed student of housing." Although not all tenements were "immaculate," she found no "accumulations of filth," "no dilapidation or extreme disrepair." Still, the newest and best tenements remained too expensive for the very poor, who still crowded into old, unsatisfactory buildings, and no one argued that New York's working class was housed very well. By and large, New York's tenements were less dangerous, unsanitary, and unhealthful, but the great problems—how to prevent the housing situation from deteriorating again under the impact of population growth, how to assure working people housing they found satisfactory at a price they could afford, and how to provide minimally decent housing for the poor—still had not been solved.[62]

The businessmen and reformers who formed the City Homes Association in 1900, the first Chicago organization to focus on housing reform, brought in one of Veiller's closest associates, Charles Ball, to run their operation, and, in 1907, they managed to secure his appointment as head of the city's Sanitary

Bureau, which he ran for the next 21 years. Although almost no model housing was built before 1920, in 1902 and 1910, the association persuaded the city council to pass tenement ordinances, which were the counterparts of the New York Tenement Act of 1901. The ordinances set out sanitary standards and building codes, which depended for enforcement on inspection. In practice, inspection proved a weak reform tool. Not only were there too few inspectors, but the system invited graft. According to Philpott, City Council members passed the 1901 ordinance so readily because they realized it was a "four-flush law," that is, "one which politicians passed for the purpose of soliciting graft in return for *not* enforcing it." The association also sponsored the Municipal Lodging House for homeless men—excluding blacks, who were not allowed to stay there—and the development of city parks and playgrounds, created by displacing thousands of poor people and leveling their homes. Neither the members of the association nor the settlement workers who supported their project showed any sympathy for the "protests of the uprooted families."[63]

In both Chicago and New York City the problem of housing for the poor remained unsolved partly because Veiller and most other influential Progressive era housing reformers refused to extend the role of government beyond restrictive legislation. Although Veiller seemed radical and dangerous to real estate and construction interests, he remained fundamentally conservative. Veiller believed that America's urban housing crisis could be solved—though not quickly— within the context of the market, and he rejected public housing on both economic and political grounds. Model municipal tenements, he argued, could never house more than a tiny fraction of the working class. Even more, public construction actually would curtail housing supply by discouraging private builders unwilling to compete with the government. Nor could government's involvement be contained. There would be no "limit to the scope of municipal building operations if once they were begun. If cities . . . are to become landlords at all, where should the wage line be drawn between those for whom they should and . . . should not provide? Where in practice, would the line be drawn in American cities where democracy reigns supreme, and the limit of public bounty would be ultimately fixed by popular vote?" Public housing would become another form of outdoor relief, demanded by everybody, generously doled out by politicians anxious to curry favor and build strong machines.[64]

For Veiller, the wretched housing that disfigured the lives of half the people who lived in New York had two great sources: greed and neglect. Regulation and inspection, he felt, could check both. Without destroying economic incentives by curtailing profits, they would insure that builders and landlords supplied the working class with safe, clean, sanitary housing. Willing to stretch, although not to cross, the fictive boundary between public responsibility and private prerogative, Veiller advocated an individual solution to a massive social problem.

Government would not build, buy, or subsidize housing. Instead, it would control the behavior of individual builders and landlords. It would prevent them from doing harm (if it could), but how could it force them to do good? This is the question Veiller did not answer.[65]

Nor did any of the other serious approaches to the housing problem cross the boundary between public and private. Some reformers, appalled especially by congestion and crowding, advocated the garden city solution popularized in England by Ebenezer Howard, who wanted to uproot the working class from cities and move them into planned new towns in the countryside. But no garden cities were built in America. More important was zoning (developed first in Germany), which united housing reformers and the new city planning profession early in the twentieth century. Planners and reformers hoped "zoning would improve urban housing and living conditions by controlling population distribution." Businessmen often supported it because they felt it would "protect their financial interests." In New York City, a coalition of reformers and businessmen passed "America's first comprehensive zoning code" in 1916, but it suffered the same inherent weakness as housing reform: it was a negative policy that "could not clear slums," house the poor, or "establish criteria for satisfactory residential development."[66]

Not only builders and landlords objected to housing reform by regulation and inspection. By World War I, younger reformers familiar with European housing legislation and anxious to push state and local governments to positive, constructive action also attacked the restrictive or "negative" approach. However, until the New Deal, they had no chance to try their alternatives. In retrospect, the sorry history of public housing since then hardly makes them seem more prescient than Veiller and his colleagues. If Veiller could not recognize the contradictions between quality, cost, and profit, his critics could not foresee how the degradation of public responsibility in America would rob public housing of its potential and leave it just another form of welfare.[67]

Progressive era housing reformers not only failed to improve housing for the poor; they also helped build the ghetto. "The period between 1870 and 1915," claims Kenneth Kusmer, "may be called the formative years of the black ghetto in the United States." In these years, Southern blacks, attracted by industrial opportunity, began to drift into Northern cities. Although few "clear cut" ghettos appeared, the degree of residential segregation increased as the racism of the period, industrial relocation, and inexpensive mass transit reshaped American cities.[68]

In Chicago, before World War I, existing black neighborhoods accommodated the small but growing black population, which increased from 34,691 in 1870 to 44,103 by 1910. In each of the next two decades, the black population more than doubled; in 1920 it was 109,458 and in 1930, 233,803. After World

War I, Chicago faced a housing crisis as the city's population growth exceeded its housing supply, and where the growing black population threatened to move into adjacent white neighborhoods, racial tensions flared. Whites used two tactics to prevent blacks from crossing the color line. One was violence: they beat blacks who moved into their neighborhoods and bombed their homes. Nor were the police any protection in racial clashes, because they usually sided with whites. The other tactic was forced exclusion, accomplished either through deed restrictions or racial covenants. The former, "covering a single parcel or a whole subdivision, was common" early in the century; racial covenants by which residents formally agreed not to sell their property to blacks became widespread in the 1920s.[69]

The history of Chicago's blacks, and of blacks in every other city, did not recapitulate the experience of European immigrants. No immigrant group ever lived in neighborhoods as segregated as the black ghetto. With each decade, as they left the center of cities for new homes in the suburbs, European immigrants and their children lived in less segregated surroundings. By contrast, black segregation, higher from the start, continued to increase. European immigrants were allowed, indeed encouraged, to move out of ethnic enclaves; blacks were prevented from leaving the ghetto. Even though blacks often lived closer to industrial jobs than European immigrants, they held far fewer of them, because racial discrimination concentrated them in unskilled and domestic work. In every way, blacks should have been more mobile than European immigrants. Their early migration to cities coincided with industrial expansion; they came in "moderate numbers"; they were Protestant and spoke English; they were eager for work. But they confronted racism and laws that deprived them of their civil rights. An 1853 Illinois law, abandoned only slowly, legally forbade them from entering the state. They could not vote until 1870. Schools were segregated legally until 1874. Most of all, they were relegated to menial "nigger jobs," paid badly, and often laid off. Even when they wanted to buy housing within the Black Belt, they faced special problems because banks demanded a larger down payment and charged them a higher interest rate. Indeed, their carrying charges were so high they found it "impossible to keep up repairs." Moreover, white landlords "were lax about upkeep," and the city "neglected all poor areas and all districts with Negro residents, poor or otherwise. So deterioration in Negro-occupied property continued. . . . The Black Belt was a ghetto-slum and there was no way out of it."[70]

In the summer of 1919, a terrible race riot erupted when white youths attacked and drowned a black youngster who swam across a generally acknowledged color line that divided a section of Lake Michigan. In the week-long riot that followed, 38 people were killed; 537 injured; and about 1,000 left homeless. As one way to ease the tensions that had led to racial violence, the Chicago

Commission on Race Relations, created to study the riots, urged the city to improve its "housing problem by 'constructive means,' " by which it meant restrictive legislation, zoning, model homes, and, especially, "better Negro housing." Although the commission did not recommend segregation, in practice its report called for housing reform based on two principles: "the business creed and the color line."[71]

Throughout the 1920s, Chicago's housing reformers and settlement workers—often, of course, the same people—did nothing to discourage segregation. In fact, they often reinforced it. Leading settlement workers had been active in all aspects of housing reform; they had served on the Riot Commission; they had advised leading philanthropists and other civic leaders about housing problems. With their base in immigrant neighborhoods, staffed by well-educated residents with serious research interests, closely connected with the University of Chicago, their experience and data made them the leading authorities on the city's social conditions. There were, of course, shades of difference in their points of view. Jane Addams, Edith Abbott, Sophonisba Breckenridge, and Florence Kelley led the left wing of the settlement movement. They understood how blacks had been exploited and denied opportunity. Nonetheless, when it came to practical policies, no differences separated them from their more openly racist colleagues in the settlement movement. The more liberal settlement leaders advocated economic and political equality, but not social equality; worked to improve black living conditions within the ghetto; and accepted segregation either as inescapable or desirable. All of them refused to integrate their settlement houses. Even when the racial composition of their neighborhoods changed, most settlements remained white islands, and the handful of settlements opened to serve blacks were "always few, always separate, and always unequal."[72]

By 1930, what did Chicago's housing reformers and settlement workers have to show for fifty years of hard work? Chicago had over seventy settlements and boys' clubs almost all for whites only. Private developers had built three segregated, model projects that were too expensive for most of the families who lived in tenements. The city had passed tenement ordinances that it could not enforce because most families were too poor to pay the rent on houses which met the minimum standards. The advent of the automobile had begun to eliminate "the filthy stables and dreadful manure heaps," but, "For all their effort, housing reformers and neighborhood workers had not been able to unmake the slum, and they had helped to make the ghetto." Reform by regulation and model housing worked no better in Chicago than in New York. Mixed with racism, the limitation of public responsibility by the profit motive proved lethal to every attempt to build decent, low-cost housing. And so it has remained ever since.[73]

Housing reform stands as a metaphor for the reorganization of cities in the early twentieth century. Although it united new urban experts around a single issue, the limits they accepted made real solutions impossible, and, in the end, their achievements were more organizational than substantive. They adapted the structure of city government to the transformation of urban life and built new, specialized public and private organizations dedicated to the amelioration of great civic problems. Reformed city governments spent more money on public functions and probably delivered services more efficiently and with less corruption. Nonetheless, as business interests, buttressed by racism, increased their control over policy, experts retreated before the fictive boundaries between public and private and declined to propose solutions that seriously interfered with the market. As a consequence, they scarcely touched the fundamental problems of the urban poor.

7 Reorganizing the Labor Market

Between 1880 and 1920, modern American business burst out of its nineteenth century shell. In eleven of sixteen major industries, average factory size doubled during the last third of the nineteenth century. Manufacturing employed 2,700,000 people in 1880; 4,500,000 in 1900; and 8,400,000 in 1920. By any measure, output increased even more than employment as electric power drove faster, more sophisticated machines that revolutionized manufacturing processes. Other changes were organizational. Corporations flung their operations outward across the country; some of the largest formed vertical monopolies by integrating their manufacturing operations with the production of raw materials and the marketing of finished goods; and large sprawling collections of buildings built of new, flexible materials increasingly replaced the old, multistoried mills.

The major problems faced by big business were managerial not technological. Because business entered the new era with managerial and labor practices rooted in early and mid-nineteenth century industrial experience, it confronted major organizational bottlenecks. Old hierarchical chains of command descended from owners through plant superintendents to foremen who exercised great authority on the shop floor and frustrated attempts to coordinate vast, complex operations strung out through several sites. The control by skilled workers of manufacturing processes left management unable to plan effectively and vulnerable to informal shop-floor restrictions on output. Informal hiring practices and frequent layoffs fostered a large pool of surplus labor with a staggering turnover rate. As great masses of workers gathered in huge settings, a new worker militance erupted in union growth and the great confrontations between capital and labor of the late nineteenth and early twentieth centuries. In Chicago, between 1881 and 1900, 593,000 employees struck 17,176 establishments in 1,737 strikes; in Milwaukee, 38,977 workers struck 1,722 employers in 187 strikes; in New York City, in the same years, the number of workers on strike nearly reached a million.[1]

The new industrial era forced American business to reorganize. "Managerial capitalists replaced all-purpose autocrats. The new administrators substituted departmental or regional units that performed" special "functions such as marketing, research and development, and 'welfare work' for the old chain of command." In short, business invented modern management. It also developed four major strategies to extend its control over labor. First was repression. With the help of local police, state militias, and the National Guard, business crushed strikes. The use of federal troops for the first time in the great railroad strike of 1877; the hanging of Joe Hill in 1916; and the destruction of the Industrial Workers of the World (IWW) in the Red Scare following World War I: these are only three examples among, literally, thousands which show that unions confronted not only the power of big business with its scabs and private armies of Pinkertons but the collusion and organized violence of the state. As a second strategy, management attempted to wrest control of the manufacturing process from foremen and skilled workers. The use of time-and-motion studies to set and enforce faster piece rates, as advocated by Frederick Taylor and the apostles of scientific management, was one tactic; another was the introduction of technology designed, as David Noble argues, to gather control of the manufacturing process in the hands of management.[2]

Third, progressive businesses introduced policies designed to win worker loyalty, decrease labor turnover, and raise productivity. Their individual efforts have been called welfare capitalism. Unable to solve all their labor market problems by themselves, they joined with labor and academic reformer-experts to support social insurance legislation: workman's compensation, unemployment insurance, and pensions. Still, early social insurance suffered from the reluctance of public authorities to interfere with private prerogatives and the market, and, soon, conflicting interests ripped apart the fragile coalitions that had supported it. Not surprisingly, in the end, it was labor that gained the least. Even more, Progressive era legislation introduced the distinction between public assistance and social insurance that has dominated the history of social welfare in twentieth century America. Even though social insurance premiums had only a marginal relation to benefits, the insurance model removed the stigma of relief and welfare and distinguished beneficiaries from the irregularly employed or otherwise dependent poor who remained outside the labor force, shunted aside, sometimes locked up in institutions. In this way, the early architects of social insurance

180

cemented the association of relief or welfare with social and economic marginality, where it has remained stuck ever since.

Management's fourth strategy for adjusting its labor supply was its support for policies that cleared the labor market of workers newly made unproductive by technological development. Anxious to rid their factories and offices of workers insufficiently speedy and productive, yet afraid of the impact on the work ethic and labor relations of a large, demoralized class of casual labor, management looked for ways to eliminate unwanted workers not only from their workplaces but, as well, from the workforce. Here, major tactics included the abolition of child labor, immigration restriction, forced retirement, and eugenics. As part of the reorganization of capitalist labor markets, an inexorable drive for greater efficiency and higher production forced one group after another either out of the workforce or into the ghettos of unskilled, dead-end employment at its margins. The "massive growth of institutions stretching all the way from schools and hospitals on the one side to prisons and madhouses on the other," wrote Harry Braverman, "represents not just the progress of medicine, education, or crime prevention, but the clearing of the marketplace of all but the 'economically active' and 'functioning' members of society." Even a contemporary labor market economist like Don Lescohier recognized the same process. "Short hours of labor," he pointed out, "are practical only when employees have physical and nervous vigor so that they can work hard and fast. They inevitably make unemployable the slow and weak."[3]

Among the first workers made increasingly unproductive in the early twentieth century were children and youths. As technology reshaped the youth labor market, young people exchanged work for school. Only a few decades later, the same revolutions in sources of power and technology that made young people redundant lessened industrial reliance on unskilled immigrant labor. Only when industrialists no longer wanted immigrant labor, did they throw their weight behind the immigration restriction movement, which, at long last, triumphed with the infamous quota restrictions of 1921 and 1924. Rejected, redundant, useless people could not be left simply to starve and die. After all, the problem with some of them was only their youth; they would in time be needed, and their exclusion from the market was redefined as a problem of education. The problem with others was old age; they never would be needed again. Their exclusion, originally a problem of welfare, was transmuted into a new stage in the life course: retirement. Others, immigrants, were needed periodically and could be excluded as required through public policy. Finally, some people were defined as incapable because they were sick, handicapped, dangerous, or defective. Theirs was a problem not only for welfare and criminal justice but, equally, for science and medicine. Although, for the most part, networks of institutions

181

kept them from intruding on the marketplace or on the time of those who served it, when institutions became too expensive or too transparently barbarous, other modes of control guaranteed their quiet marginality. Today, the major control is medical and its technique the use of drugs. Earlier in the century, the last line of defense was assigned to the new science of eugenics. Its most dramatic tactic was sterilization.[4]

Eugenics and the Causes of Dependence

In the early twentieth century, a new theory—eugenics—justified immigration restriction and the harsh, punitive treatment of paupers and other dependent people. Despite its veneer of respectable objectivity, eugenics supplied a scientific basis with which to write the old distinction between the worthy and unworthy poor into social policy. For over a century, with scant success, poor law officials, legislators, and charity reformers had tried to drive away or lock up the dependent poor. Still, they continued to demand outdoor relief, drove up taxes, littered the country with their illegitimate children, filled poorhouses, and made a mockery of scientific charity. In eugenics, at last, officials and reformers found both an explanation of the problem and a set of policies for its ultimate solution. From its inception, eugenics had close ties to welfare. It offered an explanation for the intractable problem of pauperism; stimulated the creation of new state institutions for special classes of defectives; and gave local welfare officials a scientific way to substitute authoritative distinctions for their customarily loose, casual discriminations between categories of dependents.

Eugenics, wrote Charles Davenport, one of its most important advocates, "is the science of the improvement of the human race by better breeding." Sir Francis Galton founded eugenics as a scientific field in late nineteenth century Britain when he tried to apply Darwin's concept of natural selection to human inheritance. Galton (1822–1911), and his disciple Karl Pearson, who cofounded the new science of biometrics in 1900, helped spread eugenic thought to America. Although Galton had been interested mainly in the biological pedigree of the rich and well born, American eugenicists, eager to show that mental illness, feeblemindedness, and other defects could be traced primarily to inborn, immutable individual qualities, applied his ideas primarily to the problem of dependence. The most famous of the early American studies was Richard Dugdale's analysis of poorhouse populations in a New York county in the 1870s, especially

182

his portrait of the Jukes family, which had been breeding paupers, criminals, and other defectives for generations. The Jukes family, so Dugdale argued, had cost taxpayers a small fortune. In fact, anger at the amount spent to relieve dependent people helped fuel the eugenics movement. So did the failure of social policy. After all, by late in the nineteenth century, no one could claim that major social institutions worked very well or that very much progress had been made in the long-standing struggle against crime, pauperism, and mental illness. Now, eugenics offered a simple, scientific explanation: whatever the defect—and it might pop out as criminality, insanity, feeblemindedness, or moral imbecility—its origins lay deep and ineradicably within dependent people themselves. Eugenics, then, tossed the mantle of science over the ancient distinction between the worthy and the unworthy poor.[5]

At first, eugenics spread slowly, though not on account of any reluctance to use hereditarian explanations. Rather, the mechanism by which traits of personality and character were transmitted remained obscure. Indeed, most people who thought about the role of heredity believed in the inheritance of acquired characteristics, which was a modestly hopeful position that left scope for reform and improvement. However, by the early twentieth century, in Germany, August Weismann's theory of the "immortality of germ plasm" and the rediscovery of Gregor Mendel's genetic principles boosted eugenics's fortunes by discrediting older ideas about the inheritance of acquired characteristics. One result was fear. Because defectives, with their "weak minds in strong and oversexed bodies," threatened to engulf respectable, normal, white native Americans whose fertility had been declining steeply, there remained only one way to save America from the menace of the feebleminded, that is, from future mobs of criminals, crazy people, and moral imbeciles: halt their reproduction. Eugenic reformers initially stressed the importance of special institutions, where noncriminal defectives could be incarcerated throughout their fertile years. In 1878, with Josephine Shaw Lowell as principal promoter, New York became the first state to create a school for feebleminded girls; other states followed not long afterward. In 1896, Connecticut became the first state to legislate against the marriage of defectives. Its example, too, soon was copied by several states.[6]

Sterilization seemed even easier and more reliable than stuffing unfortunate people in institutions or preventing their marriage. However, until very late in the nineteenth century, castration for men and removal of the ovaries for women were the only methods of sterilization available, and both altered the body's endocrine balance, which even many eugenicists found too extreme. With the development of the vasectomy and salpingectomy, sterilization became easy and virtually without physical consequence, and these new surgical techniques unleashed more aggressive campaigns for sterilization. Indiana passed the first sterilization law in 1907. In 1927, in the famous *Buck* v. *Bell* case, the United

States Supreme Court, led by Justice Oliver Wendell Holmes, affirmed the constitutionality of sterilization. Stephan Jay Gould has demonstrated that Holmes based his decision on fabricated evidence he should have questioned more seriously. Instead, the Court lent its authority to the most extreme tactic of eugenic crusaders. In fact, aside from public education, sterilization was the only state-sponsored social improvement in which America led the world. The first American sterilization laws were passed 20 years earlier than those in other countries. Although thirty-one states had passed sterilization laws by 1931, most were vague and sometimes unenforceable. California led the nation in sterilization with 6,255 between 1909 and 1929. In all, by 1931, 12,145 sterilizations had been recorded across the country. By the end of 1958, the figure was 60,926.[7]

In 1910, Charles Davenport, the country's leading eugenics promoter, persuaded Mrs. E. H. Harriman to underwrite a eugenics research laboratory at Cold Spring, Long Island. Eventually, she endowed the laboratory and transferred its care to the Carnegie Corporation. The opening of Cold Spring marked the golden age of eugenics, which faltered only after the Nazis showed where its implications led. As a social movement, eugenics embraced some of the country's best reform talent. Wisconsin economist Richard Ely and Charles Van Hise, president of the state's university, counted themselves among its advocates, as did David Starr Jordan, founding president of Stanford. Indeed, despite some internal controversy over sterilization, eugenics forged a place for itself among the principal reforms of the Progressive era. For it seemed an effective way to enlist science in the cause of social uplift. Eugenics had intimate links, as well, with immigration restriction and mental testing. It justified the exclusion of the new immigrants from southern and eastern Europe, who, eugenicists argued, carried defective genes and, also, legitimated the continued suppression of black aspirations for the same reasons. Its links with the mental testing movement were especially close because early intelligence testers thought they were evaluating inherited capacity.[8]

In New York State, in 1911, the State Board of Charities founded a Bureau of Analysis and Investigation to pursue eugenic research. In its initial report, the bureau defined its purpose:

> To understand better the source of some of the evils which are disastrously affecting mental and moral qualities, and that their racial meaning may be made clear and proper methods suggested for improvement, it is essential that the data of human inheritance, embodied in the records of charitable and reformatory institutions, shall be analyzed, classified, and interpreted.

The bureau pointed to the immense sum spent by the state on its institutions for dependents. "There can be no doubt," it contended, "that a large proportion of the money . . . is required for the maintenance of defective and hereditary paupers." The implications for policy were clear. As the bureau bluntly asserted, "The public welfare demands that degenerates shall be prevented from the reproduction of their kind."[9]

By 1918, Chester Lee Carlisle, M.D., director, Bureau of Analysis and Investigation, and superintendent, Division of Mental Defect and Delinquency of the State Board of Charities, believed he had found the real roots of dependence. In "Seeking the Ultimate Causes of Dependence," the final chapter of a long report, he stated them bluntly. They were, of course, eugenic. "The story of the poor," he wrote, "is best read in the annals of cases of mental defect, affective deviation and all the other psycopathic reactions of conduct. . . . All such types constitute the subnormals of the human race." In affluent times, even the defective "carried along on the general stream of community prosperity," became "self-supporting." However, when "the economic horizon" turned "less rosy, when the needs of necessitous times" demanded "the utmost functioning ability of adequately developed human individuals, just then" were "these subnormals . . . unable to keep up the pace and . . . pushed out of the main stream of citizen activities" to "settle as social flotsam along the shores of the back waters of our communities." Certainly, environment had some effect on behavior. Although a hygienic environment improved "chances for survival" and determined an individual's "rise or fall in the sense of dependency," "ultimately," success in the "struggle to survive" was "determined by the individual's ability (or lack of ability) through psycho-somatic endowment to establish himself as an efficient economic unit." If he failed, he became a "potential or actual sociologic liability" and "his environment . . . a social nuisance." In other words, defectives clogged the marketplace. Happily, eugenics finally had discovered how to free social and economic mechanisms from the drag of accumulated human defect. Indeed, when the spotlight of modern diagnosis focused on dependent people, paupers would disappear. "In the place of the almshouse" would "stand the community clinic, the hospitals adapted to care for every type of mental and physical defect or disorder and the vocational village for the socially handicapped." The patient would replace the pauper, and experts would assure "accurate diagnosis, discriminating placing and scientifically supervised after-care to help him at all times make adequate mental and physical adjustment to the world of reality, according to his innately defective, constitutionally crippled capacity whatever it may be." Through the judicious deployment of eugenic tactics—institutions, sterilization, individuation, and supervision—medicine and science would abolish pauperism and free the marketplace for "normal minds and bodies." Eugenics, in short, promised to reach the goals for which poor law reformers had struggled so hard and unsuccessfully for more than a century.[10]

By the early 1930s, the racism inherent in eugenic thought, the scientific softness of most research in the field, and its disappointing payoff for policy all

Weakening of eugenics
1. Nazi Germany

had weakened eugenics's scholarly and popular appeal. The uses to which it was put in Hitler's Germany dealt the movement a crippling blow. Crippling, though not fatal: for the alleged failures of social and educational reform in the 1960s predictably enough elicited a new wave of neo-eugenic scholarship that argued for the innate intellectual inferiority of black Americans and the inheritability of criminal tendencies. Despite devastating scientific criticism, sociobiology—as the new eugenics has come to be called—flourishes, and for much the same reasons, and with much the same dangers, as the old.

inferiority of black Americans

areas: biology: new eugenics

Welfare Capitalism and the Labor Market

In the late nineteenth century and first three decades of the twentieth century, many of the major innovations in American welfare practice originated in the private sector. Large corporations experimented with social insurance and new labor market policies far more daring than almost any government innovations. Not only were corporations free of the political restraints of government, they were more competent. In the early twentieth century, federal and state governments, like mid-nineteenth century businesses, were small, inefficient, and relatively uncoordinated. Large corporations that had developed "strategies to deal with diversified national markets," therefore, innovated more easily and led "in the formulation of welfare procedures and the provision of welfare services." With some irony, the reluctance to exercise public responsibility had so crippled the development of government capacity that it fell to the leaders of private industry to pioneer key aspects of the American welfare state.[11]

When Don Lescohier, a Progressive era economist, formerly superintendent of Minnesota's Public Employment Office, chief statistician of Minnesota's Department of Labor and Industries, and associate professor of economics at the University of Wisconsin, published his analysis of the labor market in 1919, an experienced reader would have been struck by how little had changed in the last 40 years. With few exceptions, Lescohier's description of the labor market could have been written in 1880 as well as in 1919. Clearly, labor policy had not caught up with the great changes in industrial structure. Although several corporations had experimented with the techniques of welfare capitalism, its great age lay just ahead in the 1920s. In fact, Lescohier's underlying point was that business, not outside agitators or inexorable market forces, had caused its own labor problem. Through its callous equation of labor with other raw materials,

business, not market forces, caused its own labor problem

failure to minimize fluctuations in labor demand through intelligent planning, and inattention to the human and social consequences of the great reserve army of surplus labor it kept so well stocked, American business had alienated its workforce. The consequence was as clear as it was chilling. "Unless those who control our industrial policies accept responsibility for those hardships [that workers suffer], and recognize that the worker's relation to production is and must be different from that of the raw material or the machine, we will have to face, sooner or later, a demand for a social and economic system that will concern itself.[12]

The American labor supply, Lescohier argued, had five features:

1 the fluctuating but unceasing flow of immigrant laborers;
2 an ever present labor reserve;
3 the decentralized character of that reserve;
4 excessive labor turnover; and
5 a defective system of labor distribution.

The causes were complex, but all of them could be traced in one way or another to the fluctuating demand for labor and to employers unwilling to plan ahead by anticipating slack times and spreading their production over the course of the year. By and large, employers accepted the seasonal and cyclical demands for their products and in slack times simply laid off excess workers. They counted on the labor reserve to keep a ready supply of hands at their factory gates, always eager for work. Rarely able to count on steady employment, workers suffered from this irregularity far more than from low wages. Indeed, the average daily or weekly wage in an industry offered no guide whatsoever to the average annual earnings of most workers. To make matters worse, workers had no reliable way of learning about job openings elsewhere. Labor turnover—at least 100 percent a year on the average in large companies—was staggering. Often desperate for work, workers would travel thousands of miles on the rumor of available jobs. Others, especially with families, remained stuck, dependent on the earning of their wives and children.[13]

Lescohier tried to convince employers that conventional labor practice worked against their best interests. They lacked loyal workers; productivity suffered because new workers continually had to be trained; estranged and hostile, workers disrupted production with strikes; inadequately protected, they suffered unnecessary accidents; underfed and overworked, they lost more time through sickness than through any other cause. Irregularly employed, in the end, they even lost their will to work. As their attachment to the labor market itself weakened, they became casual workers. Lescohier warned:

> *The subtle danger of casual work, which silently accomplishes serious results, is*

187

that it develops a habit of irregular work in those who depend upon it for a livelihood.
. . . Men easily learn to like frequent idle days. . . . to the laborer who learns to
support himself by odd jobs casual labor is as dangerous as the tentacles of a devilfish.[14]

Late in the nineteenth century, some employers had recognized the urgency of new labor policies and introduced the earliest form of welfare capitalism: industrial villages. Most famous was Pullman, Illinois, built by the railroad magnate George Pullman between 1881 and 1884. Others were Steelton, Pennsylvania; Gary, Indiana; Leclaire, Missouri; and many smaller, less well known towns in the North and South. Industrial villages offered workers decent, affordable housing and a variety of amenities, such as schools, churches, and entertainment. Although they varied from one another, all of them were designed to increase worker loyalty, reduce labor turnover, and dampen union activity. They were definitely not philanthropies. Rents were to provide a decent return on capital investments; and improved worker health, contentment, loyalty, and stability were supposed to boost corporate profits. Most leases stipulated that workers who were fired, left voluntarily, or joined strikes would be evicted, and most towns deliberately lacked places where workers could hold large meetings to discuss collective grievances. As the experience of Pullman proved, hard times exposed the limits of early welfare capitalism. When his company's profits dropped, Pullman cut wages and raised rents. The result was the great Pullman strike of 1894, crushed only when President Grover Cleveland, despite the protest of Illinois's Governor John Altgeld, sent in the army. Although Pullman illustrates most dramatically the unstable base of a community erected on paternalism and profits, most other model towns also slid away from their original goals, especially when European immigrants, unwilling to submit to corporate supervision of their leisure hours, began to flood American industries. As a strategy of welfare capitalism, company towns were a dead end.[15]

After 1900, welfare capitalism became a national movement. A variety of regional and national organizations promoted welfare work: in 1904, the National Civic Federation created a Welfare Department; many large corporations appointed "welfare secretaries"; and universities began to train students for industrial welfare work. In 1906, two Chicago institutions—The Chicago Institute of Social Science and the Chicago Commons—first offered courses in industrial welfare. Yale followed in the next year. By 1916, similar courses flourished in more than 150 engineering schools.[16]

World War I accelerated the speed with which big business adopted welfare capitalism. Anxious to boost production and prevent disruptive labor disputes, Congress created a Council of National Defense whose Advisory Committee set up a Committee on Labor, which, in turn, spun off a Committee on Welfare Work composed primarily of industrialists noted for their welfare programs.

188

Reorganizing the Labor Market

However, even without federal encouragement, businessmen subsidized welfare activities to deflect labor militance and slow union growth. Especially in the steel industry, the balance of power between capital and labor shifted for a few years as the war increased demand and virtually cut off the supply of immigrant labor. As workers, aware of their enhanced power, eager for a share of wartime profits, joined unions at an accelerated pace, business turned to welfare capitalism, which, as Brandes observes, "was a protective device aimed largely at trade unionism, the common devil which brought American businessmen together as no other issue did." Underlying business concern with productivity, wages, and unions, lurked the fear of bolshevism, for the Russian revolution had frightened American capitalists who "had dreaded a labor uprising for years." Aware of the disruptive potential of demobilization, they "translated their fear into support for welfarism."[17]

The enormous growth in the factory workforce, the problem of Americanizing immigrants, and the dramatic spread of labor militance all made business leaders receptive to the message of labor economists like Lescohier. Without curbing labor turnover, attacking the problem of casual labor, and winning worker loyalty, business could anticipate not only more strikes but also the diffusion of radical influence fueled, so they thought, by the Bolshevik revolution. "Overnight," says Nelson, "the employment department and employment manager became standard features of a progressive factory, superseding the old-time foreman, welfare secretary, and to a lesser degree, the efficiency engineer." In the process, American business quickly created the field of personnel management. The National Association of Employment Managers, only formed in 1918, attracted more than 2,000 people to its 1919 convention and more than 5,000 in 1920.[18]

What were the major features of welfare capitalism in the 1920s? David Brody describes them this way:

> The welfare plans proliferating in the 1920s were designed to meet the major hazards of modern industrial life. One group of schemes encouraged men to acquire property. Some companies operated savings plans, often with the incentive of high interest rates or special bonuses. Many firms adopted homeownership plans that provided employees with various kinds of technical assistance and financial aid. Stock-purchasing plans exerted special appeal. . . . Other programs protected workmen and their families from losses resulting from accident, illness, old age, and death. Group insurance valued at $7.5 billion covered close to six million workers in 1928. More than 350 companies gave pensions in 1929. Besides granting these basic protections, companies improved plant conditions and safety, provided medical services and visiting nurses, underwrote sports and classes, distributed land for gardening, and assisted workmen in all manner of personal problems.[19]

Neither the impact nor uniformity of welfare capitalism should be overstated.

189

Plans varied greatly in different regions of the country and between rural and urban areas, and they never covered more than a minority of workers even in large, prosperous firms. According to one survey, 6.5 percent of firms with fewer than 500 employees had personnel departments compared to about 30 percent of those with 500–2,000 employees and 50 percent of those with more than 2,000. Some activities were more widespread: "over 90 percent of the companies surveyed operated safety programs; 70 percent, group insurance; 60 percent, mutual aid associations. But only one out of five provided formal pension plans, stock purchase opportunities, or savings and loan facilities." Even more, welfare capitalism left some of workers' most important problems untouched. Companies made very little effort to reduce unemployment; "the steady decline of hours since the 1890s leveled off after 1920"; and wage rates increased only half as fast as labor productivity.[20]

Although the 1920s were stagnant years for organized labor, welfare capitalism could take little of the credit. The militant wing of the labor movement had been smashed, and rising real wages had dampened enthusiasm for unions by improving the standard of living among steadily employed industrial workers. "Labor leaders of the 1920s," says Brandes, "to a man disliked welfarism and clearly hated employee representation [company unions]." What ordinary workers thought is less clear, although Gerald Zahavi's suggestive case study of Endicott Johnson points to a complex, contingent, and fragile "negotiated loyalty." In the end, "the performance of American capitalism in the 1920s" gave welfare capitalism whatever credibility it had, and when even the most progressive employers cut back their welfare programs and laid off workers during the Great Depression, the fragile base of worker quiescence and loyalty crumbled. With almost lightning speed, workers turned "actively and fiercely against their employers."[21]

Despite its inability to win the undivided loyalty of workers, check the growth of the labor movement, survive depression unscathed, or assure all workers decent, regular wages and safe, humane working conditions, welfare capitalism remains an important episode. Indeed, translated into the more mundane language of fringe benefits, welfare capitalism revived and flourished, and for much the same reasons. Even more, personnel management continued its meteoric career, aided by the incorporation of the new psychology as well as the new labor economics. Captured early by corporate interests, industrial psychology allied itself firmly with its new employer. Instead of disinterested professionals, industrial psychologists emerged in the 1920s as "servants of power," concerned with productivity, worker adjustment, and the deflection of militance. The road from the early welfare secretaries to the latest specialists in union decertification seems long, but it is, as history goes, unusually direct.[22]

Workmen's Compensation and the Origins
of Social Insurance

Between 1909 and 1920, forty-three states passed legislation that required employers to compensate their employees for injuries sustained at work. Nonetheless, the narrow boundaries of public responsibility restricted the scope and effectiveness of the new legislation, and, in the end, workmen's compensation emerged as one more lame attempt by state governments to solve a serious problem through regulation.[23]

Founded in 1906 and led by economists and political scientists, the American Association for Labor Legislation (AALL), according to Lubove, "created and sustained the organized social insurance movement in the United States" and "testified to the emergence of the social scientist as an influence in legislation and reform." Workmen's compensation was its first major victory. John Andrews, executive secretary of the AALL from 1908 to 1943, had been a student of John L. Commons, the Wisconsin economist, whose influence dominated the association. The "Wisconsin approach to labor legislation" promoted social insurance; stressed "scientific investigation and the employment of experts"; and advocated a specific method of administration: the industrial commission, which Commons called "a fourth branch of government." Through research and the application of expert knowledge, industrial commissions were supposed to divorce social policy from politics and arrive at disinterested recommendations that reflected the "general will." In 1911, Wisconsin created an Industrial Commission that combined several offices, including the administration of the new workmen's compensation legislation, and several other states soon tried to follow Wisconsin's example. The Wisconsin approach to social insurance also stressed prevention. Insurance, Commons and his colleagues argued, should be designed not so much to relieve dependence as to prevent it. In time, this stress on prevention, as contrasted with policies focused more sharply on relief, became one of the most contentious issues in the American history of social insurance.[24]

Workmen's compensation became the first widespread form of American social insurance because it served an unusually wide range of influential interests: labor, big business, insurance companies, and academic reformer-experts. Labor's interests were clear. America had appallingly high industrial accident rates. In 1904, 28 of every 10,000 railroad workers died in an accident; in 1916, 1 in 10 was injured. For coal miners, rates were even higher. In 1906, 48 of every 10,000 were killed. Put another way, between 1900 and 1906, the mortality

191

rate for American coal miners averaged 33.5 compared to 9.1 in France, 10.3 in Belgium, 12.9 in Great Britain, and 20.6 in Prussia. In 1905, one writer who wanted to demonstrate the greed of American capitalism showed that two years earlier 11,066 workers had been injured on American railroads compared to 172 in Austria. Either by distance traveled or number of passengers, "American railroads killed and injured many times their European counterparts." Still, the 328 American railroad workers killed between 1888 and 1908 were only 10 percent "of an estimated 35,000 killed and 536,000 injured workers in American industry each year." In one U.S. Steel plant in South Chicago alone, 46 men were killed and 598 wounded in 1906. Accidents were more common in the United States than in Europe, one observer commented, "partly because of the higher pressure under which our work is carried on and partly because of the rapid introduction of a new element of labor unfamiliar with our methods of mechanical production, but largely because of our general attitude of indifference toward human life itself."[25]

Although often injured so badly they never could work again, workers found it difficult to collect compensation, and the families of workers killed in industrial accidents rarely received more than a token settlement. Although they had a theoretical right to sue, injured workers who took their cases to court confronted common law doctrines that favored employers. "Fellow servant" precedents exonerated employers from responsibility when they could prove that accidents happened as a result of the negligence of other employees. Nor could workers collect damages if they had been injured through their own neg-ligence or had continued working in conditions they knew to be dangerous.[26]

In the late nineteenth century, state legislatures began to modify liability laws. By 1908, sixteen states had abolished the "fellow servant" rule; about twenty had "modified the assumption of risk doctrine"; and several had softened "contributory negligence to allow recovery under the law of 'proportional neg-ligence.'" As liability laws eased, injured workers began to sue far more often, and they frequently won. In one sample, between 1875 and 1905 the number of workmen's compensation cases increased from 92 to 736 per year, and juries in an appellate court "decided in favor of the employer in only 98 of 1043." To protect themselves against rising, unpredictable compensation costs, busi-nesses bought liability insurance, whose value soared from $200,000 in 1887 to $35 million in 1912.[27]

Even though injured workers could pursue their claims in court with fewer restrictions, they still faced serious obstacles. Litigation was expensive and slow; businesses took a long time to pay awards, if they paid at all; and awards frequently were inadequate. (Indeed, juries lacked almost any standards by which to fix the amount of awards.) Despite the number and size of policies they wrote, insurance

high premium
low reward

companies could not solve either the problems of injured workers or their employers, and, in fact, they came under attack from all sides because they allegedly "collected large sums in liability premiums, but distributed only a small portion to injured workers. Much of the premium dollar was consumed in profit and administrative overhead." Nonetheless, insurance companies also faced uncertainty, because they had almost no way to predict the magnitude of claims or the size of awards.[28]

ok in theory

In theory, workmen's compensation laws would mitigate the problems of labor, business, and insurance. Injured workers and their families would be assured prompt, adequate compensation without the delay, uncertainty, and expense of a trial. Businesses not only would be spared expensive litigation; they would know how much compensation would cost, and, as long as they remained the carriers, private insurance companies would improve their public relations, decrease their legal expenses, and increase their capacity to predict their obligations.

emphasis on prevention

Its emphasis on prevention was one reason why workmen's compensation so attracted academic reformer-experts. Under the threat of higher premiums, employers would reduce the demand for workmen's compensation by paying more attention to safety. Workmen's compensation, they predicted, would add "a tremendous incentive for the promotion of safety as a business proposition and bring together the officers of the state" and "the manufacturers on a common ground in the work of reducing accidents." Consequently, a "vast amount of safety discussion and organization" accompanied the workmen's compensation movement, and, everywhere, the two problems were discussed together. One result was the formation, in 1913, of the National Council for Industrial Safety.[29]

Even with its potential to serve many interests, a consensus in principle on workmen's compensation did not arise quickly or easily. At first, Samuel Gompers and the AFL preferred liberalized liability laws to workmen's compensation, which they feared would favor employers and undermine the influence of labor unions. Indeed, Gompers, unimpressed by the academics who ran the AALL, distrusted their "rhetoric of disinterested benevolence," which, he thought, "disguised a struggle for power between himself and self-proclaimed friends of the working class." By the second decade of the twentieth century, however, Gompers and other labor leaders, their initial reluctance overcome, now fought over the details rather than the principle of proposed legislation. Business support also solidified slowly. Although a conservative faction predictably resisted any extension of government responsibility, the leading businessmen who organized the National Civic Federation (NCF) in 1900 argued that workmen's compensation would help capital reach an accommodation with the conservative wing of organized labor, head off the impending entrance of labor into politics, and deflect the threat of socialism. In fact, after 1908, spurred by its president, Seth Low, the NCF led the campaign for business support of workmen's compensation.[30]

difficulty in passing

Agreement in principle was only one hurdle. As legislatures worked on compensation laws, they had to resolve sticky, contentious issues. Should compensation be provided through state funds or private insurance companies? Should participation in compensation insurance be voluntary or compulsory? How should rates be fixed? What value should be placed on specific injuries? How long should workers have to wait to collect compensation? How should compensation awards be enforced? Should injured workers retain their right to sue? In some instances, as in Missouri, conflicts between business and labor over these issues delayed the passage of compensation legislation for years. In states where labor had a strong influence on legislation, as in Arizona, injured employees could choose their remedy, although a strong counterattack by business interests eventually rescinded this advantage. On the whole, however, workmen's compensation laws reflected business interests: very few allowed injured workers to sue; most were voluntary; and the majority relied on private insurance companies rather than state governments, even though the former had higher administrative costs. Some states created no special administrative agency and left enforcement to the courts, with disastrous consequences for injured workers. (Court enforcement created such great problems that by 1919, thirty-four of the forty-five states with workmen's compensation laws had created industrial commissions to administer them.) Worst of all, rates remained too low. Because of labor's influence, some were pegged at more than half of a worker's customary wages, but, in practice, their low ceilings, rarely more than ten dollars a week, and limited durations, not usually more than 300 or 400 weeks in cases of total disability or death, meant that injured workers and their families still suffered an often crippling loss of income.[31]

laws reflected business interests

Importance of laws (despite limits)

Despite their limits, the early workmen's compensation laws were important in three ways. First, they represented a hesitant but irreversible step from charity toward entitlement, for they at least established the principle that workers injured in industrial accidents had a right to compensation. Second, the industrial commissions that administered most of them had an important impact on government. They were major vehicles for the ascendant influence of academic experts on public policy; they fostered the myth that disinterested expertise could derive impartial, correct solutions to social problems unmuddied by politics; and they added to government bureaucracy a new layer with a vested interest in its own survival. Industrial commissions clung to the administration of workmen's compensation laws—usually their major responsibility—even when they overlapped with or duplicated other components of the emerging welfare structure. The existence of industrial commissions, therefore, insured the continuation "of workers' compensation laws and perpetuated a state-by-state approach to disability." Finally, through workmen's compensation the federal government "made its entrance into the modern social welfare system." In 1914, the U.S. Commissioner of Labor Statistics convened a conference to standardize "accident forms and statistics" and agreed to serve as secretary and publish the proceedings of the new International Association of Industrial Accident Boards and Commissions (IAIABC).[32]

Nonetheless, the narrow boundaries of public responsibility once again corrupted social innovation and restricted government to reform by regulation. Workmen's compensation had conflicting, incompatible purposes. For it could not both assure injured workers an adequate income and keep employers' costs low. Workmen's compensation was supposed to support workers injured in industrial accidents; improve relations between business and labor; and reduce the waste, uncertainty, cost, and hostility endemic where accident rates were high and liability a decision of the courts. In the process, it was to infringe as little as possible on private economic interests by making sure costs did not even nibble at profits and private insurance companies did not suffer. With these constraints, it was, of course, the injured worker who lost.

Unemployment Insurance and the Limits of Voluntarism and Prevention

Unemployment is a modern concept. It assumes the transmutation of work into employment; presupposes the reorganization of production into a collection of jobs that mediate the relation between labor and subsistence; and requires the intervention of a market in which work becomes a prerogative contingent on the sale of labor. None of these conditions existed throughout most of human history. With daily life centered on the land, production based in households, and age and gender roles fixed by custom, no one lacked useful work. Indeed, when few people sold their labor, work could not mean employment; it was, rather, the purposeful expenditure of human energy on useful tasks.[33]

European governments introduced unemployment insurance early in the twentieth century. Britain passed the first unemployment insurance act in 1911. Between 1919 and 1930, ten other countries followed. In America, not until 1932—more than twenty years after the first state passed a workmen's compensation bill—did Wisconsin enact the nation's first unemployment legislation.

The depression of the 1890s, the threat of labor militance, and fear of radicalism began to shake American businessmen, reformers, and public officials out of their complacent and self-serving explanations of unemployment. Even then, their early palliative responses, such as potato patches, small-scale public works projects, or special funds, offered only temporary relief. A few enlightened businessmen who realized that unemployment hurt employers as well as workers and national labor leaders thought they could reduce unemployment and mitigate its consequences by themselves, with minimal help from government. In the end, their efforts only showed once more the limits of voluntarism. Nor did the experts do much better. Early in the twentieth century, influential American social scientists developed their own solution. Although they called for government action, their plan depended on incentives and assumed the ability of businessmen to curb unemployment by reforming their labor policies, if only they tried hard enough. This, too, proved a fantasy.[34]

American economists considered unemployment both a labor market and a moral problem. In most industries, the irregular demand for labor left all but a small proportion of workers periodically unemployed, and the absence of an organized regional or national labor market kept them uninformed about the availability of work elsewhere. Irregular work not only reduced "the amount of the workman's earnings"; it induced bad habits, undermined character, and eroded the will to work. From the economists' view, employers who refused to smooth out their labor needs confused their short- and long-term interests. No amount of short-term profit could compensate for the consequences of a labor force that lost its skills, energy, and, even, its will to work. No labor reserve was worth the potential militance and disorder of a hostile, dissipated working class.[35]

The economists' analysis of unemployment led in two complementary directions. The first was toward labor-exchanges, implemented after 1910 in Great Britain on a national scale. In theory, labor-exchanges integrated information about the availability of work on a regional or national basis; retrained workers displaced by technology; steered young people away from dead-end jobs; and gently removed unemployables from the labor market. However, in neither Britain nor the United States did theory and practice coincide. After 1910, several American states and cities started labor exchanges, none of which met their goals. Only the federal government's United States Employment Service, operated briefly during World War I and quickly dismantled, could claim any success, though it, too, was riddled with problems. No matter how well they were run, public employment offices encountered one insuperable obstacle. Most employers, "either hostile, indifferent, or contemptuous," remained unwilling to use their services. Nor did labor, with its distrust of government, embrace them. Gompers, for instance, argued that "state employment offices . . . would provide a means of spying on the workers."[36]

Reorganizing the Labor Market

Economists also pointed to the need to stabilize the demand for labor. Here a few businessmen led the way, and attempts to both reduce and mitigate unemployment figured prominently in some of the welfare capitalism schemes of the 1920s. Firms attempted to reduce unemployment by staggering production more evenly over the course of the year. They tried to soften the consequences of the unemployment they could not avoid by creating reserve funds which would pay limited benefits until they were exhausted. A few companies also guaranteed workers employment for a minimum number of weeks or days each year. Nonetheless, employer-sponsored unemployment funds never covered more than a small number of workers. Between 1916 and 1934, employers started at least twenty-three funds, covering 60,000 workers, but not more than sixteen operated at any one time. At their peak in 1931, about "50,000 workers, most of whom had hard-to-replace skills or high seniority, were eligible to receive out of work benefits." Nor did the companies that offered plans represent a cross-section of industry. Rather, before the depression, without exception they were small or medium-sized firms that "manufactured traditional consumer goods. . . . for which there was a fairly constant demand." Even the most well-known company-based unemployment plans—at the Dennison Manufacturing Company in Massachusetts, which initiated the first company plan in 1916; the Leeds and Northrup Company of Philadelphia; and the S. C. Johnson Company of Racine, Wisconsin—foundered in the 1930s. Reserves, which had been calculated on the basis of the depression of 1920–22, quickly vanished after 1929. Nor could even well-managed companies in noncyclical industries count on steady consumer demand during the years of the Great Depression.[37]

Although they did not expect employers to stabilize production voluntarily, Wisconsin economists—John Commons, Don Lescohier, William Leiserson, John B. Andrews—agreed with welfare capitalists that by themselves individual firms could reduce the amount of unemployment among their workers. The Wisconsin approach became known as the "American Plan." Unemployment, they argued, should be fought through prevention. As an incentive, they advocated compulsory unemployment insurance paid by employers into segregated reserve funds. Each employer's account would remain distinct, and businesses that promoted steady employment would pay lower premiums. The alternative, a pooled insurance fund, they contended, would degenerate into simply another form of relief with no incentive for employers to curb unemployment by attacking its underlying cause. Here, the economists pointed to Great Britain and Germany where unemployment insurance payments had exceeded contributions. With most restrictions on eligibility and length of coverage removed, unemployment insurance in these countries, so they said, had turned into just another demoralizing form of outdoor relief.[38]

By the late 1920s, social insurance advocates based in Ohio—led by Isaac

197

Rubinow, Abraham Epstein, and Paul Douglas—had challenged the American Plan's emphasis on prevention. Given its most influential statement in the 1932 report of the Ohio Commission on Unemployment, the "Ohio Plan" considered prevention a fantasy. By themselves, few firms could stabilize employment. "Insurance," argued Rubinow, "is based on the assumption that the risk itself is inevitable, however much it may be reduced." Rather than prevention, the main purpose of insurance was to help unemployed workers and stimulate purchasing power. Incentives for employers were pointless. The profit motive, wrote Epstein during the Great Depression, was "sufficient inducement and no penalty levied through an unemployment insurance contribution can equal the loss now encountered through inability to keep their factories going." Nor should reserves be segregated, because insurance was "soundest and most economical when it" covered "the widest spread of people subject to the risk." Only pooled funds could assure a fund large and flexible anough to meet any contingency.[39]

Neither the American Plan nor the Ohio Plan converted the national leadership of the AFL to unemployment insurance before the Great Depression. Unemployment insurance, charged Gompers, undermined voluntarism, invited government interference with labor, and, in Europe, had failed to reduce unemployment "one iota." Unions, he claimed, could solve the unemployment problem themselves by bargaining for shorter workdays, "restricting the supply of labor and . . . prolonging the available work." In fact, unions had several potential tactics: "high membership fees, long apprenticeships, the restriction of output, agitation for curbs on immigration, regulation of overtime, work sharing, and opposition to incentive schemes of the sort proposed by" advocates of scientific management. Government's only role was to provide public works—not relief— during depressions. For Gompers, voluntarism was the " 'cornerstone' of the house of labor."[40]

Despite Gompers's opposition, support for unemployment insurance surfaced within state and local unions inspired by the success of the British Labour Party, and, in the 1920s, radical unions representing workers in the needle trades "adopted the most far-reaching unemployment insurance plans of the postwar decade." Nonetheless, even before the Great Depression, unemployment in "the depressed clothing, fur, and hat industries" overwhelmed union reserves. With their leadership weak, their members divided by "Communist agitation," and their unemployment funds bankrupt, these radical unions proved "unsuccessful in reforming their industries and compensating their members." Once again, voluntarism had failed.[41]

When interest in unemployment insurance revived during the Great Depression, the AFL changed its position and, at its 1932 convention, "approved unemployment insurance by an 'overwhelming margin.' " Thereafter, labor

198

"provided most of the backing for unemployment insurance" and some business groups "most of the opposition." (Some businessmen were attracted to unemployment insurance because of its potential impact on purchasing power.) Labor favored the Ohio Plan; it wanted "benefits first, and prevention if and when possible." With labor's support, state campaigns for unemployment insurance legislation gathered momentum. Wisconsin passed the country's first unemployment insurance act in 1932; next came New York in 1935. Still, only three other states followed before the Social Security Act, signed in September, 1935, made unemployment insurance compulsory. Nonetheless, labor's influence proved powerful and decisive. Union leaders "largely determined the major features" of the first unemployment laws, and no state passed an unemployment law opposed by labor. With the exception of Wisconsin, everywhere, the primary goal of the early legislation "was to sustain the unemployed worker rather than to force the employer to prevent unemployment."[42]

Early unemployment insurance hardly replaced lost income. In most cases, benefits were small, about ten dollars a week, and limited to 10 weeks each year. Even so, it took decades of agitation and a major depression before American state legislatures joined the European countries that had passed unemployment insurance laws years earlier. By comparison, the struggle over workmen's compensaton seemed quick and easy. Three states—Minnesota, Wisconsin, and New York—had passed workmen's compensation acts in 1909; eight more states followed the next year; and within less than a decade workmen's compensation was nearly universal. By contrast, unemployment insurance proved tough to sell. Mild as it was, its intervention in the labor market offended the self-appointed guardians who policed the boundaries of public responsibility. More than workmen's compensation, unemployment insurance touched the lurking fear of entitlement that had haunted charity and relief in America for over a century. Academic indictments of labor policy lacked the impact of lawsuits by injured workers and high insurance premiums. Nothing disguised or reduced industrial accidents in the way prosperity undermined the case for unemployment insurance. Labor unions could not claim the ability either to look after their injured members or reduce the incidence of injury in the same way the AFL had asserted its capacity to deal with unemployment by itself. The European example suggested that unemployment insurance degenerated into a dole. Even the academic experts disagreed about its purpose and basis. For these reasons, no strong coalition ever formed around unemployment insurance in the way one had around workmen's compensation. As labor switched its stance, powerful business opponents hardened their opposition, and state legislatures had to choose sides. In the end, they picked labor. For all their bluster, the depression had left opponents of unemployment insurance with nothing to offer. With a decade to prove their ability to reform the labor market by themselves, welfare capitalists

199

demonstrated nothing so much as the limits of voluntarism. Nor had the Wisconsin academics done much better. As the Great Depression devastated the world economy, it seemed, to say the least, quaint to imagine that with a modest incentive individual firms could defy the business cycle.

Old Age and Economic Redundancy

Throughout the latter nineteenth century, the federal government operated one large, important social insurance scheme: veterans' pensions. Between 1867 and 1912, expenses for veterans' pensions—an enormous program—swelled from $21 million to $153 million, and in 1913, veterans' pensions accounted for 18 percent of all federal expenditure. In fact, a year earlier Rubinow had used veteran's pensions as a precedent to point out that America did indeed have a system of social insurance. It was, he rightly observed, "idle to speak of a popular system of old-age pensions as a radical departure from American traditions, when our pension roll numbers several hundred thousand more names than that of Great Britain." Military pensions were not, he stressed, simply rewards for service. To the contrary, they were "an economic measure which" aimed "to solve the problem of dependent old age and widowhood."[43]

This massive contribution made by the federal government to economic security began with 1862 legislation granting pensions to Civil War veterans. Pension eligibility expanded in 1890 to cover any veteran who had served at least 90 days or to his dependents. Neither combat experience nor injuries during the Civl War were prerequisites. The only condition was inability to perform manual labor, a criterion usually satisfied by old age. (In 1906, another amendment made age 62 officially the start of the period of "permanent specific disability," and later laws raised the amount of benefits.) In the late nineteenth and early twentieth centuries, at least one of every two elderly, native-born white Northern men and many of their widows received a pension from the federal government. Pensions were the largest expense in the federal budget after the national debt. Through its veterans' pensions, the United States federal government, as Rubinow observed, spent much more on old-age assistance than did Britain, which usually is thought to have been far in advance of America in the development of a welfare state. (Britain passed its first old-age insurance legislation in 1908.) In Massachusetts, to take a specific example, "three times as many people were receiving over ten times as much support under rubrics of aid to

Veterans Pensions and largest expense

old soldiers and their dependents as through local poor houses and outdoor relief and state pauper institutions and other asylums." In effect, the veterans' pensions formed a rudimentary system of old-age assistance for the respectable working class. After about 1910, as the Civil War generation and its dependents began to die and cohorts ineligible for veterans' pensions reached their sixties, pressure for a new form of old-age assistance surfaced. Although working-class groups and unions argued for a continuation of noncontributory pensions, they lost, and when the federal government tried to design a permanent system of economic security for the elderly in the 1930s, it followed a dramatically different approach that reflected another strong current in the drive for pensions for the elderly—their elimination from the workforce.[44]

As the speed of industrial production increased, older workers, so employers thought, lacked the stamina and dexterity essential to maximum production in new, competitive environments within business, industry, and, even, some public bureaucracies. Worried about competition, concerned with driving production faster and higher, employers looked for ways to strip their labor force of superannuated workers. Herein lay the origins of pensions and retirement.

Old age long had been a serious problem for all but the wealthy. With no private pensions or social security, men did not retire. They worked until they dropped or were fired. Without work, old people had three options: they could live on their savings, move in with their children, or go to the poorhouse. Of these, the second was the most common because very few people had earned enough to save for their old age. Military pensions helped some elderly workers in the late nineteenth and early twentieth century, and, as life insurance became more common, some fortunate widows did manage to stay independent. Nonetheless, the best recent research estimates that in the nineteenth century most old people with adult children lived with them. More than any other factor, a lack of family (as chapter 4 has shown) distinguished the old people in poorhouses from those who escaped confinement.[45]

In the late nineteenth century, the elderly's problems intensified. For one thing, there were more of them. The proportion of the populaton over sixty increased from 4.1 percent to 6.4 percent between 1850 and 1900. Among immigrants, who, with the exception of blacks, included the people with fewest resources, the proportion more than sixty-five years old rose from 4.0 percent to 9.3 percent between 1870 and 1900 compared to a rise from 2.9 percent to only 3.3 percent among native-born whites. After 1900, the proportion of elderly people who lived with their children began to drop sharply. One response was the transformation of poorhouses into old-age homes (as described in chapter 4); another was the explosion of "private institutions for the aged." Almost "two-thirds of the 1,200 benevolent homes operating in 1939 were founded between 1875 and 1919." In fact, by the 1920s, a revolt against institutional care for the

201

elderly, parallel to the revolt against children's institutions, stimulated the introduction of pensions.[46]

The "pension idea" also had other sources, of which the most important
was the mounting campaign to push older workers out of the labor force. Confronted with both labor's demands for a shorter workday and escalating competitive pressures, industrialists turned to new technology in their relentless drive
for higher productivity in less time. Older workers, they feared, simply could
not work fast enough, and opposition to them hardened between 1880 and
1915. Everywhere, social attitudes turned against the elderly. Earlier in the
century, writers had praised the "usefulness" and "merits of age." By contrast,
after the Civil War, "Instead of depicting the elderly as stately and healthy,
more and more observers described them as ugly and disease-ridden." By the
second decade of the twentieth century, "if not before," according to Achenbaum,
"most Americans were affirming the obsolescence of old age."[47]

Even organized labor joined the campaign for exclusion as it traded the
prerogatives of older workers for shorter workdays and discovered in pensions—
considered as a deferred wage—a bargaining chip which could be used to extract
concessions from employers even during depressions. "By inviting the speedup
in return for the shorter working day," claims Graebner, "labor organizations
bargained away the job rights of older workers who could not produce at higher
speeds and of the unemployed, who could be absorbed only if output levels
remained stable."[48]

Late in the nineteenth century, a few private industries—first, American
Express, in 1875—pioneered limited pension plans, which spread slowly in the
next few decades. Only after 1910, as part of industry's new concern with
scientific management, labor turnover, and increased productivity, did increasing
numbers of firms introduce pensions. Between 1910 and 1920, about twenty-
one firms a year started plans, and in the heyday of welfare capitalism in the
1920s, the figure rose to about forty-five, boosted, especially, by tax advantages
introduced in 1916. Still, the impact of private pensions remained limited. "As
of 1932, only 15 percent of American workers were potentially covered under
the plans, and perhaps 5 percent of those who needed benefits were receiving
payment." Nor did corporate pensions continue benefits to workers' widows.
In fact, "only 10 percent . . . legally obligated the company to any kind of
payment." Trade union pension plans had even less impact. In 1930, "only
about fifteen internationals and a few locals had pension programs." Those firms
and unions that introduced pensions, Graebner stresses, were not concerned
primarily with the economic problems of the elderly.

> For the corporation and the union, the pension was a device for recruiting and
> holding personnel and for prosecuting the on-going struggle for survival and dom-

[handwritten margin note: increase in pension plans, but still limited]

inance within the capitalist system. Social justice—the relief of old-age dependency—appears to have been singularly unimportant in motivating the corporation and only one of several goals for the union.[49]

Pensions spread most widely and quickly in the public sector. As municipal reformers streamlined city governments in the name of efficiency, they, too, tried to clear urban workforces of their older, allegedly incompetent members. In a number of instances, their interests partially coincided with those of aging city workers who lacked the income to retire. Indeed, pensions promised a partial solution to the worries of teachers, firemen, and policemen, none of whom earned enough to save very much for their old age. Still, as the representatives of city employer groups recognized, retirement and pensions were not unambiguous benefits. For they arbitrarily forced workers out of the labor force, onto a much lower pay scale, regardless of their health and competence. Although Chicago introduced the first teachers' pensions in 1895, no other cities followed its lead for 15 years. Then, between 1911 and 1915, thirty-three state legislatures introduced compulsory retirement and pensions for teachers; in twenty-one of them, the funds were built with contributions from both public funds and the teachers themselves. By the late 1920s, retirement funds for policemen, firemen, and teachers had become nearly universal.[50]

In 1911, Massachusetts became the first state to pass pension legislation covering all state employees. Although most other states had passed pension laws by 1923, this early legislation, limited in its coverage and benefits, had only a marginal impact. By 1935, state old-age assistance reached only one-fourth the number of people covered by federal—mainly military and civil service—pensions. In some cases, courts declared the legislation unconstitutional, and some governors vetoed it. Most of the hostility to state pensions came from business groups, whose "effective opposition" undercut the "intensive drive" mounted by pension or old-age insurance advocates in the 1920s. This business opposition, as Lubove contends, was more than a matter of ideology: "To concede the need for a pension program was to concede that welfare capitalism, voluntarism, had failed"[51]

In 1920, after a long, complex, political debate that had lasted 25 years, the federal government passed the first general retirement plan for its employees, which still remains the "core of federal civil service retirement." Although two major associations of retired federal workers (whose fights with each other eventually ended in court) had lobbied long and hard for retirement legislation, the law passed only when "business-oriented reformers decided that superannuation in the government service was too costly to endure." With the exception of a government contribution to a start-up fund, the new law, funded wholly by employee contributions, pointed American pension and retirement legislation in the direction it eventually would follow: that is, compulsory savings rather than a "real welfare state" which guarantees economic security out of general revenues. "The decision to construct a surrogate welfare state, premised on individual rather than social responsibility," Graebner underlines, "was not made in 1935, but in the decade after 1910." Although the influence of retired federal workers did make the legislation "more generous and humane than" it "otherwise would have been," most of their energy had been absorbed by "a defensive reaction against proponents of economic efficiency." Indeed, the forces in favor of "increased efficiency were the dominant component in the political history of retirement."[52]

In both industry and government, supervisors and older workers found ways around new retirement plans, which usually allowed exceptions in special circumstances for workers with undiminished skill and stamina. In practice, supervisors used these loopholes to employ workers who could not afford to retire, and, despite attempts to exclude them from work, participation rates of the elderly in the labor force did not drop sharply until after the introduction of Old Age Assistance in the 1930s. In this context, increasingly formal retirement rules did not reflect a kind, paternalistic streak in government or industry. To the contrary, an attempt to increase efficiency by depersonalizing the relations between management and labor, the rules reflected the hegemony of capitalist social relations throughout the workplace. "The pension," writes Graebner, "was expected to free those who made personnel decisions from the fetters of personalism, to transform a human situation into a bureaucratic one."[53]

By the 1920s, with "the appearance of a new social insurance leadership," old-age security had assumed first priority in the social insurance movement. Campaigns launched by the Fraternal Order of Eagles; the American Association for Old Age Security, founded in 1927 and led by Abraham Epstein; and in the 1930s, the Townsend movement, which advocated pensions of $200 each month for the elderly, eventually swept the country and forced the administration to put old-age security at the top of its legislative agenda. Indeed, by the 1920s, for reasons that had as much to do with class as dependence, the elderly had emerged as America's most effective lobby for social insurance. Unlike any other strand in the social insurance movement, old-age security cut across class lines. Because only the very wealthy could look forward without fear to old age, old-age security, as a social movement, did not need to draw support primarily from the working class. Instead it tapped the great new white-collar classes that taught the nation's schools, manned its swelling bureaucracies, and dominated its emerging service sector. With strong roots in the articulate, educated middle classes, old-age security broke loose from its earlier association with poor relief; forged ahead of every other kind of social insurance; and earned its privileged place as the only irreversible and untouchable welfare program in American history.[54]

Finally, if it need be said, the history of old-age security reveals once again the limits of voluntarism. For all the claims of welfare capitalists, industry protected only a small fraction of its workers; despite their stress on self-reliance and voluntarism, unions assisted even fewer; and in the Great Depression, most industrial and union pension plans went bankrupt. Only government had the resources and authority to offer economic security to the nation's elderly. Nonetheless, the reluctance to extend public authority into economic relations circumscribed government activity at every level. In the end, the federal government built a semiwelfare state out of individual contributions. Directed toward workers employed steadily for many years, excluding whole classes of badly paid, irregularly employed labor, for decades public old-age security deflected help away from those who needed it most.[55]

[handwritten margin notes: limits of volunteerism; strength of gov resources; indiv. contrib; = semi-welfare state]

8 Reorganizing the Nation

Peggy Terry remembered the impact of the Great Depression on her family in an Oklahoma town:

> I first noticed the difference when we'd come home from school in the evening. My mother'd send us to the soup line. . . . everybody had to bring their own buckets to get soup. . . . Then we'd go across the street. One place had bread, large loaves of bread. Down the road just a little piece was a big shed, and they gave milk. My sister and me would take two buckets each. And that's what we lived off for the longest time.
>
> I can remember one time, the only thing in the house to eat was mustard. My sister and I put so much mustard on biscuits that we got sick. And we can't stand mustard till today.

Reporter Lorena Hickok wrote about the suffering she found in a North Dakota town on a bitterly cold day in late October, 1933:

> For themselves and their families they need everything. Especially clothing. 'How about clothes?' the investigator asked one of them. He shrugged. "Everything I own I have on my back," he said. He then explained that, having no underwear, he was wearing two pairs of overalls, and two, very ragged denim jackets. His shoes were so far gone that I wondered how he kept them on his feet. With one or two exceptions none of the men hanging about the church had overcoats. Most of them were in denim—faded, shabby denim. Cotton denim doesn't keep out the wind very well. . . . When we came out to get into the car, we found it full of farmers, with all the windows closed. They apologized and said they had crawled in there to keep warm. . . . The women and children are even worse off than the men. Where there has been any money at all, it has gone for shoes for the children and work clothes for the men. The women can stay inside and keep warm, and the children can stay home from school.

206

Reorganizing the Nation

Between 1929 and the summer of 1933, official unemployment in America climbed from 3.2 percent to 24.9 percent. In Cleveland, unemployment reached 50 percent; in Akron, 60 percent; and in Toledo, 80 percent. Consumption expenses dropped 18 percent; construction, 78 percent; manufacturing output, 54 percent; and investment, 98 percent. In 1932, the automobile industry operated at 20 percent capacity. The Great Depression lay across the land.[1]

Even before the Great Depression, the inadequacy of the federal government had become painfully apparent. Indeed, few of the administrative reforms that had reshaped national corporations and city governments had been applied to the federal government. Like a small nineteenth century firm, the government lacked the means to coordinate increasingly complex, national business. With the election of Herbert Hoover, engineer, humanitarian, and modern manager, all of this appeared about to change. Hoover brought bright technicians into government and sponsored major studies of recent economic and social trends. Clearly, it seemed as though modern organizational and managerial models were about to reshape the federal government. Strangely, though, in office Hoover backed away from vigorous, federal action, and, as the depression worsened, he moved increasingly to the right. It was left to Franklin Delano Roosevelt and the New Deal to reorganize the federal government and, with it, national life. By the time FDR took office, voluntary agencies had exhausted their human and financial resources, and states and cities, teetering on the edge of bankruptcy, clamored for federal aid. Across the country, unemployed workers agitated for more relief, staged rent strikes, and rioted for food, and, not long after FDR's election, the Townsendites, Huey Long's share-the-wealth movement, and demagogues like Father Coughlin galvanized their followers into social movements that demanded quick, simple, sometimes frightening, solutions to the social and economic crisis.[2]

FDR did not intend to tamper with the fundamental structure of American capitalism. To the contrary, he wanted to save it, and he responded to the crisis with a flurry of legislation in his famous first hundred days. Unable to offer a quick, permanent solution to economic dependence and insecurity, he tapped his experience as governor of New York to create the nation's first federal relief system. Very shortly thereafter, warned of horrible suffering and rioting to come in the winter of 1934, he added a temporary but massive program of civil works. When the crisis eased, he turned relief of "unemployables" back to the states, where he thought it belonged, and introduced a new public works program to soak up employable people the private sector still could not absorb. At the same time, he charged a special committee of experts with devising a comprehensive and permanent system of economic security based on contributory insurance.

Despite his mounting political strength and the variety of options among which he could choose, FDR, worried about the reactions of both business and

207

Southern agriculture, drew back from the protean possibilities of the moment and built a semiwelfare state that used the power of the federal government to crystallize the distinction between social insurance and public assistance and reinforce income inequality. With the major public employment program, the Works Progress Administration, sharply curtailed by the late 1930s, with agricultural and domestic workers excluded from most social security programs, the new semiwelfare state offered little immediate help to the poor. Indeed, all things considered, the newly formed Congress of Industrial Organizations (CIO), made possible by the Wagner Act, became the New Deal's greatest gift to the working class. In the end, Hitler's armies and Japanese bombs, not the New Deal, lifted America out of the Great Depression. Still, it is wrong to dismiss the significance of New Deal social legislation. Emergency programs did prevent mass starvation and, very possibly, massive social disorder. Social security did introduce the idea of entitlement into national policy and establish federal responsibility for a wide range of human problems. Even more, the new legislation vastly augmented the size and scope of the national government, altered the very nature of federalism, and reorganized relations between the national state and its citizens.

Public Welfare in the 1920s

In the 1920s, technical experts presided over the reorganization of states' welfare apparatus into specialized departments that centralized fiscal control, systematized procedures, evaluated results, wrote new poor laws, tightened supervision of public and private agencies, and spent more money. Between 1917 and 1920, state legislatures passed 400 new public welfare laws; by 1931, mothers' pensions in all states except Georgia and South Carolina supported 200,000 children; and in constant dollars, public welfare expense, fueled especially by mothers' pensions, increased 168 percent between 1903 and 1928. Put another way, with 1913 as a base of 100, public welfare expenses increased from 70 in 1903 to 279 by 1928. Still, per capita spending on welfare by government remained low. Between 1913 and 1929, per capita federal spending rose from $.09 to $.25; state spending from $.78 to $1.85; and city spending from $1.65 to $3.12. Of all public welfare expenses, even in 1928, the federal government paid 58 percent—mostly veterans' pensions; states, 19 percent; and counties and cities, each 11 percent. Despite the widespread assumption that voluntary

208

agencies outspent government for welfare, public spending for relief exceeded private by a ratio of three to one.[3]

In the two decades before the Great Depression, private social work also changed. One major trend was the development of specialized casework (discussed in chapter 6): by the end of the 1920s, about half of the country's social workers considered themselves caseworkers, and many worked in specialized settings as medical social workers, visiting teachers, vocational guidance specialists, probation officers, psychiatric social workers, and personnel officials in private industry. Although their numbers had increased rapidly, their influence remained limited: only 8 percent of the country's 6,809 hospitals (about half in New York and Massachusetts) had social service departments in 1931; there were only 275 visiting teachers in thirty-four states; and only one-third of the country's factories had personnel departments. Despite an expansion of social work schools from five to forty-five between 1915 and 1930, the number of trained workers grew slowly and remained a minority within the occupation. In fact, social work schools enrolled only about 2,000 students, of which a mere 10 percent completed the course. Clearly, as an occupation, social work held limited attraction. Almost all of the country's 31,241 social workers in 1930, of whom 24,592 were women, ³/₄ *women* were paid very badly. The average staff salary in a social agency was $1,517 in 1925 compared to $1,844 for an elementary school and $2,434 for a high school teacher. At the same time, social workers' autonomy decreased as community chests and social service exchanges (discussed in chapter 6) coordinated their activities, agency administrators monitored their work more closely, and increased state supervision and funding eroded the boundaries between public and private. Between 1924 and 1928, in six large cities the share of funds from voluntary sources dropped from 22 percent to 19 percent of private agency budgets while the public contribution increased from 38 percent to 41 percent. (The rest came from endowments and earnings.)[4]

The increasingly rational, modern structure of welfare should not be overemphasized. From another point of view, in the late 1920s, the "uneven development of social work" was its most arresting character. "It is possible," observed Sydnor Walker, "to find every practice of the nineteenth century, however bad and officially outgrown, still followed in some spot not necessarily remote. The past is by no means left behind; there is ample opportunity to compare the standards of fifty years ago with those of today by travelling only a short distance from the centers which represent social work in its most advanced form." Indeed, despite nearly two decades of centralization, public welfare remained an overwhelmingly local responsibility, and the local boards that dispensed poor relief still composed a confused, bewildering administrative pattern. Most decentralized was Massachusetts, whose 355 towns and counties each formed distinct units for poor relief. (In most other states, only the counties were units.)

In Pennsylvania, approximately 525 laws still governed poor relief in 1934; in its 67 counties, 967 persons legally administered poor relief in 425 poor districts, 366 of which crowded into 15 counties. In New Hampshire, 700 different officials administered public relief in 245 separate county, city, and town units of which 140 had fewer than 1,000 people and only 14 more than 5,000. In Ohio's 88 counties, as late as 1934, 1,535 local government units retained some responsibility for poor relief.[5]

Soon after the onset of the Great Depression, state, local, and private welfare expenses skyrocketed. In eighty-one cities, the combined amount of public and private relief from about $42 million in 1929 to $70 million in 1930 and $170 million in 1931. These figures, which register the dramatic spread of unemployment and hunger, reveal only the tip of the desperation and destitution across the nation, for public and private agencies could meet only a fraction of the need. Equally important, many of the newly destitute, desperate to avoid the stigma of pauperism, turned first elsewhere, everywhere, anywhere, before they asked for help. In his great study of New Haven's unemployed during the depression, E. Wight Bakke identified the sequence of alternatives that preceded relief. At first, they sought help from friends, relatives, and others of their class. Indeed, they could take "occasional loans or even outright gifts of house furnishings and food from" their "economic equals with no damage to" their "sense of self-support." But gifts from those "of a higher economic category which did not involve the possibility of return assistance" remained "different": they were "charity" and, as such, challenged their "claim to independence." Bakke outlined the ten-step sequence in which unemployed workers sought help from different sources. The major breaks occurred between steps 3 and 4, 5 and 6, and 7 and 8, because at each of these points workers violated their own sense of independence.

1 Accrued benefit rights.
2 Commercial credit.
3 Savings of others than head of the family.

4 New working members of family not normally expected to earn.
5 Borrowing on property.

6 Clan aid—loans to gifts.
7 Friends—loans to gifts.

8 Government work relief.
9 Associations in which individual has membership.
10 Community assistance—cash to commodity.[6]

Clearly, unemployed workers turned to relief only as a last resort. "The

210

unemployed man who asks for assistance from a relief agency has obviously admitted failure in his attempt to be independent and self-supporting." He could not escape the fact that a new relationship "separated him . . . from his fellows." Of the 2,000 representative New Haven family heads Bakke interviewed in 1933, 988 were unemployed. Reinterviewed 2 years later, only one-quarter of them had sought relief, and half of those had been in contact with relief agencies before their current unemployment. Of the 12 percent who asked for relief for the first time between 1933 and 1935, only 10 percent had applied in less than 3 months; 17 percent, in less than 6; and 30 percent, after one year. "Even after two years of unemployment 40% of this applying-for-the-first-time group were 'getting by' somehow without public assistance. . . . after the full force had been felt of relief policies declared by some at the time to have killed self-reliance!"[7]

To most observers, then and since, the men and women who finally swallowed their pride and appeared at relief offices differed sharply from the chronically dependent relief population of the past. "Contemporaries," James Patterson notes, "concentrated neither on old poverty nor on low income. Their focus, so intense that it virtually blotted all else from vision, was unemployment, which the unprecedented depression had driven to catastrophic proportions." Many Americans usually had lived in poverty: the disabled, the handicapped, women who headed families or lived alone, old people without children to care for them, and the nonwhite had always been especially vulnerable. Nor was unemployment a new experience for native white working men. Nonetheless, in more prosperous times, even in earlier depressions, it had been possible to preserve the fiction that a sharp line separated those who asked for relief from the rest of the working class. Aside from physical disability, so many said, improvidence, laziness, or some other character defect distinguished people who asked for help. By 1930, massive, swelling unemployment had destroyed (temporarily as it turned out) these easy stereotypes, and people everywhere spoke of the "new" unemployment: a mass of respectable, hard-working family men unable to find work.[8]

According to one national study, in 1934 the average person on relief was a white male household head, age 38, with an elementary school education and 10 years' work experience in the occupation "he considered his customary or usual one," usually semi- or unskilled work in the "manufacturing or mechanical trades." The "most significant fact about the average urban worker on relief in 1934," the report claimed, "was that he had lost the last job at his usual occupation in the winter of 1931–32" or 2 years earlier. Only about 17 percent of the relief population consisted of "broken families or lone persons," and female household heads were only about 14 percent of the total. "Contrary to

211

an erroneous popular impression," concluded the report, "workers on urban relief rolls in 1934 were not industrial misfits who had never worked nor persons with an irregular work history. Unemployed workers on relief . . . were a relatively experienced group of workers." Similarly, in New York City, the Social Service Exchange reported that 82 percent of applications in January, 1930, came from people who had never asked for relief before. In 1931, the exchange processed 663,000 applications, twice as many as in the previous year. Even white-collar workers suffered. "We are now dealing with all classes," Harry Hopkins told the National Council of Social Work in 1933. "It is no longer a matter of unemployables and chronic dependents, but your friends and mine."[9]

Still, it must be remembered, unemployment hardly was a new experience for men who headed working-class families. Even the vaunted prosperity of the 1920s had a soft underbelly. Steadily employed skilled workers enjoyed rising incomes with which they joined the culture of consumption promoted by the brash, new advertising industry. But farmers suffered a decade-long depression, and unskilled workers often found themselves either without work or with wages too low to lift their families out of poverty. In 1927, for instance, Leila Houghteling surveyed "467 families of unskilled wage earners, married and with at least one child, in Chicago." Although more than two-thirds of them worked regularly, "the earnings of the chief wage earner were insufficient to provide a standard of living equal to that provided by the budget of the United Charities for dependent families." When E. Wight Bakke surveyed unemployed workers in New Haven in 1933, he found that "for three-fourths . . . this was not the first major spell of unemployment." During the past 10 years, the average worker had been unemployed for 1 year and 2½ months. Even this statistic, Bakke emphasized, "underestimates the irregularity of work and makes no reference at all to short-time schedules." Although the skilled and semiskilled had fared better than the unskilled, the great majority of men in each category had been unemployed. Indeed, only one-quarter of his sample "recalled no major spell of unemployment." The Great Depression, therefore, did not create unemployment as a serious problem. Irregular, insecure work had always disfigured working-class experience and prevented all but a fortunate minority from ever finding any sort of security. The sharp line separating the independent, self-supporting worker from his contemporaries who asked for help always had been a figment of ideology.[10]

Even so, the Great Depression was an unprecedented disaster: (1) because of the scale of industrial and financial collapse; (2) because of the magnitude of its unemployment, which soon exhausted all the usual sources of help; (3) because it reached into the ranks of salaried and professional workers who generally had escaped unemployment; (4) because skilled workers, lulled by rising real incomes in the 1920s, had begun to enjoy a level of modest affluence and consumption never before known to their class; and (5) because the customary cyclical recovery seemed increasingly evanescent and unlikely.

Before the New Deal: Governments, Relief, and Protest in the Great Depression

The consequences of sudden, massive unemployment fell first on local governments, which, as they had for 300 years, retained primary responsibility for poor relief. Although local governments and private agencies tried to increase relief payments, even in the most liberal cities they remained pitiful. Mostly, people received only a little food. In Detroit, for example, the cost of relief "rose from $116,000 in February 1920 to $1,582,000 two years later." Still, the amount of relief was only $3.60 a week for a family of two adults. Baltimore gave only an average of $0.80 a week in commodities. In 1932, those lucky enough to get relief in New York City—only one-quarter of the unemployed— had to scrape by on an average of $2.97 a week. Woefully unprepared, local governments lacked both the administrative capacity and financial resources to alleviate the crisis. Consequently, they turned for help to their state governments, which, unfortunately, in most cases, also lacked the money, organization, and sometimes even the will to respond effectively.[11]

Nor could private agencies cope with massive unemployment and suffering. Many buckled under the pressure and dissolved; some rationed their limited resources; others resisted involvement with relief and unemployment. For instance, although some settlement houses approached relief and unemployment energetically, joined appeals for federal help, sponsored "social action programs," and supported the New Deal, others became outspoken critics of the government social programs and "ignored social issues." The "decisive factor," according to Trolander, was "the presence or absence of a Community Chest in any given city." The "joint funding of private social agencies" explains "why settlements varied in social outlook and why the settlement reform impulse weakened." Community Chests, dominated by wealthy business interests, controlled the budgets and, by indirection, policies of the agencies they funded. The "well-to-do people" who held the "purse strings of private charity were adamantly opposed to the New Deal," and "with the rise of the Community Chest, they had extended their control over private charity."[12]

Large cities with high unemployment rates felt the crisis first. During the 1920s, counties and municipalities spent between 55 and 60 percent of all public funds. Two-thirds of their income came from property taxes, some from the states, and a tiny amount from the federal government, excluding veterans' pensions, which were not administered by local governments. When the Great Depression eroded their tax base, local governments could hardly meet the payments on the $9 billion debt they had acquired during the 1920s, let alone find much extra for welfare. Indeed, "By early 1933 nearly one thousand local governments had defaulted on their debts." Nor could voluntary agencies, their funds depleted by the crisis, supplement public funds. Although a few state governments took an "unusually reactionary" position and did almost nothing, most tried to respond constructively to the emergency. One of the most notable was New York, whose governor, Franklin Delano Roosevelt, also confronted a major crisis. During the first quarter of 1931, New York cities with a population greater than 30,000 spent more than $15 million on public and private relief compared to just under $4 million during the first quarter of 1929. In the same period, public expenses jumped 184.4 percent. Nor could private agencies relieve depleted city treasuries. "By the spring of 1932," Bremer reports, "social services in New York City had been disrupted almost beyond recognition. Nearly four hundred private agencies had disappeared since 1929 (about one-third of the 1929 total)," and the city's Home Relief Bureau reduced its aid for those families still on its rolls to "two dollars and sixty-seven cents a week." Faced with the breakdown of private and public welfare, Roosevelt called a special session of the state legislature to pass the "Wicks Act," which created the Temporary Emergency Relief Association (TERA) in September, 1931. The TERA gave FDR, as president, a model for the first federal relief program in American history.[13]

The TERA, directed by Harry Hopkins, gave matching grants to localities and made New York the first state to create a program of emergency unemployment relief. Equally important, it supervised "the way in which monies were spent . . . and . . . set professional standards for administrators." Although it was supposed to last only 10 months and spend $20 million, the TERA lingered until 1937 and eventually spent $50 million. Even though municipalities spent $1.6 billion and private agencies $30 million in the same years, everyone recognized that "relief fell far short of need." Indeed, work relief absorbed only a fraction of those who needed jobs. In August, 1932, for instance, although 32,000 people worked on relief projects, another 88,000 who had been approved waited for work. In the end, the experience of the TERA only underlined the impotence of state and local governments, which cut "cultural, recreational, health and child welfare services" and diverted money from education. "No one knew how far such cuts would be made . . . unless Federal funds could be

214

secured for relief." Whatever their earlier reservations about federal relief, whatever their commitment to home rule and states' rights, by 1933 few state and local officials still resisted Washington's assistance. To the contrary, governors and mayors lobbied hard for federal money. Indeed, only one source had the resources to attack the Great Depression and relieve its casualties: it was, of course, the federal government.[14]

Hoover's reluctance to initiate a federal relief program surprised the social workers and reformers who had supported him for president. They expected the former international relief administrator, manager, and engineer to energize the federal government and harness its resources to progressive social reform. Given Hoover's background, their expectations were reasonable, but they remained unmet. Hoover's first response to the unemployment crisis was the appointment of an Emergency Committee for Employment in October, 1930, directed by Colonel Arthur Woods. (In 1931, the committee was reorganized as the President's Committee on Unemployment Relief.) With no funds for relief, the committee accomplished little, and Hoover rejected its recommendations for "federal road building, rural electrification projects . . . urban housing. . . . a national bureau for gathering unemployment statistics, 'a nationwide system of public employment offices,' and a national plan for unemployment insurance." Indeed, as the depression worsened, Hoover increasingly stressed voluntarism and the local basis of relief:

> This is not an issue as to whether people shall go hungry or cold in the United States. It is solely a question of the best method by which hunger and cold shall be prevented. It is a question as to whether the American people on one hand will maintain the spirit of charity and mutual self-help through voluntary giving and the responsibility of local government as distinguished on the other hand from appropriations from the Federal treasury for such purposes. . . . The basis of successful relief in national distress is to mobilize and organize the infinite number of agencies of self-help in the community. That has been the American way of relieving distress among our own people and the country is successfully meeting its problem in the American way today.

By 1932, even Hoover had to admit that the American way needed federal help, and in July he signed a relief bill that created the Reconstruction Finance Corporation (RFC), which "offered states $300 million in federal funds. . . . to be lent, not given, and deducted from future highway grants." The RFC increased the amount of federal money flowing to states from about $100 million in the 1920s to $240 million in 1932–33. Woefully inadequate, the new funds hardly resolved the problem, although they did force states to improve their administrative practices. For the RFC examined applications carefully; made only short-term grants; and "forced state developed relief services to maintain acceptable practices," if they wanted their funds renewed. When the program ended in 1933, an expert at the Russell Sage Foundation reported that as a result of the RFC, "All but four states have now some form of state-wide relief organization, more or less effectively developed; and social workers of training, experience and good professional standards have been brought into positions of influence in more than half of them."[15]

Not all members of Congress shared Hoover's opposition to federal relief. From the time Congress convened in 1931 until the first important federal relief legislation in 1933, senators, especially Costigan of Colorado, La Follette of Wisconsin, and Wagner of New York, held hearings whose records offer "the most vivid, the most telling and the most accurate picture in existence of the unemployment relief problem; the extent of the destitution during the early years of the depression, and the struggles of local and private agencies to meet increasing needs" with "inadequate funds." In 1931, one of Wagner's bills that called for federally funded public works, an expanded federal employment service, and unemployment insurance passed the House and Senate, only to be vetoed by Hoover.[16]

By 1932, "Many observers were warning that the desperate conditions facing Americans might produce a revolution." Wealthy businessmen, "prominent journalists and politicians agreed that revolution, rather than prosperity, might be right around the corner. William Allen White wrote in the fall of 1931 that effective relief would be 'the only way to keep down the barricades in the streets this winter.' Several normally conservative labor leaders joined in the prediction of revolution." Although no revolution arrived, anger and frustration among the unemployed often boiled over into militant action. Thousands of unemployed workers looted food stores; (afraid of their contagious effect, the press usually did not report food riots); indeed, Irving Bernstein reports, "By 1932 organized looting of food stores was a nationwide phenomenon." Anthracite coal miners bootlegged coal; others joined demonstrations demanding increased relief, which often ended in fights with the police. Elsewhere, especially in Harlem, unemployed councils organized rent strikes, forcibly prevented evictions, and led demonstrations at relief offices, where they pioneered the sit-down strike as a form of nonviolent protest. In Pittsburgh, Father James R. Cox, a priest "known as the Mayor of Shantytown," drew 60,000 people to a rally at Pitt Stadium, and 12,000 followed him to Washington to present their case to Hoover. In the spring, 1932, about 5,000 veterans and their families descended on Washington, where they camped in old, unused, partially demolished buildings or in tents, and asked for early payment of pensions due them in July, 1943. Congress refused their request, and Hoover, who would not meet them, ordered

unlike today [handwritten marginal note]

the army, led by General Douglas MacArthur and Major Dwight Eisenhower, to rout them from the Capitol. A. Everette McIntyre, then a federal trade commissioner, told Studs Terkel:

> The police encircled them. There was some brick-throwing. A couple of the police retaliated by firing. A bonus man was killed and another seriously wounded. . . . To my right . . . military units were being formed. . . . A squadron of cavalry was in front of this army column. Then, some staff cars, and four trucks with baby tanks on them, stopped near the camp. They let the ramps down and the baby tanks rolled out into the street. . . . The 12th Infantry was in full battle dress. Each had a gas mask and his belt was full of tear gas bombs. . . . They fixed their bayonets and also fixed the gas masks over their faces. At orders, they brought their bayonets at thrust and moved in. The bayonets were used to jab people, to make them move. . . . The entire block was covered by tear gas. Flames were coming up, where the soldiers had set fire to the buildings to drive these people out.[17]

Emergency Relief and the Expansion of the Federal Government

No one really knew what to expect of FDR. Despite a decent record as governor of New York, he seemed neither daring nor innovative. His vague, contradictory campaign speeches left his real opinions and plans, if he had any, unclear. Nonetheless, within his first hundred days as president, he astounded everybody with a legislative barrage that transformed the role and structure of the federal government. As part of his redefinition of federal responsibility, FDR, for the first time, put the national government directly and massively into the business of relief. Nonetheless, he did so unwillingly. When the first emergency passed, he returned relief, other than work programs for the unemployed, back to the states, where he thought it belonged.[18]

Roosevelt had to act quickly. When he took office, he confronted a deepening depression, massive suffering and unrest around the country, a banking system tottering on the brink of collapse, bankrupt mayors and governors demanding help, worsening unemployment, farmers unable to sell their crops or pay their debts. Everywhere, people looked to the new government for fast, decisive action. Still, he faced constraints that would hobble any national government, whatever its intentions. One of them was the nature of federalism

Federalism plus [handwritten marginal note]

itself. Another was the small, weak, undeveloped administrative capacity of the national government.

Neither relief nor social insurance are among the responsibilities assigned to the national government by the Constitution, and, of course, all powers not directly granted to the national government are reserved to the states. How, then, was the national government to justify its excursion into welfare? The answer had to be by "indirection," aware, always, of the tricky constitutional basis of its expanded activity and the possibility that the Supreme Court might invalidate its whole program for reform, as, indeed, it seemed to do in 1935 when it declared the National Recovery Act (NRA) unconstitutional. Nonetheless, the government could develop its own public works projects; set labor conditions for federal contractors; attach conditions to grants-in-aid offered to states, as long as states remained theoretically free to refuse them; impose regulations on interstate commerce; or draw on its vague constitutional authority "to provide for the ... general Welfare." Of these, grants-in-aid became the most important and effective method, because whatever their attachment to states' rights or reservations about federal money, states by and large have been unable to resist the temptation of federal dollars. In fact, the grant-in-aid system developed and expanded, though not invented, during the New Deal became the template for federal-state relations in the decades that followed.[19]

grants in-aid [handwritten marginal note]

States' rights set limits to federal expansion as powerful, if less formal, than the Constitution and Supreme Court. In the 1930s, Patterson points out, states' rights "was a vital ideology," shared by a varied coalition in Congress. Even Edwin Witte, who came to Washington from Wisconsin to direct the Committee on Economic Security, which formulated the social security legislation, remained "skeptical of both the wisdom and constitutionality of national administration" and shared the fears of many people in his home state that the federal government might undercut their progressive innovations in unemployment insurance and other areas. More often, states' rights reflected a fear that federal influence would disrupt cozy local practices and political arrangements, raise taxes, give too much money to people on relief, or interfere with race relations. Indeed, in the South, states' rights often was little more than a cover for racism.[20]

The national government's limited size and administrative weakness confronted New Deal agencies with an enormous task when they began to build the administrative structures with which to launch the federal government into new responsibilities on an unprecedented scale under emergency conditions. Some of the most fascinating, important, and untold history of the New Deal lies precisely in this area: the way in which the national government created the infrastructure of the national state.[21]

In the nineteenth century, Theda Skocpol writes, America was governed by a unique system of "courts and parties." "The courts regulated and defended property rights," and the "party-dominated electoral-administrative system freely handed out economic benefits and loosely knit together a diverse society." Well suited to an "expanding, decentralized economy," this mode of government began to break down in the late nineteenth and early twentieth century with "the advent of corporate concentration and the emergence of a truly national economy and society." Nonetheless, old interests blocked any fundamental change in the structure of government, which altered "slowly and in fragmented ways during the Progressive era." Without established bureaucracies, like those in European countries, presidents led "administrative expansion and federalizing reforms," which Congress resisted. Even during World War I, "administrative expansion . . . was ad hoc and staffed by officials predominantly recruited from business." Therefore, the Great Depression found the United States with "a bureaucratically weak national government, and one in which existing administrative capacities were poorly coordinated."[22]

President Roosevelt did not permit the national government's administrative underdevelopment to deter him. His early legislation, which demanded immediate action, depended on a quick, effective, and massive expansion of the federal government. To an amazing degree, it happened. Consider the administrative task of the Federal Emergency Relief Administration—created by congressional action on May 12, 1933—modeled after FDR's emergency relief program in New York, and led by its director, Harry Hopkins. The FERA began with $500 million: the first $250 million consisted of matching funds to be given to the states ($1 federal for every $3 in public money raised from all sources and spent in the states during the preceding 3 months); the remaining $250 million was a discretionary fund to be spent by the FERA itself where the need appeared greatest. Hopkins took office on May 22, 1933, and approved the first grants the following day. Between May, 1933, and June 30, 1936, when it was finally terminated, the FERA had spent over $3 billion. The FERA had to put the national government into the relief business for the first time, improve state administrative procedures, and persuade states to increase their spending. As Hopkins's associate Josephine Brown observed, when Hopkins took office, "he undertook to administer the biggest single business ever developed in any country." Between late May and the end of December, 1933, the FERA had allocated over $324 million to forty-eight states and all the Territories. By March, 1934, nearly 3,700,000 families and single people were receiving relief; one month later the figure jumped to 4,500,000. All of this called for an expansion of staff throughout the country. "In more than three thousand county administrative units and in over a thousand additional town and municipal units, social service staffs were rapidly built up to a total of approximately 40,000 by October,

219

1934." In all, the FERA employed about 120,000 people.[23]

The states spent FERA funds on both work relief and direct relief. At first, they paid for work relief in kind rather than cash; however, after March, 1934, all work was paid for with wages, even though direct relief often came in the form of grocery orders or, most unsatisfactory of all, orders on commissaries or central warehouses. (The federal government also had started a surplus food program, directed more to increasing farm income than to feeding the hungry.) Benefits varied greatly from state to state. In May, 1934, a family in Kentucky received $6.78 each month; in New York, $45.12. Sometimes, in order to spread relief more widely, states lowered benefits. Because standards remained arbitrary and artificial, the size of the relief rolls was a poor guide to the extent of need. Hopkins well understood relief's inadequacy. He knew that the states' manipulation of eligibility requirements always kept an "underdetermined number of needy people" off the rolls. Indeed, the FERA "never could discover" the full number "or devise a satisfactory way" to reach them.[24]

What was it like to apply for relief? Writing to Harry Hopkins, Lorena Hickok described the humiliation and agony in New York City:

> You go first to a schoolhouse in your neighborhood designated as a precinct Home Relief office. If you are the kind of person the government really should be interested in helping, you go there only as the last resort. You have used up all your resources and have strained the generosity of your relatives and your friends to the breaking point. Your credit is gone. You couldn't change a nickel's worth at the grocery store. You owe several months' rent. The landlord has lost his patience and is threatening to throw you out. Maybe you've already gone through an eviction or two. . . . If your children happen to attend the school where you must go to apply for relief, it just makes it that much tougher. . . . There will be a policeman around, maybe several. A lot more would be there inside of three minutes if you caused any commotion. . . . If you get by the policemen—and some people, I have been told, take one look at him, lose their courage, and turn around and go home—you have to tell some man at the door what you're there for. If you've got any pride, it hurts. . . . You go into a room filled with people. Up at the front a line of makeshift desks, where interviewers are taking down the stories of relief applicants. You sit on a bench in the back of the room. And there you wait, wondering if they're going to make you sell the radio, which wouldn't bring in enough to feed the family two days. You're apt to wait a long time—and it doesn't improve your morale. Eventually you get your turn. Maybe the questions aren't so bad, but you hate answering them, just the same. . . . Finally you get out—and go home to wait. An investigator will call at your house . . . and ask more questions.[25]

Even with its funds channeled through the states, the national government retained unprecedented control through its administrative regulations. FERA regulations forced state and local governments to expand and reorganize their

220

relief administration. Eventually, every state except Maryland set up special emergency relief agencies separate from their existing welfare departments. Indeed, the FERA hoped to link "Federal, state and local" government agencies into "one closely-knit system." The system, of course, never was as closely knit as the FERA wanted. The size of relief grants, the balance between cash and in-kind payment, eligibility requirements, and the competence and cooperation of local administrators all varied too much. Nonetheless, the degree to which states altered their relief practices and conformed to federal regulations, the speed with which the FERA created a national administrative structure, and the scope of its operations—all of which were unprecedented—were harbingers of the future of government and its relation to the people in America.[26]

The FERA proved the effectiveness of the grant-in-aid system. Even though states had clamored for federal aid because they claimed to be stretched to their financial limits, they found money to match the new federal grants. Although the proportion of emergency relief funds provided by the federal government rose from 62.2 percent to 71.6 percent between 1933 and 1934, the amount of money spent by states increased from about $104 million to $189 million and the amount spent by local governments from $197 to $233 million. Later matching grants also stimulated greater state spending. For instance, in Massachusetts, in the thirty years after 1936, following the introduction of old-age assistance and aid to dependent children, both matching grant programs, the amount of money raised by the state increased from $8.5 million to $76 million and from local revenues from $20 million to $49 million, even though the proportion of costs paid by the federal government nearly doubled.[27]

matching grants

Grants-in-aid also forced states to improve their standards and practices by providing more adequate assistance, hiring more professional personnel, and increasing their administrative equity and efficiency. Even more, the extension of the grant-in-aid system changed the nature of American federalism. In a federal system, as Derthick points out, government functions are shared in two ways. One, which is set out in the Constitution, allocates them by level. The other, "which evolved through the medium of the grant system until it has become the prevailing approach, is for all major functions to be shared." In this way, the New Deal set in motion not only an extension of governmental responsibility or an increase in public spending on social welfare; it also stimulated a profound and enduring shift in the nature of federalism and, hence, in the character of American government itself.[28]

Because it hoped both to create as uniform a program as possible and to raise administrative standards, the FERA set "uniform minimum wages," prohibited racial, religious, and political discrimination, and made public agencies responsible for public funds. As public agencies increasingly were identified as the source of relief funds, private agencies concentrated more on casework and therapeutic intervention. The FERA thereby reshaped the practice of social work by heightening the role of public agencies and sharpening the division of responsibilities between them and the private sector.[29]

Nonetheless, private social workers, especially women, exerted an unprecedented influence on government policy during the New Deal. For the New Deal "brought to Washington a remarkable group of women who would rise to positions of power and prominence in many of the new government agencies," and their personal interaction created an important and influential women's network within the New Deal. The women's network, in fact, was one of the important forces continually pushing FDR and the New Deal to expand the federal government's role in social welfare. Led by Eleanor Roosevelt and Frances Perkins, secretary of labor and the first woman cabinet member, most network members had been born in the 1870s and 1880s. They were second-generation Progressive reformers who followed in the footsteps of the great pioneers: Jane Addams, Florence Kelley, Julia Lathrop, and M. Carey Thomas (president of Bryn Mawr). Clustered in the new divisions of the federal government, they thought of themselves as social reformers rather than feminists and self-consciously brought a woman's viewpoint to the New Deal. Together, they exerted a critical influence on social welfare policies. For instance, "The Mothers' Pension plan incorporated into the final [Social Security] bill as Aid to Dependent Children . . . was based on a report written by Katherine Lenroot and Martha M. Eliot of the Children's Bureau, with the help of the former Children's Bureau chief, Grace Abbott." Grace Abbott also persuaded Frances Perkins to include a section prohibiting child labor in the Fair Labor Standards Act, which Perkins and Lenroot drafted. After new social legislation had passed, members of the network played key roles in its administration. To take one example, aside from the Children's Bureau, which always had been led by women, Molly Dewson, an important network member, served on the new three-member Social Security Board from 1937 to 1938. Ellen Woodward succeeded her for a six-year term. "Jane Hoey headed the Bureau of Public Assistance, and Sue Shelton White worked in the legal department." Nonetheless, the network members failed to "institutionalize even the limited gains" they had "won in the 1930s," and, as they aged, no new generation replaced them. By the end of World War II, "the women's network was nearing its end as well." The death of FDR, says Susan Ware, the network's historian, was "the final blow."[30]

Another, if more intermittent, pressure for expansive social welfare policies arose from the unemployed. The Great Depression, write Piven and Cloward, "saw the rise and fall of the largest movement of the unemployed this country has known." Almost wherever she went, Lorena Hickok, hired by Harry Hopkins to report on the administration of federal relief, commented on this public protest either boiling over or simmering, ready to explode. In August, 1932, she wrote Hopkins:

> I still feel that vast numbers of the unemployed in Pennsylvania are 'right on the edge,' so to speak—that it wouldn't take much to make Communists out of them. The Communists are decidedly not friends of the government. They openly say they hope the Administration program will fail. They want bloodshed. They say so themselves.

Communists, socialists, and other radical groups organized councils of the unemployed. Although only a tiny fraction of unemployed workers formally joined them, all over the country thousands of workers not affiliated with any social movement or political party joined in the demonstrations and protests they sponsored. The unemployed's protests forced several states and cities to participate in the new federal programs, which were voluntary and required matching funds. When relief appropriations became an issue in Ohio, 7,000 unemployed workers "marched on the state capitol." When the federal government discontinued relief to Colorado in the winter of 1934 because of the state's failure to pay its share of the costs, "mobs of the unemployed rioted in relief centers, looted food stores, and stormed the state legislature." Within 2 weeks, the legislature passed a new relief bill. Around the nation, local groups led similar events. Still, no national organization existed, and, everywhere, leaders of the unemployed complained about the chaotic, unorganized nature of the movement.[31]

Nonetheless, militant unemployed workers could be proud of their accomplishments. As Roy Rosenzweig points out, "First, they resolved the immediate individual grievances of their members with particular success: They won relief adjustments, blocked evictions, and reconnected the gas and electric for thousands of unemployed." Second, as organizations, they not only "helped create pressure . . . for higher levels of relief and larger relief appropriation, but also for more equitable and less degrading administrative practices at relief stations." Third, in the 1930s, they were "the first groups . . . to propagandize and agitate openly and actively for unemployment insurance," which they helped "revive . . . as a serious issue." Less tangible but at least as important, they helped unemployed workers understand "that their condition was not their own fault," and they "helped raise the political and social consciousness of the thousands of workers who passed through" their "ranks." Indeed, many of the early rank and file members of the CIO, as well as its leaders, "came directly out of the unemployment movement." So did many black leaders influential two decades later in the early civil rights movement. Especially in urban ghettos like Harlem, the unemployed movement for the first time brought blacks and whites together in the militant pursuit of social justice.[32]

The Contradictions of Work Relief

Early in the depression, pressure for work relief arose from two sources: "the survival among middle-class people of the traditional attitude toward work as a duty, and . . . the newer attitude of the working class stressing the obligation to work." However, as the costs of work relief—and, consequently, taxes—rose, as government appeared to compete with private enterprise, as problems with the organization and administration of work relief surfaced, middle-class enthusiasm for work relief waned. By 1940, "a great body of support" encouraged "the elimination of work relief and the substitution therefor of a presumably less costly and less competitive dole."[33]

The inability of New Deal agencies to resolve the tensions inherent in work relief had historic precedents. With the exception of the occasional farm, attempts to put the inmates of poorhouses to work usually had failed. Indeed, the inability of poorhouses to integrate a program of useful work into their routine remained a constant criticism throughout the nineteenth century. Nor had public works, never really tried on a massive scale in America, successfully united productive and efficient labor with relief. When private charities committed to the association of work with relief confronted the problem of setting their clients to work, all they could do was resort to breaking stone or cutting wood. This failure of work relief did not result from a lack of will or intelligence on the part of administrators or from the indolence of their clients. Rather, it reflected the contradictions between work relief and American political economy.

Federal Employment in the Early New Deal

New federal employment programs tried to put young people—who often lacked training as well as jobs—to work. The first, the Civilian Conservation Corps (CCC), authorized in March, 1933, sent men 18–25 to work camps, primarily in rural areas. (The government started a few camps for women as well, which remained independent of the CCC.) The War Department, the only branch of the government with enough experience, administered the program through existing agencies. At its peak, in August, 1935, the CCC employed 505,000 young men in 2,600 camps. It closed in 1941 when the problem of manpower became a shortage rather than a glut. The National Youth Administration (NYA) (1936), technically part of the Work Projects Administration (WPA), sponsored part-time jobs for young men and women still in school and, for those out of school, near their homes and in residential centers, intended,

224

in effect, as vocational boarding schools. Most students aided were in high school, and their families had to be on relief. Before the expansion of the program for defense training in 1941, the number of students aided hovered around 400,000. Even though the CCC and NYA had educational components, both (unlike other major social reform movements) deliberately bypassed the public educational system. "New Dealers like [Aubrey] Williams, director of the NYA," point out David Tyack and his colleagues, "were convinced that few teachers would have the courage to teach the truth about the injustices of American society, and that educators regarded many people as uneducable, and the present system of schooling did not equip either youth or adults to cope with the massive dislocation of society." Nonetheless, the New Deal did funnel money into schools through relief and public works.[34]

As part of the National Recovery Act, the government created the Public Works Administration (PWA) in June, 1933. Although the PWA, headed by Harold L. Ickes, secretary of the interior, had broad authority to finance public works projects, in practice, it did no construction itself. Instead, it loaned money to state and local governments and to private firms. Ickes, determined to construct high-quality projects and prevent his agency from turning into a pork-barrel, reviewed all proposals carefully with his engineering, law, and finance divisions. As a consequence, the PWA moved slowly, and, although it funded the construction of important public facilities, it did not stimulate employment quickly. Indeed, contractors, not required to use workers on relief, seldom did so.[35]

To supplement the FERA's inadequate work relief programs, alleviate the suffering and disorder predicted for the winter of 1933–34, and inject some purchasing power into the economy, the national government launched the Civil Works Administration (CWA) in November, 1933. On November 9, Hopkins had persuaded President Roosevelt to accept the new jobs plan; by January, the CWA employed 4 million people. The CWA was not relief or a dole. Rather, it reflected the administration's highest priority: to put the unemployed back to work. Unlike the FERA, the CWA paid its workers wages negotiated by the Public Works Administration in collective bargaining agreements. However, in contrast to the PWA and, later the Work Projects Administration, it "assumed the complete responsibility to undertake projects, hire workers, and place applicants according to their skill." In its short 4-month life, the CWA employed professionals, artists, and white-collar workers as well as craftsmen and unskilled laborers. It was the greatest public works experiment in American history. Given the haste with which it was constructed and the staggering administrative task it faced, the CWA's achievements were heroic.

> Despite record-freezing cold, gangs of construction and repair men fanned out over the landscape, building and widening roads, clearing sites for recreation centers,

225

and grading runways for airports. Hundreds of miles of ditches were opened to install water mains and sewer conduits, while schools, hospitals, libraries, and other public buildings got replastered walls, new coats of paint, and even decorative murals. Hardly a community failed to receive some lasting benefit—a paved street, an athletic stadium, a new playground. The CWA sent visiting nurses to the poor in city slums and bookmobiles to remote regions of the South. It pumped $1 billion of purchasing power into the stagnant economy.

Half the CWA's workers came from the emergency work relief rolls of the FERA, and the others, with no means test applied, from the ranks of people who needed jobs. At its peak, in January, 1934, the CWA employed 4,260,000 workers. "Not until 1971," points out Schwartz, "would a mere tenth of the 4 million jobless" employed by the CWA "enjoy the status of public employees." In February, 1934, the FERA, the CWA, and the CCC assisted about 8 million households with 28 million people or 22.2 percent of the American population.[36]

Dominated by "businessmen and efficiency experts, many of them independent Republicans and holdovers from the Hoover 'New Era,' " the CWA worked more "like an emergency employment corporation . . . than charitable made work." Indeed, within the CWA, the management and efficiency experts edged the social workers from power by consciously abandoning casework, rejecting a means tests, and relegating them to a minor role within the agency. As a result, when fiscal conservatives, Southern democrats, and business groups, alarmed at the CWA's potential effect on wages, not to mention its cost, attacked the agency, social workers were notably absent among its defenders.[37]

President Roosevelt had always thought of both the FERA and CWA as temporary—responses to crises and not permanent solutions—and he was easily persuaded by the arguments of conservatives like Bureau of the Budget Director Lewis Douglas who warned him that "thousands would settle into government-made jobs if civil works continued" while " 'political forces' generated by prolonging the CWA might become so great that it might be impossible to end it." In January, 1934, FDR warned the National Emergency Council that the CWA "will become a habit with the country. We want to get away from the CWA as soon as we can." FDR's policy reflected conventional worries about the effect of relief on work incentive and initiative. He warned Congress that "continued dependence upon relief induces a spiritual and moral disintegration fundamentally destructive to the national fibre. To dole out relief in this way is to administer a narcotic, a subtle destroyer of the human spirit." Even Hopkins, early in his administration, said that the job of the FERA was "to see that the unemployed get relief, not to develop a great social work administration throughout the United States." When the CWA ended, its workers either were dropped or transferred to the FERA. Although the FERA tried to develop work relief programs in all communities with more than 5,000 people, it paid much lower wages and employed far fewer people. Even more, it, too, was targeted for abolition. In fact, within a month after the decision to close down the CWA, Congress passed the Emergency Relief Appropriations Act, which effectively terminated the FERA as well.[38]

The administration had decided on a new strategy. The federal government would assume responsibility for the relief of "employable" unemployed workers through a new national program of work relief. Victims of a "nationwide depression" with national, not local, causes, they were, said FDR, the responsibility of the federal government. To put all of the employable people now on relief to work, "pending their absorption in a rising tide of private employment," was a duty "dictated by every intelligent consideration of national policy." By contrast, the new legislation turned the relief of the "unemployables" back to the states, where, according to President Roosevelt, it belonged. People "who could not maintain themselves independently" would be "cared for by local efforts. . . . It is my thought that in the future they must be cared for as they were before."[39]

Whatever FDR might say, state and local governments still lacked the resources, and often the will, to run adequate relief programs without federal prodding. Indeed, critics both inside and outside the administration opposed the cutbacks, predicted serious consequences, and proposed alternative policies. Even Harry Hopkins joined the call for a federal department of welfare, and Frances Perkins, secretary of labor and chair of the Committee on Economic Security, appointed a distinguished group of public welfare officials and social workers to an Advisory Committee on Public Employment and Relief, which "strongly recommended an enlarged work program, without any relief eligibility requirement, for all who needed employment, and Federal grants to the states for general relief for the benefit of all persons in need" and incapable of work. The proposed new federal work program, it argued, could absorb no more than 50 percent or 60 percent of families currently assisted through the FERA. Social workers also protested the end of the FERA, in which they had a great deal more influence than in the CWA. Confronted with mass unemployment, angry at the federal government's withdrawal from relief, social work, according to Brown, at last discarded the vestiges of scientific charity and openly supported public relief. Indeed, one social work faction, "critical not only of the government's relief and work programs, but of the New Deal as a whole and of the moral validity of the prevailing economic order," created the militant Rank and File movement within social work and published the radical journal, *Social Work Today*.[40]

Critics who predicted hardship when the FERA ended were right. The period of transition between the FERA and the WPA was "a time of confusion and near chaos in the history of public relief," a period of "uncertainty, insecurity, and even terror for the relief client," who with no "secure work relief and . . .

227

no sure niche in developing categorical programs" needed to rely on the limited, inadequate general relief offered by hard-pressed state and local governments. In Denver, to take an example, "Diets of relief families were found to provide only: 51 percent of the necessary calories; 40 percent of the phosphorous needed; from 30 to 40 percent of the required protein and iron; from 20 to 30 percent of the needed calcium and vitamin A; from 10 to 20 percent of the required vitamins B and G; and only 5 and 6 percent, respectively, of the essential vitamins C and D." In California, in 1941, families on relief received about 21 percent less than a "subsistence budget"; in Texas, where "no relief at all" was "available to thousands of needy families," the relief given fell "far, far short of meeting recipients needs." According to one report, the return of relief to local governments, "paralyzed" the states' "plans for meeting human needs."

> Its most compelling effects may be found by all who seek them; in hovels beneath viaducts, in early deaths encouraged by the diseases of hunger, in high infant mortality rates, in juvenile delinquency, in crowded hospitals for the insane, in the degradation of the body and of the spirit among our neighbors—*the men, women, and children whom we keep alive but to whom we deny an opportunity to live.*[41]

The WPA and the Substitution of Work for Relief

As jobs, "not the dole," became the "keystone of federal aid," Congress approved the creation of the Works Progress Administration (after 1939, The Work Projects Administration) in 1935. Within a year, it employed more than 3 million people. Despite superficial similarities between the WPA and the CWA, great differences separated the two agencies. The WPA, first of all, decentralized its operations. With the exception of the Arts Program and a few others, "most WPA undertakings were planned and sponsored by state and local units, with ninety-five percent of all money going to the latter." The WPA also boosted the authority of social workers, who were sent to investigate all applications for relief. "In sharp contrast to the CWA (where conceivably more than one person per family could hold a job), the WPA would employ only one member at any one time; and family size, makeup, and monthly budgets figured in eligibility." The new means test meant that many unemployed workers, previously employed by the CWA, were unable to qualify for work with the WPA. Wages on the WPA became a particularly delicate issue. Wary of encouraging workers to remain on public projects, the WPA "drew up an elaborate scheme of differential payments" called "security wages," pegged, supposedly, between wages in the private sector and relief.[42]

WPA projects included all sorts of work, from repairing highways to cataloguing archives and recording the stories of ex-slaves. Although it employed

228

skilled workers, most of its labor force was unskilled or semiskilled, and a plurality of its funds, 38.9 percent, were spent on the construction of highways, roads, and streets. Between 1935 and 1942, the WPA spent over $15 billion. However, the high turnover on its projects make impossible any estimation of how many individuals it actually employed. The largest number at any one time was 3 million, and its rolls never dropped below 1.4 million. Because the average WPA worker lived in a family with 3.76 people, the total number helped by the WPA was very high. Nonetheless, the WPA reached only a fraction of the eligible people, by one estimate, only a quarter of the eligible unemployed. "At all times there were 350,000 to 900,000 unemployed certified for WPA employment but not used" because of lack of money, and between 1,500,000 and 2,300,000 people at all times "were on relief, but not certified for WPA employment." Nor did it pay adequate wages. "Particularly for the semi-skilled, the total wages per year were often only 65 to 70 percent of that originally intended." In the South, the proportion was much lower, perhaps only 30 to 40 percent of a worker's total needs.[43]

When social workers attacked the relatively small amount allocated to the WPA, their colleagues inside the administration replied "by calling attention to the assault on the government's program from the right, which threatened, they claimed, its very existence." Not only Republicans in Congress "but . . . the nation's press, largely Republican in political outlook, and . . . business organizations from the U.S. Chamber of Commerce down . . . had succeeded in convincing large sections of the public that WPA was a 'boondoggle.' " Any liberalization of wages or coverage, a leading administration official told the National Conference of Social Work, "would bring the program down." Businessmen worried about the WPA's effect on the labor market and wage rates; they feared public employment would delay recovery by driving up their costs and prices. Sensitive to this pressure, the administration tailored its appropriations for work relief to the fluctuations of the labor market.[44]

Although the WPA lasted until World War II eliminated unemployment, Congress slashed its budget nearly in half in 1937, when economic conditions appeared to improve a little. Although funds were raised slightly the next year during the renewed depression, they were cut sharply again in 1939 when Congress ordered everyone employed eighteen months or more fired. When it cut those employed for eighteen months, Congress clearly "intended to force project workers to seek private employment." The problem, of course, was that the private sector could not absorb the displaced workers. Indeed, the economic statistics used by the administration to defend its reduction in WPA employment proved poor predictors of the availability of private sector jobs for WPA workers. Of 775,000 workers in twenty-three cities dropped because of the new 18-month rule, only 7.6 percent had found private jobs within three to four weeks

229

and 12.7 percent within two to three months. "In industrial centers like Buffalo, Cleveland, Cincinnati, Detroit, and Birmingham, the proportion with jobs was about one in six; in eight of the twenty-three cities it was about one in ten."[45]

Historians and contemporaries have given New Deal work relief programs mixed verdicts. Virtually no one—even their sponsors in the federal government—has argued they lacked faults. The disagreement centers more on how completely they failed. The answer looks different from the point of view of an unemployed worker who exchanged his tiny relief benefits and the constant scrutiny of a social worker for higher wages and greater independence on a CWA or WPA job than from the perspective of a social scientist confronted with data on inadequate coverage, wretched wages, and low productivity. However, put that way, the question of whether work relief succeeded or failed does not lead in very interesting directions. More to the point is why it faced so many obstacles. For the New Deal experience highlights the contradictions that always undercut work relief in American society.[46]

Consider first the problem of administrative capacity. The national government only turns to massive public works projects in times of emergency. Especially in peacetime, it lacks any division capable of rapidly mobilizing millions of workers around specific tasks. Its choice is between a tight, coherent program that starts too slowly to ease the crisis or a loose, disjointed one whose projects lack adequate planning and supervision. In the New Deal, the experience of the Public Works Administration (PWA) showed how the lack of an administrative infrastructure delayed the development of a construction program funded by the federal government. The early experience of the FERA, and to some extent the brief history of the Civil Works Administration (CWA) and the problems of the WPA, showed what happened when programs were launched without very much planning and without an administrative structure securely in place. Recall, too, that when the federal government wanted to launch the CCC quickly it had to turn to the War Department, which was the only federal agency capable of undertaking the task.

Public works projects have conflicting goals, which are difficult, if not impossible, to reconcile. They should not be merely make-work; they are supposed to be useful and efficient. It follows that they should be able to employ qualified workers, offer incentives for good work, and fire those who prove incompetent. However, the other goal of public works is to provide as many jobs as possible. They have to hire the unskilled; they can offer few incentives; they cannot discharge some workers simply because they have less competence than others. Indeed, critics who complained that projects were overstaffed and work shoddy forgot that providing jobs was the fundamental purpose of the program. This dilemma of efficiency versus numbers or of the quality of work versus the amount of relief constantly hampered New Deal work relief projects.

230

"These two elements—the quality of the personnel, and the integrity of the project," wrote two contemporary observers, often conflicted, "dividing the relief administration itself into two camps: one interested primarily in seeing that the largest possible number of relief clients—and only actual relief clients—be assigned to WPA projects and paid WPA wages; the other, aiming primarily at high-class and voluminous production."[47]

How to determine eligibility for public works projects is a related dilemma. The goal of policy is to reach the people most in need of help. But how should that group be defined? Every criterion discriminates against some group that deserves inclusion. The WPA tried to solve the problem by requiring that 90 percent of its workers come from relief rolls and that only one person per family could hold a WPA job at the same time. These rules worked against those who had been unemployed recently; they discriminated against women, who only made up between 12 and 19 percent of the WPA workforce at any time; and they hurt large families, who sometimes received less when one member worked for the WPA than when they had survived on direct relief from the FERA.[48]

Incentives provide another quandary. By definition, public works jobs are temporary. They are seen as an expedient to tide workers over for a short time until more jobs open in the private sector. They do not offer a career. Indeed, in theory they should remain less attractive than private sector jobs, because the attachment of workers to them should be discouraged. Given these assumptions, public project employees have little reason to labor intensively. They will not earn higher salaries, greater job security, or promotion. With no incentives offered employees, it is no surprise that the efficiency and quality of work suffers. As Bakke observed when he explained why WPA workers often appeared not to work very hard, "Work relief can provide little of the incentive to efficient work which might reside in the possibility of promotion. It is certain that no job which offers so little chance for advancement can hope to stand very high as a stimulator to greater efficiency."[49]

Authority relations between workers and supervisors on public projects are ambiguous. Given the temporary nature of the jobs, the high turnover in workers, the lack of incentives, and the absence of customary sanctions, let alone the frequent lack of experienced or trained workers, supervisors face a difficult task when they try to promote efficient, high-speed production. At the same time, the workers, neither employees nor welfare clients in the ordinary sense, are expected to work hard and remember that public generosity has provided them with jobs. In practical terms, this means they should work as hard, or harder, than any employees in the private sector while they forgo normal workers' rights, such as collective bargaining or strikes. "Say what you will," Bakke points out, "relief employment is a form of public welfare, and not the accepted form of employer-employee relationship. Both the public and administrators feel there

231

is something anomalous in the situation when work-relief workers strike and picket." This anomaly underlined the fact that "the relationship of project manager to relief worker is different from the ordinary relationship of an employer to his workers."[50]

Problems

① Wages, of course, are an especially difficult issue in public works projects, because none of the criteria with which they can be set are satisfactory. They can be pegged to relief standards. That is, a worker can receive as wages only what he or she would be given as direct relief. However, this undercuts the incentive to work and, as well, usually pays workers much less than equivalent jobs in the private sector. At the other extreme, public works project wages can match those in the private sector. By adding to the expense of work relief, this policy can decrease the total number of workers employed. It also discourages workers from seeking jobs in the private sector. A third option is to set wages somewhere in between relief standards and private pay scales, with some variation for skill level. Here there is a danger that public wage scales will depress private ones and undercut union efforts to raise wages in industries with which they compete.

All of these policies were tried during the New Deal and none of them worked well. Although it set a low minimum wage, the FERA by and large paid relief wages, at first often in commodities rather than cash. The CWA and, at first, the WPA were supposed to pay "security wages," which were between relief standards and prevailing wage scales, and usually supplied only a fraction of what it took to support a family. As a result, for most workers, WPA project pay remained inadequate, and the "security wage" policy soon broke down. As early as November, 1935, Hopkins permitted "state administrators to pay 10 percent of all WPA workers in the state a wage scale determined on the basis of prevailing wages," and several months later, he recommended to Congress "that the prevailing hourly wages be paid," though with a monthly maximum. Congress approved the new regulations, and until 1939, "WPA wage rolls were based on prevailing rates of pay of each community where a WPA project existed." Nonetheless, this policy, too, had major problems because it "led to great variance in pay for equal work . . . caused much unnecessary confusion," and failed "to provide the unskilled and semiskilled WPA worker with sufficient income for the basic needs of life." In areas with strong unions, union rates became the standard, and employers objected that this policy raised their costs; in the South employers complained that WPA wages exceeded what they normally paid.[51]

② The relation between jobs, training, and skills remains another problem for public works projects reflected in the experience of the New Deal. What responsibility should public works projects assume for developing the skills of their employees or for helping them make a transition away from jobs in ob-

solescent industries? How useful is work experience that leaves a person unprepared and unable to find decent work in the private sector when more jobs
become available? The CWA and the WPA, for instance, employed nearly as
many women in sewing rooms as did the entire garment industry. They often
paid them more than they might have made in the private sector for sewing by
hand at a time when machines dominated the industry. What future would
these women have when the WPA ended? The question, of course, became
moot because of the need for workers in the defense industry after 1940, but
the question, nonetheless, remains an example of the general problem. So
does the question of the kind of experiences offered young people by the CCC
and the NYA. In the long run, is it helpful to teach rural skills to young people
who will spend their lives in cities? Were "large sums expended on fruitless
training for overcrowded or obsolete occupations?" Without adequate studies,
contemporaries could only speculate about the relevance of vocational training
offered by the CCC and NYA. Nonetheless, the issue remains important and
unresolved. The question is this: is it possible to combine relief with useful
vocational training? Does the attempt to put the two together compromise both
so badly that it worsens the problems it sets out to solve? The answer, as Ken
Auletta shows, is no more clear—and no less important—now than in the
1930s.[52]

Public works projects are political creations. Their size, focus, regulations,
and stability depend on political considerations rather than on the factors that
govern employment in the private sector. This political dependence creates
special problems both for the individuals who work on public projects and for
levels of government other than the one that initiates them. New Deal work
relief rolls, for instance, fluctuated with pressures on the administration and
with congressional appropriations. Workers did not know how long their jobs
would last, and the uncertainty dampened their morale. At the same time, state
and local governments never knew what the federal government intended.

> Appropriations and allotments might be curtailed; projects might be completed with
> no new projects to take their places. The local community might suddenly find
> itself called upon to provide . . . general public assistance funds for former W.P.A.
> workers. . . . Neither the local governments nor the state governments knew what
> the national government was going to do, so that orderly planning, appropriating,
> and administering were out of the question.[53]

In the end, not only conservative employers and their allies criticized the
public works strategies adopted during the New Deal. So did many who supported
government-led efforts to relieve distress and promote economic security. Two
social workers wondered, for instance, whether the money spent on the relatively

small group who benefited from the NYA would have been better used to help their families more directly. Lewis Merriam of the Brookings Institution, another critic, evaluated the WPA on four criteria: "(1) its efficiency in constructing public works and rendering needed services, (2) its efficiency as a relief agency, (3) its effect on state and local finance, and (4) its political implications." He found it wanting on each score and argued "that a more efficient relief system would have been developed under the original 1933 relief legislation which provided grants-in-aid to the states and for which the WPA was substituted." Others, like Bakke, recognized the programs' limits but stressed the psychological superiority of work over direct relief. Government administrators also acknowledged many of the programs' inadequacies but argued that they were the best that could be pushed through Congress, especially in the face of growing public hostility.[54]

In retrospect, whether the New Deal relief programs succeeded or failed, whether the administration had options that were both better and equally realistic, are less compelling issues than the irreconcilable tensions that ran through the first great American experiment with federal work relief. For these showed the incompatibility of massive public work relief with America's capitalist economy and federalist political structure.

The same great forces—the constraints of political and economic structure—also undercut the attempt to create a system of economic and social security. The result was a complex, incomplete, uniquely American semiwelfare state.

The Limits of Social Security

Within less than 50 years, social security, a controversial innovation that vastly extended the reach and responsibility of the federal government, became an impregnable national institution. Even a conservative president, Ronald Reagan, had to promise to rescue social security with only the most minor modifications. The social security crisis—the projected bankruptcy of its reserve fund—hardly was unexpected; the system's architects in the 1930s knew that demand would outstrip resources by the 1990s. Still, they helped preserve the fiction that social security was a perpetual insurance fund built on contributions which it returned with interest. By pointedly distinguishing social security from relief, they froze the distinction between social insurance and public assistance into federal policy, where it has been stuck over since, and built a regressive system that reinforced economic inequalities. As salesmanship, their strategy was brilliant. For by dissociating social insurance from relief, they won public allegiance to welfare for the middle classes.[55]

Social
insurance
vs.
relief

In 1935, President Roosevelt turned leftward in the "Second New Deal." The "fundamental reason" for his shift, claims McElvaine, "is clear. His constituents had already turned in that direction and it was politically necessary for the President to move to catch up with his followers." In 1934, the "smoldering coals" of worker discontent had "burst into flame," and almost 1.5 million workers took part in some 1800 strikes." Everywhere, the "message was clear. Roosevelt had given workers hope; they did not intend to let the President, businessmen, or even their own union leaders stand in the way of fulfilling that hope." In California, "discontented" Democrats took over the party and nominated Upton Sinclair for governor. Sinclair, who had run twice before as a Socialist, was defeated only by a campaign that "set a standard for distortion and lies that was not equaled until the 1972 presidential election."[56]

At the same time, three movements with "national significance" grew "stronger every day." They were Senator Huey Long's "Share-the-Wealth Movement"; Father Charles Coughlin's radio broadcasts attacking capitalists, communists, and Jews; and Francis Townsend's plan for a flat federal pension for the elderly. Indeed, the "organized and insistent" elderly, their share of the population growing, had become a potent political force. Townsend proposed that the federal government give a pension of $200 a month to everyone over the age of sixty on the condition that they stop working and spend the entire amount during the month. A 2 percent tax on financial transactions was to finance the scheme. Townsend supporters flooded Congress with mail, which the architects of social security, including Edwin Witte, director of the Committee on Economic Security, took very seriously. "I think," Witte wrote to a top member of his technical board's staff, "that the Townsend movement has become a terrific menace which is likely to engulf our entire economic system," and Secretary of Labor Frances Perkins recalled, the Townsend plan "both drove us and confused the issue." Without it, "it is possible that the old-age insurance system would not have received the attention which it did at the hands of Congress." Even though Congress remained unlikely to enact the plan (the House voted against it 206–56 in April, 1935), Witte feared the Townsend plan might lead the elderly to "demand extravagant, gratuitous pensions," and he blamed it for draining support away from the Economic Security Act and making its passage more difficult.[57]

Pressure from the left also came from Congress. In the 1934 elections, the Democrats became the first incumbent party in American history to increase its congressional strength in an off-year election. Of the new congressmen, thirty-five "were clearly to the left of the President." FDR, says Leuchtenberg, "was riding a tiger, for the new Congress threatened to push him in a direction far more radical than any he had originally contemplated." Although the president answered with a legislative volley, his response fell far short of radical hopes or, even, of expectations aroused by the president's more militant and class-conscious rhetoric. The Wheeler-Rayburn bill regulated, but did not abolish, utility holding companies; the Wagner Act protected labor's right to organize and created the National Labor Relations Board; the Banking Act "centralized control of the money market in the Federal Reserve Board"; the Rural Electrification Administration tried to bring electricity to the 90 percent of the nation's farms without it; the Wealth Tax Act made taxes slightly more progressive, although it "did almost nothing to redistribute wealth"; and the Economic Security Act created the basis for America's peculiar, semiwelfare state.[58]

The architects of social security tried to construct a self-funding system resembling private insurance. "I believe," said FDR, "that the funds necessary to provide this [old age and unemployment] insurance should be raised by contribution rather than by an increase in general taxation." "Thoroughly familiar" with Wisconsin's social legislation and the "philosophy underlying it," claims Arthur Altmeyer, first chairman of the Social Security Board, the president "continued to regard social security primarily as a comprehensive system of contributory social insurance providing basic protection to Americans against all major personal hazards," and he brought in Edwin Witte, chairman of the University of Wisconsin's economics department, to direct the top-level Committee on Economic Security (CES), which, in 1934, he charged with drafting social security legislation.[59]

Altmeyer's assessment of FDR's position combines the three principles of what Jerry Cates calls the "conservative social insurance ideology" underpinning American social security policy. The first, "risk selection," means that social insurance does not try to eliminate all economic need. Rather, it focuses on "carefully selected contingencies" and pays benefits when an event—widowhood, unemployment, industrial accident, a sixty-fifth birthday—happens. By eliminating a means test, "risk selection" dissociates insurance from poor relief and shields its recipients from stigma. It also often pays benefits to people who have other income or property. Workers, according to the second principle, should contribute to their own insurance not only to contain public costs, but, even more, to prevent them from demanding unreasonably high benefits. Benefits themselves, the remaining principle holds, should reflect wages, although the match need not be perfect, and poorly paid workers might receive a higher proportion of their wages as benefits. Still, the importance of incentives in a free enterprise system means that benefits should not be equal. The effect of these principles is clear: by design, social insurance does not redistribute income. To the contrary, it reinforces inequality.[60]

Demographic projections had convinced the CES staff that a reserve fund for old-age insurance could not remain solvent throughout the late twentieth century. They knew it would run dry, and they recommended that general tax revenues eventually subsidize the reserves. However, FDR refused to accept the committee's recommendation and ordered it to devise a compromise that would make the system appear perpetually able to meet its own expenses with no additional tax revenue. Despite the administration's preference for contributory insurance, in 1935 the first social security legislation chose to protect those elderly who had not worked long enough to earn benefits. For this reason, the federal government offered matching grants to the states for old-age assistance while it set in motion the contributory system of old-age insurance that soon became synonymous with social security. Unemployment insurance also was designed to pay for itself through the combined contributions of employers and workers. In fact, the CES tried to devise ways to give employers and state governments incentives to minimize unemployment and to devise and pay for their own plans. Nobody paid much attention to the economic implications of the Economic Security Act's other components. Aid to Dependent Children, slipped into the act by the Children's Bureau as another program of matching grants to the states, was considered an inexpensive way to help widows with young families. Nor did the other titles of the act—aid to the blind, increased appropriations for the Public Health Service, vocational rehabilitation, and infant and maternal health—cost very much.[61]

Neither Witte nor President Roosevelt viewed social security primarily as a way to stimulate economic growth, which was a more important objective of other programs. In fact, their rejection of Keynesian theories reinforced their commitment to contributory insurance and reluctance to raise taxes to pay for welfare. "Like Roosevelt," claims Schlabach, "Witte and most members of the technical board were not impressed with Keynesian doctrines. Witte criticized them as too abstract, and scarcely grasped the idea that deficit spending might increase the nation's total wealth." Consequently, he urged the CES to acknowledge that economic recovery lay "largely outside" its task. However, his technical board, which included Keynesian economist Alvin Hansen, forced Witte to bend slightly by admitting that all plans "must be weighed in the light of their effects upon economic recovery. Other members of the CES, notably Frances Perkins, stressed the importance of the measure in stimulating consumption, and even FDR finally acknowledged the promotion of economic growth as one of the bill's objectives."[62]

The CES also rejected expensive welfare measures because it wanted to draw a sharp line between public assistance and social insurance. "The most obvious characteristic" of the economic security system that emerged from the New Deal, according to James Patterson, "was its primary reliance on contributory social insurance and its concomitant distaste for welfare," or public assistance. This "American emphasis, moreover, was unique; other western nations developed a blend of social policies, including family allowances, health services, housing allowances, and assistance, that benefited poor and nonpoor alike and obscured the distinction between social insurance and welfare." The "objective difference" between the two, argues Eveline Burns, "lies in two characteristics of social insurance that are not found in public assistance." First of all, "the law specifies with precision the conditions governing eligibility, and the nature and amount of the benefit. Second, the specific conditions do not include a requirement to undergo a test of means or need." With one exception, the original social security legislation froze the distinctions between insurance and assistance into national policy. Categorical old-age assistance was the one program which blurred the distinction between the two because the original legislation required no means test. However, a 1939 amendment to the Social Security Act, which made categorical old-age assistance dependent on need, cleared up the anomaly. Through its administration of the act, the Social Security Board, under Altmeyer's leadership, argues Cates, manipulated the distinction between social insurance and public assistance to edge the program away from any policies that threatened to move it in a more redistributive direction. Convinced that threats to social security came more from public assistance and flat plan advocates (like the Townsendites) on the left than from conservatives, Altmeyer and his staff denigrated general relief and forced progressive states, most notably California, to modify their liberal policies.[63]

The resilient distinction between social insurance and public assistance reflects the long-standing suspicion of relief or welfare. There remains, even today, a lurking assumption that many of those who ask for help neither need nor deserve it. By contrast, social insurance is acceptable because, so it is believed, it is earned. With their own wages, workers contribute to funds—supplemented by employers—that will support them in periods of unemployment or in old age. Even though they may take out far more than they contribute, they can argue that they have paid their way. Equally important, social insurance is popular because its benefits cross class lines. Almost everyone is eligible for social security retirement benefits, and, of course, many wealthy people have been able to add its nontaxable—now very lightly taxed—payments to income from stocks, bonds, property, or other nonwage sources. In the same way, even though few well-to-do people need unemployment insurance, by no means is unemployment

238

only a problem of the poor. Rather, it touches a surprisingly large share of the population during their working lives. It comes, then, as no surprise that welfare programs for the middle class—social security, Medicare, unemployment insurance—have been defined as social insurance; that they carry no stigma; and that their benefits are more generous than those paid by public assistance, which, after all, is strictly for the poor.[64]

From early in his administration, FDR emphasized his preference for a collaborative approach that left as much responsibility as possible to the states. In practice, this goal created intricate problems for the architects of social security, who found the federal issue the most difficult one with which they had to deal. "The question of national versus state," writes Schlabach, "was more troublesome than any of the other . . . major guideline decisions." The CES resolved the federal-state issue more easily for old-age security than for unemployment insurance. Few objected to state administration of old-age assistance, and the advocates of national old-age insurance made a compelling case based on the "actuarial soundness of distributing the risk broadly and the interstate character of the labor market, with its high mobility of workers between states during their long period of contribution." However, the "national versus state" controversy "erupted most hotly over unemployment compensation." Most of Witte's leading staff members preferred a national system, though Witte himself favored a strong role for the states. "A national system," its advocates argued, "promised the advantages of uniformity in unemployment compensation and easy protection of workers who moved interstate," and, they added, "national administrators would be more efficient and honest than state officials." Others, including Witte, feared leaving unemployment insurance completely at the mercy of national politics; they wanted to leave progressive states room to maneuver; they thought it better to let the states resolve some of the more controversial issues themselves; and they feared the Supreme Court would find a national system unconstitutional. In the end, the CES recommended a compromise: the combined federal-state system that Congress eventually accepted. In this way, New Deal policy reinforced state and local variations in welfare benefits and froze into place the complex, multi-layered, decentralized pattern that had distinguished relief and welfare in America since early in the nation's history.[65]

The CES knew it was walking through a minefield. Indeed, opposition came from all political directions. The right feared the government would "dissipate" the "huge reserves . . . in unwise public" spending and, then, collect money all over again when benefits became due. The left argued that the new system "placed the entire burden on the employees themselves through an income tax and on employers through a payroll tax," which, they predicted, would have the same result as a sales tax, because employers would shift their new tax burden to consumers. Southerners were more unexpected opponents. During the hearings on the Economic Security Act, Senator Byrd spoke for Southern fears that social security might "serve as an entering wedge for federal interference with the handling of the Negro question in the South." Southern senators, he pointed out, wanted to prevent the federal government from withholding funds from states whose administration of old-age assistance discriminated against blacks. Witte told Byrd that "it had never occurred to any person" on the CES "that the Negro question would come up in this connection," and he agreed to modify the bill to permit Southern states a great deal more administrative autonomy.[66]

As the CES worked on the bill, Witte consulted with leading businessmen, and several of them, including Gerard Swope of General Electric, Marion Folsom of Eastman Kodak, and leaders of the National Retail Dry Goods Association, supported it. Nonetheless, although the editor of the New Republic claimed that FDR's administration had "always been too timid in the face of the opposition of employers," most business representatives, such as the national Chamber of Commerce and the National Association of Manufacturers, opposed the act.[67]

Although they proved less influential than conservatives, sponsors of more radical alternatives were also important. First, they forced the administration to respond quickly. Without the threat from the Townsend forces, for instance, both FDR and Congress might have acted much more slowly. Even more, radical and liberal alternatives show that the peculiar shape of the American semiwelfare state was not inevitable. To the contrary, it emerged from a choice among possibilities made at a uniquely protean moment in American history.

Indeed, the CES itself recommended a more comprehensive program, including a system of national health insurance and an ongoing public works program. As it had for decades, the American Medical Association successfully squashed health insurance, and President Roosevelt rejected a permanent system of public works. More dramatic was an alternative approach to economic security embodied in the Lundeen bill, introduced by Senator Lundeen of Minnesota, and supported "by a coalition of left-wing unemployed worker groups, some labor unions, radicalized liberals, and the Communist party." The bill called for generous flat benefits based on local wages and administered without a means test by local "commissions elected by workers and farmers' organizations," which also would design special insurance programs. All costs would be paid "by the federal government out of taxes on individual and corporate income in excess of $5,000 per annum and inheritance and gift taxes."[68]

In her testimony in favor of the Lundeen bill, labor economist Mary Van Kleeck pointed out that it went beyond merely "providing compensation for the unemployed." Instead, it committed the federal government "to a reversal

240

of its policies which at present are restricting production of goods and even of food which the people need, in order to increase prices." The government had tried to "sustain business by direct loans . . . to conserve the claims of mortgage holders and other creditors, and to maintain and increase prices by actual curtailment of production in agriculture and industry." Instead of recovery, the result was "widespread unemployment and . . . decreased purchasing power." By contrast, the Lundeen bill proposed to "raise the standards of living of the people" by redistributing income and unleashing the nation's tremendous productive capacity. If passed, the bill would give "an enormous stimulus to production in the basic industries, including the production of food, which is alarmingly inadequate for the needed health diet of the American people."[69]

Van Kleeck advocated an approach to economic security deliberately rejected by FDR and the CES. The question of economic security, she argued, could not be divorced from the problem of economic recovery. Only by stimulating demand would the government encourage productivity and increase employment. By contrast, the Economic Security Act would reduce purchasing power and act as a brake on employment. The payroll tax, intended to pay for unemployment insurance, she claimed, would "be passed on to the consumer in higher prices, thus forcing workers to pay for their insurance in higher costs of living." Even if workers did not contribute directly from their wages, a payroll tax "constitutes a down drag on the wage scale, since it enters into the cost of production." The great leap in output made possible by technological advance had increased profits far more than employment or wages. As a consequence, capital now lacked an outlet for investment; unemployment remained high; workers could not afford the necessities of life; and demand stayed too low to stimulate production. The only way out of the dilemma without restructuring the economy—which she favored—was to redistribute wealth through a tax on incomes and profits, not payrolls.[70]

Lewis Merriam, a social welfare expert with the Brookings Institution, also attacked the American social security system shortly after its creation and proposed an alternative based on very different principles. Unlike Van Kleeck, Merriam rejected the role of relief in promoting economic recovery. Even so, when he assessed the American system against three broad, reasonable criteria—universal coverage, comprehensiveness, and coordination—he found it wanting in every respect. Impressed especially by New Zealand's new social insurance scheme, Merriam recommended that the United States reject the reserve fund concept and adopt a modern means test. "Expenditures for relief and social security," he argued, "must be made from current income." The "insurance reserves" of the "national government," he pointed out, consisted "only of its own obligations to pay in the future. Consequently, the reserve system does not and cannot

241

actually lessen the burden on future generations," and he predicted the exhaustion of the reserve fund in the 1990s. Merriam rejected not only the reserve fund but also the distinction between social insurance and public assistance. All aid, he said, should be based on need. Hostility to a means test arose from factors that could be eliminated: "a modern means test should make the individual or the family eligible for assistance when and if the resources fall below a sum, or a schedule of sums, set forth in law. What sums should be allowable should be determined upon the basis of sound research."[71]

In the 1940s, few people would have argued that the American welfare state was adequate, comprehensive, or well coordinated. Still, neither Merriam's, Van Kleeck's, nor other major alternatives received even a serious hearing. Each in its own way violated the major principles on which the American social security system had been erected. The Lundeen bill never had a chance, not only because of its association with the Communist party, but, even more, because the New Deal hoped to shore up capitalism without a major redistribution of power and income. Besides, its proposals threatened to increase wages and interfere with the labor market. Merriam's proposals foundered because the federal government wanted to pretend it could finance social security without raising taxes and because of nearly universal hostility to a means test in any form. Indeed, Merriam's proposed merger of social insurance and public assistance blurred the very distinction so carefully crafted into the American semi-welfare state.[72]

In practice, its own labor legislation proved the New Deal's major alternative to its patchy, inadequate social insurance policies. In fact, the unionized working class, which became one of the Democratic party's key constituencies during the 1930s, gained at least as much from New Deal labor legislation as from social security. Indeed, more than public assistance or social security, New Deal labor legislation increased its power, earning capacity, and economic security. In 1933, section 7(a) of the National Recovery Act for the first time aligned the federal government with labor's right to organize. Although employers found ways to subvert labor's new rights, section 7(a) revived organized labor, which had been devastated by the business offensive launched against it in the 1920s. By early 1935, FDR, aware of the wide "discontent with the pro-business character of the early New Deal," proposed "more progressive policies aimed at winning the support of workers and farmers," and liberal congressmen fought hard for Senator Robert Wagner's bill "to create a National Labor Relations Board to conduct elections for collective bargaining and regulate labor practices." Despite his initial reluctance to support Wagner's bill, Roosevelt wanted to retain his solid labor support and signed it into law on July 5, 1935. Although court challenges delayed its implementation for 2 years, the Wagner Act's passage "encouraged worker militancy by demonstrating that the New Deal Congress would protect and defend the workers' right to organize and bargain collectively."[73]

Mass production workers could be less sure of support from the conservative, white, male AFL than from Congress. When the federation ended a rubber workers' strike in Akron, Ohio, in 1935, "enraged workers . . . stood on street corners, tearing up their union cards, refusing even to vote on the contract." At the next AFL convention, the tension between the craft and industrial unions erupted in a conflict between the federation's leadership and John L. Lewis, president of the United Mine Workers. When the federation delegates voted down his "industrial union strategy," Lewis left the AFL and, together with other industrial union leaders, formed the Committee for Industrial Organization (CIO). Militant, exciting, committed to social justice, the CIO pioneered the sit-down strike and in 1937 won a major victory over General Motors, the world's largest corporation. Unlike the AFL, the CIO organized women and blacks. In the 1930s, the number of female union members tripled, and blacks and whites for the first time joined together in large, interracial unions. By 1937, only 2 years after its organization, the CIO had more members, 3,700,000, than the AFL, 3,400,000, and throughout the country, union membership skyrocketed. Between 1933 and 1940, the number of unionized workers tripled. Within manufacturing, they increased from 9 to 34 percent, in mining from 21 to 72 percent, in transportation from 23 to 48 percent, and in construction from 54 to 65 percent.[74]

In 1937, the Supreme Court held the Wagner Act constitutional, and, a year later, with the Fair Labor Standards Act, the New Deal extended its protection of labor with a minimum wage, maximum work week, and prohibition of child labor, although federal legislation still excluded the most exploitive categories of work, including those which employed large numbers of blacks. Through collective bargaining, unionized workers even gained health care and other benefits that Congress failed to provide. As Paul Starr observes, "What Social Security failed to achieve in industrial welfare, the Wagner Act provided an alternative means of pursuing. So in the 1940s, when Congress again declined to add health insurance to Social Security, workers sought protection against the costs of illness through what John R. Commons once called the 'private legislation' of collective bargaining." Truly, labor had made enormous gains. "A new kind of workers' power," Green concludes, "had been mobilized in countless factories and communities. For the first time, millions of industrial workers asserted rights that had to be respected, and created organizations that finally gave them control over their world." Here, more than in social security or public assistance, was the New Deal's great legacy to the American worker.[75]

The New Deal and Black Americans

The New Deal's legacy to black Americans was even more ambiguous and ironic than its impact on the white working class. New Deal agricultural policies hurt Southern blacks by forcing land out of production and shrinking the base of black employment. Although farmers were supposed to share their federal crop subsidies with their displaced workers, few did so. The consequence was widespread, rural black poverty and the acceleration of black migration to cities, where, of course, they found little work. Of all groups during the Great Depression, black men had the highest unemployment rates, and black women, confined largely to argiculture and domestic service, did little better. Indeed, statistics hardly tell the story of how, with labor cheap, employers shamelessly exploited domestics by forcing them to work harder for lower pay. Nor did the New Deal protect the most important black civil rights: FDR, afraid of losing Southern support, refused, repeatedly, to endorse an antilynching law.[76]

Most New Deal welfare programs officially tried to prohibit discrimination. Even so, blacks received less than their fair share of either jobs or relief. Only the Public Works Administration showed "how federal power could be used creatively to benefit black Americans." Nonetheless, of all New Deal programs, the most important for blacks, claims Nancy Weiss, was the WPA. "The relief program literally became the salvation of millions of unemployed Americans. Blacks were no exception." Although local relief administrators discriminated against blacks, Aubrey Williams and Mary Mcleod Bethune, Director of its Division of Negro Affairs, made the National Youth Administration the most racially progressive agency in the federal government. Still, the New Deal failed to use its most important welfare legislation, social security, to increase blacks' economic security. By excluding agricultural and domestic workers, the Social Security Act left two-thirds of employed blacks with no protection for old age or unemployment. The act also failed to prohibit racial discrimination. Indeed, by relying on state administration, the Economic Security Act guaranteed blacks an unequal share of benefits. At the same time, New Deal housing policies also discriminated against blacks and promoted residential segregation, because the Federal Housing Authority redlined black neighborhoods and refused to insure mortgages within them.[77]

Despite President Roosevelt's reluctance to fight discrimination, his popularity with blacks soared, thanks, partly, to Eleanor Roosevelt, whose outspoken commitment to racial justice, support for the NAACP, speeches to interracial audiences, and meetings with black leaders all convinced blacks that, for the

244

first time, there was "someone in official circles in Washington whom they could trust." "Most black people," asserts Weiss, "knew they were getting less economic assistance than whites, and most of them needed more than they got." Still, "they got something," and New Deal relief "kept many families *political* from starving." Because it did not exclude blacks from its benefits, the New *implication* Deal "was a sufficient departure from past practice to make Roosevelt look like a benefactor of the race."[78]

The result was dramatic. In 1936, blacks exchanged their historic commitment to the party of Lincoln and voted for Roosevelt. In black neighborhoods, he "won anywhere from 60 to 250 percent more votes . . . in 1936 than in 1932." In New York, he increased his percentage of the vote in black districts from 46 percent to 81 percent; in Cincinnati from 29 percent to 65 percent; and in Detroit from 31 percent to 66 percent. The vote was a personal triumph for FDR rather than for the Democratic party. In 1936, 71 percent of black businessmen, professionals, and leaders interviewed in a national poll supported Roosevelt; only 44 percent called themselves Democrats. Blacks, concludes Weiss, "did not vote for reasons of racial advantage. Rather, they behaved like most other poor people in the United States. In short, they responded to the New Deal on economic rather than on racial grounds." FDR had brought blacks into the new coalition that sustained the Democratic party. At first, only a very small fraction of eligible voters in Northern cities—often disenfranchised in the South—their vote had little impact on election results. Still, the impact of blacks on the New Deal, and of the New Deal on blacks, cannot be gauged in the short run. Ironically, the New Deal launched policies that in the 1960s linked together in unanticipated ways to reshape American cities and their politics. New Deal agricultural policies, reinforced after World War II by technology, drove blacks off the land and into Northern cities, where their concentrated power has become the backbone of Democratic strength. Within cities, a lethal combination of discrimination, redlining, and industrial decline eroded opportunities, sustained catastrophic levels of unemployment, and gnawed at the structure of black families. A small New Deal program designed for widows *New Deals* now sustains millions of black women and children. Both the great, crumbling *legacys to* urban ghettos with their staggering unemployment and reliance on welfare and *blacks* the energetic, intelligent black Democratic mayors who increasingly led big cities are among the New Deal's legacies to black America.[79]

Assessing the New Deal

The limits of the early American welfare state glare so brightly they deflect attention away from the magnitude of the New Deal's achievements. As the National Resources Planning Board observed in 1942, "The years 1930 to 1940 witnessed a vast expansion of governmental activity in providing income to needy or presumably needy persons, which will undoubtedly stand out as a major social development in our times." The growth of government spending for public aid summarizes the story. In fiscal year 1913, all levels of government spent about $21 million on public aid. By 1932, the amount had increased to $208 million. In 1939, it jumped to $4.9 billion. In both 1913 and 1923 public aid consumed only 1 percent of all government expenses; by 1933 it took 6.5 percent; and by 1939, 27.1 percent. Expressed another way, in 1913 all levels of government spent $0.22 for public aid per capita; $0.57 in 1923; and $37.80 in 1939. In 1913 and 1923, these public expenses were only 0.1 percent of national income; in 1939, they were 7.1 percent.[80]

New Deal legislation forced states as well as the federal government to expand their commitment to social welfare. A veritable "flood of progressive legislation followed" the Social Security Act "as state after state proceeded to take advantage of its benefits." In 1932, Wisconsin was the only state with a system of unemployment insurance; in 1935, eight states had unemployment insurance laws; 2 years later they were universal. The Social Security Act also forced states to improve the quality of their administration and professionalize their staffs. Even though the federal government paid a larger portion of the cost of public aid, the absolute amount of state and local contributions increased dramatically: in 1932, the state and local government share of public aid expense was 97.9 percent and the federal share 2.1 percent. By 1939, the state and local proportion had dropped to 37.5 percent. Nonetheless, the amount contributed by state and local governments had risen from $203 million to about $1.9 billion since 1933.[81]

In the late 1940s, Eveline Burns, one of the country's leading authorities on social insurance, observed how difficult it was to describe the American social security system. After she surveyed the system, Burns concluded, "the predominant impression that would be made on an impartial observer of the present so-called system is its lack of rationality. No consistent philosophy appears to underlie" the way in which America answers "the major issues that face any nation aiming to provide itself with a relatively acceptable and stable social security program." The result was a sprawling, inadequate, incoherent series of

246

programs that left many people in need. "Needy people," she wrote, "are denied access to any form of public aid largely as a result of the accident of where they live or the length of time they have lived in a particular area, or their possession of certain characteristics, such as age, that are irrelevant to the question of need."[82]

By the 1940s, America had acquired a unique, unsatisfactory, semiwelfare state. The New Deal had expanded vastly the role of the federal government and altered its relation to the states. States spent much more for welfare, which they administered more professionally. Government had assumed a degree of responsibility for economic security unprecedented in the nation's history. Still, the new structure had been erected partly on an old foundation. It compromised with, rather than superseded, the local basis of relief. It modified but did not erase archaic distinctions between the worthy and unworthy or the ablebodied and impotent poor; it created walls between social insurance and public assistance that preserved class distinctions and reinforced the stigma attached to relief or welfare; in no way did it redistribute income or interfere with welfare's role in the regulation of the labor market and the preservation of social order. With a few changes in details, but not in structure, adequacy, or role, this was the welfare state inherited by the reformers of the 1960s who wanted to wage war on poverty.

PART III

FROM THE WAR ON POVERTY TO THE WAR ON WELFARE

9 The War on Poverty

and the Expansion

of Social Welfare

The bifurcation of welfare into social insurance and public assistance trapped the architects of John F. Kennedy's New Frontier and Lyndon B. Johnson's Great Society who wanted to wage war on poverty. For it ruled out any serious attempt to redistribute wealth, guarantee incomes, or tamper with the structure of American capitalism. Indeed, as his concessions to the steel industry and tax cut made clear, John F. Kennedy did not intend to antagonize business or modify its power and privileges. Neither did Lyndon Johnson. Rather, through the magic of economic growth, they expected simultaneously to strengthen American capitalism, ameliorate suffering and injustice, and reduce the impact of racism on black Americans.[1]

Despite innovations and the addition of one important new role, American social welfare continued to serve its historic purposes. Racial conflict, urban riots, militant welfare clients, and increased out-of-wedlock births among black women impelled a search for new ways to preserve social order and discipline. Unemployment induced by technology, functional illiteracy, or inadequate education; fear of Soviet competition; new manpower theories; and the realization that welfare regulations discouraged work, all encouraged the use of welfare policy to shape and regulate labor markets. The increased Democratic dependence on the votes of urban blacks insured the continued use of welfare as a source of political mobilization, and the shock and outrage aroused by the rediscovery of poverty, hunger, and malnutrition in the early 1960s spurred the improvement and extension of social welfare to relieve human suffering. To these conventional uses of welfare, the civil rights movement added a new element: for the first time, social welfare policy became one strategy for attacking the consequences of racism in America.

Civil Rights and the Origins of the War on Poverty

As racial tensions worsened in the North as well as the South, the civil rights movement transformed the historic links between race, poverty, and opportunity into a national disgrace. It began, of course, in the 1950s in the South. Recall its landmarks: the 1954 Supreme Court decision in *Brown* v. *Board of Education* that deliberate school segregation was unconstitutional; Martin Luther King's leadership of the 1956 bus boycott in Montgomery, Alabama; President Eisenhower's 1957 decision to send troops to Little Rock, Arkansas, to enforce the desegregation of Central High School; the first civil rights legislation to pass Congress since Reconstruction; the sit-in movement that began in 1960, eventually enlisted 50,000 people and desegregated public facilities throughout the South. In the South, segregationists shot civil rights workers and bombed black churches. On May 11, 1963, "More than 2,500 Birmingham blacks took to the streets . . . and pioneered a form of social protest new to the 1960s: the urban riot"; on July 18, 1964, "the first northern ghetto riot of the decade erupted in Harlem"; in August 1965, the massive Watts riot exploded in Los Angeles. The analyses that followed the riots argued what everybody really knew already: poverty was an issue of race as well as class.[2] "The civil rights movement, which developed in the late 1950s and early 1960s," notes Harrell Rodgers, "began to center attention on the desperate economic condition of millions of Americans. Civil rights workers maintained that millions of minority and white Americans were ill-housed, ill-clothed, medically neglected, and malnourished." In August, 1963, when Martin Luther King led 200,000 people in the March on Washington, he demanded jobs for blacks as well as voting rights and an end to racial discrimination. Even from a more cynical point of view, measures to combat poverty, improve living conditions, and reduce discrimination had to rank high within any effective strategy for quieting the ghettos and restoring social order. With its influence on a Democratic party in need of blacks' votes, the civil rights movement became the most effective poor people's movement in American history. Even more, as it extended its targets from segregation and voting to housing, jobs, welfare, and education, the civil rights movement became the crucible of a "new citizen movement" whose emphasis on local democracy, or community action, blossomed into grass-roots campaigns for social justice and institutional reform—and, later, opposition to the war in Vietnam—across the country.[3]

Civil rights activists joined other antipoverty workers to attack the "suitable home" provision in state Aid to Dependent Children (ADC) regulations. New state policies drafted after the passage of federal Aid to Dependent Children in 1935 continued the limitation of aid to "suitable homes" that had been a feature of early mothers' pension laws. Despite pressure from the Social Security Board and Bureau of Public Assistance, some states, especially in the South, implemented tougher "suitable home" regulations to deny aid to nonwhites and children born out-of-wedlock, who had become targets of an increasingly virulent antiwelfare backlash in the late 1940s. Some welfare critics worried about the effect of welfare on the supply of cheap black labor. In Louisiana, for instance, one member of a 1945 Grand Jury concerned with welfare costs observed, "what the people who make these criticisms are chiefly interested in is cheaper servants. It makes no difference to them one way or the other what happens to Negro children. They are not interested in whether the mother has someone to leave the children with or not. What they want is to get a cook at $5 a week as they used to." A pervasive fear that welfare encouraged immorality sharpened concerns about labor supply and fraud. In Arkansas, in 1959, to take one instance, Governor Faubus thundered, "By taxing the good people to pay for these programs, we are putting a premium on illegitimacy never before known in the world." Given these fears, "restrictive welfare policies," Winifred Bell points out, "became increasingly viable devices for applying social and economic sanctions against misbehaving, nonconforming, and impoverished parents and their children. . . . Negro and illegitimate children . . . were their primary victims." Not surprisingly, both the civil rights and antipoverty movements joined together to attack these "suitable home" provisions enacted to reduce the number of blacks on welfare and curb the sexuality of unmarried black women.[4]

The most visible grass-roots antipoverty campaign with links to the civil rights movement was the welfare rights movement, represented by the National Welfare Rights Organization (NWRO), founded in June, 1966. The NWRO embraced a coalition of "middle-class organizers, social scientists, and other intellectuals, lawyers, and church supporters" joined by CORE (Congress of Racial Equality) and a network of blacks and whites, mobilized through the civil rights movement. However, poor black women formed the movement's backbone. Indeed, NWRO was the "first national protest of poor women" in American history. "For the first time," writes Guida West, the movement's historian, "thousands of women, previously isolated, stigmatized, and intimidated by the power of the welfare authorities, came together and collectively exerted their influence on public policy." For a few years, the movement grew in size and strength as its members mounted demonstrations in welfare offices, "protested in the streets, lobbied in Washington and in the state capitals, and fought in the courts." Although it did not persuade the federal government to adopt a "guaranteed minimum income program for the poor as part of national social policy," NWRO "played a major role in reshaping the food stamp program, in expanding other nutritional and health programs for poor children and mothers, and in securing other policies that added to the basic resources of poor families." Measured by the number of its formal members, NWRO was a small and not very powerful organization. But numbers (as with the Unemployed Councils in Harlem in the 1930s) are an inadequate guide to influence. As an assertion of the strength and competence of poor women; as a demonstration of the potential power in the fusion of race, class, and gender; as a channel for helping poor women transform their ideas of welfare into entitlement—aside from its part in expanding welfare benefits and increasing the AFDC rolls—NWRO remains a remarkable and significant episode in American social history.[5]

The War on Poverty: Other Sources and Strategies

The *war on poverty* (the phrase was Lyndon Johnson's, in his inaugural speech in January, 1964; the idea of a comprehensive assault on poverty, however, had been formulated by John F. Kennedy, before his assassination) did not end racism and discrimination, eliminate the causes of poverty, transcend the split between social insurance and public assistance, solve the intractable problems of work relief, or erase the stigma attached to welfare. Nevertheless, between the early 1960s and the mid-1970s, new or expanded government programs, much more than economic growth, reduced poverty, hunger, malnutrition, and disease; increased the access of the poor to important social services; and lowered barriers to political participation, employment, housing, and education for black Americans. At the same time, strengthened by the civil rights movement, new community action programs reshaped urban politics. Their achievements lay less in specific accomplishments—indeed, some were spectacular failures—than in the stimulation of grass-roots social action and the nurturance of a distinctive, new generation of reformers who moved out of neighborhoods and into public offices across the country.

The war on poverty's sponsors mounted no attack on the distribution of economic power or resources. Instead, they fixed their attention on opportunity, not inequality. They wanted to give everyone a chance to compete, unhindered by accident of birth, for the sweet rewards of success. No approach to poverty could be more conventional, or more American. Ever since the early nineteenth century, reformers had wrestled with the intractable persistence of poverty in the land of abundance. Unwilling to explain poverty as an inescapable consequence of American political economy, they had two alternatives. One was to place the blame squarely on individuals and to redefine poverty as evidence of moral or intellectual incompetence. The other was to see it as the result of artificial and unjustifiable barriers unnecessary, indeed inimical, to the open and competitive structure of American life. In practice, explanations drifted between both poles, with emphasis on individual incapacity stressed in periods of pessimism about reforms that did not work and explanations that focused on barriers to opportunity underpinning periods of optimism about the possibilities of change. This is why opportunity so often became defined as education and why education has occupied so special a place in American reform. Education, so it was often argued, could soften the rough edges of capitalism by making Americans equal, not in condition but in opportunity to compete and achieve. Education became a painless panacea, a way, in time, to solve every social problem without recourse to conflict or redistribution. The good society became, in short, a horse race without handicaps. In the context of economic growth and limitless abundance, even the losers need not suffer.[6]

Poverty warriors drew on an influential, current theory of juvenile delinquency, which they expanded into a more general explanation of the source of poverty—blocked opportunities. By the early 1960s, the theory of delinquency, which had emerged as a national issue in the preceding decade, had shifted from individual to community pathology, that is, from a question of mental health to one of social organization. Argued most forcefully by Richard A. Cloward and Lloyd E. Ohlin in *Delinquency and Opportunity*, the new theory located delinquency's major source in the frustration and rage aroused in poor youngsters by the contrast between the promise and delivery of opportunities. A Ford Foundation grant helped Cloward and Ohlin organize Mobilization for Youth in New York City. The project combined a number of activities, including employment programs, work preparation, vocational guidance, skill training, remedial education, home visits, and neighborhood service centers, all designed to boost poor, especially minority, youngsters over the structural barriers to social mobility. More than an important project, Mobilization for Youth became the template for the Kennedy administration's assault on delinquency.[7]

The theory of cultural deprivation offered a supply side explanation of poverty that complemented the emphasis on blocked opportunity and denatured its potential radical sting. Institutional barriers, in particular, segregation and other forms of racial discrimination, did exist, to be sure, but the major problem remained the inability of poor children to take advantage of education and other channels for social mobility already in place. They lacked the repertoire of cultural skills and family supports that prepared more advantaged youngsters for school and work. Therefore, their education had to commence early and proceed differently. They had to be prepared for learning; they needed a "headstart." Cultural deprivation, for all the good will of its theorists, patronized the poor by reinforcing stereotypes of empty, childlike incompetence. What did it imply, after all, to label people as lacking a culture? (Similar images of poor and dependent people were widespread throughout the social sciences during the early 1960s. Think of the Sambo metaphor applied to slaves by historians; the image of poor immigrants to America as degraded and demoralized; or the view of Third World peoples as underdeveloped and in need of an injection of the achievement ethic by the American witch doctors of social science.) A supply side view, such as cultural deprivation, is, after all, very serviceable. It assigns the key role in social improvement to intellectuals and their acolytes, and it diverts attention away from the structural barriers to opportunity. It is the safest basis on which to mount a war on poverty, and, as a couple of centuries' experience shows, is about the least effective. Blocked opportunity and cultural deprivation conflicted with the poverty war's emphasis on community action, because the active participation of the cultureless is not very important or helpful. Indeed, blocked opportunity/cultural deprivation and community action pulled the antipoverty movement in contradictory directions. Given their respective political loadings, the outcome was never in serious doubt.[8]

Concern about juvenile delinquency and about cultural deprivation added two sources of the poverty war to the concerns of the civil rights movement; another source was the realization that urban renewal had ripped apart great American cities. After World War II, the federal government had subsidized urban freeway construction; guaranteed low-interest mortgages in suburbs; sanctioned redlining in cities; and, under the banner of urban renewal, destroyed far more of the poor's housing than it had replaced. When it spent money on housing for the urban poor at all, the government too often had funded shoddy, badly planned, massive new ghettos. As Jane Jacobs showed in her influential book, *The Death and Life of Great American Cities*, urban renewal seemed an absurd reversal of sane, compassionate social policy. With the incentive of inexpensive homeownership, those who could afford suburban housing quickly began to flee inner cities. The consequences were the deterioration of inner city tax bases, housing stock, and infrastructure and the concomitant rise of crime, poverty, and racial segregation.[9]

By the early 1960s, it was clear that public relief worked as badly as urban renewal. Benefits, everywhere inadequate, varied from state to state; regulations broke up families and discouraged work; administrative practices degraded recipients and reinforced the stigma attached to welfare; and welfare departments seemed bloated, ineffective, and callous bureaucracies. Even before the draconian welfare cutbacks in 1961 in Newburgh, New York—the culmination of the first post-World War II attack on welfare—spurred Congress to hold hearings on public assistance, Kennedy (as has every subsequent president) had made welfare reform a priority. Of course, everyone recognized that jobs were the best alternative to welfare, and, by 1961, both Republicans and Democrats agreed on the need to retrain unemployed workers. The recessions of the 1950s, the implications of technology and automation, the failures of urban schools, economists' new theories of human capital, and the threat of Soviet scientific superiority all had combined into the search for a national manpower policy, which became another key source of antipoverty programs.[10]

By the early 1960s, as a "sense of failure" grew "among participants in each of the major fields of public action that reached most deeply into the lives of the poor," remembers James Sundquist, one of the architects of the Economic Opportunity Act, strands of "innovative thought and action . . . converged" into the program that became the war on poverty. Nobody, claims Sundquist, "can say how much of the new thought and experimentation had made an impression directly on President Kennedy by 1962 or 1963," or whether the galvanizing impact supposedly exerted by Michael Harrington's exposure of poverty in *The Other America* is apocryphal. What is clear is that before his assassination Kennedy had decided to launch a major, coordinated attack on poverty, which Lyndon Johnson quickly decided to make one of the first priorities of his new administration. However, by no means did the Economic Opportunity Act (1964), the official charter of the war on poverty, create all of the important antipoverty activities of the critical years between 1961 and 1976. In fact, until Nixon abolished the Office of Economic Opportunity (OEO), in 1974, its spending never accounted for more than 3 percent of all federal social welfare expenses, or 6 percent of all federal funds for the poor.[11]

The antipoverty measures developed under Kennedy, Johnson, and Nixon can be sorted into programs with four overlapping purposes: to promote opportunities, stimulate community action, introduce new services, and expand transfer payments. Together, in only 8 years, between 1965 and 1972, they fueled a massive increase—from $75 billion to $185 billion—in federal spending for social welfare. In constant dollars, social welfare spending increased at an

257

average rate of 4.6 percent between 1950 and 1965 and 7.2 percent between 1965 and 1976. It accounted for 7.7 percent of the GNP in 1960, 10.5 percent in 1965, and 16 percent in 1974. Whether or not all this money and the programs it supported were a true war on poverty, they greatly extended the role and responsibilities of the federal government and altered the relations between citizens and the state.[12]

Programs to promote opportunity concentrated on four areas: juvenile delinquency, civil rights, job training, and education. (See the appendix to this chapter for more detail.) Their success was mixed. Juvenile delinquency did not decrease, and unemployment among black teenagers rose to disastrous levels. The match between jobs, skills, and experience is, conservatively, no better today than in 1960. Indeed, evaluations of the early economic opportunity programs are discouraging. The Manpower and Development Training Programs had a modest success with the fraction of the relevant population they trained; the Job Corps, on the other hand, failed. Nor, as other than a form of work relief, did the Comprehensive Employment and Training Act (CETA) have any very great success. All of these programs foundered on the contradictions that have plagued public works and training programs in America since the New Deal. Education programs did better. Initial negative evaluations of Operation Headstart gave way to more positive reports after a few years. The critical factor appeared to be programs designed to help youngsters retain the advantages with which they left preschool. Upward Bound did help significant numbers of poor adolescents prepare for college, and the financial assistance provided through loans, grants, and work study made higher education possible for thousands of young people from families with low or modest incomes. Still, the massive flow of funds to schools that served poor children made no dramatic impact on the quality of urban education, which, as report after report has documented and despite a few shining exceptions, remains a scandal.[13]

More than any other factor, the Vietnam War crippled the war on poverty. The Office of Economic Opportunity received less than 10 percent of the most conservative estimate of what it needed to reach its goals. As Michael Harrington emphasizes, "It never cost even one percent of the federal budget and never reached the 'takeoff' point that is normal in most federal programs." In 1966, Sargent Shriver, director of the OEO, went with an "ambitious, long-range budget" to President Johnson, who told him "that because of the expenditures in Vietnam, there was not enough money to fulfill his request." When Shriver suggested raising taxes, Johnson replied it was impossible on the eve of a congressional election. At any rate, the war would be over in a year. "In 1967 there would be no problems."[14]

In fact, the war on poverty did most to increase opportunity through its support of the civil rights movement. Although Johnson enforced the Civil

Rights Acts lamely, and the Congress did not authorize the Equal Employment Opportunity Commission to initiate suits against employers until 1972, the combination of a tight labor market, a shift in white opinion, increased educational attainment, and civil rights legislation did improve blacks' occupational and economic achievements. Between 1960 and 1970, for instance, the proportion of black males in white-collar jobs increased from 11 percent to 28 percent compared to a much smaller rise, from 37 percent to 43 percent among whites. To take another example, between 1959 and 1977 the median income of black male employees increased from 59 percent to 69 percent of the median for whites. Black family income, however, changed very little relative to white because of the growth of families headed by women. The civil rights movement notwithstanding, by the 1980s about half of all black children and their mothers lived in poverty; most black male teenagers were unemployed; and black participation in the labor force dropped "from 74 percent in 1965 to 53 percent in 1978."[15]

Community action was a novel and explosive strategy. By implication, it defined powerlessness as one key source of poverty and created direct links between local activists outside established urban political structures and the federal government. The definition of a community action program as one "developed, conducted, and administered with maximum feasible participation of the residents" was slipped quietly and almost without comment into Title II of the Economic Opportunity Act. Despite its low key introduction, the Office of Economic Opportunity took "maximum feasible participation" very seriously. An early OEO bulletin said that, "Above all," an acceptable antipoverty plan, "must be a program in which projects are carried out not *for* the community, but rather *by* the community—with external financial assistance—to attack community problems." By funding community agencies, the federal government—not by accident, but by design—threatened to bypass local politicians and shift the balance of political power. OEO officials often defined city politicians and established city agencies as part of the problem rather than as instruments for its solution, and they viewed community action as a source of institutional change as well as an important method for the delivery of services. In theory, each city was supposed to form a broad, inclusive, multipurpose agency to coordinate antipoverty activity. In fact, partly as a response to the howl of opposition from local politicians, OEO funded many special purpose agencies, and in 1967 Congress amended the EOA to force OEO to fund only agencies at least tacitly approved by state governors. At the same time, Congress reduced OEO's discretion by earmarking antipoverty money for special purposes. The big winner was the popular Operation Headstart, followed by Legal Services and Upward Bound. By 1967, OEO had discretion over less than half—$323 of $846 million—of its appropriation. The end came in 1974, when Nixon closed OEO, transferred its remaining programs to other government departments, and created the Community Services Administration to administer remaining community action programs within the Department of Health, Education, and Welfare.[16]

In their outstanding study of community action, *Dilemmas of Social Reform: Poverty and Community Action in the United States*, Peter Marris and Martin Rein emphasize two major sources of the program's rocky history: its mixed purposes and its unwillingness to confront conflict as an inescapable component of social life. Community action was supposed to serve three different goals. "Participation was . . . to restore dignity, redistribute power, and ensure that wherever possible, the poor themselves were recruited for the jobs that the projects would create." Two conceptions of their role pulled the officials who implemented community action in different directions. One of them emphasized the liberation of ideas more than their consequences and "interpreted community action as a stimulus to invention, a means to break out of patterns of service and administrative structures which seemed unable to recover their relevance without outside intervention." The other wanted to build "a new structure of social planning that would not merely innovate, but determine how these innovations were to be integrated in a new balance of community leadership and institutional responsibilities." Where the "first accepted the pluralistic basis of American political life, and tried to exploit its potential vitality," the other considered "this pluralism as itself a crucial obstacle," which it "tried to subordinate to a master plan." Pulled in both directions at once—toward disorderly creativity and disciplined planning—community action never gained the capacity to forge a strong, coherent identity.[17]

Community action officials, Marris and Rein point out, often suffered from their unwillingness to confront the inescapable reality of conflict and their attachment to unrealistic expectations of consensus. Community action, after all, was about power and resources, and not everyone could win. Trapped like the Progressive era reformers before them in the conventions of American liberalism, poverty warriors too often identified conflict with social pathology and refused to choose sides, but, "Only as an agency became partisan, and chose between its possible roles, could it recover its coherence." The most important "general conclusion" of their study, claimed Marris and Rein, was this: no American reform movement "can hope to supplant the conflicts of interest from which policy evolves." A commitment to neutrality emasculates reform, which can succeed "only . . . as an advocate not as judge."[18]

Nonetheless, it would be wrong to say that community action failed. For it was a national movement with important consequences. It reshaped national-local relations; redefined the nature of poverty, as partly a consequence of powerlessness, and the prerequisites of reform—as including local participation;

260

energized and legitimized nascent, grass-roots social action; and launched a new kind of public servant. The Community Action Program, observe Peterson and Greenstone, "contributed to a larger change in political institutions and relationships." Combined with other antipoverty programs, it "helped reverse black exclusion from important positions in local politics." "Within the administration of social policy," write Marris and Rein, "a new kind of public servant had become crucially important, at once more independent of established authority and more responsive to the people. . . . Of all the innovations of community action, this may prove the most important: it created the professional reformer, and invented an organizational framework appropriate to his function." Although the achievements of community action have been attenuated in the 1980s, they have not been destroyed. So far at least, the war on welfare has been unable to stifle what Harry Boyte has called the new citizen's movement or to unseat the new political leaders in city halls, civic agencies, and state houses throughout America.[19]

The Expansion of Social Welfare

Between 1962 and 1974, federal legislation transformed the nature of service delivery across the nation. New programs expanded the federal government's role as a provider of social services, and a variety of forces accelerated federal spending along its existing parallel tracks: social security and aid to families with dependent children. President Nixon's antiwelfare rhetoric notwithstanding, government welfare spending and public housing increased most dramatically during his administration; Nixon, in fact, proposed to restructure social welfare more fundamentally than any of his predecessors since Franklin Roosevelt.

The transformation of social service began with the Public Welfare Amendments of 1962 and culminated with the Social Security Amendments, especially its Title XX, of 1974. One change was the increase in federal spending, which surged between 1963 and 1972 from $194 million to $1.7 billion. In the next year, Congress capped Title XX spending at $2.5 billion annually. As spending increased, legislation, as Neil Gilbert describes, altered social services along five dimensions, "clientele, provisions, delivery, finance, and planning." The expansion of eligibility broadened the social mix of clients. Earlier, most services had been restricted to individuals and families eligible for welfare; now, many services became available "free of charge to all without regard to income" or at a graduated cost. In the first year after eligibility standards had been loosened, 30 percent of Title XX recipients already were exempt from means tests. The kinds of services funded by the federal government also diversified. In 1962, social services "aimed primarily at preventing or reducing poverty" through "intensive social casework." Amendments passed in 1967 reduced the prominence of casework and promoted "more tangible" services, and under Title XX diversification blossomed as Nixon's "New Federalism," which decentralized decision making and left states "free to support whatever social services" they considered "appropriate." In the first quarter after Title XX, only 9.5 percent of services were classified as "counseling" compared to 11 percent day care, 6.5 percent "homemaker/chore," 12 percent "health-related," 2 percent housing improvement, and 3 percent "transportation." Services no longer emphasized primarily the reduction of dependency; instead, they aimed increasingly at "enhancing human development and the general quality of life." Service delivery altered as well. After 1967, the federal government greatly increased its "purchase of services from private sources," and Title XX eased the rules for the calculation of states' share of matching funds. The result was an "enormous expansion in the systematic use of public funds to purchase services delivered by voluntary agencies." To take just one example, between 1962 and 1973, government payment to Jewish-sponsored agencies grew twenty times, from $27 million to $561 million. At the same time, the criteria for allocating federal funds shifted "from state grantsmanship to population parity." That is, under Title XX the allocation of federal funds was tied strictly to formulas based on state population. When grantsmanship no longer was critical, states began to exchange their emphasis on "qualifying" for a heightened commitment to social planning. Together, these legislative shifts transformed the relation of social services to American society. As Gilbert observes:

> What these changes have in common is that each in its own way enlarges the strands—of consumers, planners, service providers, and public bodies—that weave social service into the fabric of society. Their collective impact is to strengthen the institutionalization of social service nationwide. . . . More types of public and private service agencies, more consumers from all classes, and more state governmental bodies throughout the country have a greater stake than ever before in the establishment of enduring social service networks that form an integral part of modern society.[20]

As a result of this expansion of social services, poor people began to receive a smaller share of their benefits as cash. Between 1972 and 1974, cash payments to the poor declined 5.3 percent while purchases of social services for the poor rose 42.7 percent and the purchase of medical care for them increased 37.1 percent. Much of the money went to administrators, not poor people. In Baltimore, in the late 1970s, for instance, administrative costs were 33 percent of cash welfare payments; in Indianapolis, 30 percent; in San Francisco, 49 percent; and in Washington, 60 percent.[21]

The transformation of social services dramatically affected the role of voluntary agencies. In America, public and private have always been mixed. As early as the eighteenth century, local governments contracted with private individuals for the care of the poor. When government responsibilities expanded in the New Deal, some commentators predicted the decline of voluntarism, which had subsisted on a combination of government subsidy and public reluctance to assume direct responsibility for social services. Others tried to carve out a new role and purpose for voluntarism; "most social work spokesmen," Ralph Kramer observes, "assigned to the governmental agency the mass, routine, and remedial tasks, while the voluntary organization was free to experiment, set the pace and standards, and assert its superiority in quality if not in quantity." Recent trends have complicated the ability of voluntary agencies to play their self-assigned roles as social innovators. First, their market share of service provision has declined. The spending ratio of government to nongovernment agencies for services is about ten to one, and the social legislation of the 1970s moved the government into areas previously claimed by private agencies. Despite an absolute increase in the amount of dollars raised, the real value of voluntary contributions also declined. For example, "Individual giving as a proportion of personal income dropped 13 percent between 1960 and 1976." Partly as a consequence of decreased contributions, partly as a result of government policy, voluntary agencies have become increasingly dependent on public funds. In 1974, of all the revenues of nonprofit organizations, $23 billion came from governments and $25 billion from all other sources. Like all social services, voluntary agencies have used their increased public money to reach a more socially diverse group of clients with more tangible services. As so much more of their income came from government sources, voluntary agencies more frequently became service contractors, circumscribed by the specifications of their customers, rather than innovators and pioneers. Only the "appearance of new types of voluntary organizations, such as alternative agencies, quasi-governmental organizations, and a proliferation of self-help, mutual aid, and consumer-oriented associations" kept alive voluntarism's innovative spirit as established agencies, constrained by their dependence on public funds and the conservatism of their own bureaucracies, largely abandoned invention and advocacy.[22]

New social programs increased the availability of three types of services: social work, health care, and legal assistance.[23] Legal service lawyers pioneered class action suits in areas of vital importance to poor people: medical aid, landlord-tenant relations, state housing laws, consumer credit, and welfare administration, to name some of the most important. With more than 2,000 "lawyers in slum communities throughout the nation," legal service offices provided "a remarkable quantity of routine services, which the poor needed as much as other groups and obtained far less often." Neighborhood health centers, much like the Sheppard-Towner clinics of the 1920s, though small in number—at its peak their budget was $130 million—also must rank high among the war on poverty's successful strategies for promoting institutional change and improving services for poor people. Unfortunately, in 1972, Nixon began to phase them out.[24]

On a far grander scale, Medicare and Medicaid worked a modest revolution in health care. In 1963, one-fifth of Americans below the poverty line had never been examined by a physician, and poor people made far less use of medical facilities than others more fortunate. In 1970, after Medicare and Medicaid, the proportion who had never been examined dropped to 8 percent, and the proportion of the poor who visited a physician at least once a year was nearly the same as among everyone else. At the same time, the number of prenatal visits of poor women to doctors rose dramatically, and, between 1965 and 1972, the overall infant mortality rate dropped 33 percent. Among blacks, it declined even faster, and in some poor areas, infant mortality was cut in half. Between 1950 and 1980, black infant mortality dropped from 4.4 percent to 2.2 percent, while the white rate declined from 2.7 percent to 1.1 percent. Life expectancy also rose, from 69.1 years to 74.4 for whites and from 60.8 to 69.5 for blacks. Most of the reduction in the difference between black and white rates happened after 1965.[25]

Despite these gains, the price of expanded medical coverage has been an escalation of health care costs far beyond inflation. At the price of physician support, the government put virtually no ceiling on costs, and, with increased demand, costs ballooned so rapidly that some commentators—focusing on physician fraud, "medicaid mills," and the inadequacy of care actually provided poor people—have called doctors, nursing home operators, and other health care professionals the principal beneficiaries of Medicare and Medicaid. Regardless of who benefited most, the division of federal medical insurance into two very different systems for the elderly and the very poor reinforced the wall between social insurance and public assistance that distinguished America's semiwelfare state. As Paul Starr observes:

> Though adopted together, Medicare and Medicaid reflected sharply different traditions. Medicare was buoyed by popular approval and the acknowledged dignity of Social Security; Medicaid was burdened by the stigma of public assistance. While Medicare had uniform national standards for eligibility and benefits, Medicaid left the states to decide how extensive their programs would be. Medicare allowed physicians to charge above what the program would pay; Medicaid did not and participation among physicians was far more limited. The objective of Medicaid was to allow the poor to buy into the "mainstream" of medicine, but neither the

federal government nor the states were willing to spend the money that would have been required.[26]

The transformation of social services and voluntarism passed largely unnoticed by nonprofessionals, as did another development of equal importance. For in the same years, expenses for income maintenance quietly exploded. Nearly "half of the income of the bottom fifth of the population," Piven and Cloward stress, "is derived from social welfare benefits. The poorest people in the country are now as much dependent on the government for their subsistence as they are on the labor market." This expansion of benefits came from three sources: new in-kind programs, additions to public welfare rolls, and the implementation of a "retirement wage." New in-kind programs, which included housing, nutritional supplements, and food stamps, grew especially fast. Indeed, between 1964 and 1974, the proportion of federal social welfare spending absorbed by in-kind benefits mushroomed from 3 percent to nearly 20 percent.[27]

Lyndon Johnson proposed the first major new housing legislation since the New Deal: the Housing and Urban Development Acts of 1965, notable especially for the creation of the Department of Housing and Urban Development, and 1968, which followed a summer of arson and riots in ghettos across the country. The latter called for "600,000 federally subsidized housing units for lower-income families every year for the next ten years." (During the preceding 20 years, the annual average had been only 40,000.) The major methods were federally insured mortgages for low-income families repayable at costs they could afford and federally subsidized mortgages for the construction of low-income rental housing. In 3 years, the Nixon administration, which implemented the new law, sponsored the construction of 1.3 million units for low-income families, which was more "than all previous administrations combined." Nonetheless, with mounting evidence that the new programs worked badly, Nixon, despite vigorous objections, ended them in 1973 and started an experiment with allowances with which poor people could choose their own housing. Even though most observers counted federal housing policy as a failure, new programs, it should be remembered, greatly reduced overcrowding and lessened the proportion of people living in substandard housing. In 1940, 20 percent of all American households, and 40 percent of minority ones, were overcrowded. That is, they housed more than one person per room. By 1950, the proportion had dropped to 16 percent, by 1970 to 9 percent, and by 1976, to 5 percent. Figures for the proportion of families in substandard housing followed a similar decline.[28]

Between 1965 and 1972, federal spending for nutritional programs other than food stamps, which included school lunches and dietary supplements for women and young children, increased from $870 million to over $1.8 billion.

In the same years, spending on food stamps rose from $36 million to nearly $1.9 billion. Between 1969 and 1974, the food stamp program grew ten times. Food stamps had originated as a small program during the New Deal, more as a way to supplement farm income than to feed the poor. In 1961, the Kennedy administration revived the program at a modest level, and by the late 1960s, those people eligible for welfare could buy food stamps at substantially less than their face value. When a 1968 TV documentary dramatized the extent of malnutrition, hunger became a national issue. Although Senator George McGovern first pressed the issue with a Senate investigation, President Nixon responded quickly by proposing a vast expansion of the food stamp program. In December, 1970, a bipartisan majority in Congress made food stamps available without cost to poor families and at a modest price to families whose income exceeded the official poverty line. In this way, alone among social welfare programs, for over a decade the food stamp program threatened the structural distinctions—the boundary between the working poor and welfare recipients and the wall between social insurance and public assistance—on which the American semiwelfare state had been erected. Indeed, one expert called the new food stamp program, "the most important change in public welfare policy since the passage of the Social Security Act." To skip ahead in the story, it is not surprising that one of the first victories in President Ronald Reagan's war on welfare was the restriction of food stamps to the officially poor.[29]

Food stamps as well as other new government nutritional programs significantly reduced hunger. In 1977, a Field Foundation team that returned to "poverty-stricken areas of the Bronx, Appalachia, Mississippi, and Texas, which had been their laboratory a decade earlier," found a massive improvement in nutrition. One physician, a member of the team, summarized the change:

> There can be little doubt that significant change has occurred since 1967. . . . Nowhere did I see the gross evidence of malnutrition among young children that we saw in 1967. . . . It is not possible any more to find very easily the bloated bellies, the shriveled infants, the gross evidence of vitamin and protein deficiencies in children that we identified in the late 1960's.

Thanks to nutrition and food stamp programs, they reported, the hunger problem had "virtually been eliminated."[30]

Despite the rash of new programs, two old ones—the core of public assistance and social insurance—grew most dramatically. Together, AFDC and social security accounted for most federal social welfare dollars. In 1972, for instance, cash transfers, primarily AFDC, social security, and public employee and railroad pensions, accounted for 43.3 percent of all federal social welfare spending. In 1960, 7.1 million people received public assistance. By 1974, their number had more than doubled to 14.4 million. Nearly all of the growth resulted from Aid to Families with Dependent Children, which, as James Patterson points out, "increased from 3.1 million in 1960 to 4.3 million in 1965 to 6.1 million in 1969 to 10.8 million by 1974."[31]

Much of the increase reflected a deterioration of the economic conditions and living standards of black Americans, who made up an increasing proportion, though not a majority, of AFDC recipients. The mechanization of Southern agriculture, which drove blacks off the land and into Northern cities, was one source of the increase. Another, related, was the increasing number of women who headed families on account of separation or divorce, as contrasted to death. (Recall, Aid to Dependent Children had been conceived in the New Deal as a small program for widows with children, and so it had remained for nearly thirty years.) Other developments, as Patterson points out, also accelerated the growth of the AFDC rolls. Northern states in some instances permitted payment to families with unemployed fathers (AFDC-UP); wealthy states increased both the income level for eligibility and the amount of benefits; the Supreme Court struck down residency requirements, the denial of aid to families with "employable mothers," and the "absent father rule." At least as important, the proportion of eligible families who applied for aid jumped dramatically, as did the proportion of applicants assisted. "Together, these forces resulted in a fantastic jump in the participation of eligible families in AFDC, from perhaps 33 percent in the early 1960s to more than 90 percent in 1971." This historic leap reflected the intersection of a variety of forces: the militance unleashed by the civil rights movement; the pressure of community activists who informed poor people of their rights, led protests at local welfare offices, and formed the National Welfare Rights Organization; the success of legal service attorneys at challenging restrictive administrative practices; and the commitment of federal officials who "encouraged and abetted . . . the thrust from the grass roots."[32]

The elderly emerged as the biggest winners in the expansion of America's semiwelfare state as spending on social insurance exploded. The reason had less to do with the number of elderly than with social class. Social security cut across class lines. Like public education, it offered at least as much to the middle classes as to the poor. Its constituency, therefore, was broad, articulate, effective, and, above all, respectable. In 1970, social security payments to the elderly, $30.3 billion, were about ten times higher than federal payments for AFDC, $2.5 billion. By 1975, the gap had widened: social security cost $64.7 billion and AFDC, $5.1 billion. Throughout the latter 1970s and early 1980s, disparities increased even more: in 1984, social security spending, which was indexed to inflation, had mushroomed to $180.9 billion while AFDC, which was not, had risen only to $8.3 billion. As a result, the federal government spent most of its social welfare dollars—between 1965 and 1971 about 75 percent—on the nonpoor.[33]

The dramatic increase in social security payments resulted from a series of amendments, especially those passed between 1969 and 1972, several of which raised benefits more than inflation. Between 1963 and 1973, minimum benefit levels increased 135 percent compared to a 45 percent rise in inflation, and the maximum benefit rose 270 percent. Congress indexed benefits in 1972, raised the income threshold after which benefits decreased, improved widows' benefits, extended Medicare to the disabled, combined previously separate public assistance programs into one new federally funded program (SSI), and, for the first time, set uniform national minimum benefits. (As Trattner observes, the federal government's escalation of "all public assistance for the adult poor who were clearly unemployable, while continuing to ignore others in need, further demonstrated the lasting strength of . . . the belief that a plan of social protection for those who appeared to be capable of working would undermine the free enterprise system.)[34]

These changes in social security reflected a fundamental transformation of the principles underlying the American social security system. As John Myles points out, original social security benefits deliberately did not exceed minimum wages; instead, they gave minimal support to people no longer able to work. In sharp contrast, its 1969–72 amendments made social security a "retirement wage" that encouraged workers to withdraw from the labor force whatever their physical condition. (Myles argues that explanations of the transformation based on demography or voting strength don't work, especially when international comparisons are made. Instead, he offers the intriguing hypothesis that employers, with the acquiescence of labor, in effect, used the state to trade a deferred wage for continued increases in current wage costs.) Nonetheless, social security did not become more equitable. Workers with larger incomes received higher benefits, and, because one generation's contributions usually did not cover its entitlements, younger workers paid a substantial share of the retired's benefits. Another way to highlight how social security differs from public assistance and helps the nonpoor is this: in 1972, 58 percent of social security and railroad retirement benefits went to people who otherwise would have been poor; for public assistance, the proportion was 87 percent. In subsequent years, with the indexing of social security and the relative stagnation of public assistance, the gap turned into a chasm.[35]

One other major cash transfer program expanded in the mid-1970s: unemployment insurance. As unemployment rose in 1975, Congress increased the number of weeks for which benefits were paid, extended coverage to 12 million previously excluded workers, and used federal funds, not payroll taxes, to finance the program's expansion. "In March 1975 a weekly average of 5.9 million persons received $1.5 billion in unemployment insurance benefits . . . more than five times the number during the last year of the Johnson administration, and the costs increased eightfold."[36]

By the late 1960s, federal social welfare had become a tangle of more or less unsatisfactory programs disliked by nearly everyone, including President Richard Nixon, who, to almost everyone's surprise, became the first president to propose a way to cut through the welfare jungle. In August, 1969, he called "for a Family Assistance Plan that would have guaranteed all families with children a minimum of $500 per adult and $300 per child per year, or $1,600 for a two-parent family of four. FAP promised to sustain the incentive to work and supplant welfare dependency. A poor family could keep the first $60 per month of income without losing any government aid, and half of income above that, up to specified maximums, at which points benefits would vanish." Though he denied it for political reasons, Nixon's FAP was a guaranteed income plan. (To test whether a guaranteed income would destroy work incentives, the government sponsored income maintenance experiments in a few communities. The results, however, were inconclusive.) Nixon's plan failed; so did a similar proposal by President Jimmy Carter. The reason was primarily ideological. Both plans refused to make benefits completely contingent on willingness to work. By threatening to aid the unworthy poor and breaching the distinction between public assistance and social insurance, FAP violated the structural foundations of American welfare. Even though only a few years earlier, work requirements attached to AFDC benefits had proven—for understandable reasons—a colossal failure, the link between work and welfare, which, after all, did little more than reaffirm the long-standing reluctance to help the ablebodied poor, remained unshakable.[37]

Despite the claims of right-wing ideologues, the expansion of social welfare did not retard economic growth, exacerbate social problems, or discredit old-style liberalism. In fact, data show quite the opposite. Between 1960 and 1980, the proportion of Americans living in poverty declined 60 percent, from 18 percent to between 4 percent and 8 percent, according to John Schwarz. The reason was government programs, not economic growth. Although disposable income increased 24 percent between 1965 and 1972, without government programs 21.3 percent of Americans still would have lived in poverty in 1965 and 19.2 percent in 1972. Government intervention boosted half of the 19 percent above the official poverty line. Put another way, these figures illustrate the decline in poverty after transfer payments (that is, various forms of public assistance and social insurance) have been added to income. By contrast, before transfer payments, poverty hardly declined at all. In 1965, 19.5 percent of families were poor before transfer payments; in 1972, the proportion was 17.7 percent. Pretransfer poverty did not decline, because economic growth did not help poor

269

people who remained outside the labor market: for example, retired workers, elderly widows, or female family heads with young children. In fact, transfer payments reduced poverty among the elderly more than among any other group. In 1971, transfer payments lifted 57 percent of pretransfer poor households with an elderly head out of poverty compared to 30 percent of those headed by someone younger. Between 1959 and 1980, the proportion of elderly poor people dropped from 35.2 percent to 15.7 percent. Government programs, Schwarz concludes, reduced poverty at a rate five or six times faster than economic growth.[38]

Nor did government antipoverty programs erode the work incentive. During welfare's expansionary phase, unemployment grew very slowly, and employment rose faster during the period of welfare's greatest expansion than during the preceding 15 years. According to one estimate, without any expansion of welfare, employment might have risen only an additional 1 percent. Nor were children from welfare families disproportionately prone to go on welfare when they set up their own households. Indeed, an important University of Michigan national study of income over time found that for most AFDC families welfare is a temporary, not a permanent, resource.[39]

There is, however, a less sanguine way to read the evidence. Because of inflation, the actual value of AFDC and other social welfare outlays declined during the 1970s, and, despite Medicare and Medicaid, America remained the only modern Western nation without national health insurance. Even more, figures that show a reduction in poverty rest on the official poverty line. First set in 1955, the boundary is calculated by taking the cost of a "thrifty" diet, multiplying it by three (weighted by family size and other factors), and calling the figure that results the poverty line. Often criticized cogently, the official poverty line has little to recommend it except bureaucratic convenience and the assurance that anyone whose income falls beneath it is unequivocally poor. Any truly comprehensive measure of poverty in America would have to include the millions of people whose income falls on just the other side of the line. Official poverty counts, moreover, rest on cross-sectional analysis. They are snapshots which do not show how many people slip into poverty over any period of time. The one major analysis that substitutes a dynamic for a static analysis shows a very different picture: during a 10-year period only about 8 percent of its sample was poor at any one time, but about 25 percent fell into poverty, most for brief periods, at some point. Still another problem is estimating the reduction of poverty by services and transfer payments. What is their dollar value? What assumptions, for instance, can one make about the value of Medicare or Medicaid as an income supplement? Individual people vary in the amount of medical care they consume, and, certainly, there is no reason to suppose that poor people would (or could) have spent an equivalent amount on medical care had these new programs not been available.[40]

Poverty is as much a relative as an absolute condition. It should be measured as much against prevailing standards of adequacy as against arbitrary and absolute definitions. For this reason, many students of poverty prefer a measure based on relation to median income. People are poor, according to this measure, if their income falls below a certain fraction (usually one-half) of the median income. This, of course, is a measure of inequality as well as poverty. It can be made to show not only how large a fraction of the population is poor but what share of national income they receive. What influence did the expansion of social welfare have on income inequality, or as two careful scholars call it, "relative poverty"? The answer is, none at all. Among individuals, the incidence of "relative poverty" was 15.6 percent in 1965 and 15.7 percent in 1972. For families, the same two proportions were 12.4 percent and 12.5 percent. By contrast, during the same years, the proportion of "absolute poverty" for individuals dropped from 15.6 percent to 11.9 percent, and for families from 12.4 percent to 9.3 percent. Although the great expansion of social welfare helped individuals climb out of absolute poverty, it did little to make Americans more equal.[41]

By 1975, the citizen's wage paid to elderly Americans ranked eleventh out of comparable payments in fifteen capitalist democracies. American policy at least ranked ahead of Switzerland, the United Kingdom, West Germany, and Australia. However, on a 1977 ranking that included all expenditures for income security in several of the same countries, the United States ranked last. West Germany, for instance, spent 26.5 percent of its GNP on income security; the United Kingdom, 17.1 percent; and the United States, 13.7 percent. American social policy looks especially mean when its support for families is compared to other Western, industrialized countries. Alfred Kahn and Sheila Kammerman, who conducted a careful, eight-nation study of income transfers for families with children, found, "When it comes to relieving parents of some of the costs of rearing children, the United States does less than any of the other countries." The United States is the only country that lacks a family allowance; more than any other, it relies on public assistance; its poor parents with children have lower relative incomes; fewer incentives to work; and less assistance with retraining, job placement, and child care than in any other advanced democracy.[42]

Nonetheless, although it failed to reach many of its goals and left America with only a semiwelfare state, and not a very inclusive or equitable one by international standards, the great expansion of government social spending between the early 1960s and the mid-1970s had a major impact in five areas. First, it vastly increased the proportion of the most disadvantaged Americans assisted

271

by their government; it virtually guaranteed them a minimally adequate diet and health care; and it lifted a significant fraction of them, especially the elderly, out of extreme poverty. Second, it mobilized the power of the federal government behind the civil rights movement and thereby helped reduce discrimination and increase the accessibility of jobs to minorities. Third, the OEO's emphasis on community action nourished and intensified the growing citizen's movement, or grass-roots revolution, that already has reshaped urban politics and launched a new generation of leaders into government and social service. Fourth, it altered the relations between citizens and the state by making the federal government the most important source of income for a large fraction of the population; stringing direct, new lines of communication between the federal government and local groups; and using public authority to monitor and enforce antidiscrimination measures in employment, housing, education, and social welfare, and to regulate the environment and the workplace. Fifth, all of the above point unequivocally in at least one direction: the federal government has the resources and the administrative capacity with which to stimulate and sustain progressive social change. Its current failure is a matter of will, not potential. In this recognition there is at least some small cheer for dark days.

Appendix

Here are major examples of war on poverty programs by category:[43]

Delinquency. In 1961, the creation of the President's Committee on Juvenile Delinquency, in May, and, in September, the signing of the Juvenile Delinquency and Youth Offenses Act were the major attempts to grapple with youth crime. Richard Cloward's appointment as director of the Office of Juvenile Delinquency in HEW signaled the influence of his theories and of Mobilization for Youth on the administration's plans.

Job training. The first in a series of new job training programs was the Manpower Development and Training Act (1962) originally intended "to train the technologically displaced," but soon "expanded and redirected to the hard core unemployed." In 1964, the Economic Opportunity Act added the Neighborhood Youth Corps; a residential program for teenagers, the Jobs Corps (the largest and most controversial of the manpower training programs); and a variety of smaller programs. In 1967, the Concentrated Employment Program gave "block grants to community groups for comprehensive attacks on employment programs," and the Work Incentive Program tried to "train and place welfare recipients." In 1973, the Nixon administration consolidated most public job training programs in CETA (the Comprehensive Employment and Training Act).

Education. Operation Headstart, probably the most popular program created by the Economic Opportunity Act, funded special preschool programs for disadvantaged children. Later, Operation Follow Through tried to prevent Headstart alumni from losing their early advantages; Upward Bound helped bright, poor youngsters prepare for college; and the Higher Education Act of 1965 "authorized scholarships and low interest loans" for undergraduates and "expanded the work-study program" created a year earlier as part of the Economic Opportunity Act.

Discrimination and opportunity. The Civil Rights Act (1964) and the Voting Rights Act (1975), the first major civil rights legislation since Reconstruction (a "limited measure" had been passed in 1957), tried to expand political opportunities by guaranteeing voting rights, to increase economic opportunities by ending discrimination in employment and education, and to extend social opportunities through attacking segregation in public accommodations and housing.

10 The War on Welfare

Half a million *more* people live below the poverty level than in 1965, when then-President Lyndon B. Johnson launched the "War on Poverty," and there are 4.4 million more impoverished people today than when President Reagan took office. The policies of the present administration have effectively unleashed a war on the poor.

—JESSE JACKSON, *Philadelphia Inquirer,* December 15, 1985, p. 7–H

In the last several years, city governments have slashed services; state legislatures have attacked general assistance (outdoor relief to persons ineligible for benefits from other programs); and the Reagan administration has launched an offensive against social welfare and used tax policy to widen the income gap between rich and poor. The result has been an ongoing war fought along the historic divide between public assistance and social insurance. With weak defenses, public assistance and other programs for the poor have suffered badly, and the assault on them continues. Social insurance, by contrast, has proved nearly impregnable; even Ronald Reagan's popularity could do no more than nick the battlements defended so ably by social security's articulate, middle-class beneficiaries.[1]

As industries deserted older American cities for the Sunbelt or the Third World and the economy shifted toward high tech and service; as federal policies encouraged the exodus of middle-class families to suburbs; as racial segregation increased, and urban schooling deteriorated, once well-paid, ex-industrial workers faced a future of joblessness or low-paid unskilled labor; minority unemployment—especially among young people—soared; and official poverty rates climbed most steeply among women. The "new American poverty" (to use Michael Harrington's phrase) was structural and feminized. A compassionate and comprehensive social welfare system might have mitigated its effects, but only a revolution in social and economic policy could strike at its causes. As it happened, social welfare became even less adequate, and policy accelerated the forces that built the new structure of poverty.[2]

The New Poverty

Consider, first, the feminization of poverty. Karin Stallard, Barbara Ehrenreich, and Holly Sklar report the basic facts:

> Two out of three poor adults are women and one out of five children is poor. Women head half of all poor families and over half the children in female-headed households are poor: 50 percent of white children; 68 percent of black and Latin children. A woman over 60 years of age is almost twice as likely as her male counterpart to be impoverished. One-fifth of all elderly women are poor. For elderly black women the poverty rate in 1981 was 43.5 percent; for elderly Latina women, 27.4 percent. Among black women over 65 living alone the 1982 poverty rate was about 82 percent.

Although poverty among women has always been high, these figures represent increases. Between 1970 and 1978, for instance, the number of women family heads beneath the official poverty line rose 38.7 percent. Reasons for the feminization of poverty are not hard to find. Deindustrialization; the lack of day care; poor education; inadequate child support; increased numbers of female-headed families and teenage pregnancies; ineligibility for social security among elderly women; the absence of family allowances; tax and welfare policies that decrease the incomes of women who work at the low-paying service jobs which make up the bulk of their opportunities for paid employment: together, these powerful forces trap many women in poverty.[3]

In the United States in the 1970s, more than 38 million jobs "were lost through private disinvestment." In 1979 alone, automobile manufacturers announced that twenty plants with more than 50,000 workers would shut down.

275

As a result, many of their suppliers—about one hundred plants with 80,000 employees—also would close. Between 1960 and 1978, the steel industry lost 20 percent of its total jobs, almost all in production, and in the last few years, the shutdowns have accelerated. One can argue over precise statistics: exactly how many workers will lose their jobs because of deindustrialization. By whatever count, however, the numbers are enormous. Nor are they spread evenly across the country. The industrial base of older cities has been decimated. Between 1975 and 1979, for example, Philadelphia lost 128,000, 1 of 6 jobs. Small communities dependent on single industries have been devastated as well. Every plant closing, as Bluestone and Harrison point out, has "ripple" effects: "decreased retail purchases in the community, a reduction in earnings at supplier plants, and increased unemployment in other sectors" followed by "increased demand for public assistance and social services, reduced personal tax receipts, and eventually layoffs in other industries, including the public sector." Manufacturing workers and their families displaced by plant closings often lose income permanently. Various studies show that many take early retirement or remain unable to find work; others skid down the occupational ladder by taking jobs in expanding service industries that pay badly. A *Fortune* study of 4,100 Ohio steelworkers displaced two years earlier found that "35 percent . . . were forced into early retirement—at less than half of their previous salary. Another 15 percent were still looking for work and 10 percent were forced to move. . . . Of the remaining 40 percent, some took huge wage cuts." The result is a new structure of poverty. In the past, poverty rates followed unemployment closely. When unemployment dropped, so did poverty. Now, this historic relation, as Michael Harrington shows, has nearly been broken. In the 1970s, he writes:

> every time unemployment went up, so did poverty. This reflected the impact of joblessness upon marginal workers, upon the last hired and first fired, upon blacks, Hispanics, and other minorities, and upon women. What is new now is that the dislocated worker is to be found in industries such as auto and steel, which in past times suffered, at the worst, temporary layoffs that did not threaten the unemployed with poverty. In the recession of 1974–75, the number of the official poor went up by a million and a half; between 1979 and 1982, the increase was about eight million.

These shifts in occupational structure—the replacement of industrial work by a service and high-tech economy—are why economic recovery will not reduce either unemployment or poverty beyond levels that, not long ago, belonged only in recessions.[4]

Another description of the new American poverty surfaced in the last few years. America, it is said, most articulately by Ken Auletta, now has an "underclass": perhaps 9 million of the "25 to 29 million Americans officially classified as poor." The "underclass," writes Auletta, consists of four "distinct categories":

> (a) the *passive poor*, usually long-term welfare recipients; (b) the *hostile* street criminals who terrorize most cities, and who are often school dropouts and drug addicts; (c) the *hustlers*, who, like street criminals, may not be poor and who earn their livelihood in an underground economy, but rarely commit violent crimes; (d) the *traumatized* drunks, drifters, homeless, shoppingbag ladies and released mental patients who frequently roam or collapse on city streets.

Auletta's description of the underclass has a nineteenth century ring because it compounds various forms of dependence and deviance into one convenient and derogatory category defined more by behavior than poverty. Long-term poverty, crime, and mental illness blend into a serviceably updated image of the unworthy poor. But how is one to distinguish the *passive* from the nonpassive poor? Why is it helpful to lump people with such varied problems as drug addicts, women supported by AFDC, and former mental patients in one category? Will it point policy in useful directions or increase compassion for the victims of America's structure of inequality? Even if, as I believe, the answer is no, the concept of an "underclass" serves a useful rhetorical purpose for the war on welfare. By drawing a sharp line between the working class and the very poor, it fractures a potential source of political mobilization, justifies mean and punitive social policies, and keeps the working poor at low-paid jobs, any jobs, to avoid descent into the underclass.[5]

In fact, as a metaphor, the underclass obscures more than it reveals. It glosses over differences in condition that require varied forms of help, and it passes lightly over two salient features of poverty and welfare in America: their widespread and transient character. In the Michigan study, which followed a large sample of American families for 10 years, one-quarter of individuals in the sample lived in families that dropped below the official poverty line at some point during the decade, and a similar proportion relied on some form of public welfare, although at any one point in time only 2 percent needed income from welfare sources. Both poverty and welfare use, however, lasted relatively briefly, and children whose parents relied on welfare were no more likely to need public assistance as adults than were others in the sample. What the study shows, in short, is that poverty is more accurately perceived now, as before in American history, as a point on a continuum rather than a sharp, clearly demarcated category of social experience. In truth, the forces that push individuals and families into poverty originate in the structure of America's political economy. Some of us are lucky, not different.[6]

Sources of the War on Welfare

Even if the sources of the new poverty remained beyond reach, or politically untouchable, its effects could have been softened by an expansion of the social welfare policies initiated in the late 1960s and early 1970s. This did not happen. Instead, victims of the new poverty confronted city, state, and federal governments determined to roll back the welfare state and decimate trade unions. How does one account for this implacable determination to dismantle the welfare state at the very time its growth was so urgent? Politics and ideology, certainly, provide one answer: the election of a government philosophically opposed to the welfare state. Still, the question remains, what has given antiwelfare politics their current success? Public hostility to welfare cheats or black women on AFDC is not an adequate answer. Politicians often have whipped up public outrage with images of steaks in welfare freezers and Cadillacs in the parking lots of public housing. Rather, the reason for the success of antiwelfare politics lies in a conjunction between the temper of the electorate and one diagnosis of the source of America's economic problems.

Oil shortages, inflation, and rising unemployment have left American voters receptive to a war on welfare. In the 1960s and early 1970s, an unreflective, though brand new, assumption led to an optimistic assessment of America's future. Permanent economic growth would fuel continuous prosperity and provide the resources to absorb and resolve social problems with neither conflict nor sacrifice. This faith in the benefits of unlimited growth underpinned national policy, the emergence of a counterculture, and the relatively relaxed attitude toward the expansion of social welfare. However, in 1973, the oil embargo neatly sliced the underpinnings away from assumptions of permanent abundance, and individuals' difficulty simply finding gasoline for their automobiles became emblematic of the new task confronting families: maintaining—not expanding—a standard of living. As inflation and unemployment followed the energy crisis, the resumption of buoyant growth became increasingly evanescent, and, everywhere, ordinary people reverted to an older psychology of scarcity, now tinged by the anxiety and resentment that accompanies downward mobility and, particularly, in America, the fear that their struggles and sacrifices will not insure a better life for their children. In the search for scapegoats and ways to trim public expenses that followed predictably, welfare and its clients, especially its black clients, were inevitable and early targets, displacing attention from the falling profits and return on investments that, even before the first oil crisis, had signalled the end of unlimited growth.[7]

278

The War on Welfare

As business and government determined to reverse the direction of social policy and end the tacit post-World War II pact between capital and labor, greedy trade unions and generous social welfare benefits became leading explanations of America's declining productivity and profits. Welfare, so it is said, has eroded work incentives by allowing too many people to live in idleness with relative comfort. Not only a drain on a tight national treasury and a handicap to American business, welfare, the argument continues, pushed wages to record heights and allowed unions to win outrageous settlements. Indeed, attacks on welfare and unions are two prongs of the same offensive. (They come together especially clearly in regulations denying food stamps to workers who quit their jobs "without good cause" or participate in strikes.)[8]

In a powerful explanation of the war on welfare, Piven and Cloward argue that the Reagan administration incorrectly identified capital shortage and declining investment as the source of America's economic problems, which it proposed to solve "by reducing the share of the national product that goes to the working class—by cutting taxes on business and wealth, by dismantling government regulation of business, and by slashing the income-maintenance programs" that *"limit profits by enlarging the bargaining power of workers with employers."* Economists of all political viewpoints, they contend, agree that "income-maintenance programs have weakened capital's ability to depress wages by means of economic insecurity, especially by means of manipulating the relative numbers of people searching for work." Income-maintenance programs, they continue, do more than reduce economic insecurity and raise wages.

> Economic insecurity makes workers vulnerable, it also saps their strength to make other demands in the workplace. When people fear for their subsistence, they accept onerous and dangerous working conditions. They work harder, and they work longer. They more readily accept discipline, follow orders, and submit to humiliation. An insecure labor force is thus a more productive labor force and a cheaper one, quite apart from wage levels.

It is an old story. In the late 1960s, the federal government expanded social welfare primarily to insure social order and mobilize the votes of black Americans; in the 1980s, another of welfare's historic goals—the regulation of the labor market—and an attempt to mobilize political support among affluent and middle-income voters combined to fuel a war on welfare.[9]

Assumptions about human nature and the role of voluntarism underlie the war on welfare. One, as Piven and Cloward point out, is "the archaic idea that people in different social classes have different human natures and thus different basic motivations." Because their motivations vary, the affluent and the working poor do not respond to the same incentives. "The affluent exert themselves in response to rewards—to the incentive of increased profitability yielded by lower

279

taxes. Working people respond only to punishment—to the economic insecurity that will result from reductions in income support systems." This is the logic of cutting the taxes of the rich and the social benefits of the poor.[10]

Another major assumption reflects the myth of voluntarism. Through voluntarism, it is argued, the private sector will replace and improve upon the services and supports formerly provided by the federal government. Ronald Reagan has claimed this reliance on voluntarism, individual initiative, and the private sector as the traditional American approach to social problems. On January 15, 1983, he told the New York Partnership, Inc.:

> We passed our reforms in Washington but change must begin at the grass roots, on the streets where you live. And that's why on Sept. 24, I announced that we were launching a nationwide effort to encourage citizens to join with us in finding where need exists and then to organize volunteer programs to meet those needs.
>
> The American people understand the logic of our approach. A recent Roper poll found a large majority believe that Government does not spend tax money for human services as effectively as a leading private organization like the United Way.

Of course, Reagan reflected an enduring American myth, not reality. Voluntarism never met most of the needs of dependent Americans. Some form of public assistance has always been crucial. Even more, as inadequate as they were to meet crises in the past, voluntary agencies have become even less capable in the present. Not only have they lost their role in income maintenance; more recently, escalation of government contracts for services with the private sector made them dependent, as never before, on money from public sources. Serious cutbacks in public funds, therefore, have left voluntary agencies with less money to spend on the increased numbers of needy people whose benefits have been terminated or reduced by the war on welfare.[11]

Cities and Austerity

The first round in the war on welfare was the imposition of austerity on city governments, especially New York in 1975. Throughout the 1950s and 1960s, the gap between New York's revenue and expenditures increased. One reason was the decline in private sector jobs: in the decade before 1974, the city lost 230,000 jobs or 7.5 percent of its 1964 total. The city compensated for job loss by adding public employees. In the same decade, it created at least 132,000 public municipal jobs, thereby offsetting half the private job loss and averting a major political and economic disaster. The city paid for its new workers partially with federal grants and subsidies, first for highways and urban renewal,

280

later for virtually every civic function. At the same time, it converted operating expenses, which could not be financed through borrowing, into capital expenditures, which could. The city also won new and expanded assistance from the state for universities, health care, schools, and other areas. To finance its seasonal cash flow problem, New York issued "budget notes" secured with anticipated taxes, including ones on abandoned property on which, everyone knew, none would ever be collected. The result, of course, was massive debt. Between 1967 and 1974, the city's debt more than tripled. Debt service on the city's $13 billion obligation consumed a seventh of the entire city budget.[12]

Banks played a key role in the city's fiscal crisis, first by encouraging it to borrow more than it should, then by calling in their debts. Indeed, banks had snapped up tax-free municipal bonds, which, in fact, climbed from 21.6 percent of bank portfolios in 1965 to 50 percent a decade later, thereby reducing banks' effective tax rate from 33 percent in 1960 to 14.3 percent in 1974. In 1974, although banks knew the city would have serious trouble meeting its loan payments and finding money to pay for the social needs generated by the recession, they raised their interest rates, despite the concomitant decrease in the Federal Reserve discount rate and Treasury bills.

The first serious signs of trouble appeared in October, 1974, when a securities issue sold poorly. Between October, 1974, and March, 1975, the city's largest banks began to bail themselves out of the New York bond market; in February, Bankers Trust declined to underwrite a new bond issue; by April the city could not even sell short-term securities at record rates; and banks refused to roll over $3 billion in short-term notes. By June 30, it appeared as though the city would not be able to meet the payments on its $12.3 billion debt. This was the fiscal crisis of New York.

Most of the causes usually trotted out to explain New York's fiscal crisis disintegrate on close inspection. In many of them, the scapegoat is the public sector—especially, welfare, salaries, pensions, and unions—whose alleged extraordinary expense precipitated the fiscal crisis. In fact, New York only appeared to spend more money, per capita, on income maintenance than other cities, because elsewhere county and state governments bore a larger share of the cost. Standard city functions did not cost more in New York than elsewhere.[13] Nor, by comparative standards, was the proportion of New York's population on welfare—in February, 1975, 12.6 percent—especially large.[14] As for complaints that most welfare recipients could find work, two-thirds of them were less than ten years old. Nor were municipal workers and their pensions to blame: contrary to popular perception and the occasional extreme example, a private consulting firm reported that average New York City pensions were not out of line with pensions paid in other large cities. In fact, they had increased less than inflation during the past decade.

Some people did make money from the public sector: namely, those who ran private services and charged inflated rates for private day care or nursing homes. Banks and corporate projects with reduced or abated tax assessments also profited from the city. If the World Trade Center, which paid no taxes, had been assessed the same rate as other privately owned buildings, the city would have collected $65 million a year. Instead, the center created a glut of office space, which lowered real estate assessments.

Thus, New York's fiscal crisis cannot be blamed on a bloated public sector and its greedy employees. Rather, it emerged from the transformation of the city's economy, the concomitant loss of jobs, the narrow self-interest of banks, and federal policies that drained money from the city to subsidize the mechanization of Southern agriculture (which drove poor blacks to Northern cities) and to pay defense contractors, disproportionately located in the Sunbelt. Between 1965 and 1967, the federal government took $7.4 billion more out of New York State than it spent there for all purposes.

Private sector representatives who wanted to attack the emerging strength and militance of the public sector precipitated the city's fiscal crisis and, then, restored fiscal health to the city at the expense of its most disadvantaged citizens. New York's poor, not its corporations, paid the bill for the city's return from the edge of bankruptcy. The price of New York's rescue was a program of austerity, whose cornerstones were MAC, the Municipal Acceptance Corporation, and the EFRB, Emergency Financial Control Board, that removed effective control from elected officials and vested it primarily in representatives of the city's financial and corporate leaders. The austerity program, essentially drawn up by a leading law firm and Felix Royhatyn, a partner in an important investment house, also gave a windfall to the city's creditors by exchanging at face value the city's bonds, which were selling at as much as 40 percent discount, for new securities that paid higher interest. Austerity decimated essential services throughout the city. As New York's bondholders and banks profited handsomely, its ordinary citizens experienced a swift deterioration in the quality of their day-to-day lives. Reduced wage and tax expense freed capital; layoffs in New York frightened municipal workers in other cities and helped persuade unions to accept lower wages; and the crisis itself allowed capital to experiment with new forms of control over government. Indeed, business leaders, who had remained aloof from city government, began "moving directly for power. The new institutions imposed on New York City by its creditors may be prototypes for more general forms of control, to be used on other cities and states and perhaps even for federal planning."[15]

Elsewhere, as the federal deficit soared, national leaders began to define the nation's problems in the same terms used earlier to characterize New York's, and their proposed solutions—austerity and reduced democratic control—paralleled those adopted in the city. The issues defined by New York's leaders as the source of the city's fiscal crisis, "too large a welfare state, inflationary wages, free services, and government—rather than market-regulated production," Tabb points out, "are now taken to be at the heart of our national economic crisis. And the same cures—cutbacks of social programs, lower wages, and reduced consumption to finance private sector investment—have become the mainstream orthodoxy." This is why New York's fiscal crisis was the first skirmish in the new war on welfare.[16]

States and General Assistance

Other skirmishes took place in state capitols across the country as governors and legislators attempted to roll back state programs of general assistance that gave money to people ineligible for federal income-maintenance programs. By the mid-1970s, twenty states restricted general assistance to so-called unemployables; nine states assisted "employables" as well; others had no program. Grants usually were small: Pennsylvania, one of the most generous states, in 1980 gave only $172 a month. In the 1970s, two forces turned general assistance into a major issue. One was the explosive growth in the number of recipients. In Pennsylvania, between 1973 and 1974, and 1978 and 1979, the number of individual general assistance recipients increased from about sixty-six thousand to one hundred twenty-nine thousand; in New York City between December, 1974, and 1979, it rose from about forty-nine thousand to ninety thousand. The general assistance rolls expanded at precisely the time when the fiscal crisis hit cities and states with its greatest impact. Strapped for cash, state governments looked for ways to cut expenses, and general assistance—especially its ablebodied, employable recipients—became a prime target. Once again, under the banner of welfare reform, state and local governments attacked outdoor relief of the ablebodied.[17]

First to purge "employables" from general assistance was Massachusetts, in 1975. Other states tried to follow. In New York, where state law prohibited a formal purge, tightened administrative procedures and new regulations reduced the size of the rolls. A California county even reintroduced a poorhouse. One of the longest and toughest campaigns against general assistance took place in Pennsylvania, where Governor Dick Thornburgh fought for 2 years before his reform of general assistance passed the state legislature in December, 1982. The new legislation restricted aid to "employables" to 3 months a year, required them to work at public service jobs, and made it much more difficult for new applicants to receive aid. Unlike Massachusetts, where money saved by cutting general relief was used to reduce state spending, Thornburgh promised to use it to increase welfare grants to families with children and to fund job training and placement programs. Although supporters of "Thornfare," as the new measure was dubbed, trotted out familiar stereotypes of welfare and its clients, the governor and his senior officials argued their case in terms of financial necessity and equity. "Because our resources are so limited," wrote Governor Thornburgh, "we have no choice but to choose, and I choose to help the helpless first; to encourage self-reliance in the able-bodied second, and to do what we can with any real problems that may remain after that." Secretary of State Helen O'Bannon stressed the potential of the state's job training and placement programs and emphasized that "welfare reform," expected to reduce caseloads only 9 percent, would remove young, single, employable persons "from a system that fosters dependency, and channel them into programs that will encourage self-sufficiency and employment."[18]

Despite their surface plausibility, arguments for Thornfare, as critics pointed out, were seriously flawed. Ablebodied people sliced from the welfare rolls would increase competition for a shrinking number of jobs. In Philadelphia and Pittsburgh, where most of the cuts would take effect, about fifty people would compete for every opening. Even more, "most general assistance recipients, while having some work experience," lacked "the kind of stable employment histories that" would "make them attractive to prospective employers," and the history of affordable job training programs was, in fact, dismal. Few people stayed on general assistance for more than 2 years; most used it for short-term help; and "employable" itself, as nearly two centuries of welfare reformers had discovered, was a slippery, imprecise, and subjective concept.[19]

Indeed, Thornburgh's reform of general assistance promoted neither equity nor opportunity. The savings were not very great, and the average monthly benefit increased only about 5 percent. Mainly, it cut tens of thousands of people from general assistance rolls. True, neither violence nor crime surged, as some of the measure's opponents had predicted, and the state saved even more money than its supporters expected. But there has been a serious human cost. In July, 1982, before the new provisions took effect, the average length of stay of poor men and women in Philadelphia's boarding homes was 6 days, and the total nights of shelter (length of stay multiplied by number of people) was 6,525; by March, 1984, the length of stay had climbed to 45 days and the nights of shelter to 22,687. In 1982, the city spent $2 million on shelter; in 1984, the projected cost was $3.9 million supplemented by a one-time federal grant of $2 million. Almost all of the men and women in the city's shelters were "destitute. Almost all would have been receiving general assistance before the eligibility rules changed." Truly, the reform of general assistance forced cities to reinvent the poorhouse.

Nor were the results of job training and placement programs encouraging. The Community Work Experience Program, designed to give public service jobs to general assistance recipients, had placed only one of every eight participants. In March, 1984, the Pennsylvania Employables Program, designed to use tax credits to train people on welfare and help them find jobs, placed 195 of 3,600 who had registered in jobs and 247 in vocational courses, and employers had claimed only $70,000 of the $25 million set aside by the state as tax credits to encourage them to employ welfare recipients. In September, 1984, a report issued by the Advocacy Committee for Emergency Services claimed, among other criticisms, that "an estimated 25.8 percent of those affected by the law experienced worsened health" and that "cuts and reductions in benefits have placed 'an untenable burden on families and charitable and social service agencies'. . . . those cut off from year-round cash aid also had their medical assistance coverage reduced." Even in the late twentieth century, it proved impossible to reduce outdoor relief without imposing hardship and suffering.[20]

Few general assistance recipients were launched into stable, decently paid jobs. Instead, unemployment and competition for badly paid, short-term jobs increased. The withdrawal of even the minimal cushion offered by general assistance dampened worker militance and encouraged workers to accept low pay and bad conditions. As it solved fiscal problems at the expense of the poor and used welfare policy to discipline the expectations of the workforce, across the country the reform of general assistance, as much as the imposition of austerity in New York and other cities, assumed a strategic role in the national war on welfare.

The Federal Government Wages War on Welfare

The federal government deployed the heaviest artillery in the war on welfare. It claimed, of course, only to root out waste and fraud. The truly needy, it assured Americans, would be cushioned by a social "safety net." The safety net, however, proved more a rhetorical illusion than a policy. David Stockman, Reagan administration budget director, said that the list of safety net programs "was a happenstance list, just a spur of the moment thing that the [White House] press office wanted to put out." Martin Anderson, then White House domestic policy advisor, admitted, "Providing a safety net for those who cannot or are not expected to work was not really a policy objective. The term safety net was political shorthand that only made sense for a limited period of time."[21]

At first, the Reagan administration tried to cut both social insurance and public assistance, but the political forces supporting social security proved so potent that the administration quickly withdrew, settling for a few minor adjustments in benefits. In the 1984 election, Ronald Reagan denied any intention, ever, of trimming social insurance for the elderly. Indeed, the 1985 controversy over social security was not about the principles on which it rests or its major benefits. Instead, resistance to a minor reduction in the rate of increase proved a major obstacle to the passage of a budget for the next fiscal year. Nonetheless, the administration did succeed in trimming one aspect of social insurance whose constituency seemed, incorrectly as it turned out, incapable of mounting a sustained protest: namely, the disabled.

The administration's attack on disability assistance shows how the new war on welfare can be fought with administrative regulations as well as new legislation or formal changes in eligibility. In 1956, Congress created the disability program as an amendment to the Social Security Act and restricted its benefits to "people 50 years old and older whose disabilities were expected to be permanent." In 1960 and 1965 it extended benefits to disabled workers of any age solely on the basis of their inability to work for at least 1 year. These more liberal standards boosted the cost of the program enormously: from $533 million in 1960 to $3 billion in 1970 and $15.3 billion in 1980. Congress amended the law in 1980 "to require periodic review of all cases, starting in January 1982," but the Reagan administration accelerated the review by 10 months. In 7 months, benefits to 106,000 people ended. Between March, 1981, and April, 1982, 400,000 cases were reviewed and "190,948 recipients were ruled ineligible." From all over the country came stories of severely disabled people cut off from their only source of income. Even the administration admitted that some of them committed suicide. When former recipients challenged the termination of their benefits, "administrative law judges employed by the Social Security Administration ruled in favor of claimants, against the Government, in 55 percent of all cases." New York State's commissioner of social services told an interviewer, "There is no question in my mind. Persons who cannot work have had their benefits terminated by our agency, working on instructions from the Social Security Administration. We were simply following Federal guidelines"; in Wisconsin, "the director of the state agency that reviews disability cases for the Federal government," characterized the "current attitude toward mental disability claims" as " 'deny, deny, deny.' "[22]

Income-maintenance and social service programs fared worse than social insurance. Especially during his first year in office, President Reagan persuaded Congress to enact deep cuts. Here are some examples: by 1983, under complex, new regulations, 408,000 people had lost their eligibility for AFDC and 299,000 had lost their benefits. The average loss of benefits per family was $1,555 per year. Through these reductions federal and state governments saved $1.1 billion in fiscal 1983. Other regulations restricted eligibility for food stamps and sliced $2 billion out of the program's $12 billion budget and $1 billion from the school lunch program that otherwise would have cost $3.5 billion. Spending on Medicaid dropped 3 percent in fiscal year 1982, 4 percent in 1983, and was projected to decline another 4.5 percent in 1984. Extended unemployment insurance benefits were cut back—in 1975, with unemployment at a level comparable to today, "78 percent of jobless Americans received unemployment insurance benefits" compared to 39 percent at the end of 1983—and CETA, the major federal job training program, which employed 306,000 people, was terminated at a time of high unemployment. In 1981, appropriations for housing were a third less than they had been the year before under President Carter; they were cut even more deeply in the next year. The social service block grant to the states was chopped 20 percent in 1981, although two previously federally funded programs were added to it. Between 1980 and 1984, the number of states that used AFDC to supplement the wages of a working mother with three children who earned 50 percent of the official poverty line dropped from forty-seven to twenty-four; if her income matched the poverty level, the number providing a subsidy decreased from thirty-three to one. In the same years, the income of a mother in the identical circumstances, who earned half the poverty level, dropped, on the average, by nearly $2,000, or nearly 20 percent. In 1984 dollars, her AFDC dropped from $1,862 to $83; her food stamps rose slightly from $1,239 to $1,599, and her income tax status switched from a $91 credit in her favor to a $461 liability. As a result, her total income dropped from $11,150 to $9,179.

Reductions in the value of income-maintenance and related programs, it should be pointed out, did not start with President Reagan. They began, rather, in the mid-1970s when appropriations and benefit levels failed to keep pace with inflation. Between 1972 and 1984, to take one example, the combined value of food stamps and AFDC for a mother with three children and no other income dropped about 22 percent; the maximum AFDC benefit itself dropped 37 percent. In 1972, its highpoint, the combined AFDC and food stamp benefits for a family of four (in 1984 dollars) averaged $8,894; by 1980 it had slid to $7,486; and in 1984, to $6,955, which was only $240 more than its 1960 level. Nonetheless, the decline in the actual value of welfare had different meanings before and after the Reagan administration. Prior to the Reagan administration, the decrease in welfare benefits reflected a reluctance to raise benefits to match inflation and paralleled a more general, widespread decrease in purchasing power. Under the Reagan administration, even as inflation moderated, cuts continued as part of a campaign to roll back the semiwelfare state. In sum, the percentage changes in outlays as a result of government action between 1982 and 1985 were:

Unemployment insurance −6.9 percent
AFDC −12.7 percent
Food stamps −12.6 percent
Child nutrition −27.7 percent
WIC +4.4 percent
Housing assistance −4.4 percent
Low-income energy assistance −8.3 percent [23]

Tax policies, the relation between income level and benefit loss, the size of the "poverty gap," and official poverty rates all illustrate how the dynamics of social policy shifted under the Reagan administration. The 1981 and 1982 tax cuts rewarded the rich and punished the poor. Together, between 1980 and 1984, changes in income tax policy and increases in social security taxes left families with an income below $10,000 a year with a $95 net loss; by contrast, families with a $75–$100,000 income gained $403; with a $100,000–$200,000 income, $2,269; and with an income above $200,000, $17,403. In the same years, the distance between the poverty level and the income tax threshold, which had widened during the 1970s, narrowed; in other words, poor people now had to pay taxes on poverty level incomes. In 1975, "the tax cuts were so structured that the tax threshold was raised 21.7 percent above the poverty line." By 1982, the situation was reversed; the poverty level exceeded the tax threshold by 11.5 percent; by 1984, the distance had increased to 17.2 percent and was expected to grow even greater after 1985. At the same time, poor families lost far more benefits than affluent ones. Between 1980 and 1984, the dollar loss in benefits for households with less than $10,000 in income averaged $1,340 compared, for example, to $390 for households with incomes between $40,000 and $80,000.[24]

The history of the "poverty gap" after 1980 points to the escalation of income inequality during the Reagan administration. (The "poverty gap is the amount of dollars that would be required to give all persons an income equal to the poverty line.") The poverty gap, in constant 1983 dollars, increased from (in millions of dollars) $32,980 in 1979 to $47,082 in 1983. At the same time, the overall poverty rate, not surprisingly, began to climb. Between 1966 and 1979, the rate had declined from 14.7 percent to 11.7 percent. After 1980, it started to rise; by 1983, it was 15.2 percent. "Between 1979 and 1983," reports Bob Drogin in the *Los Angeles Times*, "the number of poor children soared by 3.7 million to 13.8 million. . . . By the most recent estimate, 22.2% of America's children under 18—the highest rate in two decades—live in impoverished families."[25]

The War on Welfare

Statistics highlight the dimensions of the war on welfare's impact. More poignant are individual stories: the hardship of disabled people suddenly deprived of their sole income; the surge in the number of homeless; the dramatically increased pressures on soup kitchens. In 1967, the Physician Task Force on Hunger accompanied the team of United States senators investigating hunger in America, and found severe hunger and malnutrition throughout the country. A decade later, the Task Force reported that food stamps and other new government programs had eliminated malnutrition as "a severe problem among the poor." In 1985, when the Task Force set out again to assess the impact of recent government policies on hunger and disease, it found that "hunger had returned as a serious problem across this nation. To be sure, hunger is not yet as bad as two decades ago, but the situation has greatly deteriorated." The Task Force found evidence everywhere. Nearly three-quarters of the cities and towns reporting to the U.S. Conference of Mayors in late 1984 reported an increase in "the need for emergency food assistance. . . . During 1984 the number of facilities—soup kitchens and food pantries—increased 15% . . . and the total number of meals provided increased by more than 50% across the nation, while individual cities reported even greater increases: Dallas-100%, Chicago-182%, and Boston-200%." Trends in malnutrition and other health-related consequences of poverty are difficult to chart over time. Nonetheless, the studies reviewed by the Task Force all pointed to the association of poverty and hunger with increased infant mortality, growth failure, disease, and early adult death. The implications are clear: the growth in poverty, the cutback in food and nutrition programs, and the increased expense of medical care mean that malnutrition, disease, and mortality all are rising once again. Here, in the twenty million Americans who go hungry at some point each month, is one legacy of Ronald Reagan's war on welfare.[26]

The Future of Welfare

How successful the war on welfare will be remains uncertain. Piven and Cloward argue that a built-in bureaucratic opposition with a national constituency will check Ronald Reagan's efforts to roll back the welfare state. "There now exists," they write, "an enormous array of agencies and programs oriented to popular grievances. . . . for all its zeal, it [the Reagan administration] cannot simply eliminate the huge and intricate state apparatus. . . . Nor can that apparatus be effectively disciplined either, for much of it lies beyond federal reach. . . . It stands as a source of internal bureaucratic opposition." Indeed, Reagan, as Richard Nathan and his associates document, has not succeeded in turning the social welfare clock back to 1932. In fact, so far he has turned it not much further back than 1970. Still, since Piven and Cloward wrote, actual and proposed cuts in social programs have intensified. If he succeeds in passing income tax legislation that eliminates the deductibility of state and local taxes, Reagan will force state legislatures and city councils to trim their social programs even further, and, as Piven and Cloward argue elsewhere, "The way bureaucratic functionaries exercise discretion in determining initial or continuing [welfare] eligibility is very much influenced by shifts in the political climate."[27]

Clearly, the president has not exhausted his ammunition. Even more, the experience of the last 4 years lowers some of the anxiety about cutting welfare. Contrary to many predictions, there were no riots in cities; crime did not increase; and, even without the votes of the poor, Ronald Reagan won the presidency in 1984 with a resounding victory. Indeed, although all the causes of urban violence identified by commissions that studied riots in the 1960s intensified, there has been no repetition of the violence that rocked American cities less than 20 years ago, and Americans' concerns with violence have shifted from riot to street crime, from cities on fire to the New York subway vigilante, Bernard Goetz. One powerful reason why riots are less likely in the future is the heightened sophistication of the apparatus of repression. Cities have invested heavily in modern riot control technology; they will not be caught unprepared again. For those who want to roll back the welfare state, this means it may no longer be necessary for welfare to play one of its historic roles: the preservation of social order. Angry blacks in the increasingly segregated ghettos of America's cities can be contained with guns, grenades, and tanks; the threat of hunger and homelessness will persuade them to work, whatever the pay and conditions; at worst, cities can be turned into reservations, isolated, patrolled, left to deteriorate and to die. This is one way to reduce welfare by eliminating the problem.[28]

Welfare in America never will be satisfactory. It cannot escape the contradictions between its goals—deterrence, compassion, discipline and control, and patronage—or resolve the tension between entitlements and the market. Real reform would have to replace the division between social insurance and public assistance that underlies the semiwelfare state with full employment for fair pay complemented by a social wage guaranteed to everyone unable to work or find a suitable job. Employment, welfare, income, and industrial policy need to be meshed together, not left to dangle at tangents or clash. Adequate, appropriate training throughout the life course, restraints on industrial relocation or other decisions that destroy jobs, and a reorientation of discourse about poverty must accompany full employment and the social wage. It is time to transcend

290

the old debate about the relation between welfare and the work ethic. It has continued inconclusively for at least two centuries, and there is no reason to believe that, now, it can be resolved definitively by social science. Instead, another working hypothesis may prove more useful: work is integral to human life. Almost everyone wants to feel engaged, productive, and purposeful. Given a choice, most people will select work—as long as it is neither degrading, dehumanizing, nor exploitative—over idleness and dependence. Americans need construct no spurious social experiments; they can look to other countries for evidence that productivity and a highly developed social welfare state can coexist. Instead of trying to frighten people into work with the threat of homelessness or starvation, we could induce them to work with decent pay, improved social relations in the workplace, increased participation in planning and management, and social policies that do not penalize them for taking jobs. And we could enable them to work by creating jobs, expanding child care facilities, and supporting working families.[29]

It also is time to shed the old myths. Voluntarism never was and never will be able to meet the needs of poor and dependent Americans. Public welfare always has supported more dependent people than private relief. In fact, it is virtually impossible to disentangle the private from the public in social welfare. Their boundaries, always protean, have never been less distinct than in the late twentieth century, when governments provide most services by purchasing them from private agencies. Most extreme poverty arises from economic and social forces, from sickness and disability, or from childhood and old age, but not from character. No sharp line divides the very poor from the rest of us; the distinction between the worthy and unworthy poor has always been a convenient but destructive fiction. Nor are poor people passive, degraded, and demoralized. Throughout American history they have shown remarkable resilience, an ability to survive extraordinary hardships and manipulate social programs and institutions to their own purposes, whatever their official intent.

Government can mount programs that reduce, or augment, the rate of poverty and its attendant hardships, especially hunger, malnutrition, and disease; it can destroy or revitalize cities; widen or narrow inequalities in income; and promote or retard the expansion of civil rights. Government can also enlarge or roll back the welfare state. In a nation as smart, inventive, and rich as America, the continuation of poverty is a choice, not a necessity. Social policy always has emerged from a selection among alternative possibilities. The American semi-welfare state was not inevitable, and its future is ours to choose.

NOTES

Introduction

1. The definition of welfare here is the same as the one I used in *Poverty and Policy in American History* (New York, Academic Press, 1983), p. 4, "*Welfare* here is a broad term that refers to the provision of relief and rehabilitation for dependent people. It encompasses both private and public action and activity both inside and outside of institutions." Throughout most of American history, people spoke of relief, not welfare. As a term, welfare only came into common use in the second decade of the twentieth century. At first, it was a positive term, used to differentiate old relief practices from newer, more adequate ones. Just when it acquired its contemporary stigma is not clear.

2. For a contemporary example of the problems posed by local variation in welfare benefits, see, "Courts Balk Minnesota on Slashing Welfare Benefits," *New York Times*, September 22, 1985.

3. Alan Wolfe, *The Limits of Legitimacy: Political Contradictions of Contemporary Capitalism* (New York: Free Press, 1977), pp. 108–175.

4. Ira Katznelson, *City Trenches: Urban Politics and the Patterning of Class in the United States* (New York: Pantheon, 1981), pp. 45–72.

5. There are important parts of welfare's story to which I either have alluded briefly or neglected for one reason or another in this book. The most important are health insurance and the role of foundations. Medical history, including health insurance, is a flourishing specialty, and readers can find adequate discussions elsewhere. By contrast, the history of foundations requires a great deal of work, and its secondary literature is not rich. Fortunately, the situation should be remedied in the near future by work now in progress. One of the major themes of this book, as I note below, is the self-activity of the poor on their own behalf and the strategies they developed to cope with their circumstances. The history of welfare looks very different when the historian perches on the shoulder of a poor person and looks outward than it does when the story is told from the perspective of governments, agencies, or reformers. In this book, the story is told mainly from the latter point of view. In future work, I plan to shift the perspective. Two examples of history from the perspective of relief clients are my essays, "Families and Welfare: A Philadelphia Case," in *Poverty and Policy* and, "The History of an Impudent Poor Woman in New York City from 1918 to 1923," paper delivered at Davis Seminar, Princeton, January, 1985.

Chapter 1 / The Origins and Failure of the Poorhouse

1. Although outdoor relief—or, our modern euphemism, public welfare—is as old as the colonies, as American as Thanksgiving, there is, in contrast to England, almost no modern American historical writing about poor laws, and outdoor relief remains one of the dirty little secrets of American history. Even the one brief American flurry of interest in poor law history virtually ignored outdoor relief. Primarily in the 1920s and 1930s, a series of books sponsored by two pioneers in social welfare, Edith Abbott and Sophonisba Breckenridge, traced the history of poor laws in various states. All of them emphasized the origins and history of poorhouses and told a dreary tale of meanness and misery gradually supplanted by professional administration and specialized institutions that took children, the insane, and the sick out of poorhouses. These accounts reflected their authors' primary purpose, which was not to write social history. Rather, they wanted to stimulate the nascent growth of state power in social welfare, the development of specialized institutions, and the professionalization of social work and public administration. See, for example, Grace Abbott, *Public Assistance* (Chicago: University of Chicago Press, 1940) and Sophonisba Breckenridge, *Public Welfare Administration* (Chicago: University of Chicago Press, 1927; rev. ed., 1938). For a recent biography, see Lela B.

Costin, *Two Sisters for Social Justice: A Biography of Grace and Edith Abbott* (Urbana and Chicago: University of Illinois Press, 1983). For overviews of the history of social welfare in America, see James Leiby, *A History of Social Welfare and Social Work in the United States* (New York: Columbia University Press, 1978); Walter I. Trattner, *From Poor Law to Welfare State*, 3d ed. (New York: Free Press, 1984); David M. Schneider, *The History of Public Welfare in New York State, 1876–1940* (Chicago: University of Chicago Press, 1938); David M. Schneider and Albert Deutsch, *The History of Public Welfare in New York State, 1867–1940* (Chicago: University of Chicago Press, 1941). Blanche Coll, *Perspectives in Public Welfare* (Washington, D.C.: U.S. Government Printing Office, 1969) and "Public Assistance in the United States: From Colonial Times to 1860," in *Comparative Development in Social Welfare*, ed. E. W. Martin (London: Allen and Unwin, 1972) pp. 128–158; June Axinn and Herman Levin, *Social Welfare: A History of the American Response to Need* (New York: Dodd, Mead, 1970).

2. David M. Gordon, Richard Edwards, Michael Reich, *Segmented Work, Divided Workers: The Historical Transformation of Labor in the United States* (New York: Cambridge University Press, 1982), pp. 48–99; Maurice Dobb, *Studies in the Development of Capitalism*, rev. ed. (New York: International Publishers, 1967), chs. 1–2; Charles Tilly, *As Sociology Meets History* (New York: Academic Press, 1981), ch. 7; Daniel Rodgers, *The Work Ethic in Industrial America, 1850–1920* (Chicago: University of Chicago Press, 1978), p. 30; Kaestle, *Evolution of an Urban School System, New York City, 1750–1850* (Cambridge: Harvard University Press, 1973) p. 102; Katz, Doucet, and Stern, *Social Organization of Early Industrial Capitalism* (Cambridge: Harvard University Press, 1982), chap. 1; David Montgomery, "The Shuttle and the Cross: Weavers and Artisans in the Kensington Riots of 1844," *Journal of Social History* (Summer, 1972), pp. 411–446.

3. Richard A. McLeod, "The Philadelphia Artisans 1828–1850," Ph.D. diss. Univ. of Missouri, 1971, pp. 35 and 54–74, is good on these points. See, also, Bruce Laurie and Mark Schmitz, "Manufacture and Productivity: The Making of an Industrial Base: Philadelphia, 1850–1880," in Theodore Hershberg, ed., *Philadelphia: Work, Space, Family, and Group Experience in the Nineteenth Century* (New York: Oxford University Press, 1981), ch. 2.

4. McLeod, "Philadelphia Artisan," p. 61.

5. There are many studies of population mobility in nineteenth century America. The first book to call attention to the phenomenon was Stephan Thernstrom, *Poverty and Progress: Social Mobility in a Nineteenth-Century City* (Cambridge: Harvard University Press, 1964). For a review of the field and the presentation of somewhat less problematic data than most other studies, see Katz, Doucet, and Stern, *Social Organization*. ch. 3.

6. "Letters to the Secretary of State on the Subject of Pauperism," first published in the *Columbia Republican*, in the fall of 1853, in New York Secretary of State Annual Report on Statistics of the Poor, 1855, New York Senate Documents, No. 72, 1855, p. 79; Nancy Cott, *The Bonds of Womanhood: "Women's Sphere" in New England, 1780–1835* (New Haven: Yale University Press, 1977), pp. 23–46; Joan Underhill Hannon, "Poverty in the Antebellum Northeast: The View from New York State's Poor Relief Rolls," *Journal of Economic History*, XIV, No. 4 (December, 1984), pp. 1028–1031 (quote p. 1030; newspaper quote, pp. 1030–1031); Grace A. Browning, *The Development of Poor Relief Legislation in Kansas* (Chicago: University of Chicago Press, 1935), pp. 76–84.

7. Benjamin Joseph Klebaner, "Public Poor Relief, America 1790–1860," Ph.D. diss., Columbia University, 1952, pp. 74–75.

8. Priscilla F. Clement, "The Response to Need: Welfare and Poverty in Philadelphia. 1800–1850," Ph.D. diss., University of Pennsylvania, 1977, pp. 267–270; Barbara Lawrence Bellows, "Tempering the Wind: The Southern Response to Urban Poverty, 1850–1865," Ph.D. diss., University of South Carolina, 1983, pp. 199–201.

9. Matthew Carey, "Essays on the Public Charities of Philadelphia," (1828), p. 171, reprinted in David J. Rothman, ed., *The Jacksonians on the Poor: Collected Pamphlets* (New York: Arno Press and New York Times, 1971).

10. Carey, "Essays," pp. 167, 172; Bellows, "Tempering the Wind", p. 204.

11. Carey, "Essays," p. 173.

12. McLeod, "Philadelphia Artisan," p. 151; Walter Channing, "An Address on the Prevention of Pauperism," p. 35, in Rothman, ed., *Jacksonians*.

13. Carey, "Essays," p. 11.

14. As an example of the problem of widows, see the case history in Michael B. Katz, *Poverty and Policy in American History* (New York: Academic Press, 1983), pp. 18–54.

15. The best way to get a sense of how families survived and of the awesome pressures under which they lived is to read the case histories compiled by agents and visitors for various voluntary societies, such as charity organization societies.

16. On life insurance, see Viviana A. Zelizer, *Morals and Markets: The Development of Life Insurance in the United States* (New York: Columbia University Press, 1979). In most medium-sized cities around the middle of the nineteenth century, about one-quarter to one-third of families owned their own homes. In big cities the proportion was smaller, about 11 percent in Philadelphia and probably less than half that in New York. For a discussion of property ownership in the nineteenth century, see Katz, Doucet, and Stearns, *Social Organization*, ch. 4. For an estimation of the proportion of elderly who lived with their children see, Steven Ruggles, "Prolonged Connections: Demographic Change and the Rise of the Extended Family in Nineteenth Century England and America," Ph.D. diss., University of Pennsylvania, 1984.

17. Klebaner, "Public Poor Relief," pp. 612–613.

18. Bellows, "Tempering the Wind", p. 199.

19. Gerald N. Grob, *Mental Institutions in America: Social Policy to 1875* (New York: Free Press, 1973), p. 81. On the development of social institutions in this period see also, David J. Rothman, *The Discovery of the Asylum: Social Order and Disorder in the New Republic* (Boston: Little Brown, 1971) and Katz, Doucet, and Stern, *Social Organization*, pp. 349–391.

20. In addition to the sources already cited on institutional development see, Barbara Brenzel, *Daughters of the State: A Social Portrait of the First Reform School for Girls in North America, 1846–1905* (Cambridge: MIT Press, 1983); F. Kaestle, *The Evolution of an Urban School System*; Michael B. Katz, *The Irony of Early School Reform: Educational Innovation in Mid-Nineteenth Century Massachusetts* (Cambridge: Harvard University Press, 1968); Klebaner, "Public Poor Relief in America; W. D. Lewis, *From Newgate to Dannemora: The Rise of the Penitentiary in New York, 1796–1848* (Ithaca: Cornell University Press, 1965); Robert M. Mennel, *Thorns and Thistles: Juvenile Delinquents in the United States, 1825–1840* (Hanover, N.H.: University Press of New England, 1973).

21. McLeod, "Philadelphia Artisan," pp. 26–27.

22. The classic statement of the problem of time and work discipline in this period is, E. P. Thompson, "Time, Work Discipline, and Industrial Capitalism," *Past and Present* 38 (December 1967), pp. 56–97. See also, Herbert Gutman, *Work, Culture, and Society in Industrializing America* (New York: Knopf, 1976), ch. 1.

23. Katz, *Irony*, pp. 207–209; Lewis, *From Newgate to Dannemora*, p. 90; Mennel, *Thorns and Thistles*, pp. 51–52; Grob, *Mental Institutions*, p. 176.

24. Christopher Lasch, "Origins of the Asylum," in C. Lasch, ed., *The World of Nations: Reflections on American History, Politics, and Culture* (New York: Basic Books, 1973); Harry Braverman, *Labor and Monopoly Capital: The Degradation of Work in the Twentieth Century* (New York: Monthly Review Press, 1974), pp. 279–280.

25. Geoffrey W. Oxley, *Poor Relief in England and Wales, 1601–1834* (London, Vermont, and Vancouver, B.C.: David and Charles, 1974); Ursula R. Henriques, *Before the Welfare State: Social Administration in Early Industrial Britain* (London and New York: Longmans, 1979); M. A. Crowther, *The Workhouse System, 1834–1929* (Athens, Ga.: University of Georgia Press, 1981); Leiby, *History of Social Welfare*, p. 9; Klebaner, "Public Poor Relief," S. E. Wiberly, "Four Cities: Public Poor Relief in Urban America," Ph.D. diss., Yale University, 1975.

26. Klebaner, "Public Poor Relief," p. 682; James Leiby, *History of Social Welfare*, pp. 39–40; Elizabeth Wisner, *Social Welfare in the South: From Colonial Times to World War I* (Baton Rouge, LA: Louisiana State University Press, 1979), pp. 11, 23.

27. Klebaner, "Public Poor Relief," pp. 71–72; Wisner, *Social Welfare*, p. 40.

28. Thomas R. Hazard, *Report on the Poor and Insane in Rhode Island* (Providence, R.I.: J. Knowles, 1851; New York: Arno Press, 1973), pp. 85–87. The practice of auction or vendue resembled the older British custom of "roundsmen," where the poor were sent round from farm to farm, often to work for farmers who had made a low bid for their care. "Roundsmen" kept agricultural wages low because laborers had to compete for jobs with paupers. No one yet has tried to learn whether vendue system played a similar role in America.

29. Consider just one example. In 1870, 15,343 people were helped for some period of time in New York state's poorhouses at a cost of $1,681,470. In the same year, 101,796 people received public outdoor relief at a cost of $911,855. The cost per person in the poorhouse was $109.59; for outdoor relief it was $8.96. New York Board of State Charities, 13th annual report, p. 113; Joan Underhill Hannon, "The Generosity of Antebellum Poor Relief," *Journal of Economic History*

XLIV:3 (September 1984), p. 814 and "Poverty in the Antebellum Northeast," pp. 1019–1031.

30.　In 1880, a committee of the New York State Assembly prefaced their recommendation for drafting a new poor law by observing that "The laws of the government of poor-houses and for the relief of the poor in the several towns, counties, and cities of this State are administered according to no uniformity of interpretation, fixed by an appellate authority, having jurisdiction therein, but according to the caprice or interest of the various officers exercising authority therein." [New York] Assembly Document No. 57, February 13, 1880, "Report of Committee on General Laws of 1879, in Relation to Poor houses and Relief of the Poor. Roy M. Brown, *Public Poor Relief in North Carolina* (Chapel Hill: University of North Carolina Press, 1928), pp. 73–74; Amos G. Warner, *American Charities: A Study in Philanthropy and Economics* (Boston: Crowell, 1894), pp. 141–143. Warner was professor of economics and social science at Stanford and formerly superintendent of charities for the District of Columbia and general agent of the Charity Organization Society of Baltimore. His book was widely used and often reprinted.

31.　William C. Heffner, *History of Poor Relief Legislation in Pennsylvania* (Cleona, Pa.: published by the author, 1913), pp. 39–145; Klebaner, "Public Poor Relief," p. 69.

32.　Klebaner, "Public Poor Relief," pp. 682–683.

33.　"Report of the Committee on the Pauper Laws of this Commonwealth [1821]," hereafter referred to as Quincy Report, p. 32 and "Report of the Secretary of State [of New York] in 1824 on the Relief and Settlement of the Poor," hereafter referred to as Yates Report, pp. 1069, 1081, 966, 942, both reprinted in David J. Rothman, ed., *The Almshouse Experience: Collected Reports* (New York: Arno Press and New York Times, 1971).

34.　Yates Report, pp. 942 and 1041.

35.　Yates Report, 966; Samuel Chipman, *Report of an Examination of Poorhouses, Jails, etc. in the State of New York and in the Counties of Berkshire, Massachusetts; Litchfield, Connecticut; and Bennington, Vermont, etc.* (Albany, New York: Executive Committee of the New-York State Temperance Society, 1834), passim.; Klebaner, "Public Poor Relief," pp. 602–603; "Report of the Committee Appointed by the Board of Guardians of the Poor of the City and Districts of Philadelphia, to Visit the Cities of Baltimore, New-York, Providence, Boston, and Salem [1827]," hereafter referred to as Philadelphia Report, p. 28, reprinted in Rothman, *Almshouse Experience;* "Franklin," "Letters to the Secretary of State on the Subject of Pauperism," p. 80.

36.　Quincy Report, pp. 17 and 31; Yates Report, pp. 952 and 966. Charles Burroughs, "A Discourse Delivered in the Chapel of the New Almshouse, in Portsmouth, N.H. Dec. 15, 1834 on the Occasion of its First Being Opened for Religious Service," pp. 49–50 and R. C. Waterston, "An Address on Pauperism, Its Extent, Causes, and the Best Means of Prevention; Delivered at the Church in Bowdoin Square, February 4, 1844, pp. 19–20, both reprinted in David J. Rothman, ed., *The Jacksonians.*

37.　Quincy Report, p. 51.

38.　Burroughs, "Discourse," p. 56.

39.　Quincy Report, p. 4.

40.　Yates Report, p. 941; Burroughs, "Discourse," pp. 3–10.

41.　Bellows, "Tempering the Wind", pp. 181, 250.

42.　Yates Report, 952, 1056.

43.　Yates Report, p. 993.

44.　Yates Report, p. 1061.

45.　Yates Report, pp. 967 and 952; Wisner, *Social Welfare,* pp. 32–33.

46.　Yates Report, p. 952.

47.　Yates Report, pp. 956–957; Quincy Report, pp. 5–10.

48.　Quincy Report, p. 8; Yates Report, p. 995.

49.　Quincy Report, p. 25; Yates Report, p. 984; Burroughs, "Discourse," p. 91.

50.　Quincy Report, pp. 34–35; Yates Report, 1007–1008; Bellows, "Tempering the Wind," p. 213.

51.　Yates Report, p. 1060, 995.

52.　Yates Report, p. 943, 1041, 1047; Quincy Report, p. 19.

53.　Quincy Report, pp. 28–30; Yates Report, pp. 1009–1111; Walter Channing, "An Address on the Prevention of Pauperism," 1843, pp. 62–63, reprinted in Rothman, *Jacksonians on the Poor.*

54.　All the books on institutions previously cited tell a similar story of decline. Grob's account in *Mental Illness* (pp. 174–175) is especially graphic and his explanation detailed and convincing.

55.　New York State Senate, "Report of Select Committee to visit Charitable Institutions supported by the State, and all city and county poor and work houses and jails. In Senate, January 9, 1857.

No. 8, p. 3; Charleston commissioners quoted in Bellows, "Tempering the Wind", p. 224.

56. Clement, "Response to Need," pp. 43–64; 156–164.
57. "Franklin," "Letters," pp. 97–98; Warner, *American Charities*, p. 150.
58. Warner, *American Charities*, p. 152.
59. Brown, *Public Poor Relief*, pp. 114–119.
60. On the professionalization of psychiatry see, Grob, *Mental Illness*; on social work, Roy Lubove, *The Professional Altruist: The Emergence of Social Work as a Career: 1880–1935* (Cambridge: Harvard University Press, 1965); on school superintendents, David Tyack and Elisabeth Hansot, *Managers of Virtue: Public School Leadership in America, 1820–1980* (New York: Basic Books, 1982).
61. Clement, "Response to Need," p. 400; Klebaner, "Public Poor Relief," pp. 180–183.
62. Clement, "Response to Need," pp. 337–8, 170, 400.
63. Clement, "Response to Need," p. 335; Warner, *American Charities*, pp. 155–159; Bellows, "Tempering the Wind", p. 235.
64. "Franklin," "Letters", p. 108; Warner, *American Charities*, pp. 152–154; Brown, *Public Poor Relief*, p. 160.
65. Warner, *American Charities*, p. 150.
66. New York Senate Report, p. 4.
67. Warner, *American Charities*, p. 160; New York Senate Report, pp. 4–5.
68. Priscilla F. Clement, "The Response to Need", pp. 172–173, 307–309.
69. *Fifth Annual Report of the Board of State Commissioners of Public Charities*. State of New York. In Senate, April 4, 1872. No. 97, pp. 37–42; Grace A. Browning, *The Development of Poor Relief Legislation in Kansas* (Chicago: University of Chicago Press, 1935), p. 51.
70. "Franklin," "Letters," pp. 103–104.
71. Brown, *Public Poor Relief in North Carolina*, p. 80; Klebaner, "Public Poor Relief," p. 200; Bellows, "Tempering the Wind", pp. 243–249, is good on the problems of providing work in poorhouses.
72. New York Senate Committee, p. 6.
73. "Franklin," "Letters", p. 92.
74. New York Senate Committee Report, pp. 3–9; *Second Annual Report of the Board of Commissioners of Public Charities*. State of New York. In Senate, March 22, 1869. No. 61, pp. lxxi–lxxiii; Bellows, "Tempering the Wind," p. 226.
75. *Fifth Annual Report of the Board*, p. 64.
76. *Fifth Annual Report of the Board*, p. 64.

Chapter 2 / Outdoor Relief

1. Ira Katznelson, *City Trenches: Urban Politics and the Patterning of Class in the United States* (New York: Pantheon, 1981), p. 6; on the key role of service delivery in American politics, see also Douglas Yates, *The Ungovernable City: The Politics of Urban Problems and Policy Making* (Cambridge: MIT Press, 1977).
2. The most complete account of outdoor relief in American history (although it takes the story only until 1860) is, Benjamin Klebaner, "Public Poor Relief in America, 1790–1860," Ph.D. diss., Columbia University, 1952, pp. 254–482. For outdoor relief in the South, see pp. 310–315. For his summary of its persistence, see p. 350; on controversies over cash vs. in-kind relief, see, pp. 351–358. Joan Underhill Hannon's recent analyses of relief trends and their meaning in nineteenth century New York are important contributions to the topic. See "Poverty in the Antebellum Northeast: The View from New York State's Poor Relief Rolls," *Journal of Economic History* 44 (1984), pp. 1007–1032; "The Generosity of Antebellum Poor Relief," *Journal of Economic History* 44 (1984), pp. 810–821; "Poor Relief Policy in Antebellum New York State: The Rise and Decline of the Poorhouse," forthcoming, *Explorations in Economic History* (1985).
3. *Proceedings of the Twenty-Seventh Annual Convention of the County Superintendents of the Poor of the State of New York, Held at Thousand Island Park, June 29, 30, and July 1, 1897* (no publisher listed: 1879), p. 20. Hereafter, the proceedings of the annual conventions of the county superintendents will be referred to in the notes as, County Superintendents, Report.

4. Ernest Bicknell, "Observations on Official Outdoor Poor Relief," *Proceedings of the National Conference on Charities and Corrections*, v. 24 (1897), p. 252.
5. [Commonwealth of Pennsylvania] *Forty-eighth Annual Report [for 1917] of the State Board of Public Charities*, Official Document No. 2 (Harrisburg, Pa., 1918), pp. 183, 187–188; Julia B. Rauch, "Unfriendly Visitors: The Emergence of Scientific Philanthropy in Philadelphia, 1878–1880," Ph.D. diss., Bryn Mawr, 1974, p. 252.
6. John K. Alexander, *Render them Submissive: Responses to Poverty in Philadelphia, 1760–1800* (Amherst, Mass.: University of Massachusetts Press, 1980), pp. 91–92, 97, 118; Priscilla Clement, "The Philadelphia Welfare Crisis of the 1820s," *The Pennsylvania Magazine of History and Biography*, CV: 2 (April 1981), pp. 162–164; Klebaner, "Public Poor Relief," p. 280.
7. Klebaner, "Public Poor Relief," pp. 334, 370. See p. 322 for the classic arguments dressed up with Republican rhetoric.
8. Klebaner, "Public Poor Relief," p. 450; Clement, "The Philadelphia Welfare Crisis," p. 163; [Commonwealth of Pennsylvania] *Pennsylvania Board of Charities Annual Report for 1875* (Harrisburg, Pa., 1875), pp. 449, 451.
9. Klebaner, "Public Poor Relief," pp. 370–374.
10. Frederic Almy, "The Relation between Public and Private Charities," *The Charities Review* 9 (1899): pt. 1, pp. 2–30, pt. 2, pp. 65–71.
11. Almy, "Relation between Public and Private," p. 67.
12. Almy, "Relation between Public and Private," pp. 67–68; Kathleen D. McCarthy, *Noblesse Oblige: Charity and Cultural Philanthropy in Chicago, 1849–1929* (Chicago: University of Chicago Press, 1983), p. 68.
13. All discussions about the reasons for variation in relief policy must remain speculative until historians do research on the topic. Virtually none exists at the moment. On the differences between elites in late nineteenth century New York City, see David C. Hammack, *Power and Society: Greater New York at the Turn of the Century* (New York: Russell Sage Foundation, 1982), esp. pp. 303–326. On the class character of the controversy over outdoor relief early in Philadelphia's history, see Alexander, *Render them Submissive*, pp. 89–94. For a contemporary hint that the battle lines may still be similar in debates over welfare, see Michael J. Piore, *Birds of Passage: Migrant Labor and Industrial Societies* (Cambridge: Cambridge University Press, 1979), pp. 89–90.
14. Almy, "Relation between Private and Public Outdoor Relief," pp. 70–71.
15. For examples of its financial difficulties, see *Seventeenth Annual Report and Proceedings of the Meeting of the Charity Organization Society of Buffalo, New York 1893–1894* (no publisher), pp. 3–4; and *Thirty-first Annual Report of the Charity Organization Society of Buffalo 1908* (no publisher) pp. 10–11.
16. In 1900, the State Board of Charities reviewed all the institutions in Erie County that received any public funds. That review is the basis of the information here. States differed in the type of subsidy systems they used. On Pennsylvania's method of funding hospitals, see Rosemary Stevens, "Sweet Charity: State Aid to Hospitals in Pennsylvania, 1870–1910," *Bulletin of the History of Medicine* (58: 1984), pp. 287–314, 474–495.
17. Michael Katz, "The Configuration and Social Structure of Erie County Institutions in 1900," in Michael B. Katz, and associates "Appendix to Final Report NIMH Grant #RO1MH32-520," November, 1981.
18. Seth Low, "The Problem of Pauperism in the Cities of Brooklyn and New York," [New York] *Sixth Annual Conference of Charities (1879)*, pp. 202–203; unless otherwise noted, all references to the controversy over outdoor relief in Brooklyn are from the Brooklyn *Daily Eagle*, 1878–1880.
19. County Superintendents, 6th Report (1876), p. 18.
20. County Superintendents, 8th Report (1878), p. 4. Figures for the increase in the number of children placed with agencies or in asylums are from the annual reports of the New York State Board of Charities. Figures there indicating an astronomical increase in the number placed with the Children's Aid Society are incorrect. They reflect a changed basis for reporting, as the CAS reports themselves show.
21. At a meeting of the Kings County Board of Supervisors, one of the opponents of the abolition of outdoor relief asserted that there had been an "increased number of arrests for petty larceny of provisions." (Brooklyn *Daily Eagle*, January 25, 1878), p. 2. On tramps, see Michael B. Katz, *Poverty and Policy in American History* (New York: Academic Press, 1983), pp. 157–181; and Eric C. Monkkonen, *Walking to Work: Tramps in America, 1790–1935* (Lincoln: University of Nebraska Press, 1984). Studies of children's institutions in the nineteenth century usually show

that parents hoped to reclaim their children. See, for example, Barbara M. Brenzel, *Daughters of the State: A Social Portrait of the First Reform School for Girls in North America, 1856–1905* (Cambridge: MIT Press, 1983). Case records from charity organization societies also show that parents thought of orphanages or placements as temporary expedients for periods of crisis. They show that these were the alternatives to which parents turned only when, all other sources of income exhausted, they were desperate. The ideology of family breakup is discussed in chapter 4. No historian has studied the sources of credit with which poor families sustained themselves, but the importance of credit leaps out from any reading of charity case records. Contemporary studies of localities that ended outdoor relief (or general assistance) invariably show similar patterns of hardship and response; Gilbert Y. Steiner, *Social Insecurity: The Politics of Welfare* (Chicago: Rand McNally, 1966), p. 9.

22. William J. Trembath, "Public Outdoor Relief vs. Private Charity," Association of Directors of Poor and Charities [Pennsylvania], Forty-fourth Annual Meeting, *Proceedings* (Lancaster, Pa.: 1919), p. 71.

23. County Superintendents, 30th Convention (1900), p. 25; 4th Convention (1874), p. 9.

24. County Superintendents, 8th Report (1878), pp. 33–34.

25. County Superintendents, 9th Report (1879), p. 30; 6th Report (1876), p. 16.

26. County Superintendents, 17th Report (1887), p. 76.

27. County Superintendents, 9th Report (1879), p. 47.

28. County Superintendents, 7th Report (1877), p. 31.

29. County Superintendents, 14th Report (1884), p. 38; 8th Report (1878), p. 31.

30. County Superintendents, 7th Report (1877), p. 23. The case for breaking up families will be discussed in a subsequent chapter.

31. County Superintendents, 7th Report (1877), p. 18; 5th Report (1875), p. 6; 10th report (1880), p. 15; 22nd Report (1892), p. 35.

32. County Superintendents, 7th Report (1877), p. 29; 17th Report (1887), pp. 42, 77; 14th Report (1884), p. 96.

33. County Superintendents, 9th Report (1879), p. 47; 22nd Report (1892), p. 114; 14th Report (1884), pp. 47–49.

34. County Superintendents, 11th Report (1881), pp. 9–10.

35. Frederic Almy, "Public Outdoor Relief and Congestion," *Survey*, 25 (March 25, 1911): 1059.

Chapter 3 / The Theory and Practice of Scientific Charity

1. Examples of very good histories that ignore the public role in favor of an exclusive concentration on voluntarism are: Carroll Smith Rosenberg, *Religion and the Rise of the American City: The New York City Mission Movement 1812 to 1870* (Ithaca: Cornell University Press, 1971); Mary Ryan, *Cradle of the Middle Class: The Family in Oneida County, New York, 1790–1865* (New York; Cambridge University Press, 1981); and Paul Boyer, *Urban Masses and Moral Order in America 1820–1920* (Cambridge: Harvard University Press, 1978). Histories of welfare and poverty since the New Deal usually have an opposite problem: they give little attention to the continued, important role of voluntarism. Raymond A. Mohl, *Poverty in New York 1783–1825* (New York: Oxford University Press, 1971), p. 20, gives a list of voluntary associations for the relief of some sort of poverty in New York City in 1825.

2. Boyer, *Urban Masses and Moral Order*, pp. vii–ix.

3. Mohl, *Poverty in New York*, pp. 138–143.

4. Carroll Smith Rosenberg, *Religion and the Rise of the American City*, pp. 45–49.

5. Smith Rosenberg, *Religion and the Rise of the American City*, pp. 47–49; Mohl, *Poverty in New York*, pp. 190–191; Boyer, *Urban Masses*, pp. 24–25.

6. Boyer, *Urban Masses and Moral Order*, pp. 22–27.

7. Mohl, *Poverty in New York*, p. 197. Smith Rosenberg, *Religion and the Rise of the American City*, pp. 92–96, 187–203; Boyer, *Urban Masses*, pp. 24–27.

8. Mohl, *Poverty in New York*, pp. 99, 203–206. Jay P. Dolan, *The Immigrant Church: New York's Irish and German Catholics, 1815–1865* (Baltimore: Johns Hopkins University Press, 1975), p. 129.

9. Dolan, *Immigrant Church*, pp. 122–128.

10. The story of Catholic charity in America has hardly been told by historians, who usually ignore or slight its efforts. The Protestant coloration of the history of American social reform truly is remarkable. Dolan, *Immigrant Church*, pp. 129–138; John O'Grady, *Catholic Charities in the United States: History and Problems* (Washington, D.C.: National Conference of Catholic Charities, 1930), pp. 200–201; Gail Farr Casterline, "St. Joseph's and St. Mary's: The Origins of Catholic Hospitals in Philadelphia," *The Pennsylvania Magazine of History and Biography*, CVIII:3 (July, 1984), pp. 289–314.

11. Mohl, *Poverty in New York*, pp. 154–155.

12. Boyer, *Urban Masses*, pp. 34–41; Mohl, *Poverty in New York*, pp. 181–185.

13. Boyer, *Urban Masses*, pp. 34–43.

14. Boyer, *Urban Masses*, p. ix; Mohl, *Poverty in New York*, p. 117–118, 138; Smith Rosenberg, *Religion and the Rise of the American City*, pp. 92–94.

15. Boyer, *Urban Masses*, pp. 86–89.

16. Boyer, *Urban Masses*, pp. 89–91.

17. Boyer, *Urban Masses*, pp. 89–93. For accounts of similar organizations in Boston and Chicago, see Nathan Irvin Huggins, *Protestants Against Poverty: Boston's Charities, 1870–1900* (Westport, CT: Greenwood, 1971), pp. 16–26. Kathleen D. McCarthy, *Noblesse Oblige: Charity and Cultural Philanthropy in Chicago, 1849–1929* (Chicago: University of Chicago Press, 1982), pp. 53–56.

18. Boyer, *Urban Masses*, pp. 89–94.

19. Mary Ryan, *Cradle of the Middle Class*, pp. 105–127; McCarthy, *Noblesse Oblige*, pp. 6–11; Smith Rosenberg, *Religion and the Rise of the American City*, pp. 97–124.

20. Smith Rosenberg, *Religion and the Rise of the American City*, p. 98; Suzanne Lebsock, *The Free Women of Petersburg: Status and Culture in a Southern Town, 1784–1860* (New York: Norton, 1984), pp. 196–197.

21. Lebsock, *Free Women of St. Petersburg*, pp. 196–224.

22. Lebsock, *Free Women of Petersburg*, pp. 215–236.

23. On the strike of 1877 and its context, see Robert V. Bruce, *1877: Year of Violence* (Indianapolis and New York: Bobbs-Merrill, 1959) and Jeremy Brecher, *Strike*; for a good review of recent literature on developments in the South, see George M. Fredrickson, "Birth of a Nation," *New York Review*, November 8, 1984, pp. 39–42. Also useful on the period is, Samuel Rezneck, "Distress, Relief, and Discontent in the United States during the Depression of 1873–1878," *Journal of Political Economy* 58 (December 1950), pp. 494–512. On tramps, see the essays in Eric H. Monkkonen, *Walking to Work: Tramps in America, 1790–1935* (Lincoln: University of Nebraska Press, 1984).

24. For two examples of the importance of gratitude and deference in the actual process of friendly visiting, see Michael B. Katz, *Poverty and Policy in American History* (New York: Academic Press, 1983), ch. 1 and "The History of an Impudent Poor Woman in New York City from 1918 to 1923," unpublished manuscript, 1984.

25. Josephine Shaw Lowell, *Public Relief and Private Charity* (New York: Putnam's, 1884); S. Humphrey Gurteen, *Handbook of Charity Organization* (Buffalo, New York: published by the author, 1882).

26. Robert H. Bremner, "Lowell, Josephine Shaw," in Edward T. James, ed., *Notable American Women* (Harvard University Press, 1971), v. 2, pp. 437–439. William Rhinelander Stewart, *The Philanthropic Work of Josephine Shaw Lowell* (New York: Macmillan, 1911).

27. Lowell, *Public Relief*, pp. i, 94, 98; *Fourth Annual Report of the Central Council of the Charity Organization Society of the City of New York*, January 1st, 1886 (Central Office: No. 21 University Place, New York City, 1886), p. 19.

28. Lowell, *Public Relief*, pp. 4–5.

29. Lowell, *Public Relief*, pp. 54–58, 66–67.

30. Lowell, *Public Relief*, pp. 94–95.

31. Lowell, *Public Relief*, pp. 66–69.

32. Lowell, *Public Relief*, pp. 89–90, 92–96.

33. Lowell, *Public Relief*, pp. 99–100.

34. In 1899, the New York Supreme Court ruled that the board could not investigate institutions which did not receive state funds. Lowell objected strenuously to the ruling, which, she said, violated state law. Lowell, *Public Relief*, pp. 84–85; Stewart, *Philanthropic Work*, pp. 462–466.

35. Lowell, *Public Relief*, pp. 105–109.

36. T. Guilford Smith, "Stephen Humphreys Gurteen," *The Charities Review* v. VIII (March–February 1898–1899), pp. 364–367. On Gurteen, see also, Boyer, *Urban Masses*, pp. 150–153.

37. Gurteen, *Handbook*, p. 3.

38. Gurteen, *Handbook*, p. 11.

39. Gurteen, *Handbook*, p. 38.

40. Gurteen, *Handbook*, pp. 22–23.

41. Gurteen, *Handbook*, pp. 44–45.

42. Gurteen, *Handbook*, pp. 43–46.

43. Gurteen, *Handbook*, pp. 48, 120, 123.

44. Gurteen, *Handbook*, pp. 120–123. (italics in original)

45. Gurteen, *Handbook*, p. 127.

46. Gurteen, *Handbook*, pp. 123–173.

47. Gurteen, *Handbook*, pp. 174–186.

48. Gurteen, *Handbook*, pp. 125–129.

49. Gurteen, *Handbook*, p. 141 Italics in original.

50. Gurteen, *Handbook*, pp. 35, 167–168, 79–91, 176; Lowell, *Public Relief*, pp. 108–109.

51. Gurteen, *Handbook*, pp. 197–202.

52. Gurteen, *Handbook*, p. 186.

53. Daniel Calhoun, *The Intelligence of a People* (Princeton: Princeton University Press, 1973), pp. 203–204. I am indebted to Calhoun's persuasive discussion of tensions over sex roles in the middle decades of the nineteenth century for this point. Another excellent indication is the sudden war against abortion waged by doctors and legislators, starting roughly in the 1860s. See, James Mohr, *Abortion in America: The Origins and Evolution of National Policy* (New York: Oxford University Press, 1978).

54. Stewart, *Philanthropic Work*, pp. 190, 208, 210.

55. The best single source for an overview of the history of charity organization is, Frank Dekker Watson, *The Charity Organization Movement in the United States: A Study in American Philanthropy* (New York: Macmillan, 1922).

56. Huggins, *Protestants against Poverty*, pp. 154–157; Almy, "Relation between Private and Public Outdoor Relief," p. 24.

57. Huggins, *Protestants against Poverty*, pp. 60–65; Watson, *Charity Organization Movement*, p. 272. For charity organization's experience in other cities, see Olivier Zunz, *The Changing Face of Inequality: Urbanization, Industrial Development, and Immigrants in Detroit, 1880–1929* (Chicago: University of Chicago Press, 1982), pp. 260–279; McCarthy, *Noblesse Oblige*, pp. 53–72; Kenneth L. Kusmer, "The Functions of Organized Charity in the Progressive Era: Chicago as a Case Study," *Journal of American History* 60 (December, 1973), pp. 657–678; Julia B. Rauch, "Unfriendly Visitors: The Emergence of Scientific Philanthropy in Philadelphia, 1878–1880," Ph.D. diss., Bryn Mawr, 1974; Lillian B. Brandt, "Growth and Development of AICP and COS (A Preliminary and Exploratory Review)," Report to the Committee on the Institute of Welfare Research Community Service Society of New York, 1942 and *The Charity Organization Society of the City of New York 1882–1907*, Twenty-Fifth Annual Report for the Year Ending September Thirtieth Nineteen Hundred and Seven (New York: United Charities Building, 1907); and Watson, *Charity Organization Movement*, passim.

58. Watson, *Charity Organization Movement*, pp. 202–203; 262–263; Almy, "Relation between Private and Public Outdoor Relief," p. 26; Genevieve C. Weeks, "Oscar C. McCulloch: Leader in Organized Charity," *Social Services Review* 39 (1965), pp. 209–221; Frederick D. Kershner, Jr., "From Country Town to Industrial City: The Urban Pattern in Indianapolis," *The Indiana Magazine of History* XLV, 4 (December, 1949), pp. 327–338.

59. Atlanta (1905); Raleigh (1903); Richmond (1906); San Antonio (1906); Savannah, Staunton, Virginia, Lynchburg, Virginia, Wheeling, West Virginia, Columbus, Georgia, and Pensacola, Florida (all 1909), Birmingham, Jacksonville, and Charlotte, North Carolina a year later, and Memphis in 1913.

60. Watson, *Charity Organization Movement*, pp. 347–358, p. 412; David C. Hammack, *Power and Society: Greater New York at the Turn of the Century* (New York: Russell Sage Foundation, 1982), pp. 151, 155, 178; John Reed, "Introduction," in Konrad Bercovici, *Crimes of Charity* (New York: Knopf, 1917), n.p.; for a brief account of Bercovici's colorful career (which included a successful suit against Charlie Chaplin over the theft of material), see "Konrad Bercovici," *New York Times* (December 28, 1961), p. 27.

Chapter 4 / The Transformation of the Poorhouse

1. Gerald Grob, *Mental Institutions in America: Social Policy to 1875* (New York: Free Press, 1973), pp. 272, 276, 279, 282; 280; Walter I. Trattner, *From Poor Law to Welfare State: A History of Social Welfare in America*, second edition (New York: Free Press, 1979), pp. 75–77; David M. Schneider and Albert Deutsch, *The History of Public Welfare in New York State 1867–1940* (Chicago: University of Chicago Press, 1941), pp. 14–16.

2. For a detailed discussion of the survey and the results of a reanalysis of a sample of the data, see Michael B. Katz, *Poverty and Policy in American History* (New York: Academic Press, 1983), pp. 90–133, 259–270.

3. [New York State] Board of Commissioners of Public Charities, *Fourth Annual Report*, In Senate, February 13, 1871.

4. Alice Willard Solenberger, *One Thousand Homeless Men: A Study of Original Records* (New York: Russell Sage, 1911), p. 122.

5. Mary Roberts Smith, *Almshouse Women: A Study of 228 Women in the City and County Almshouses of San Francisco*, Leland Stanford, Jr. University Publications in History and Economics, vol. 3 (Palo Alto, Calif.: Stanford University Press, 1896), p. 26; *Paupers in Almshouses*, p. 9.

6. Katz, *Poverty and Policy*, pp. 116–129.

7. For a detailed discussion of these trends with supporting graphs and tables, see, Katz, *Poverty and Policy*, pp. 57–89, 243–258.

8. Susan Grigg, *The Dependent Poor of Newburyport: Studies in Social History, 1800–1830* (Ann Arbor, Michigan: UMI Research Press, 1984), pp. 32–38; Eric H. Monkkonen, *The Dangerous Class: Crime and Poverty in Columbus, Ohio, 1880–1885* (Cambridge, Mass.: Harvard University Press, 1975), pp. 112, 115; [U.S.] Department of Commerce: Bureau of the Census, *Paupers in Almshouses 1910* (Washington: Government Printing Office, 1915), pp. 9–10; Carol Haber, *Beyond Sixty-five: The Dilemma of Old Age in America's Past* (New York: Cambridge University Press, 1983), pp. 82–107.

9. For a discussion of tramps, see Katz, *Poverty and Policy*, pp. 157–181 and Eric H. Monkkonen, *Walking to Work: Tramps in America, 1790–1935* (Lincoln: University of Nebraska Press, 1984).

10. *Second Annual Report of the Board of State Charities, State of New York*. Senate Document No. 61. March 22, 1869, p. lviii; *Fourth Annual Report of the Board of State Commissioners of Public Charities. New York*. Senate Document No. 70. February 13, 1871, p. xv; *Fifth Annual Report of the Board of State Commissioners of Public Charities. New York*. Senate Document No. 97. April 4, 1872, p. 38.

11. *Thirteenth Annual Report of the State Board of Charities. State of New York*. Senate Document No. 25. February 5, 1880; *Proceedings . . . 1876*, pp. 31–35, 55–56; *Proceedings . . . 1877*, pp. 29–30.

12. Oscar Craig, "American Administration of Charity in Public Institutions," *Annual Report of the State Board of Charities* (Albany: James Lyon, 1893), pp. 14–15, 39; Alice Stoneaker, "County and Municipal Institutions," National Conference on Charities and Corrections, *Proceedings*, 1903, p. 376; Schneider and Deutsch, *History of Public Welfare*, p. 278; Charles E. Rosenberg, "From Almshouse to Hospital: The Shaping of the Philadelphia General Hospital," *Milbank Memorial Fund Quarterly/Health and Society* 60:1982, pp. 108–154.

13. Alice Willard Solenberger, *One Thousand Homeless Men* (New York: Russell Sage, 1911), pp. 124, 161–162.

14. Eric H. Monkkonen, *Police in Urban America, 1860–1920* (New York: Cambridge University Press, 1981), pp. 87, 94–96, 99.

15. Quoted in Monkkonen, *Police*, pp. 90–92.

16. Monkkonen, *Police*, pp. 107–108.

17. Michael B. Katz, Michael J. Doucet, and Mark J. Stern, *The Social Organization of Early Industrial Capitalism* (Cambridge: Harvard University Press, 1982), pp. 242–284; John Modell and Tamara K. Hareven, "Urbanization and the Malleable Household: An Examination of Boarding and Lodging in American Families," *Journal of Marriage and the Family*, 35 (August 1973), pp. 467–479.

18. Solenberger, *Homeless Men*, p. 314.

19. Alice Willard, "Reinstatement of Vagrants Through Municipal Lodging Houses," National Conference on Charities and Corrections, *Proceedings*, 1903, pp. 407–408.

20. E. R. L. Gould, "How Baltimore Banished Tramps and Helped the Idle," *The Forum* 17 (June 1894), pp. 497–504.

21. Gould, "How Baltimore Banished Tramps," pp. 497–504.

22. James L. Jackson, "The Rural Tramp," National Conference on Charities and Corrections, *Proceedings*, 1903, pp. 401–403; Raymond Robbins, "What Constitutes a Modern Lodging House," and Alice L. Higgins, "Comparative Advantages of Municipal and C.O.S. Lodging Houses, National Conference on Charities and Corrections, *Proceedings*, 1904, pp. 148–154, 155–166.

23. Willard, "Reinstatement," pp. 407–408.

24. Solenberger, *Homeless Men*, pp. 315–317.

25. Gerald N. Grob, *Mental Illness and American Society, 1875–1940* (Princeton: Princeton University Press, 1983), pp. 3–4, 8–10.

26. Willard, quoted in Grob, *Mental Institutions*, pp. 309–310; Amos G. Warner, *American Charities: A Study in Philanthropy and Economics* (Boston: Crowell, 1894), p. 269.

27. Warner, *American Charities*, p. 269; *Twenty-Third Annual Report of the State Board of Charities*. New York. Senate Document No. 9. January 15, 1890, p. 15.

28. Grob, *Mental Illness*, pp. 87–89.

29. Walter I. Trattner, *From Poor Law to Welfare State: A History of Social Welfare in America*, second edition (New York: Free Press, 1979), p. 159; Charles A. Ellwood, "Alms House Abuses and their Correction," *Proceedings of the Thirtieth National Conference of Charities and Corrections* (1903), p. 390; Grob, *Mental Illness*, pp. 83–86.

30. *Proceedings . . . 1890*, p. 6.

31. *Proceedings . . . 1888*, p. 4; *Proceedings . . . 1889*, p. 14; *Proceedings . . . 1888*, p. 4; *Proceedings . . . 1889*, p. 3; *Proceedings . . . 1890*, pp. 5, 6.

32. *Proceedings . . . 1890*, p. 5; *Proceedings . . . 1888*, p. 4; *Proceedings . . . 1889*, pp. 38, 50.

33. *Proceedings . . . 1889*, p. 50; *Proceedings . . . 1890*, p. 5.

34. David Rothman, *Conscience and Convenience: The Asylum and its Alternatives in Progressive America* (Boston: Little Brown, 1980), portrays the horrors of state mental hospitals in the late nineteenth century.

35. Grob, *Mental Illness*, pp. 94–97; Grob (p. 104) points out that the level of care in the South was the lowest in the country. The reason was the region's poverty combined with the lack of strong, central agencies at the state level.

36. Grob, *Mental Illness*, pp. 90–92.

37. Priscilla F. Clement, "The Response to Need: Welfare and Poverty in Philadelphia 1800–1850," Ph.D. diss., University of Pennsylvania, 1977, pp. 189–194.

38. Board of Commissioners of Public Charities [New York State], *Seventh Annual Report*. In Senate, March 23, 1874. No. 77, pp. 43–44.

39. William C. Heffner, *History of Poor Relief in Pennsylvania* (Cleonea, Pa.: published by the author, 1913), pp. 43–44; Alice Shaffer and Mary W. Keefer, *The Indiana Poor Law* (Chicago: University of Chicago Press, 1936), p. 40; Isabel C. Bruce, *The Michigan Poor Law* (Chicago: University of Chicago Press, 1936), p. 36; Ethel McClure, *More than a Roof: The Development of Minnesota Poor Farms and Homes for the Aged* (St. Paul: Minnesota Historical Society, 1968), p. 90; Roy M. Brown, *Public Poor Relief in North Carolina* (Chapel Hill: University of North Carolina Press, 1928), pp. 152–153; Grace A. Browning, *The Development of Poor Relief Legislation in Kansas* (Chicago: University of Chicago Press, 1935), pp. 63–64.

40. Committee on Homes and Asylums of the County Board of Supervisors [Kings County, New York], *Report*, 1877, p. 6.

41. *Report*, pp. 7, 11.

42. *Report*, pp. 25–26.

43. Charles Loring Brace, *The Dangerous Classes of New York, and Twenty Years' Work Among Them* (New York: Wynkoop and Hallenbeck, 1872), pp. 43–47, 55–59, 88, 231–233; Paul Boyer, *Urban Masses and Moral Order in America, 1820–1920* (Cambridge: Harvard University Press, 1978), 104–107; on Brace, see also, Thomas Bender, *Toward an Urban Vision: Ideas and Institutions in Nineteenth Century America* (Lexington: University of Kentucky Press, 1975), pp. 131–157, and Bruce William Bellingham, " 'Little Wanderers': A Socio-historical Study of the Nineteenth Century Origins of Child Fostering and Adoption Reform, Based on Early Records of the New York Children's Aid Society," Ph.D. diss., University of Pennsylvania, 1984, pp. 23–57.

44. Michael B. Katz, *The Irony of Educational Reform: Educational Innovation in Mid-Nineteenth Century Massachusetts* (Cambridge: Harvard University Press, 1968), pp. 163–211; Barbara M. Brenzel, *Daughters of the State: A Social Portrait of the First Reform School for Girls*

in North America, 1856–1905 (Cambridge: MIT Press, 1983); Robert M. Mennel, *Thorns and Thistles: Juvenile Delinquents in the United States, 1825–1940* (Hanover, N.H.: University Press of New England, 1973).

45. Brace, *Dangerous Classes*, pp. 285–286.

46. *Proceedings of the State Convention of Superintendents of the Poor, at an Adjourned Meeting, Held in Albany, N.Y., January 29, 1873* (Albany: Argus Co. 1873), p. 1.

47. *Proceedings of the Convention of the Superintendents of the Poor of the State of New York held in Rochester, New York., Tuesday and Wednesday, June 9th and 10th, 1874* (Rochester, N.Y.: Evening Express Printing, 1874), p. 10; *Proceedings of the Convention of the Superintendents of the Poor . . . Binghampton, June 12th and 13th, 1877* (Albany, N.Y.: Joel Munsell, 1877), p. 25.

48. *Proceedings of the Convention of the Superintendents of the Poor . . . held at Poughkeepsie, June 8th and 9th, 1875* (Albany, N.Y.: Weed and Parsons, 1875), p. 12; *Proceedings of the Convention of Superintendents of the Poor . . . Held at Buffalo, June 14th, 15th, and 16th, 1881* (Albany, New York: 1881), p. 10.

49. *Proceedings . . . 1875*, pp. 26, 27, 28; *Proceedings . . . 1881*, p. 61. *Proceedings . . . 1881*, p. 63.

50. The New York Society for the Prevention of Cruelty to Children, *First Annual Report, 1876* (New York: Styles and Cash, 1876); Susan Tiffin, *In Whose Best Interest? Child Welfare Reform in the Progressive Era* (Westport, CT: Greenwood, 1982), pp. 40–41. The methods of the SPCC are gleaned best by reading through its case histories, which, for Philadelphia, are in the Temple University Urban Archives. Comments about the SPCC by the poor are scattered through case histories of the COS and CAS.

Chapter 5 / Saving Children

1. *Proceedings of the Twenty-third Annual Convention of County Superintendents of the Poor of the State of New York . . . 1893* (Bath, NY: Press of Courier Co., 1893), p. 7. For an excellent discussion of progressivism that points out how contemporaries did not use the term "progressive," to describe themselves, see Daniel Rodgers, "In Search of Progressivism," *Reviews in American History* 10 (1982): 113–32.

2. Children also preoccupied social reform energies in other countries at the same time. For example, on Canada see Neil Sutherland, *Children in English-Canadian Society* (Toronto: University of Toronto Press, 1975). *Proceedings of the Conference on the Care of Dependent Children Held at Washington, D.C. on January 25, 26, 1909* 60th Congress, 2d Session, Senate, Document No. 721 (Washington: Government Printing Office, 1909), p. 6.

3. Christopher Lasch, *Haven in a Heartless World* (New York: Basic Books, 1979).

4. W. Norton Grubb and Marvin Lazerson, *Broken Promises: How Americans Fail Their Children* (New York: Basic Books, 1982), esp. pp. 247, 279, 283–284.

5. On changes in child psychology, see Dominick Covello, *Muscles and Morals: Organized Playgrounds and Urban Reform, 1880–1929* (Philadelphia: University of Pennsylvania Press, 1981), pp. 49–50. On Hall, see Dorothy Ross, *G. Stanley Hall: The Psychologist as Prophet* (Chicago: University of Chicago Press, 1972); a convenient collection of his writing with a good introduction, is Charles E. Strickland and Charles Burgess, eds., *Health, Growth, and Heredity: G. Stanley Hall on Natural Education* (New York: Teachers College Press, 1965).

6. Viviana A. Zelizer, *Pricing the Priceless Child: The Changing Social Value of Children* (New York: Basic Books, 1985), pp. 3–6.

7. Zelizer, *Pricing the Priceless Child*, p. 21.

8. See, for example, Jacob Riis, quoted in Roy Lubove, *The Progressives and the Slums: Tenement House Reform in New York City, 1890–1917* (Pittsburgh: University of Pittsburgh Press, 1962), p. 71; Jane Addams in White House Conference, *Proceedings*, pp. 100–101; Zelizer, *Pricing the Priceless Child*, pp. 8–10. Paul Osterman, *Getting Started: The Youth Labor Market* (Cambridge: MIT Press, 1980), pp. 53–62; G. Stanley Hall, "Child-Study and Its Relation to Education," in Strickland and Burgess, *Health, Growth, and Heredity*, p. 87.

9. White House Conference, *Proceedings*, pp. 41–42.

10. Homer Folks, "Why Should Dependent Children be Reared in Families Rather than in Institutions?" *The Charities Review* V, 2:December, 1895, pp. 140–145; Leroy Ashby, *Saving the*

Waifs: Reformers and Dependent Children, 1890–1917 (Philadelphia: Temple University Press, 1984), p. 27.

11.   David J. Rothman, *Conscience and Convenience: The Asylum and Its Alternatives in Progressive America* (Boston: Little Brown, 1980), pp. 5–10.

12.   Catherine J. Ross, "Society's Children: The Care of Indigent Youngsters in New York City, 1875–1903," Ph.D. diss., Yale University, 1977, p. 63.

13.   *New York Charities Directory. A Classified and Descriptive Directory . . .* (Charity Organization Society of the City of New York: New York, 1890), pp. 98–112, 175. Homer Folks, *The Care of Destitute, Neglected, and Delinquent Children* (New York: MacMillan Co., 1892, reprinted by National Association of Social Workers, 1978), p. 64; Susan Tiffin, *In Whose Best Interest? Child Welfare Reform in the Progressive Era* (Westport, CT: Greenwood Press, 1982), p. 64.

14.   "The Catholic Protectory of New York. Its Spirit and Its Workings from its Origin to the Present," National Conference of Charities and Corrections, *History of Child Saving in the United States*, Report of the Committee on the History of Child Saving Work at the Twentieth National Conference of Charities and Corrections in Chicago, June, 1893 (Boston: George H. Ellis, 1893), appendix, pp. 35–36.

15.   Right Reverend D. J. McMahon, Supervisor of Catholic Charities, Archdiocese of New York, "Family Influence," *White House Conference*, p. 98.

16.   Ashby, *Saving the Waifs*, p. 27.

17.   Homer Folks, "What Brought about the New York System?" p. 130; Folks, *Care of Destitute . . .*, p. 154.

18.   Ashby, *Saving the Waifs*, p. 13.

19.   Ashby, *Saving the Waifs*, p. 5. This interpretation contrasts with Paul Boyer's, who stresses the secularization of philanthropy in the late nineteenth century. Paul Boyer, *Urban Masses and Moral Order in America, 1820–1920* (Cambridge, MA: Harvard University Press, 1978), pp. 167–168.

20.   Tiffin, *In Whose Best Interest?* pp. 204–205.

21.   Tiffin, *In Whose Best Interest?* pp. 205–210.

22.   Trattner, *From Poor Law to Welfare State*, pp. 203–207. Originally, the bureau was located in the Department of Commerce and Labor and then moved to Labor, which became a separate department a year later. In 1953, it became part of the newly created Department of Health, Education, and Welfare.

23.   David J. Rothman, *Conscience and Convenience: The Asylum and Its Alternatives in Progressive America* (Boston: Little Brown, 1980), pp. 5–10.

24.   On the Abbotts and their remarkable careers, see the recent biography, Lela B. Costin, *Two Sisters for Social Justice: A Biography of Grace and Edith Abbott* (Urbana: University of Illinois Press, 1983). For antebellum reference to the state as a parent, see Michael B. Katz, *The Irony of Early School Reform: Educational Innovation in Mid-Nineteenth Century Massachusetts* (Cambridge: Harvard University Press, 1968), pp. 43–44, 187–188, 191.

25.   On the development of social science, see Mary O. Furner, *Advocacy and Objectivity: A Crisis in the Professionalization of American Social Science, 1865–1905* (Lexington: University of Kentucky Press, 1975) and Thomas L. Haskell, *The Emergence of Professional Social Science: The American Social Science Association and the Nineteenth-Century Crisis of Authority* (Lexington: University of Kentucky Press, 1975).

26.   Rothman, *Conscience and Convenience*, pp. 5–10.

27.   On the separation of politics and economics see, Frances Fox Piven and Richard Cloward, *The New Class War: Reagan's Attack on the Welfare State and Its Consequences* (New York: Pantheon, 1982), pp. 40–44. For a brilliant discussion of theories of the state in America, see Alan Wolfe, *The Limits of Legitimacy: Political Contradictions of Contemporary Capitalism* (New York: Free Press, 1977).

28.   White House Conference, *Proceedings*, p. 6; another example, from Judge Ben Lindsay, is on p. 217.

29.   White House Conference, *Proceedings*, p. 54.

30.   Nila F. Allen, "Memorandum for Miss Lathrop," U.S. Department of Labor, Children's Bureau, July 26, 1918, ms.

31.   Tiffin, *In Whose Best Interest?* p. 42; N.Y. *Eugenics Bulletin* #15 (1908) also points to the large number of children in institutions with one or two living parents. Mary E. Richmond and Fred S. Hall, *A Study of Nine Hundred and Eighty-Five Widows Known to Certain Charity Organization Societies in 1910*, reprint of the 1913 ed. published by the Charity Organization Dept.

of the Russell Sage Foundation, New York, which was issued as its pamphlet C.O. 34 (New York: Arno Press, 1974), p. 64.

32. White House Conference, *Proceedings*, pp. 53–55, 95.

33. Robert W. Hebberd, "Placing Out Children: Dangers of Careless Methods," [1899], pp. 171–172, in Robert Bremner, ed., *Care of Dependent Children in the Late Nineteenth and Early Twentieth Centuries* (New York: Arno Press, 1974).

34. Tiffin, *In Whose Best Interest?*, pp. 121–130, 232–237; Richmond and Hall, *Nine Hundred and Eight-Five Widows*, pp. 50–51; Roy Lubove, *The Struggle for Social Security 1900–1935* (Cambridge: Harvard University Press, 1968), pp. 91–112.

35. Tiffin, *In Whose Best Interest?*, pp. 130–134; Sydnor H. Walker, "Privately Supported Social Work," President's Research Committee on Social Trends, *Recent Social Trends* (New York: McGraw-Hill, 1933), v. ii, p. 1199; Walter I. Trattner, *From Poorhouse to Welfare State: A History of Social Welfare*, 2nd edition (New York: Free Press, 1979), pp. 186–187; Michael B. Katz, "The History of an Impudent Poor Woman in New York City from 1918 to 1923," unpublished manuscript.

36. White House Conference, *Proceedings*, p. 217.

37. Frank D. Loomis, White House Conference, *Proceedings*, pp. 69–70.

38. Katz, *Irony*, pp. 163–211.

39. Michael B. Katz, *Class, Bureaucracy and Schools: The Illusion of Educational Change in America* (New York: Praeger 1975), pp. 45–47. Tiffin, *In Whose Best Interest?* p. 144; Louis R. Harlan, *Separate and Unequal: Public School Campaigns and Racism in the Southern Seaboard States, 1901–1915* (Chapel Hill: University of North Carolina Press, 1968), p. 196.

40. Ross, "Society's Children," p. 55; on Progressive era reforms in curriculum and pedagogy, see Lawrence Cremin, *The Transformation of the School: Progressivism and American Education, 1876–1957* (New York: Random House, 1957); Edward Krug, *The Shaping of the American High School, 1880–1920* (Madison: University of Wisconsin Press, 1964); Marvin Lazerson, *Origins of the Urban Public School: Public Education in Massachusetts, 1870–1915* (Cambridge: Harvard University Press, 1971; and David Tyack, *The One Best System: A History of American Urban Education* (Cambridge: Harvard University Press, 1974).

41. Zelizer, *Pricing the Priceless Child*, pp. 58–64.

42. Walter I. Trattner, *Crusade for the Children: A History of the National Child Labor Committee and Child Labor Reform in America* (Chicago: Quadrangle Books, 1970), pp. 77–78.

43. Zelizer, *Pricing the Priceless Child*, pp. 85–96; Ashby, *Saving the Waifs*, pp. 69–132.

44. Trattner, *Crusade*, p. 35.

45. Trattner, *Crusade*, pp. 50–65. 131, 136, 223.

46. Mennel, Katz, *Irony*, Part 3; Schlossman, Brenzel.

47. Tiffin, *In Whose Best Interest?* pp. 217–226. Quotes from pp. 219, 226.

48. Folks, *Destitute, Neglected, and Delinquent Children*, pp. 229–234, quote p. 226; Tiffin, *In Whose Best Interest?* pp. 222–224, quote p. 224.

49. Michael B. Katz, Michael J. Doucet, and Mark J. Stern, *The Social Organization of Early Industrial Capitalism* (Cambridge: Harvard University Press, 1981), pp. 228–230; Michael B. Katz, *Poverty and Policy in American History* (New York: Academic Press, 1983), pp. 17–54.

50. Trattner, *From Poor Law to Welfare State*, p. 108; Steven L. Schlossman, *Love and the American Delinquent: The Theory and Practice of "Progressive" Juvenile Justice 1825–1920* (Chicago: University of Chicago Press, 1977), p. 188. David Rothman, *Conscience and Convenience*, pp. 10–12.

51. Quoted in Sheila M. Rothman, *Woman's Proper Place: A History of Changing Ideals and Practices, 1870 to the Present* (New York: Basic Books, 1978), p. 126.

52. Walter I. Trattner, *From Poor Law to Welfare State: A History of Social Welfare in America*, third edition (New York: Free Press, 1984), pp. 135, 142.

53. On the history of hospitals, see Morris J. Vogel, *The Invention of the Modern Hospital: Boston 1870–1930* (Chicago: University of Chicago Press, 1980); Charles E. Rosenberg, "From Almshouse to Hospital: The Shaping of the Philadelphia General Hospital," *Health and Society* 60:1 (1982), pp. 108–154; David Rosner, *A Once Charitable Enterprise: Hospitals and Health Care in Brooklyn and New York 1885–1915* (New York: Cambridge University Press, 1982).

54. New York's dispensaries were partially funded by the state and city governments. The city had twenty-nine dispensaries by 1874 and Philadelphia, thirty-three in 1877. Dispensaries treated enormous numbers of people: in New York, "134,069 patients in 1860, roughly 180,000 in 1866, 213,000 in 1874, and 876,000 in 1900."

55. Charles E. Rosenberg, "Social Class and Medical Care in 19th-Century America: The Rise and Fall of the Dispensary," in Leavitt and Numbers, *Sickness and Health*, pp. 157–171.

56. Rothman, *Woman's Proper Place*, pp. 124–126.

57. Edward T. Mormon, "Guarding Against Alien Impurities: The Philadelphia Lazaretto 1854–1893," *Pennsylvania Magazine of History and Biography* CVIII, 2 (April 1984), pp. 131–151; William R. Brock, *Investigation and Responsibility: Public Responsibility in the United States, 1865–1900* (Cambridge, Eng.: Cambridge University Press, 1984), pp. 116–147; Trattner, *From Poor Law to Welfare State*, p. 136; Rothman, *Woman's Proper Place*, p. 70. On the history of public health, see also, Barbara Gutman Rosenkrantz, *Public Health and the State: Changing Views in Massachusetts, 1842–1936* (Cambridge: Harvard University Press, 1972). Dates for the founding of other boards of health were, for example, Michigan, 1873; Pennsylvania, 1886; Connecticut, 1878; Maryland, 1874; Tennessee, 1877. (The American Public Health Association was organized in 1872; in 1878 the federal government passed the National Quarantine Act and in 1879 established the National Board of Health.)

58. Roy Lubove, *The Progressives and the Slums: Tenement House Reform in New York City 1890–1917* (Pittsburgh: University of Pittsburgh Press, 1962), pp. 83–84.

59. Joyce Antler and Daniel M. Fox, "The Movement Toward a Safe Maternity: Physician Accountability in New York City, 1915–1940," in Judith Walzer Leavitt and Ronald L. Numbers, eds., *Sickness and Health in America: Readings in the History of Medicine and Public Health* (Madison: University of Wisconsin Press, 1978), pp. 375–392.

60. Gretchen A. Condron, Henry Williams, and Rose A. Cheney, "The Decline in Mortality in Philadelphia from 1870 to 1930: The Role of Municipal Services," *Pennsylvania Magazine of History and Biography* CVIII, 2 (April 1984), pp. 153–177.

61. Walter I. Trattner, *Homer Folks: Pioneer in Social Welfare* (New York: Columbia University Press, 1968), pp. 154–155, 214–215; Judith Walzer Leavitt, *The Healthiest City: Milwaukee and the Politics of Health Reform* (Princeton: Princeton University Press, 1982), pp. 38–39, 214; S. Josephine Baker, *Fighting for Life* (New York: Macmillan, 1939), p. 253.

62. Leavitt, *Healthiest City*, pp. 67, 156–189, 213; Baker, *Fighting for Life*, pp. 127, 139.

63. Leavitt, *Healthiest City*, p. 241.

64. Rothman, *Woman's Proper Place*, p. 136, 140; Trattner, *From Poor Law to Welfare State*, p. 206.

65. Rothman, *Woman's Proper Place*, pp. 139–141.

66. Rothman, *Woman's Proper Place*, pp. 142–153; Lela B. Costin, *Two Sisters*, pp. 169–176; Kathleen W. Jones, "Sentiment and Science: The Late Nineteenth Century Pediatrician as Mother's Advisor," *Journal of Social History* 17 (Fall 1983), pp. 80–96.

Chapter 6 / Reorganizing Cities

1. Stanley, H. Howe, "The Development of Municipal Charities in the United States," National Conference of Charities and Corrections, *Proceedings* (40:1913), pp. 208–209. Jane Addams, "Modern Devices for Minimizing Dependencies," *Proceedings of the Conference on the Care of Dependent Children Held at Washington, D.C. January 25, 26, 1909* (Washington, D.C.: Government Printing Office, 1909), pp. 99–100.

2. Charles Hoffman, *The Depression of the Nineties: An Economic History* (Westport, CT: Greenwood Press, 1970), pp. 104–109.

3. Carlos P. Closson, "The Unemployed in American Cities," *Quarterly Journal of Economics* 8:4 (January 1894), pp. 168–217; Samuel Rezneck, "Unemployment, Unrest and Relief in the United States During the Depression of 1893–97," *Journal of Political Economy* 61:4 (August 1953), pp. 324–45; Leah Hannah Feder, *Unemployment Relief in Periods of Depression: A Study of Measures Adopted in Certain American Cities, 1857–1922* (New York: Russell Sage Foundation, 1936), pp. 94, 153; Melvin G. Holli, *Reform in Detroit: Hazen S. Pingree and Urban Politics* (New York: Oxford University Press, 1969), pp. 61–73; Brenda K. Shelton, *Reformers in Search of Yesterday: Buffalo in the 1890s* (New York: SUNY Press, 1976), pp. 140–150.

4. Closson, "The Unemployed," pp. 205–206; Paul T. Ringenbach, *Tramps and Reformers 1873–1916: The Discovery of Unemployment in New York* (Westport, CT: Greenwood Press, 1973), p. 42.

5. Samuel T. McSeveney, *The Politics of Depression: Political Behavior in the Northeast, 1893–1896* (New York: Oxford University Press, 1972), pp. 35–36, 224.

6. Ringenbach, *Tramps and Reformers*, pp. 135–155.

7. Quotes from Coit and Massachusetts Commission in, Feder, *Unemployment Relief*, pp. 132–133; Ringenbach, *Tramps and Reformers*, pp. 80–81, 181.

8. John McClymer, *War and Welfare: Social Engineering in America. 1890–1925* (Westport, CT: Greenwood Press, 1980), pp. 50–64.

9. Kenneth L. Kusmer, *A Ghetto Takes Shape: Black Cleveland, 1870–1900* (Urbana, IL: University of Illinois Press, 1976), p. 36; Blake McKelvey, *The Urbanization of America* (New Brunswick, NJ: Rutgers University Press, 1963), pp. 63–69.

10. McKelvey, *Urbanization of America*, pp. 37–60, 75–81.

11. Jon C. Teaford, *The Unheralded Triumph: City Government in America, 1870–1900* (Baltimore: Johns Hopkins University Press, 1984), pp. 3–6.

12. Teaford, *Unheralded Triumph*, pp. 25–26. My interpretation of urban government has been influenced by Teaford and, especially, by Kenneth Fox, *Better City Government: Innovation in American Urban Politics, 1850–1937* (Philadelphia: Temple University Press, 1977). Fox puts the development of urban government into the framework developed by Alfred Chandler for corporate reorganization in the same period. I emphasize the influence of business interests on urban development more than he does. Also very useful is Martin J. Schiesl, *The Politics of Efficiency: Municipal Administration and Reform in America 1800–1920* (Berkeley: University of California Press, 1977). Helpful more for information than interpretation are, Ernest S. Griffith, *A History of American City Government: The Progressive Years and their Aftermath 1900–1920* (New York: Praeger, 1974) and Blake McKelvey, *Urbanization of America*, and *The Emergence of Metropolitan America 1915–1966* (New Brunswick, NJ: Rutgers University Press, 1968).

13. Fox, *Better City Government*, pp. 43–48; Schiesl, *Politics of Efficiency*, pp. 25–26; Griffith, *History*, p. 34.

14. Fox, *Better City Government*, xvii–xviii; Schiesl, *Politics of Efficiency*, pp. 2–4.

15. On the reorganization of industry, see chapter 7. Teaford, *Unheralded Triumph*, outlines the accomplishments of city governments. Teaford, and most other historians argue that reform succeeded least well with police forces, which remained corrupt. However, Harring argues that the primary role of police was to protect the interests of the business class by insuring order, cleaning up the streets, breaking strikes, and harassing vagrants. The accomplishment of these purposes, he notes, was not incompatible with corruption, and he points to innovations in policing that fostered these goals. Sidney L. Harring, *Policing a Class Society: The Experience of American Cities, 1865–1915* (New Brunswick, N.J.: Rutgers University Press, 1983), esp. pp. 38–41.

16. Fox, *Better City Government*, pp. 63–89; Schiesl, *Politics of Efficiency*, pp. 96–98.

17. Fox, *Better City Government*, pp. 101, 113; Sydnor H. Walker, "Privately Supported Social Work," in [President's Research Committee on Social Trends] *Recent Social Trends* (New York: McGraw-Hill, 1933), pp. 1182–1183, 1198. Relief grants increased after a rash of family budget and cost of living studies showed the pitiful inadequacy of prevailing standards.

18. L. A. Halbert, "Boards of Public Welfare and Good City Government," National Conference of Charities and Corrections, *Proceedings* (40:13), pp. 212–221.

19. Schiesl, *Politics of Efficiency*, pp. 111–132; Ernest L. Tustin, in *Proceedings*, 45th Annual Meeting of the Association of Directors of the Poor and Commissioners of Charities of the State of Pennsylvania (Harrisburg, PA, 1920), p. 35.

20. L. A. Halbert, "Boards of Public Welfare; A System of Government Social Work," National Council of Social Work, *Proceedings* (45:1918), pp. 223–224.

21. Susan E. Davis, "The Underdevelopment of Public Welfare in Philadelphia 1913–1931," in Michael B. Katz and Associates, Appendix to Final Report NIMH Grant No. RO1MH32520.

22. Roy Lubove, *The Professional Altruist: The Emergence of Social Work as a Career, 1880–1930* (Cambridge: Harvard University Press, 1965), pp. 183–184.

23. Walker, "Social Work," pp. 1188, 1204–1206; Lubove, *Professional Altruist*, pp. 183–184. Chests often took over the Social Service Exchanges, established several years earlier in most cities to centralize information about charity recipients and prevent duplication in giving. In 1931, 94 of 113 Exchanges were under community chest auspices.

24. Scott M. Cutlip, *Fund Raising in the United States: Its Role in America's Philanthropy* (New Brunswick, NJ: Rutgers University Press), pp. 60–61; 73–74, 151–152, 202, 206, 220–224.

25. William I. Cole, "Introductory," in Robert A. Woods, ed., *The City Wilderness: A Settlement Study* (Boston: Houghton Mifflin, 1898), pp. 2–3.

26. Robert A. Woods, "Social Recovery," in Woods, *City Wilderness*, p. 273.

27. Allen F. Davis, *Spearheads for Reform: The Social Settlements and the Progressive Movement 1890–1914* (New York: Oxford University Press, 1967), pp. 3–12. The Cambridge Neighborhood House in Cambridge, Massachusetts, claims to be the first in the country, older than the New York settlements. I have not seen the documentation necessary to resolve the question.

28. Davis, *Spearheads for Reform*, p. 16; McClymer, *War and Welfare*, p. 14; Clarke A. Chambers, *Seedtime of Reform: American Social Service and Social Action 1918–1933* (Minneapolis: University of Minnesota Press, 1963), p. 16.

29. Davis, *Spearheads for Reform*, p. 16, 21, 22. Also useful on the settlement movement are, Allen F. Davis, *American Heroine: The Life and Legend of Jane Addams* (New York: Oxford University Press, 1973); Jane Addams, *Twenty Years at Hull-House* (New York: Macmillan, 1910), in which, as Davis points out, Addams creates her own legend as much as writes an autobiography; and Paul Boyer, *Urban Masses and Moral Order in America 1820–1920* (Cambridge: Harvard University Press, 1978), pp. 155–158. My favorite work from the era is Jane Addams, *Democracy and Social Ethics* (New York: Macmillan, 1902).

30. These figures are from Davis, *Spearheads for Reform*, pp. 33–35, which does not report the gender ratios in the movement as a whole or the extent to which individual settlement houses were predominantly single-sex. They are based on a sample of 724 settlement leaders.

31. Davis, *Spearheads for Reform*, pp. 36–39; John P. Rousmaniere, "Cultural Hybrid in the Slums: The College Woman and the Settlement House, 1889–1894," *American Quarterly* 22:1 (Spring 1970), pp. 45–66; Donald Fleming, "Social Darwinism," in Arthur M. Schlesinger, Jr., and Morton White, eds., *Paths of American Thought* (Boston: Houghton Mifflin, 1963), pp. 123–146.

32. Davis, *Spearheads for Reform*, pp. 40–193; Woods, *City Wilderness*, passim.

33. [Mark de Wolfe Howe] "Settlers in the City Wilderness," *Atlantic Monthly* LXXVII: CCCCLIX (January, 1896), p. 123; Davis, *American Heroine*, discusses Jane Addams's popularity. Most current interpretations of progressivism do not offer any clues to why Jane Addams should have attained such national popularity. The most useful book for thinking about the period in a way that makes her prominence comprehensible is, David Thelen, *The New Citizenship: Origins of Progressivism in Wisconsin, 1885–1900* (Columbia, University of Missouri Press, 1972), which stresses a new civic consciousness arising out of people's identification with each other as consumers.

34. Davis, *Spearheads for Reform*, pp. 185–187, 194–217.

35. Chambers, *Seedtime of Reform*, p. 116; McClymer, *War and Welfare*, pp. 192–209; the Rubinow-Kellogg correspondence is in the Minnesota Social Welfare History archives as is Rubinow's manuscript. Davis, *Spearheads* and *American Heroine* discuss Addams's fall from popularity.

36. On the development of psychiatry see Gerald Grob, *Mental Institutions in America: Social Policy to 1875* (New York: Free Press, 1973) and *Mental Illness and American Society 1875–1940* (Princeton: Princeton University Press, 1983); on nursing, Barbara Melosh, *"The Physician's Hand": Work Culture and Conflict in American Nursing* (Philadelphia: Temple University Press, 1982); on school superintendents, David Tyack and Elisabeth Hansot, *Managers of Virtue: Public School Leadership in America* (New York: Basic Books, 1982); on medicine, Paul Starr, *The Social Transformation of American Medicine: The Rise of a Sovereign Profession and the Making of a Vast Industry* (New York: Basic Books, 1982), pp. 79–232.

37. Frank J. Bruno, *Trends in Social Work*, second edition, (New York: Columbia University Press, 1957), p. 142; Lubove, *The Professional Altruist*, pp. 140–141.

38. Bruno, *Trends in Social Work*, pp. 3–5, 146; on the American Social Science Association, see Thomas L. Haskell, *The Emergence of Professional Social Science: The American Social Science Association and the Nineteenth-Century Crisis of Authority* (Urbana, Ill.: University of Illinois Press, 1977).

39. Lubove, *Professional Altruist*, pp. 49–52.

40. Lubove, *Professional Altruist*, pp. 107–108.

41. Lubove, *Professional Altruist*, pp. 48, 84, 119.

42. Lubove, *Professional Altruist*, p. 79; Bruno, *Trends in Social Work*, pp. 186–187.

43. Lubove, *Professional Altruist*, pp. 161, 164–165.

44. Lubove, *Professional Altruist*, p. 132.

45. Lubove, *Professional Altruist*, pp. 220–221.

46. Walker, "Social Work," p. 1168.

47. *Proceedings of the Thirty-Sixth Annual Convention of the County Superintendents of the Poor of the State of New York* (1906), p. 13.

48. County Superintendents, Fortieth Convention (1910), pp. 156–157.

49. County Superintendents, Forty-Third Convention (1913), pp. 50, 77.

50. Josephine Chapin Brown, *Public Relief 1929–1939* (New York: Henry Holt and Co., 1949), pp. 85–86, 229; Jacob Fisher, *The Response of Social Work to the Depression* (Cambridge: Shenkman, 1980), pp. 66–67; 235.

51. Robert H. Wiebe, *The Search for Order 1877–1920* (New York: Hill and Wang, 1967), pp. 111–112.

52. Lubove, *Progressives and the Slums*, pp. 127–128; Lela B. Costin, *Two Sisters for Social Justice: A Biography of Grace and Edith Abbott* (Urbana: University of Illinois Press, 1983), pp. 64–66.

53. Susan Ware, *Beyond Suffrage: Women in the New Deal* (Cambridge: Harvard University Press, 1981).

54. McClymer, *War and Welfare*, pp. 52–57.

55. McClymer, *War and Welfare*, pp. 74, 201, 219.

56. C. Wright Mills quoted in McClymer, *War and Welfare*, p. 220; Mary O. Furner, *From Advocacy to Objectivity: A Crisis in the Professionalization of American Social Science, 1865–1905* (Lexington, Ky.: University of Kentucky Press, 1975).

57. According to New York law, a tenement was "Any house occupied as the home or residence of three families or more, living independently of each other and doing their cooking upon the premises." To differentiate tenements from apartments, reformers drew a line marking off "those houses which in their construction and maintenance require regulation for the protection of their inmates."

58. Robert W. DeForest and Lawrence Veiller, "The Tenement House Problem," in DeForest and Veiller, eds., *The Tenement House Problem* (New York: Macmillan, 1903), p. 67.

59. Roy Lubove, *Progressives and the Slums* (Pittsburgh: University of Pittsburgh Press, 1962), pp. 9–10, 102–112.

60. Lubove, *Progressives and the Slums*, pp. 28–30; DeForest and Veiller, "Tenement House Problem," pp. 8–9.

61. Riis, quoted in Lubove, *Progressives and the Slums*, pp. 246–247. Born in Elizabeth, New Jersey, in 1872, Veiller attended City College in New York and "became interested in social problems after studying the social critics of Victorian England, Ruskin and Carlyle." In the depression of 1893, he worked for the East Side Relief Work Committee, which taught him "at the mature age of 20 years, that the improvement of the homes of the people was the starting point of everything." Between 1895 and 1897, Veiller worked in the city's Building Department as a plan examiner, where he learned a great deal about the technical aspects of the tenement problem. Then, in 1898, he became secretary of the new Tenement House Committee of the Charity Organization Society. When New York created a Tenement House Department, Veiller, also the author of several books, became its first deputy director; he virtually founded as well as directed the National Housing Association; and after 1907, he directed the COS Department for the Improvement of Social Conditions, which immersed him in the campaign against tuberculosis and in juvenile court work as well as housing. Lubove, *Progressives and the Slums*, pp. 127–128.

62. Lubove, *Progressives and the Slums*, pp. 94–166; quote from p. 166.

63. Thomas Lee Philpott, *The Slum and the Ghetto: Neighborhood Deterioration and Middle-Class Reform, Chicago, 1880–1930* (Chicago: University of Chicago Press, 1978), pp. 89, 95–102.

64. DeForest and Veiller, "Tenement House Problem," p. 44; Lubove, *Progressives and the Slums*, p. 178.

65. Lawrence Veiller, "Tenement House Reform in New York City, 1834–1900," in DeForest and Veiller, eds., *Tenement House Problem*, p. 89.

66. Lubove, *Progressives and the Slums*, pp. 221–230; 244–245.

67. Lubove, *Progressives and the Slums*, p. 179.

68. Kenneth L. Kusmer, *A Ghetto Takes Shape: Black Cleveland, 1870–1930* (Urbana: University of Illinois Press, 1976), pp. 35–36. On the development of ghettos in this period, see also Allen H. Spear, *Black Chicago: The Making of a Negro Ghetto 1890–1920* (Chicago: University of Chicago Press, 1967); Gilbert Osofsky, *Harlem: The Making of a Ghetto: Negro New York 1890–1930* (New York: Harper Torchbook edition, 1968); Howard N. Rabinowitz, *Race Relations in the Urban South 1865–1890* (Urbana: University of Illinois Press, 1980); Elisabeth Hafkin Pleck, *Black Migration and Poverty: Boston 1865–1900* (New York: Academic Press, 1979).

69. Philpott, *Slum and Ghetto*, pp. 119, 168–169, 189.

70. Philpott, *Slum and Ghetto*, pp. 116–117, 159. A number of other studies also show the fundamental differences between the experiences of blacks and white immigrants. These include: Kusmer, *Ghetto Takes Shape*; Theodore Hershberg, *et al.*, "A Tale of Three Cities: Blacks, Immigrants, and Opportunity in Philadelphia, 1850–1880, 1930, 1970," in Theodore Hershberg, ed., *Philadelphia: Work, Space, Family, and Group Experience in the 19th Century* (New York: Oxford University Press, 1981); Stanley Lieberson, *A Piece of the Pie: Blacks and White Immigrants since 1880* (Berkeley: University of California Press, 1980); and Stephen Steinberg, *The Ethnic Myth: Race, Ethnicity, and Class in America* (Boston: Beacon Press, 1981).

71. Philpott, *Slum and Ghetto*, pp. 170, 204. For a social-psychological interpretation of the riot, see Richard Sennett, *Families Against the City: Middle Class Homes of Industrial Chicago, 1872–1890* (Cambridge: Harvard University Press, 1970).

72. Philpott, *Slum and Ghetto*, pp. 274–275, 341.

73. Philpott, *Slum and Ghetto*, p. 346.

Chapter 7 / Reorganizing the Labor Market

1. Donald Nelson, *Managers and Workers: Origins of the New Factory System in the United States* (Madison: University of Wisconsin Press, 1975), pp. 3–54; Alfred D. Chandler, *The Visible Hand: The Managerial Revolution in American Business* (Cambridge: Harvard University Press, 1977); James R. Green, *The World of the Worker: Labor in Twentieth-Century America* (New York: Hill and Wang, 1980), pp. 3–99. The generalizations above make no attempt to account for the great distinctions between different types of industries in their size, growth rates, technologies, and managerial practices. Nonetheless, they are a sort of least common denominator that can be made about big business in this period. Figures for numbers of workers and strikes are from Sidney L. Harring, *Policing a Class Society: The Experience of American Cities, 1865–1915* (New Brunswick, NJ: Rutgers University Press, 1983), p. 102.

2. Edward Berkowitz and Kim McQuaid, *Creating the Welfare State: The Political Economy of Twentieth-Century Reform* (New York: Praeger, 1980), p. xi; Daniel R. Fusfield, "Government and the Suppression of Radical Labor, 1877–1918," in Charles Bright and Susan Harding, *State-making and Social Movements: Essays in History and Theory* (Ann Arbor: University of Michigan Press, 1984), p. 366; Harring, *Policing*, pp. 101–148; Nelson, *Managers and Workers*, pp. 55–78; David F. Noble, *America by Design: Science, Technology and the Rise of Corporate Capital* (New York: Knopf, 1977); Stuart D. Brandes, *American Welfare Capitalism, 1880–1940* (Chicago: University of Chicago Press, 1976).

3. Harry Braverman, *Labor and Monopoly Capital*, p. 280; Don D. Lescohier, *The Labor Market* (New York: Macmillan, 1919), p. 88.

4. Paul Osterman, *Getting Started: The Youth Labor Market* (Cambridge: MIT Press, 1980), pp. 53–62. Stan Vittoz, "World War 1 and the Political Accommodation of Transitional Market Forces: The Case of Immigration Restriction," *Politics and Society* (8,1: 1978), pp. 51–53, 57, 64–65. On the history of immigration restriction, the standard work is John Higham, *Strangers in the Land*. For a theory about the relation of immigration to the labor market, see Michael Piore, *Birds of Passage: Migrant Labor and Industrial Societies* (New York: Cambridge University Press, 1979).

5. Quote is from Charles Davenport (1911), in Mark H. Haller, *Eugenics: Hereditarian Attitudes in American Thought* (New Brunswick, NJ: Rutgers University Press, 1963), pp. 3, 26. For his discussion of Galton and Pearson, see pp. 8–20. See also, Donald K. Pickens, *Eugenics and the Progressives* (Nashville, TN: Vanderbilt University Press, 1968), pp. 3–36. The most authoritative study of the eugenics movement in America and Great Britain is, Daniel Kevles, *In the Name of Eugenics: Genetics and the Uses of Human Heredity* (New York: Knopf, 1985).

6. Haller, *Eugenics*, pp. 27–28, 47, 59–62.

7. Holmes, quoted in Haller, *Eugenics*, p. 139, see also p. 135; Picken, *Eugenics*, pp. 86–101; Stephan Jay Gould, "Carrie Buck's Daughter," *Natural History* 93 (July 1984), 18; Kevles, *In the Name of Eugenics*, pp. 107–117, 167–169.

8. Haller, *Eugenics*, pp. 59, 96, 113.

9. State Board of Charities—Department of State and Alien Poor—The Bureau of Analysis and Investigation, *Eugenics and Social Welfare Bulletin* I (The Capitol, Albany, New York, 1911),

pp. 1–2; Cornel Reinhart and William W. Culver, "The Rear Guard of Capital: Welfare Policy and the 'Unfortunate' in New York State," *Rockefeller Institute Working Papers* #14 (Fall: 1984), p. 15.

10. Chester Lee Carlisle, "The Causes of Dependency Based on A Survey of Oneida County," State of New York, State Board of Charities, Division of Mental Defect and Delinquency, The Bureau of Analysis and Investigation, *Eugenics and Social Welfare Bulletin* XV (The Capitol, Albany, New York, 1918), pp. 441, 445, 462–463.

11. Berkowitz and McQuaid, *Creating the Welfare State*, p. xiii.

12. Lescohier, *The Labor Market*, p. 16. (italics in original)

13. Lescohier, *Labor Market*, p. 3.

14. Lescohier, *Labor Market*, pp. 63, 69, 93. (italics in original)

15. Nelson, *Managers and Workers*, pp. 91–95; Berkowitz and McQuaid, *Creating the Welfare State*, pp. 4–11; Stanley Buder, *Pullman: An Experiment in Industrial Order and Community Planning 1880–1930* (New York: Oxford University Press, 1967); Jane Addams, "Industrial Amelioration," in *Democracy and Social Ethics* (New York: Macmillan, 1907), pp. 137–177. On the Pullman strike as a turning point in American history, see Nick Salvatore, *Eugene Debs: Citizen and Socialist* (Urbana: University of Illniois Press, 1982), p. 174.

16. Brandes, *American Welfare Capitalism*, p. 23.

17. Brandes, *American Welfare Capitalism*, pp. 25–27, 32.

18. Nelson, *Managers and Workers*, pp. 148, 154.

19. David Brody, *Workers in Industrial America: Essays on the Twentieth Century Struggle* (New York: Oxford University Press, 1980), p. 54.

20. Nelson, *Managers and Workers*, pp. 117–118; Brody, *Workers*, pp. 59–60.

21. Brody, *Workers*, pp. 59, 61, 74; Brandes, *American Welfare Capitalism*, p. 138; Gerald Zahavi, "Negotiated Loyalty: Welfare Capitalism and the Shoeworkers of Endicott Johnson, 1920–1940," *Journal of American History* 71:3 (December 1983), pp. 602–620.

22. Loren Baritz, *The Servants of Power: A History of the Use of Social Science in American Industry* (New York: Wiley, 1965).

23. Trattner, *From Poor Law to Welfare State*, p. 214.

24. Lubove, *Struggle for Social Security*, pp. 30–33; Berkowitz and McQuaid, *Creating the Welfare State*, pp. 37–38; Gary M. Fink, *Labor's Search for Political Order: the Political Behavior of the Missouri Labor Movement 1880–1940* (Columbia, Mo.: University of Missouri Press, 1973), p. 49.

25. James Weinstein, "Big Business and the Origins of Workmen's Compensation," *Labor History* 8:2 (Spring 1967), p. 157; Carl Gersuny, *Work Hazards and Industrial Conflict* (Hanover, NH: University Press of New England, 1981), pp. 20, 28.

26. Weinstein, "Big Business and the Origins of Workmen's Compensation," pp. 157–158; Berkowitz and McQuaid, *Creating the Welfare State*, pp. 33–34; Roy Lubove, *The Struggle for Social Security 1900–1935* (Cambridge: Harvard University Press, 1968), pp. 49–50.

27. Lubove, *Struggle for Social Security*, pp. 50–51; Berkowitz and McQuaid, *Creating the Welfare State*, p. 34.

28. Lubove, *Struggle for Social Security*, pp. 51–52.

29. Lubove, *Struggle for Social Security*, p. 64.

30. Lubove, *Struggle for Social Security*, pp. 33–34; Weinstein, "Big Business and the Origins of Workmen's Compensation," pp. 166–167.

31. Fink, *Labor's Search for Political Order*, pp. 48–53, 83–93; Lubove, *Struggle for Social Security*, pp. 58, 206–207; Berkowitz and McQuaid, *Creating the Welfare State*, pp. 38–39; Weinstein, "Big Business and the Origins of Workmen's Compensation," pp. 168–174.

32. Berkowitz and McQuaid, *Creating the Welfare State*, pp. 40–41.

33. John A. Garraty, *Unemployment in History: Economic Thought and Public Policy* (New York: Harper and Row, 1978), pp. 12–30.

34. Lubove, *Struggle for Social Security*, pp. 166–167; Daniel Nelson, *Unemployment Insurance: The American Experience, 1915–1935* (Madison: University of Wisconsin Press, 1969), p. 10.

35. Lescohier, *Labor Market*, pp. 70–71, 106–107.

36. Lescohier, *Labor Market*, pp. 145, 164–165; Nelson, *Unemployment Insurance*, p. 72.

37. Nelson, *Unemployment Insurance*, pp. 47–55.

38. Nelson, *Unemployment Insurance*, pp. 22–23, 105–106, 120.

39. Rubinow and Epstein, quoted in Lubove, *Struggle for Social Security*, pp. 171–172; Ohio

Commission on Unemployment Insurance, *Report* (Columbus, Ohio, 1932).

40. Nelson, *Unemployment Insurance*, pp. 65–67, 72.

41. Nelson, *Unemployment Insurance*, pp. 69, 79, 103.

42. Nelson, *Unemployment Insurance*, pp. 161, 183, 189, 190.

43. Lubove, *Struggle for Social Security*, p. 125 (includes Rubinow quotations); A. Achenbaum, *Old Age in the New Land: The American Experience Since 1970* (Baltimore: Johns Hopkins University Press, 1978) p. 84. Ann Shola Orloff effectively applies a "state-centered" approach to the history of old-age insurance in America, England, and Canada in her dissertation, "The Politics of Pensions: A Comparative Analysis of the Origins of Pensions and Old Age Insurance In Canada, Britain, and the United States, 1880s–1930s," Ph.D. diss., Princeton University, 1985.

44. Ann Shola Orloff and Theda Skocpol, "Why Not Equal Protection? Explaining the Politics of Public Social Welfare in Britain and the United States, 1880s–1920s," paper presented at the annual meeting of the American Sociological Association, Detroit, Michigan, September 2, 1983, pp. 49–55.

45. For estimates of residential patterns of the elderly, see Steven Ruggles's important dissertation, "Prolonged Connections: Demographic Change and the Rise of the Extended Family in Nineteenth Century England and America," Ph.D. diss., University of Pennsylvania, 1984. Lubove, *Struggle for Social Security*, p. 133. On the situation of the elderly in the nineteenth century and attitudes toward the elderly, see Carol Haber, *Beyond Sixty-Five: The Dilemma of Old Age in America's Past* (New York: Cambridge University Press, 1983). For case histories of two old-age homes, see Brian Gratton, "Boston's Elderly, 1890–1950: Work, Family, and Dependency," Ph.D. diss., Boston University, 1980, pp. 158–240. Gratton also shows (pp. 252–253, 333, 457) that the institutionalized elderly in Boston had few, if any, family members to whom they could turn for help.

46. Figures for the proportion of elderly in the population are taken from, Achenbaum, *Old Age*, pp. 60, 91. See also pp. 82–83 for figures on private homes.

47. This neat convergence of social ideology and industrial policy began to split in the 1920s. The celebration of youth, mounting unemployment, and, then, the depression all reinforced hostility to the aged. However, some newly minted personnel specialists and their employers began to appreciate the "stability and conservatism" of older workers. "Having succeeded before 1920 in creating a less tradition-bound industrial working class," reports Graebner, "post-1920 employers often experienced the most difficulty with younger workers. William Graebner, *A History of Retirement: The Meaning and Function of an American Institution, 1885–1978* (New Haven: Yale University Press, 1980), p. 19. Rubinow quoted in Achenbaum, *Old Age*, p. 48.

48. Graebner, *History of Retirement*, p. 27.

49. Graebner, *History of Retirement*, pp. 132–135, 149.

50. Graebner, *History of Retirement*, pp. 91–93; Lubove, *Struggle for Social Security*, p. 126; Gratton, "Boston's Elderly," pp. 248–249, points to an increased proportion of male old-age residents who had received some sort of relief after 1910.

51. Lubove, *Struggle for Social Security*, pp. 139–140; Orloff, "Politics of Pensions," p. 265.

52. Graebner, *History of Retirement*, pp. 57, 71, 87.

53. Graebner, *History of Retirement*, p. 149; Gratton, "Boston's Elderly," p. 111, Table III-1.

54. Lubove, *Struggle for Social Security*, pp. 136–137, 142.

55. On the deliberate policy of not using social security to redistribute income, see Jerry R. Cates, *Insuring Inequality: Administrative Leadership in Social Security, 1935–1954* (Ann Arbor: University of Michigan Press, 1983).

Chapter 8 / Reorganizing the Nation

1. Studs Terkel, *Hard Times: An Oral History of the Great Depression* (New York: Pantheon, 1970), pp. 63–64; Richard Lowitt and Maurine Beasley, eds., *One Third of a Nation: Lorena Hickok Reports on the Great Depression* (Urbana: University of Illinois Press, 1983), pp. 56–57.

2. Robert S. McElvaine, *The Great Depression* (New York: Times Books, 1984), p. 75; [U.S.] President's Research Committee on Social Trends, *Recent Social Trends in the United States*, 2 vols. (New York: McGraw-Hill, 1933); Guy Alchon, *The Invisible Hand of Planning: Capitalism,*

Social Science, and the State in the 1920s (Princeton: Princeton University Press, 1983), pp. 145–149. Irving Bernstein, *A Caring Society: The New Deal, the Worker, and the Great Depression* (Boston: Houghton Mifflin, 1985), which appeared after this book was written, is an excellent source for social and economic conditions in the early 1930s.

3. Sydnor H. Walker, "Privately Supported Social Work," *Recent Social Trends* v. 2, pp. 1198, 1199; Howard W. Odum, "Public Welfare Activities," *Recent Social Trends* v. 2, pp. 1224–1273.

4. Walker, "Privately Supported Social Work," pp. 1168–1223.

5. Walker, "Privately Supported Social Work," pp. 1196; Josephine Chapin Brown, *Public Relief 1929–1939* (New York: Henry Holt and Co., 1940), p. ix.

6. E. Wight Bakke, *The Unemployed Worker: A Study of the Task of Making a Living Without a Job* (New Haven: Yale University Press, 1940), pp. 26–29. On the strains of unemployment on family life, aside from Bakke, see Mirra Komarovsky, *The Unemployed Man and His Family* (New York: Dryden Press for Institute of Social Research, 1940) and Glen H. Elder, Jr., *Children of The Great Depression: Social Change in Life Experience* (Chicago: University of Chicago Press, 1974).

7. Bakke, *Unemployed Worker*, pp. 363–364, 342.

8. James T. Patterson, *America's Struggle Against Poverty, 1900–1980* (Cambridge: Harvard University Press, 1981), p. 42.

9. Gladys L. Palmer and Katherine D. Wood, *Urban Workers on Relief*, Part I (Works Progress Administrations, Research Monograph IV: Washington, D.C., 1936), pp. xxiii–xiv, 9, 12, 32; William W. Bremer, *Depression Winters: New York Social Workers and the New Deal* (Philadelphia: Temple University Press, 1984), pp. 66–67 (includes Wald quote); Hopkins quoted in Bonnie Fox Schwartz, *The Civil Works Administration; The Business of Emergency Employment in the New Deal* (Princeton: Princeton University Press, 1984), pp. 34–35.

10. Bakke, *Unemployed Worker*, pp. 114–115; Sydnor, "Privately Supported Social Work," p. 1183. On consumption and prosperity among working-class families in the 1920s see, Robert S. Lynd, "The People as Consumers," *Recent Social Trends*, pp. 857–911 and David Brody, *Workers in Industrial America: Essays on the 20th Century Struggle* (New York: Oxford University Press, 1980), p. 63.

11. Francis Fox Piven and Richard A. Cloward, *Poor People's Movements: Why They Succeed, How They Fail* (New York: Pantheon, 1977), pp. 61–63.

12. Judith Ann Trolander, *Settlement Houses and the Great Depression* (Detroit: Wayne State University Press, 1975), pp. 9–10, 31.

13. James T. Patterson, *The New Deal and the States: Federalism in Transition* (Princeton: Princeton University Press, 1969), pp. 26, 34–36; Piven and Cloward, *Poor People's Movements*, pp. 63–64; Martha Derthick, *The Influence of Federal Grants: Public Assistance in Massachusetts* (Cambridge: Harvard University Press, 1970), p. 26; Harold P. Levy, *A Study in Public Relations: Case History of the Relations Maintained Between a Department of Public Assistance and the People of a State* (New York: Russell Sage Foundation, 1943), pp. 16–18; Brown, *Public Relief*, pp. 14–15. James Leiby, *Charities and Corrections in New Jersey: A History of State Welfare Institutions* (New Brunswick: Rutgers University Press, 1967), p. 275; Lewis Merriam, *Relief and Social Security* (Washington, D.C.: Brookings Institution, 1946), pp. 10–11.

14. David M. Schneider and Albert Deutsch, *The History of Public Welfare in New York State 1867–1940* (Chicago: University of Chicago Press, 1941), pp. 307–414; Bremer, *Depression Winters*, pp. 65, 69; Brown, *Public Relief*, pp. 103–138. On Hopkins background, see Robert E. Sherwood, *Roosevelt and Hopkins: An Intimate History* (New York: Harpers, 1948), pp. 14–37.

15. Bremer, *Depression Winters*, pp. 85–86, 89–90; Patterson, *New Deal*, pp. 27–32; Hoover quoted in Searle F. Charles, *Minister of Relief: Harry Hopkins and the Depression* (Syracuse, NY: Syracuse University Press, 1963), pp. 9–10.

16. Brown, *Public Relief*, pp. 103–138; Bremer, *Depression Winters*, pp. 94–95.

17. Francis Fox Piven and Richard A. Cloward, *Poor People's Movements*, p. 41; Irving Bernstein, *The Lean Years: A History of the American Worker, 1920–1933* (Boston: Houghton Mifflin, 1960), pp. 422–423; Robert S. McElvaine, *The Great Depression: America 1929–1941* (New York: Times Books, 1984), pp. 90–91; Terkel, *Hard Times*, pp. 31–32.

18. The legislative accomplishments of the first hundred days included the National Recovery Administration, which tried to create codes for industries and sanctioned labor's right to organize; the Agricultural Adjustment Act, which, for the first time, subsidized farmers for not growing crops and taking land out of production; a farm credit act that consolidated farm loan agencies and ultimately refinanced all outstanding farm mortgages; the repeal of the gold standard; the creation of the Civilian Conservation Corps for unemployed young men; the Home Owners Loan Act,

which created the corporation that eventually financed the debts on one of every five private homes; the Tennessee Valley Authority; the Federal Deposit Insurance Corporation; and the Federal Emergency Relief Administration, with which the national government itself dispensed relief for the first time. William E. Leuchtenberg, *Franklin D. Roosevelt and the New Deal* (New York: Harper & Row, 1963), pp. 4–11; McElvaine, *Great Depression*, p. 113; Charles McKinley and Robert W. Frase, *Launching Social Security: A Capture-and-Record Account, 1935–1937* (Madison: University of Wisconsin Press, 1970), pp. 5–6.

19. Merriam, *Relief and Social Security*, pp. 19–21; Martha Derthick, *The Influence of Federal Grants: Public Assistance in Massachusetts* (Cambridge: Harvard University Press, 1970), pp. 4–5, 50, 68.

20. Patterson, *America's Struggle*, pp. 68, 71; Patterson, *The New Deal*, pp. 136, 138; Theron F. Schlabach, *Edwin E. Witte: Cautious Reformer* (Madison: State Historical Society of Wisconsin, 1969), pp. 115, 149–150.

21. Abe Bortz, *Social Security Sources in Federal Records 1934–1950*, U.S. Department of Health, Education, and Welfare, Social Security Administration, Office of Research and Statistics, Research Report No. 30 (Washington: GPO, 1969).

22. Theda Skocpol, "Political Response to Capitalist Crisis: Neo-Marxist Theories of the State and the Case of the New Deal," *Politics and Society*, 10:2 (1980), pp. 174–177. For an account of the growth of the federal government in the late nineteenth and early twentieth century, see Stephen Skowronek, *Building a New American State: The Expansion of National Administrative Capacities* (New York: Cambridge University Press, 1982).

23. Brown, *Public Relief*, pp. 146, 148, 173, 191, 201, 220, 236. A few years later, the implementation of the Social Security Act also was a massive administrative problem. The government had to create 400 field offices around the country to supplement a system of twelve regional offices. The new structure had to be put in place quickly in order to register all the eligible people. This meant assigning social security numbers to employers and employees, a task delegated at first to the Post Office Department; Bortz, *Social Security Sources*, p. 7; Harry L. Hopkins, *Spending to Save: The Complete Story of Relief* (New York: Norton, 1936), pp. 115–117; Sherwood, *Roosevelt and Hopkins*, pp. 52–53.

24. Brown, *Public Relief*, pp. 234, 242–243, 246; Hopkins, *Spending to Save*, pp. 99–107.

25. Lowitt and Beasley, eds., *One Third of a Nation*, pp. 47–48.

26. Brown, *Public Relief*, pp. 182–183, 196, 216.

27. Brown, *Public Relief*, p. 204; Derthick, *The Influence of Federal Grants*, p. 70.

28. Derthick, *The Influence of Federal Grants*, pp. 69, 242.

29. Brown, *Public Relief*, p. 199.

30. Susan Ware, *Beyond Suffrage: Women in the New Deal* (Cambridge: Harvard University Press, 1981), pp. 6–7, 87, 99, 101, 102, 130–131.

31. In 1935, delegates from most of the larger organizations of the unemployed held a conference in Washington, where they formed the Workers Alliance of America. Their new focus on organization, argue Piven and Cloward, deflected attention away from protest. Indeed, at the very time leaders concentrated on building a national organization, "local groups across the country were declining," primarily because the federal government had liberalized relief machinery and "absorbed local leaders in bureaucratic roles. And once the movement weakened, and the instability of which it was one expression subsided, relief was cut back." Piven and Cloward, *Poor People's Movements*, pp. 49–53, 61–77; Lowitt and Beasley, *One Third of a Nation*, p. 12; M. Naison, *Communists in Harlem During the Depression* (Urbana: University of Illinois Press, 1983), pp. 68–69, 76–79; Roy Rosenzweig, "Radicals and the Jobless: The Musteites and the Unemployed Leagues, 1932–1936," *Labor History* 16:1 (Winter 1975), pp. 52–77, " 'Socialism in Our Time': The Socialist Party and the Unemployed, 1929–1936," *Labor History* 20:4 (Fall 1979), pp. 485–509, "Organizing the Unemployed: The Early Years of the Great Depression, 1929–1933," in James Green, ed., *Workers' Struggles, Past and Present* (Philadelphia: Temple University Press, 1983), pp. 168–169; Merriam, *Relief and Social Security*, p. 11; Schneider and Deutsch, *The History of Public Welfare*, pp. 334–336; Jacob Fisher, *The Response of Social Work to the Depression* (Cambridge: Schenkman, 1980), pp. 11–12; Brown, *Public Relief*, pp. 134, 139, 263, 265; Charles, *Minister of Relief*, p. 248.

32. Rosenzweig, "Organizing the Unemployed," pp. 181–182; Naison, *Communists in Harlem*, pp. 37, 76–78. For a more skeptical view of the achievements of unemployed workers, see Patterson, *America's Struggle Against Poverty*, pp. 49–53. Bakke also stresses the lack of political interest among the unemployed he interviewed, although he stresses the potential for revolutionary protest among them. E. Wight Bakke, *Citizens Without Work: A Study of the Effect of Unemployment*

upon the Workers' Social Relations and Practices (New Haven: Yale University Press, 1940), pp. 75–81.

33. Bakke, *Unemployed Worker*, pp. 387–388.

34. Merriam, *Relief and Social Security*, pp. 352–393; Ware, *Beyond Suffrage*, pp. 111–114; Merriam, *Relief and Social Security*, pp. 345–359; David Tyack, Robert Lowe, and Elisabeth Hansot, *Public Schools in Hard Times* (Cambridge: Harvard University Press, 1984), pp. 104–105, 108–109.

35. Merriam, *Relief and Social Security*, pp. 349–350; Bonnie Fox Schwartz, *The Civil Works Administration: The Business of Emergency Employment in the New Deal* (Princeton: Princeton University Press, 1984), pp. 22, 37.

36. Schwartz, *Civil Works Administration*, pp. vii–ix; Brown, *Public Relief*, pp. 160–161, 254–262.

37. Schwartz, *Civil Works Administration*, pp. vii–ix, 28–29, 194–196, 214; Sherwood, *Roosevelt and Hopkins*, p. 56.

38. Schwartz, *Civil Works Administration*, pp. 227–228.

39. Brown, *Public Relief*, pp. 165–166, 301.

40. Brown, *Public Relief*, pp. 304–305; Donald S. Howard, *The WPA and Federal Relief Policy* (New York: Russell Sage Foundation, 1943), p. 96. Even before the New Deal, the massive increase in unemployment relief had given new importance and standing to public relief officials, who formed the American Association of Public Welfare Officials in 1930 (which became the American Public Welfare Association 2 years later). Fisher, *Response of Social Work*, pp. 66–67; 235; John Earl Haynes, "The 'Rank and File Movement' in Private Social Work," *Labor History* 16:1 (Winter 1975), pp. 78–98.

41. Charles, *Minister of Relief*, p. 225; Leiby, *Charity and Corrections*, pp. 280–287; Brown, *Public Relief*, p. 317; Fisher, *The Response of Social Work*, p. 62; Howard, *The WPA*, pp. 92–93 (italics in original).

42. Schwartz, *The Civil Works Administration*, pp. 254–256. The most complete history of the WPA is, Howard, *WPA*.

43. Merriam, *Relief and Social Security*, pp. 352–393; Charles, *Minister of Relief*, pp. 231–232; Piven and Cloward, *Regulating the Poor: The Functions of Public Welfare* (New York: Pantheon, 1971), pp. 434–440.

44. Fisher, *The Response of Social Work*, p. 150.

45. Piven and Cloward, *Regulating the Poor*, p. 113.

46. Charles, *Minister of Relief*, p. 235; Patterson, *America's Struggle*, p. 66; Bakke, *Unemployed Worker*, p. 324.

47. Lane and Steegmuller, *America on Relief*, p. 27; Charles, *Minister of Relief*, pp. 229–230.

48. Patterson, *America's Struggle*, p. 64.

49. Bakke, *Unemployed Worker*, p. 402.

50. Bakke, *Unemployed Worker*, p. 424.

51. Brown, *Public Relief*, pp. 237–239; Lane and Steegmuller, *America on Relief*, pp. 29–32; Charles, *Minister of Relief*, pp. 151–152.

52. Lane and Steegmuller, *America on Relief*, pp. 72–78, 146–152; Ken Auletta, *The Underclass* (New York: Random House, 1982), passim.

53. Merriam, *Relief and Social Security*, pp. 16, 423–424; Patterson, *America's Struggle*, p. 64.

54. Lane and Steegmuller, *America on Relief*, p. 155; Merriam, *Relief and Social Security*, pp. 412–427; Bakke, *Citizens without Work*, pp. 260–261.

55. FDR did not use the term "social security" when he appointed the Committe on Economic Security in 1934. The term came into use when it was introduced by several witnesses during congressional hearings on the bill. Arthur Altmeyer, assistant secretary of labor and first chairman of the Social Security Board, defined social security as "a specific governmental program designed to promote the economic and social well-being of individual workers and their families through providing protection against specific hazards which would otherwise cause widespread destitution and misery." Arthur J. Altmeyer, *The Formative Years of Social Security* (Madison: University of Wisconsin Press, 1968), pp. 3–6.

56. McElvaine, *The Great Depression*, pp. 225–229, 233–236, 250.

57, McElvaine, *Great Depression*, pp. 237–248; Patterson, *America's Struggle*, pp. 70–72; Frances Perkins, "Forward," in Witte, *Development of the Social Security Act*, p. vi; Schlabach, *Witte*, pp. 135–136; Witte quote in McKinley and Frase, *Launching Social Security*, p. 11; Derthick,

Influence of Federal Grants, pp. 47, 56; Merriam, *Relief and Social Security*, pp. 24–25.

58. McElvaine, *Great Depression*, pp. 250, 255–261; Leuchtenberg, *Franklin D. Roosevelt*, pp. 117, 157, 165–166.

59. Altmeyer, *Formative Years*, pp. ix–x, 4.

60. Witte, *Development of the Social Security Act*, pp. 6–7; Jerry R. Cates, *Insuring Inequality: Administrative Leadership in Social Security, 1935–1954* (Ann Arbor: University of Michigan Press, 1983), pp. 13–17.

61. Witte, *Development of the Social Security Act*, pp. 148–150; Lela B. Costin, *Two Sisters for Social Justice: A Biography of Grace and Edith Abbott* (Urbana: University of Illinois Press, 1983), pp. 221–224; Ware, *Beyond Suffrage*, p. 99.

62. Schlabach, *Witte*, p. 104; Witte, *Development of the Social Security Act*, p. 21; Jill S. Quadagno, "Welfare Capitalism and the Social Security Act of 1935," *American Sociological Review*, 49 (October 1984), p. 640; William Graebner, *A History of Retirement: The Meaning and Function of an American Institution, 1885–1978* (New Haven: Yale University Press, 1986), p. 190.

63. Patterson, *America's Struggle*, p. 76; Burns, *American Social Security System*, p. 31; Jack R. Parsons, "Origins of the Income and Resources Amendment to the Social Security Act," *Social Services Review* 36 (March 1962), pp. 51–61; Cates, *Insuring Inequality*, pp. 78, 108, 139.

64. Patterson, *America's Struggle*, p. 76; Cates, *Insuring Inequality*, pp. 5–10; Greg J. Duncan, *Years of Poverty Years of Plenty: The Changing Fortunes of American Workers and Families* (Ann Arbor: Institute for Social Research, University of Michigan), pp. 103–105.

65. Schlabach, *Witte*, pp. 114–120.

66. Merriam, *Relief and Social Security*, pp. 91–92; Witte, *Development of the Social Security Act*, pp. 143–144.

67. Schlabach, *Witte*, pp. 143–145.

68. Fisher, *The Response of Social Work*, p. 64; Witte, *Development of the Social Security Act*, p. 86; Starr, *Social Transformation*, pp. 266–279.

69. "Statement of Miss Mary Van Kleeck," *Hearings before a Subcommittee of the Committee on Labor House of Representatives Seventy-Fourth Congress First Session on H.R. 22927, H.R. 2859, H.R. 185, H.R. 10* (Washington: Government Printing Office, 1935), pp. 83–101; "Statement of Miss Mary Van Kleeck," *Hearings before the Committee on Education and Labor United States Senate Seventy-fourth Congress Second Session on S. 3475* (Washington: Government Printing Office, 1936), pp. 159–164. On Van Kleeck, see Alchon, *Invisible Hand*, pp. 167–169; on the Lundeen bill see, Quadagno, "Welfare Capitalism," pp. 638–639.

70. "Statement of Miss Mary Van Kleeck," *Hearings before the Committe on Ways and Means House of Representatives Seventy-Fourth Congress First Session on H.R. 4120* (Washington: Government Printing Office, 1935), pp. 925–927.

71. Merriam, *Relief and Social Security*, pp. 88, 464–465, 516–519, 552, 841, 869.

72. Merriam, *Relief and Social Security*, p. 869; Burns, *American Social Security System*, pp. 402–403.

73. On labor and unionism in the twenties see, James Green, *The World of the Worker: Labor in the Twentieth Century* (New York: Hill and Wang, 1980), pp. 100–129, 150; Foster Rhea Dulles and Melvyn Dubofsky, *Labor in America: A History*, fourth edition (Arlington Heights, IL: Harlan Davidson, 1984), pp. 257–264.

74. Green, *World of the Worker*, pp. 151, 157, 158, 161, 167, 173; Dulles and Dubofsky, *Labor in America*, p. 288.

75. Paul Starr, *The Social Transformation of American Medicine* (New York: Basic Books, 1982), p. 311.

76. Green, *World of the Worker*, pp. 148–150; Jacqueline Jones, *Labor of Love, Labor of Sorrow: Black Women, Work, and the Family from Slavery to the Present* (New York: Basic Books, 1985), pp. 196–213; Weiss, *Farewell*, pp. 45–46, 96–119.

77. Weiss, *Farewell*, pp. 120–135, 166–167, 173, 211; Kenneth T. Jackson, "Race, Ethnicity, and Real Estate Appraisal: The Owners Loan Corporation and the Federal Housing Administration," *Journal of Urban History* 6 (August, 1980), pp. 419–452; Mark I. Gelfand, *A Nation of Cities: The Federal Government and Urban America, 1933–1965* (New York: Oxford University Press, 1975), p. 123.

78. Weiss, *Farewell*, pp. 209–211.

79. Weiss, *Farewell*, pp. 206–208, 212, 294.

80. National Resources Planning Board, *Security, Work, and Relief Policies* (Washington: Government Printing Office, 1942), pp. 7–8, 291.

81. Schneider and Deutsch, *History of Public Welfare in New York*, pp. 355–356; National Resources Planning Board, *Security, Work, and Relief*, p. 292; Brown, *Public Relief*, pp. 320–321, 351–352; Derthick, *Influence of Federal Grants*, passim; Merriam, *Relief and Social Security*, p. 183.

82. Burns, *American Social Security System*, pp. vi, 398–399.

Chapter 9 / The War on Poverty and the Expansion of Social Welfare

1. In this discussion, the term *war on poverty* frequently is used for convenience to cover the general expansion of social welfare programs between the early 1960s and the mid-1970s; it is not confined only to those programs administered by the Office of Economic Opportunity. Strictly speaking, war on poverty is a mistaken term for the largest social welfare programs, which offered cash transfers as a form of relief, and, unlike the OEO programs, did not try to attack the causes of poverty. Also, the discussion that follows generally omits antipoverty programs specifically directed toward rural areas. On the relation of the Kennedy administration to business, see Allen J. Matusow, *The Unraveling of America: A History of Liberalism in the 1960s* (New York: Harper and Row, 1984), pp. 30–59; on the reliance on growth to resolve potential contradictions between business and social justice, see Alan Wolfe, *America's Impasse: The Rise and Fall of the Politics of Growth* (Boston: South End Press, 1981), pp. 10–12 and Sar A. Levitan and Robert Taggart, *The Promise of Greatness* (Cambridge: Harvard University Press, 1976), p. 29. Robert D. Plotnick and Felicity Skidmore, *Progress Against Poverty: A Review of the 1964–1974 Decade* (New York: Academic Press, 1975), p. 12, points out that the war on poverty's planners did not give much thought to cash transfers.

2. Matusow, *Unraveling of America*, p. 62.

3. Harrell R. Rodgers, Jr., *The Cost of Human Neglect* (Armonk, New York and London: M. E. Sharpe, Inc., 1982), pp. 52–53; Matusow, *Unraveling America*, pp. 88, 139, 196–197; Frances Fox Piven and Richard A. Cloward, *Regulating the Poor: The Functions of Public Welfare* (New York: Pantheon, 1971), p. 232–234 and *Poor People's Movements: Why They Succeed and How They Fail* (New York: Pantheon, 1977), pp. 181–263; Harry Boyte, *The Backyard Revolution: Understanding the New Citizen Movement* (Philadelphia: Temple University Press, 1980) is the source of the phrase "new citizen movement"; Nick Kotz, "Discussion," in Robert H. Haveman, ed., *A Decade of Federal Antipoverty Programs: Achievements, Failures, and Lessons* (New York: Academic Press, 1977), pp. 48–51, convincingly links the federal antipoverty programs and civil rights.

4. Winifred Bell, *Aid to Dependent Children* (New York: Columbia University Press, 1965), p. 57 (Quotes from Louisiana and Faubus, pp. 57 and 68).

5. Guida West, *The National Welfare Rights Movement: The Social Protest of Poor Women* (New York: Praeger, 1981), pp. 6, 366–368. See also, Larry R. Jackson and William A. Johnson, *Protest by the Poor: The Welfare Rights Movement in New York City* (Lexington, MA: D. G. Heath, 1974) and Piven and Cloward, *Poor People's Movements*, pp. 264–361.

6. Henry J. Perkinson, *The Imperfect Panacea: American Faith in Education, 1865–1965* (New York: Random House, 1968); Michael B. Katz, *The Irony of Early School Reform: Educational Innovation in Mid-Nineteenth Century Massachusetts* (Cambridge: Harvard University Press, 1968); Joseph A. Kershaw, *Government Against Poverty* (Washington: Brookings Institution, 1970), p. 24; James T. Patterson, *America's Struggle Against Poverty* (Cambridge: Harvard University Press, 1981), pp. 135–136; Matusow, *Unraveling America*, p. 126.

7. Richard A. Cloward and Lloyd E. Ohlin, *Delinquency and Opportunity* (New York: The Free Press, 1960); James L. Sundquist, "Origins of the War on Poverty," in Sundquist, ed., *On Fighting Poverty: Perspectives from Experience* (New York: Basic Books, 1969), pp. 8–12; Peter Marris and Martin Rein, *Dilemmas of Social Reform: Poverty and Community Action in the United States* (London: Routledge and Kegan Paul, 1967), pp. 19–20; Matusow, *Unraveling of America*, pp. 107–110.

8. For a good example of writing about cultural deprivation, see Frank Riessman, *The Culturally Deprived Child* (New York: Harper, 1962); on the Sambo image, see Stanley M. Elkins, *Slavery: a Problem in American Institutional and Intellectual Life*, 2nd edition (Chicago: University of Chicago Press, 1968); for an example of the image of Irish immigrants as cultureless, see Oscar Handlin, *Boston's Immigrants, 1790–1865: a Study in Acculturation*, rev. and enlarged edition

(Cambridge: Harvard University Press, 1959); on the need to transform the culture of developing countries, see David C. McClelland, *The Achieving Society* (Princeton, NJ: D. Van Norstrand, 1961). Gilbert Steiner has commented, "Probably no beneficiaries of a public subsidy have less real influence on the terms and conditions of that subsidy than do the recipients of public assistance. . . . Only in public assistance does it seem to be taken for granted that the interests of the group most directly and particularly affected, the recipients, will be indirectly protected in the course of the public policy struggle by some caretaker." Gilbert Y. Steiner, *Social Insecurity: The Politics of Welfare* (Chicago: Rand McNally, 1966), pp. 153–154.

9. On urban renewal and the Grey Areas project, see Scott Greer, *Urban Renewal and American Cities: The Dilemma of Democratic Institutions* (Indianapolis: Bobbs-Merrill, 1965); Jane Jacobs, *The Death and Life of Great American Cities* (New York: Random House, 1961); Marris and Rein, *Dilemmas of Social Reform*, pp. 13–14; Sundquist, *On Fighting Poverty*, pp. 13–14. See Herbert J. Gans, *The Levittowners: Ways of Life and Politics in a New Suburban Community* (New York: Random House, 1967; second edition, New York: Columbia University Press, 1982) for evidence that the lure of homeownership rather than a flight from race and urban problems fueled the great postwar exodus to suburbs. For an excellent case study of the creation of a ghetto after World War II, see Arnold A. Hirsch, *Making the Second Ghetto: Race and Housing in Chicago, 1940–1960* (New York: Cambridge University Press, 1983).

10. Patterson, *America's Struggle*, pp. 9–10, 131–133; Sundquist, "Origins," pp. 16–19; Steiner, *Social Insecurity*, p. 30; Kirsten A. Gronbjerg, *Mass Society and the Extension of Welfare 1960–1970* (Chicago: University of Chicago Press, 1977), pp. 13–15; Joel Spring, *The Sorting Machine: National Educational Policy since 1945* (New York: David McKay, 1976).

11. Sundquist, "Origins," p. 9; Plotnick and Skidmore, *Progress Against Poverty*, p. 66.

12. Plotnick and Skidmore, *Progress Against Poverty*, p. 73; James T. Patterson, *America's Struggle*, p. 164.

13. Henry Levin, "A Decade of Policy Developments in Improving Education and Training for Low-Income Populations," in Haveman, ed., *A Decade*, pp. 123–188 makes a compelling case that the manpower and most of the education programs failed. For a particularly chilling description of an urban high school, see Sara Solovich, "What Makes a School Go Bad?" *Philadelphia Inquirer Magazine*, June 16, 1985, pp. 10–12, 25–31.

14. Michael Harrington, *The New American Poverty* (New York: Holt, Rinehart and Winston, 1984), pp. 21–22.

15. Matusow, *Unraveling of America*, pp. 211–213; Phyllis A. Wallace, "A Decade of Policy Developments in Equal Opportunities in Employment and Housing," in Haveman, ed., *A Decade*, pp. 329–359; Department of Commerce and Economic Statistics Administration, Bureau of Census, *The Social and Economic Status of the Black Population in the United States, 1974*, Current Population Reports, Special Studies, Series P-23, No. 54, July 1975, pp. 30, 37; U.S. Commission on Civil Rights, *Social Indicators of Equality for Minorities and Women: A Report* (Washington: GPO, 1978), pp. 14, 18, 20.

16. Marris and Rein, *Dilemmas*, passim; Sanford Kravitz, "The Community Action Program," in Sundquist, ed., *On Fighting Poverty*, pp. 52–69; Levitan and Taggart, *Promise of Greatness*, pp. 169–187; Daniel P. Moynihan, *Maximum Feasible Misunderstanding: Community Action in the War Against Poverty* (New York: Free Press, 1969), passim.

17. Marris and Rein, *Dilemmas*, pp. 227–228.

18. Marris and Rein, *Dilemmas*, pp. 228–230. On the belief in consensus, see Rothman, *Conscience and Convenience: The Asylum and its Alternatives in Progressive America* (Boston: Little Brown, 1980), pp. 5–10. On the development of objectivity as ideology in social science, see Mary Furner, *From Advocacy to Objectivity: A Crisis in the Professionalization of American Social Science, 1865–1901* (Lexington, KY: University of Kentucky Press, 1975). On the role of social scientist as advocate, see Charles E. Lindblom and David K. Cohen, *Usable Knowledge: Social Science and Social Problem Solving* (New Haven: Yale University Press, 1979).

19. Marris and Rein, *Dilemmas of Social Reform*, pp. 221–223; Boyte, *Backyard Revolution*; Paul E. Peterson and J. David Greenstone, "Racial Change and Citizen Participation: The Mobilization of Low-Income Communities through Community Action," in Haveman, *A Decade*, p. 263.

20. Neil Gilbert, "The Transformation of Social Services," *Social Services Review* (December 1977), pp. 624–641.

21. Richard S. Morris, *Bum Rap on America's Cities: The Real Causes of Urban Decay* (Englewood-Cliffs, NJ: Prentice-Hall, 1980), pp. 18, 30.

22. Ralph M. Kramer, *Voluntary Agencies in the Welfare State* (Berkeley: University of California Press, 1981), pp. 57–76.

23. The major new services were:

Social work. The Public Welfare Amendment (1962) increased funds for community work and professional social work training and changed the Bureau of Public Assistance into the Bureau of Family Services.

Legal services. The OEO "instituted 250 legal services projects, which were directed by OEO guidelines to ensure community involvement . . . and to consider law reform as well as legal services as a major goal."

Medical care. The Johnson administration began several important health programs: nurses training; increased aid to mental retardation facilities and medical schools; scholarships for medical students and paraprofessionals; expanded birth control programs and new treatment centers for drug addicts and alcoholics; and Maternal and Child Health Programs as well as Neighborhood Health Centers. Most important, however, were Medicare for the elderly and Medicaid for those on welfare and "other medical indigents," both passed by Congress in 1966 as additions to the Social Security Act. Both programs grew quickly: in 1970, Medicare cost $7.5 billion and Medicaid, $3 billion. Plotnick and Skidmore, *Progress Against Poverty*, pp. 16–19; Matusow, *Unraveling of America*, p. 267; Levitan and Taggart, *Promise of Greatness*, p. 15.

24. Ellen Jane Hollingsworth, "Ten Years of Legal Services for the Poor," and Karen Davis, "A Decade of Policy Developments in Providing Health Care for Low-Income Families," in Haveman, ed., *A Decade*, pp. 285–314, 197–231.

25. Christopher Jencks, "How Poor are the Poor," *New York Review of Books*, xxxii:8 (May 5, 1985), p. 42; John E. Schwarz, *America's Hidden Success: A Reassessment of Twenty Years of Public Policy* (New York: Norton, 1983), pp. 47–48.

26. Paul Starr, *The Transformation of American Medicine* (New York: Basic Books, 1982), p. 370; Matusow, *Unraveling of America*, pp. 228–232; Morris, *Bum Rap*, pp. 33–50.

27. Laurence E. Lynn, Jr., "A Decade of Policy Developments in the Income-Maintenance System," in Haveman, ed., *A Decade*, p. 88; Frances Fox Piven and Richard A. Cloward, *The New Class War: Reagan's Attack on the Welfare State and its Consequences* (New York: Pantheon, 1982), p. 15.

28. Matusow, *Unraveling of America*, pp. 232–233, 236–237; Levitan and Taggart, *Progress Against Poverty*, p. 17; Schwarz, *America's Hidden Successes*, pp. 48–50.

29. Plotnick and Skidmore, *Progress Against Poverty*, pp. 52, 56; Levitan and Taggart, *Promise of Greatness*, pp. 35–36; Patterson, *America's Struggle Against Poverty*, p. 168 (includes Nathan quote).

30. Schwarz, *America's Hidden Successes*, p. 45, includes quote; Physician Task Force on Hunger in America, *Hunger in America: The Growing Epidemic* (Boston: Harvard University School of Public Health, 1985), p. 1.

31. Patterson, *America's Struggle*, p. 171.

32. Plotnick and Skidmore, *Progress Against Poverty*, p. 58; Patterson, *America's Struggle Against Poverty*, pp. 177–181; Piven and Cloward, *Regulating the Poor*, pp. 185–189. There has been a spirited debate about the role of protest and militance in expanding welfare benefits. Piven and Cloward started the argument in *Regulating the Poor* and made a forceful statement of their case on both theoretical and empirical grounds in *Poor People's Movements*, where they contend that most extensions of government assistance to the poor have resulted from the militant protest of poor people themselves. The first social scientists to construct quantitative tests of their arguments claimed that the evidence did not support Piven and Cloward's thesis. (See, Robert B. Albritton, "Social amelioration through mass insurgency? A reexamination of the Piven and Cloward thesis," *American Political Science Review* 73:1003–1011 and Eugene Durman, "Have the poor been regulated? Toward a multivariate understanding of welfare growth," *Social Service Review* 47:339–59.) Subsequent quantitative studies, however, have challenged these conclusions with evidence that supports the importance of protest. (See, for example, Larry Isaac and William R. Kelly, "Racial insurgency, the state, and welfare expansion: local and national level evidence from the postwar United States," *American Journal of Sociology* 86:1348–86, and Sanford F. Schram and J. Patrick Turbett, "Civil disorder and the welfare explosion: a two-step process," *American Sociological Review* 48:408–414.) All of these quantitative studies seem to me shot through with weaknesses. For one thing, the debate does not distinguish between the extension of welfare by the federal

320

government and the liberalization of procedures by local welfare bureaucrats who retain considerable discretionary authority. Different dynamics, certainly, must apply in each case. Even more, statistical correlations between riots and welfare in individual cities are weak evidence, especially in the age of instant news. For they do not measure the anticipatory reactions of other cities. Who can tell, even with multivariate analysis, the impact of a riot in Newark on, say, San Jose? The Piven and Cloward thesis, it seems to me, can only be tested through individual, historical case studies that try to find out not only what happened but why it happened. From the evidence I have seen, the impact of militant protest is indisputable, though, certainly, not the only important factor. Nor do Piven and Cloward say it is. In fact, most critics ignore their careful specification of the circumstances in which protest has been effective.

33.   Committee on Ways and Means, U.S. House of Representatives, *Background Material and Data on Programs within the Jurisdiction of the Committee on Ways and Means* (Washington: GPO, 1985), pp. 14–73, 329–380; Laurence E. Lynn, Jr., "A Decade of Policy Developments in the Income-Maintenance System," in Haveman, *A Decade,* p. 101.

34.   Walter I. Trattner, *From Poor Law to Welfare State: a History of Social Welfare in America,* second edition (New York: Free Press, 1979), p. 271.

35.   Committee on Ways and Means, *Background Material,* p. 3; Levitan and Taggart, *Promise of Greatness,* pp. 38, 46; John Myles, "Does Class Matter? Explaining America's Modern Welfare State," unpublished paper, conference on "Theoretical Approaches to Modern Social Politics," Center for the Study of Industrial Societies, University of Chicago, November, 1984, pp. 11, 19–43 and *Old Age in the Welfare State: The Political Economy of Public Pensions* (Boston: Little Brown, 1984); Plotnick and Skidmore, *Progress Against Poverty,* pp. 56, 59.

36.   Levitan and Taggart, *Promise of Greatness,* p. 65.

37.   Patterson, *America's Struggle Against Poverty,* p. 168. For a comparative account of the politics of a guaranteed income in Canada and the United States, see Christopher Leman, *The Collapse of Welfare Reform: Political Institutions, Policy, and the Poor in Canada and the United States* (Cambridge: MIT Press, 1980). Leman points out that proposals in each country were remarkably similar in content and timing. However, they foundered on the problem of federalism in Canada and ideology in the United States. On the failure of the 1967 WIN (Work INcentive) amendments to AFDC, see Levitan and Taggart, *Promise of Greatness,* pp. 55–59. On income-maintenance experiments, see Plotnick and Skidmore, *Progress Against Poverty,* pp. 181–182. The New Jersey experiment indicated that an income maintenance program had little effect on work incentive; the Seattle experiment showed the opposite. Plotnick and Skidmore, *Progress Against Poverty,* p. 182; Martin Anderson, *Welfare: The Political Economy of Welfare Reform in the United States* (Stanford: Hoover Institution, 1978), pp. 102–127. It is no surprise that these experiments were inconclusive. In retrospect, it seems impossible to draw conclusions on the basis of a small population suddenly immersed in a new system whle still surrounded by the old. At the least, a two-generation study would be necessary, though, even then, the influence of national culture could not be eliminated. More to the point are comparisons based on the association between unemployment rates and welfare over time; economic growth and productivity in countries with guaranteed incomes; and arguments about the connection of motivation to the social organization of work, such as offered in Samuel Bowles *et al., Beyond the Wasteland: A Democratic Alternative to Economic Decline* (New York: Anchor Press/Doubleday, 1984), and Robert Kuttner *The Economic Illusion: False Choices Between Prosperity and Social Justice* (Boston: Houghton Mifflin, 1984).

38.   The most notable ideological right-wing attack on the social programs of the 1960s and early 1970s is Charles Murray, *Losing Ground: American Social Policy, 1950–1980* (New York: Basic Books, 1984), which has been attacked with devastating effectiveness. See Christopher Jencks, "How Poor Are the Poor?" pp. 41–49 and Robert Greenstein, "Losing Faith in 'Losing Ground,' " *New Republic,* March 25, 1985, pp. 12–17. Schwarz, *America's Hidden Success,* p. 43; Plotnick and Skidmore, *Progress Against Poverty,* p. 112; Levitan and Taggart, *Promise of Greatness,* pp. 200–201; Michael Harrington, *The New American Poverty* (New York: Holt, Rinehart and Winston, 1984), p. 247.

39.   Schwarz, pp. 32–40; Greg J. Duncan, *Years of Poverty Years of Plenty: The Changing Economic Fortunes of American Workers and Families* (Ann Arbor: University of Michigan, 1984), pp. 82–83.

40.   Plotnick and Skidmore, *Progress Against Poverty,* pp. 32–40, 169–170; Rodgers, *Cost of Human Neglect,* pp. 15–30; Michael Harrington, *The New American Poverty* (New York: Holt, Rinehart and Winston, 1984), pp. 69–88.

41.   Plotnick and Skidmore, *Progress Against Poverty,* p. 82.

42. Myles, *Old Age in the Welfare State*, pp. 17, 71; Alfred J. Kahn and Sheila B. Kammerman, "Income Maintenance, Wages, and Family Income," *Public Welfare* (Fall 1983), p. 28; "Income Transfers and Mother-only Families in Eight Countries," *Social Service Review* (September 1983), pp. 448–463); "Social Assistance: An Eight-Country Overview," *The Journal* (Winter 1983–84), pp. 93–112.

43. Levitan and Taggart, *Promise of Greatness*, pp. 16–19.

Chapter 10 / The War on Welfare

1. In the mid-1970s, few social scientists realized that the expansion of social welfare was about to be checked by a war on welfare. At the worst, they thought the trajectory of welfare expansion would flatten in the next decade; at best, they forecast the federal government would follow its expansion of social benefits with a modest attack on income inequality. Nor, by and large, did they observe the emerging new structure of poverty. For a modestly optimistic prediction, see Robert A. Haveman, "Introduction: Poverty and Social Policy in the 1960s and 1970s—An Overview and Some Speculations," in Haveman, ed., *A Decade of Federal Antipoverty Programs* (New York: Academic Press, 1977), pp. 18–19.

2. Michael Harrington, *The New American Poverty* (New York: Holt, Rinehart and Winston, 1984).

3. Karin Stallard, Barbara Ehrenreich, Holly Sklar, *Poverty in the American Dream: Women and Children First* (Boston: Institute for New Communications, South End Press, 1983), pp. 6–7; Ken Auletta, *The Underclass* (New York: Random House, 1982), pp. 68–69.

4. The major growth is occurring in relatively unskilled, low-wage jobs. In the 1980s, the Bureau of Labor Statistics predicted, service industries would provide the most new job openings: 500,000 nurse's aides and janitors, 400,000 fast-food workers, 377,000 general office clerks compared to 133,000 computer operators and 112,000 programmers. Barry Bluestone and Bennett Harrison, *The Deindustrialization of America* (New York: Basic Books, 1982), pp. 35–36, 49–50, 67; Harrington, *New American Poverty*, pp. 48–49, 60. Bureau of Labor Statistics cited in Harrington, p. 48.

5. Auletta, *Underclass*, p. xvi.

6. Greg J. Duncan, *Years of Poverty, Years of Plenty: The Changing Economic Fortunes of American Workers and Families* (Ann Arbor: University of Michigan Press, 1984), pp. 2–6, 60–61.

7. Philip Slater, *The Pursuit of Loneliness: American Culture at the Breaking Point* (Boston: Beacon Press, 1970), pp. 96–118.

8. On the postwar pact between capital and labor, see Bluestone and Harrison, *Deindustrialization*, pp. 16–17; Alan Wolfe, *America's Impasse: The Rise and Fall of the Politics of Growth* (Boston: South End Press, 1981), pp. 59–60; Samuel Bowles, *et al.*, *Beyond the Wasteland: a Democratic Alternative to Economic Decline* (Garden City, NY: Anchor Books, 1984), pp. 70–75.

9. Frances Fox Piven and Richard A. Cloward, *The New Class War* (New York: Pantheon, 1982), pp. 13, 27–28; 30 (italics in original); Committee on Ways and Means, "Background Material and Data," p. 421.

10. Piven and Cloward, *New Class War*, p. 39.

11. *New York Times*, January 15, 1982.

12. My interpretation of New York City's fiscal crisis is drawn from essays in the excellent collection edited by Roger E. Alcaly and David Mermelstein, *The Fiscal Crisis of American Cities: Essays on the Political Economy of Urban America with Special Reference to New York* (New York: Random House, 1977) and William K. Tabb, *The Long Default: New York City and the Urban Fiscal Crisis* (New York and London: Monthly Review Press, 1982). Martin Shefter, *Political Crisis/Fiscal Crisis: The Collapse and Revival of New York City* (New York: Basic Books, 1985), a major contribution to the topic, appeared after this chapter was written.

13. With state contributions included, the 1974 per capita figure for New York was $432 compared to $441 in Boston, $470 in Baltimore, and $488 in San Francisco.

14. The excessive number of ineligible welfare recipients, to which some commentators pointed

as a source of waste and fraud, did not reflect any special dishonesty among New York's poor. Over two-thirds of the errors arose from agency, not client, mistakes.

15. *Wall Street Journal* quoted in Tabb, *Long Default*, p. 42; Jack Newfield, "How the Power Brokers Profit" in Alcaly and Mermelstein, *Fiscal Crisis*, pp. 296–300.

16. Matthew Edel, "New York's Crisis as Economic History," in Alcaly and Mermelstein, *The Fiscal Crisis*, p. 242; Tabb, *Long Default*, p. 122.

17. Helen B. O'Bannon, ". . . it deserves legislative support," *Philadelphia Inquirer*, February 23, 1981; Blanche Bernstein, unpublished report on General Assistance prepared for Commonwealth of Pennsylvania Senate Public Health and Welfare Committee (1980), pp. 1–2, 30.

18. Dick Thornburgh, "Welfare could collapse of its own weight," Philadelphia *Bulletin*, June 22, 1980; O'Bannon, ". . . it deserves legislative support"; Bernstein, report on General Assistance, pp. 2–22; see also her book, *The Politics of Welfare: The New York City Experience* (Cambridge: Abt Books, 1982); *Maine Times*, July 22, 1983.

19. Terry E. Johnson, "Can welfare rolls be cut? Researchers ponder it," *Philadelphia Inquirer*, June 7, 1980; Christopher Berglund *et al.*, "Report on House Bill 2044: Consequences for the General Assistance Population," unpublished report, Department of City and Regional Planning, University of Pennsylvania, May 30, 1980; Walter F. Roche, Jr., "State readies rules for welfare raises, restrictions," *Philadelphia Inquirer*, June 3, 1982.

20. Marc Kaufman and Walter F. Roche, Jr., "What the welfare cuts have wrought," *Philadelphia Inquirer*, June 17, 1984; Walter F. Roche, Jr., "Welfare changes criticized," *Philadelphia Inquirer*, September 9, 1984.

21. Physician Task Force on Hunger in America, *Hunger in America: The Growing Epidemic* (Boston: Harvard University School of Public Health, 1985), p. 91, contains Stockman and Anderson quotes, originally reported in *Washington Post*, December 4, 1983, and July 8, 1983.

22. Public outrage prompted Congress to hold its own hearings on the administration of disability insurance, and the administration has been forced to moderate its policies. Piven and Cloward, *New Class War*, p. 33. Robert Pear, "Fairness of Reagan's Cutoffs of Disability Aid Questioned," *New York Times*, May 9, 1982; Jonathan Peterson, "Under Reagan drive, eligible disabled are denied benefits, House panel told," *Philadelphia Inquirer*, May 22, 1982.

23. Committee on Ways and Means, "Background Material and Data," pp. 351, 376, 535, 537; Robert A. Pear, "The Reagan Revolution: The Plans, the Progress," *New York Times*, January 31, 1983; Physician Task Force on Hunger in America, *Hunger in America: the Growing Epidemic* (Boston: Harvard University School of Public Health, 1985), pp. 93, 96.

24. Thomas Byrne Edsall, *The New Politics of Inequality* (New York: Norton, 1984), pp. 205, 206; House Ways and Means Committee, "Background Material and Data," pp. 525–526.

25. House Ways and Means Committee, "Background Material and Data," pp. 508, 518, 524; Bob Drogin, "True Victims of Poverty: Children," *Los Angeles Times*, July 30, 1985.

26. Physician Task Force on Hunger, *Hunger in America*, pp. xiii–xiv, 4, 10, 85; Mark J. Stern, "The Emergence of the Homeless as a Public Problem," *Social Service Review* (June 1984), pp. 291–301.

27. Piven and Cloward, *New Class War*, pp. 3, 143–144; Richard P. Nathan, Fred C. Doolittle, *et al.*, *The Consequences of Cuts: The Effects of the Reagan Domestic Program on State and Local Governments* (Princeton: Princeton Urban and Regional Research Center, 1983); Richard P. Nathan and Fred C. Doolittle, "Overview: Effects of the Reagan Domestic Program on States and Localities," unpublished ms., Princeton Urban and Regional Research Center, June 7, 1984; Richard P. Nathan and Fred C. Doolittle, "Reagan's Surprising Domestic Achievement," *Wall Street Journal*, September 18, 1984. Nathan and Doolittle argue that Reagan's programs have had a major impact on the nature of federalism by revitalizing the role of state governments.

28. *Report of the National Advisory Commission on Civil Disorders* (New York: Bantam Books, 1968); Robert Fogelson, *Violence as Protest: A Study of Riots and Ghettos* (New York: Anchor Books, 1971); President's Commission for a National Agenda for the Eighties, *Urban America in the Eighties* (Englewood Cliffs, NJ: Prentice Hall, 1981).

29. On the impossibility of a satisfactory welfare system in America's political economy, I agree with the conservative critic, Martin Anderson, in his book, *Welfare: The Political Economy of Welfare Reform in the United States* (Stanford: Stanford University Press, 1978). For an analysis of declining productivity that stresses the role of the social relations of work, see Bowles, Gordon, and Weisskopf, *Beyond the Wasteland*.

INDEX

Abbott, Edith, 123, 162, 169, 177, 293*n*1
Abbott, Grace, 144, 162, 169, 222, 293*n*1
Achenbaum, A., 202, 313*nn*43,46
Addams, Jane, 123, 146, 159, 160, 162, 163, 177, 222, 307*n*1, 309*n*29, 312*n*15
Adler, Felix, 134
Agriculture: rural poverty and mechanization of, 5–6
Aid to Dependent Children (ADC), *xi*, 129, 237; suitable home, provision of, 253
Aid to Families with Dependent Children (AFDC), *ix*, 266–67
Albritton, Robert, B., 320*n*32
Alcaly, Roger E., 322*n*12, 323*nn*15,16
Alchon, Guy, 313*n*2, 317*n*69
Alexander, John K., 298*nn*6,13
Allen, Nila F., 125, 305*n*30
Almshouses, *see* Poorhouses
Almy, Frederic, 42–43, 44, 46, 57, 298*nn*11,11,12,14, 299*n*35, 301*nn*-56,58
Altgeld, John, 188
Altmeyer, Arthur J., 236, 316*n*55, 317*n*59
America on Relief (Lane and Steegmuller), 316*nn*47,51,52,54
American Association for Labor Legislation (AALL), 191
American Association for Old Age Security: old age security and, 204
American Association of Public Welfare Officials, 168
American Association of Social Workers (AASW), 164, 166
American Bible Society, 60
American Charity Organization Society, 44, 45–46
American federalism: social welfare practice and, *x*
American Federation of Labor: public relief and, 148

American Medical Association, 143, 144
American Plan, of unemployment insurance, 197–98
American Social Science Association, 164
American Sunday School Union, 63, 64
American Tract Society, 60
Anderson, Martin, 285, 321*n*37, 323*n*29
Andrews, John B., 191, 197
Antler, Joyce, 307*n*59
Arnold, George, 40
Artisans: wage laborers and, 4–5
Ashby, Leroy, 119, 120, 304*n*10, 305*nn*16,18,19
Associated Charities (Boston), 81
Association for Improving the Condition of the Poor, 172
Auctioning off the poor, 19–20
Auletta, Ken, 276–77, 316*n*52, 322*nn*3,4
Austerity, cities and, 280–83
Axinn, June, 294*n*1

Bakke, E. Wight, 210–11, 212, 234, 314*nn*6,7,10, 315*n*32, 316*nn*33,46, 49,50,54
Baker, S. Josephine, 137, 141, 307*nn*61,62
Ball, Charles, 173
Banking Act, 236
Baritz, Loren, 312*n*22
Barnett, Samuel, 158, 159
Barrel-houses, *see* Lodging Houses
Beasley, Maurine, 313*n*1, 315*nn*25,31
Bell, Winifred, 253, 318*n*4
Bellingham, Bruce William, 303*n*43
Bellows, Barbara Lawrence, 19, 294*n*8, 295*n*18, 295*nn*41,50, 297*nn*55,63, 71,74
Bender, Thomas, 303*n*43
Bercovici, Konrad, 84, 301*n*60
Berglund, Christopher, 323*n*19

324

Index

Index

Index